THE WOMEN WHO BUILT BRISTOL: VOLUME TWO

By Jane Duffus

Tangent Books

The Women Who Built Bristol: Volume Two
First published 2019 by Tangent Books. Reprinted 2021.

Tangent Books
Unit 5.16 Paintworks, Bristol BS4 3EH
0117 972 0645
www.tangentbooks.co.uk
richard@tangentbooks.co.uk

ISBN 978-1-910089-87-3

By Jane Duffus

Cover illustration: Tiitu Takalo
Cover design: Joe Burt
Inside illustrations: Tina Altwegg, Rhi Lee, Carrie Love
Typesetting: Joe Burt (www.wildsparkdesign.com)

A CIP record of this book is available at the British Library.

Printed by TJ Books using paper from a sustainable source.

This book is for Rachel (2007-2018).
My shadow.

FOREWORD

By Thangam Debbonaire MP

So many tales but so few are told. In volume two of *The Women Who Built Bristol,* Jane Duffus continues the wonderful work of volume one, which lifted a curtain on an entire part of the city's history. I hope this book will not just be a marker of progress in expanding the telling of women's stories, but stimulate a new way of seeing and experiencing our city and inspire more women.

Will we need Tangent to publish further volumes? Will women continue to be largely side lined in social political history or will women now be so visible and vocal, so involved and prominent in social and political life, that we will automatically enter the mainstream documentation process?

This book puts to bed the tired, misleading and downright inaccurate justifications for women being left out of the records: 'Maybe there just weren't any women artists/scientists/composers/politicians', or 'maybe women just don't want to be politicians/headteachers/business leaders'.

In politics, my own area of operation, it is often said that "politicians should be selected on merit, not because of their sex". Well, if only wishing could make it so. Proof abounds that for centuries male MPs have been chosen precisely because of their sex and evidently not on merit.

Each of these statements leaves out the possibility that there were women doing all these things, but whose lives were never recorded or who have been ignored. It also ignores the lives of the pioneering women who broke through the barriers.

Jane is bringing us part of the missing record of who and what makes Bristol. This book includes the shining exceptions, the pioneers and the trailblazers as well as the women who lived their lives and played their part in making Bristol but were never made aldermen or had a street named after them, whose contribution to a meeting never got mentioned in the official minutes, whose extraordinary activities never got into the local paper or, if they did, only in their husband's name.

As I read volume two, I am struck by the extraordinariness of the women, some of them extraordinary in their ordinariness. The bride-to-be who died in a boating accident with her fiancé on a pre-wedding pleasure outing. The widow who supported her children by taking in piece-work from the Easton factory making leather work boots. These stories are unfamiliar because we've rarely learnt about them in social history.

Then there are the educators, including two women who played a critical role in the establishment of what is now Badminton girls' school, and a woman who used sadistic discipline on unruly middle-class girls. For in this volume, Jane has not confined herself to those women whose force was used for good but also those whose impact on Bristol was negative, although impact there definitely was.

Some entries are about women who deliberately tried to be invisible, but the nature of their lives means that they are worthy entries. Svetlana Alliluyeva, for instance, tried to make as little impact on Bristol as she could, wanting to remain anonymous as the only surviving child of the brutal dictator Joseph Stalin. After his death, she reverted to her mother's maiden name and came to live quietly in Clifton so that her daughter could be educated without the shadow of her father's name. This was, I can attest, a failed endeavour: said daughter was at the same school as one of my sisters and everybody knew who she was.

This impact of surnames on records of women's lives is significant throughout the book. For Svetlana, the consequence of a man's surname was life-altering. For other women, the family name became the end of a woman's childhood and, somewhere between her father's surname and her husband's, many women's records were lost.

The reading of these tales is as compelling as a good detective story. As well as answering questions too little asked by historians, they joyfully slip from one woman to the next, whether alphabetically or not. As I read, I wonder what pleasure Jane has had from tracking down some of the finer geographic or genealogical details?

Sarah and Harry, the tragic unmarried couple whose vicar had to lead their funeral shortly before he should have been conducting their wedding, were buried in St John's New Cemetery in Bedminster. Apparently, Sarah and Harry's gravestone is one of only two left in a park where I used to eat my lunch when I worked at Women's Aid, then nearby.

The Women Who Built Bristol shows us worlds and lives not unremarkable and clearly not totally unrecorded, but the stories have not previously been articulated or analysed. These tales light up the corners of our happily crowded city of Bristol, its past and the future we are building with it.

As we see more of Bristol's history and of the people who shaped it, the fabric of our city makes more sense. We understand why a gravestone remains or who is commemorated by Mary Carpenter Place, for example. This links us back to our present selves.

When I walk down Wilson Street in St Paul's, which I do often, I'm thinking of the Sturge family whose accomplished women span both volumes of *The Women Who Built Bristol*. I think of Elizabeth Backwell, the UK's first woman doctor, who lived and practiced there. I think of the women I know who live and have grown up there.

This knowledge, the perspective of the present reflecting on the past and of the women who built Bristol has the capacity to enrich and inspire us all. As I read the books and absorb how such a range of women with such diverse skills and qualities leaves an impact on the city, perhaps we can start to see how our generation's range of women will leave their mark. Women moving around the city today are still building it. Being a woman must no longer default to the quiet setting, the erased surname and the purposeful yet unremarked activities.

These books are rich resources for us. We can use them to educate ourselves, our city leaders and our children. We can use them as source materials for novels, to prompt walking or running routes, to unwrap the city and to inspire us.

Thangam Debbonaire has spent most of her working life in gender equality. From activism in a refuge for young Asian-origin women in the 1980s, through seven years as National Children's Officer for Women's Aid, helping to set up support for children in refuges. To establishing domestic violence prevention programmes for young people, and work with the Domestic Violence Intervention Project (where she co-facilitated a group work programme with abusive men to stop their abusiveness), and Respect (where she helped set up a national accreditation, research and training programme to support work with abusive men). Since 2015, Thangam has continued her feminism as a Member of Parliament for the people of Bristol West. She originally trained as a classical cellist and recently formed an all-female Parliamentary string quartet. Her political interests range from climate change to refugees, school funding to autism, the EU to drugs, antimicrobial resistance to homelessness. Thangam also founded and chairs the All-Party Parliamentary Group on domestic violence perpetrators; plus she is a Labour whip and part of the Women and Equalities team.

INTRODUCTION:
THE REVENGE OF THE WOMEN

By Jane Duffus

"I am not afraid of storms for I am learning how to sail my ship."
Louisa May Alcott, 1868

The above quote is one of my absolute favourites. It speaks of female strength and courage in the face of adversity. It reminds us that women are continually swimming against the tide to affect change and resolution. That it is a quote from the hard-working Amy March in Louisa May Alcott's novel *Little Women* simply reinforces this.

The Women Who Built Bristol is a celebration of women with a tangible connection to this city who weathered their storms and got stuff done. Maybe the woman was born here, died here or lived here for a bit in the middle of her life. Maybe she is a woman who invented something, wrote something or achieved something memorable while within our metaphorical city walls. She might be a woman whose name is already recorded in other history books for whatever it is she did, or perhaps she was completely overlooked and nobody took any notice of her achievements. Then again, maybe she hid her light under a bushel or – more likely – didn't think that what she was doing was anything out of the ordinary and so would be astonished to even find herself in a book. All Bristol women who did something of public interest are welcome in this book. The only rule for entry is she must no longer be alive.

Since getting the green light for volume one of *The Women Who Built Bristol* in spring 2017, this project of finding and recording stories about forgotten women has taken over my life in a wonderful way. With a ridiculously tight schedule in order to hit the February 2018 publication deadline (AKA the suffrage centenary), I researched, wrote and edited volume one during an intense seven-month period (alongside a full-time job, family and training for multiple marathons). Looking back, I can't imagine how I got a 135,000 word book produced in such a short period of time and can't tell you how glad I am that for volume two I have enjoyed a comparatively leisurely 18-month production process.

But the tight timescale for volume one was worth the late nights and hours spent tumbling down research-related rabbit holes. I have met many fascinating living people, heard about even more incredible dead women and been humbled by the immense range of spin-off projects which have come out of the stories about the women in the book (off the top of my head: the community woodcutting of suffragist Mary Blathwayt by Cato Press in Easton; the mural of women from Hotwells and Cliftonwood in the Cumberland Basin painted by artist Amy Hutchings; a friend's daughter who had to write a school essay about someone inspiring and picked a little-known woman from the book). I have been invited to give talks in all manner of places from Women's Institute meetings to children's libraries, and from the Edinburgh Fringe Festival to a team of engineers at an international manufacturing firm. I have met a small army of people who were delivered into this world by the neonatal pioneer Dr Beryl Corner and, by extraordinary coincidence, three unconnected people who now live in houses which artist Doris Flinn once lived in and have items of her artwork she left behind. Oh, and I even 'met' one of the dead women from volume one in the form of engineer Sarah Guppy (well, actor Kim Hicks, who plays her in the splendid — and hilarious — show

Sarah Guppy: The Bridge, The Bed, The Truth[1]). Meeting one of 'my old dead women', as I affectionately call them, was something I had previously filed under 'Unlikely to Ever Happen' but, despite death creating a barrier, I would welcome the opportunity to meet a few more (within reason). What unites all these experiences is the warm and enthusiastic response to the stories about these wonderful women, and the desire from readers to learn more and share further stories.

My friend Kate Smurthwaite suggested 'The Revenge of the Women' as a possible title for volume two and in many ways that would be extremely apt. Unlike in volume one (where I only included women who had had a positive impact on Bristol), in volume two I am also including some women who were certainly not good people. A serial killer, a highway robber, a Victorian woman whom you could pay to issue corporal punishment to your headstrong daughter... these women are among those included in volume two. I felt it was important to show history in all its colours: while largely wonderful, not every single woman was a good egg. But these people are far outweighed by the women in this book who were, for instance, World War Two code breakers, pioneering engineers, nurses, pilots, teachers... and much more in between. As before, I am keen to include the stories of 'real' women: women whom you might not initially think of as warriors because they 'just' ran a shop, were 'only' a mother of quads, were 'yet another' victim of male domestic abuse... but as the bastardised saying goes, behind every strong city there is an even stronger army of women.

However, I am beyond sad to be including my friend and comrade Maryanne Kempf in this book. Mas' untimely death in May 2018 was, to use one of her own oft-repeated terms,

1 showofstrength.org.uk/productions/sarah-guppy

extremely vexatious. Mas was a generous champion of *The Women Who Built Bristol*; enthusing and tweeting about it variously from her hospital bed or the front row of the balcony at the Colston Hall. She was wonderfully supportive and at times it felt like having my own cheerleader. I take some comfort from the fact that the last time I saw Mas was at the launch party for volume one, where she insisted on running the book stall even though she was exhausted and in pain from her rapidly advancing cancer. But nobody would have known how ill she was from talking to her that evening because she was full of vim. I am not alone in missing Mas, nor her love, kindness and sheer pig-headedness.

Sadly, Mas' death is not the only personal loss I have experienced during the writing of volume two, but these recent experiences of death have caused me to see the historic stories of the dead women who fill my life in a new way and to seize the day. Time is short, the clock is ticking, we do not know when our last day will be.

Despite the fact everyone in this book is dead, there is lots to be positive about and there are many hundreds, if not thousands, more women who could be included in future editions (I already have a long list of women who might one day grace the pages of a third volume). I hope that now people are finding out more about these unsung sheroes from our past, they will be inspired to dig deeper and find out even more... because we have only just started to scratch the surface of women's untold stories.

Jane Duffus qualified as a journalist in 2001 and has since worked as a journalist and editor for numerous best-selling national magazines and publishers, as well as editing several books for other writers. After relocating from London to Bristol, Jane founded the award-winning all-female What The Frock! Comedy project in 2012 to challenge an industry that knowingly overlooks female talent, and wrote *The What The Frock! Book of Funny Women* in 2015. In addition, she continues to work as a freelance writer, editor and public speaker, and was named as one of the West Women of the Year in 2019. *The Women Who Built Bristol: Volume Two* is her fourth book. Jane takes a break from all of the above by running ridiculously long distances for kicks.

Email: janeduffusbooks@gmail.com
Twitter: @Bristol_Jane
Website: janeduffus.com

HIDDEN FROM HISTORY:
WHERE DO WOMEN COME FROM?

Since the publication in February 2018 of the first volume of *The Women Who Built Bristol*, the one question I have been asked more than any other is where I find the women to include in the books. So I thought it might be helpful to write about this, in case it inspires anyone else to dig around and find even more forgotten women. Because there is an assemblage of forgotten wonderful women out there who desperately deserve to have their achievements remembered before they get buried under one too many layers of dust. As historian and writer **Naomi Clifford** tells me: "The explosion of interest in the lives of women in history – whether it is their hitherto uncelebrated achievements or the generality of their existences – is to be welcomed as rectifying an obvious imbalance, but there is still much work to do."[2]

Volumes one and two of *The Women Who Built Bristol* each contain 250 women in their A-Z sections, although both name many more than 250 when you look at the additional women mentioned within another woman's story. For instance, volume one contains 420 individually named women throughout the entire book, and volume two has a further 498 women (discounting mentions of women already named in volume one, this comes down to 439). That's more than 850 women who history has largely forgotten, which is very careless.

But where did these 859 women come from? With volume one, it was admittedly easier to find the women. In that book, although there were probably plenty of women who were strangers to you,

2 Naomi Clifford's books include *Women and the Gallows 1797-1837 (2017) and The Murder of Mary Ashcroft (2018).* She was a valued contributor to volume one of *The Women Who Built Bristol* and her website is: naomiclifford.com

there may well have been some about whom you knew *some*thing. The pioneers in medicine (eg **Elizabeth Blackwell**, **Elizabeth Casson**, **Eliza Walker Dunbar** and other medical women not called Elizabeth, such as **Florence Barrett** and **Vicky Tryon**), the suffragists and suffragettes (eg **Annie Kenney**, **Emmeline Pethick Lawrence** and the redoubtable **Priestman** sisters), the reformers (eg **Mary Carpenter** and **Frances Power Cobbe**), writers (eg **Angela Carter**, **Helen Dunmore** and **Hannah More**) and so on. Many of these and other names might have rung a bell somewhere in the back of your memory.

For volume one, I could draw on my previous research into the South West's suffrage campaign and chapters I had written for books by other people. There were also a few '100 Women of Bristol' lists which had been published over the years that provided some jumping off points. And I picked up some clues from existing books by historians (for instance **Madge Dresser**'s comprehensive *Women And The City: 1373-2000*, as well as **Lorna Brierley** and **Helen Reid**'s *Go Home and Do the Washing!*), as well as several booklets by the grassroots Bristol Broadsides project, which published social histories during the 1980s and 1990s. But after fishing for women from these places, I only had a list of 150 suitable women to go in volume one… and I wanted 250.[3]

The remaining 100 or so were more challenging – but more fun – to find because I had to do some real detective work and think creatively to get them; my background as a newsstand journalist came in useful. A handful of the women (eg poet **Sara Coleridge** and heiress **Fanny Fust**) were suggested by people who had heard I was researching the book and volunteered their own ideas; one of the women (progressive educationalist **Susie Hopes**) was my

3 By 'suitable' I mean that the criteria for inclusion was that the individuals in *The Women Who Built Bristol* needed to be dead, have a link of some kind to Bristol (eg were born here, died here, did something memorable here etc) and, for volume one, had made a positive contribution to the city or wider world.

own mother's former headteacher; while another (cobbler **Eliza Steele**) had previously lived in a friend's house on North Street. But as these examples show, the people suggesting women for the book were people I already know, which obviously limits my reach. I have no doubt there are plenty of great suggestions from people I do not know for women to include in any future books: please do contact me if so.

One thing which is different about volume two is that this time I am including some women who had a less than positive impact on Bristol. In volume one, I only included those who had done good things. But in volume two, I want to make it clear that not all women were holier than thou. So now we have the serial killer **Amelia Dyer**, highway robber **Joan Bracey** and an assortment of other ne'er-do-wells. Although these rotten eggs are still enormously outweighed by the good hearts who contribute to the totality of life in this city.

Steve Poole, Professor of History and Heritage at the University of the West of England, says: "It's now 45 years since Sheila Rowbotham's *Hidden From History* challenged the academic establishment to recognise the shameful invisibility of women in the historical record. Although plenty has been done since then to introduce consciously feminist and gendered approaches to the past, the yawning chasms remain – especially, perhaps, in the British provinces. While the restoration of nationally prominent figures and movements has redressed the balance in part, Jane Duffus' work on Bristol indicates how little we know even now of women's history at the local level, and sets a challenging agenda for comparative research in other cities and towns."[4]

NB: I am deliberately repeating the phrase 'hidden from

4 Professor Steve Poole has written widely on his specialist subjects, which include 18th and early 19th century political movements, and the history of the Bristol and Somerset regions. He is the Director of the Regional History Centre at the University of the West of England.

history' in acknowledgement of **Professor Sheila Rowbotham**'s seminal 1973 book *Hidden From History: 300 Years of Women's Oppression and the Fight Against It*, which Steve mentions above. In her book, Sheila (now a Bristol resident) shows how class and sex, work and the family, personal life and social pressures, have shaped and hindered women's struggles for equality. And in her inscription to me in her fantastic 2010 book *Dreamers of a New Day: Women Who Invented the Twentieth Century* (itself a tribute to historical women), Sheila wrote: "To Jane, with love from Sheila Rowbotham. I hope my oldies are inspiring". The answer is yes, Sheila, they definitely are. No longer hidden from history, you have inspired me to remove the cloak of invisibility which has shrouded many of our city's great women.

WHY ARE HISTORICAL WOMEN SO HARD TO FIND?

It is important to consider *why* these women are hidden from history. As a sweeping generalisation, I would say it is because history (traditionally written by and about men) did not think these women's stories worth recording at the time, and did not want women to have any power or authority, so did not publicise their achievements (see also why women had to fight for so long to get the vote). Consequently, contemporary historians have to pick at tiny threads and unravel the most throwaway of comments in order to try and find the untold stories of our past.[5]

However, I'm not a 'real' historian. By that, I mean I have had no specific training in anything to do with history, I don't have so much as a History GCSE to my name. Instead, I am a magazine features journalist with a passion for sharing the stories

5 NB: This is a book about forgotten women from history so obviously that is my angle. However, I am aware the same applies to missing stories about working-class history in general, as well as BAME stories and other minority groups.

of forgotten women. So to gain some authoritative perspective on this, I spoke to a few real historians to see what they thought about why women have been hidden from history.

Professor Peter Fleming is a History Professor at the University of the West of England, specialising in the medieval and Tudor periods (eras in which women are, regrettably, largely hidden in both volumes of *The Women Who Built Bristol*). He suggests women are hidden from history three times. Firstly, Peter points out the medieval and Tudor periods are eras where the surviving evidence is largely only of a legal nature (which was seen as a male space), and the domestic sphere (seen as a female space) was rarely recorded until the 18th century. Secondly, cities outside of London were generally less well documented because they were seen as provincial. And thirdly, Peter reminds us that in these early eras wives were under the legal control of their husbands, so they were not as well represented in the surviving documentary evidence as men. Despite these negative points, Peter adds positively: "While women in late medieval Bristol are less well-known to historians than their male counterparts, and are largely under the shadow of the men, they are not completely unknowable."[6] So there are threads to be pulled…

Academic and suffrage historian **Dr Naomi Paxton** affirms: "There are many varied and interconnected reasons why the voices, images, writings and stories of women are hard to find in public and general histories. In short, women have not been celebrated in the mainstream as capable, intelligent, creative or powerful. Where they have been undeniably successful, their success has often been attributed to the fact they are 'extraordinary' and therefore an exception to the rule. Their stories are hard to find

6 Among many other texts, Professor Peter Fleming wrote the chapter 'Women in Bristol 1373-1600' in *Women In The City* (2016) edited by Dr Madge Dresser, as well as the pamphlet *Women in Late Medieval Bristol* (2014).

because they have been considered not part of the mainstream, not been valued by the culture or society they were part of – which has influenced subsequent historians of that period, not considered worthy of preservation or not recorded at all."[7]

In January 2019, it was reported that archaeologist **Dr Anita Radini** and microbiome scientist **Dr Christina Warinner** had been examining the plaque on a medieval woman's teeth. They noticed something unusual, in that there was the brilliant blue pigment of lapis lazuli (once a highly valued commodity) embedded in the plaque. This meant the woman had been a writer or painter of medieval manuscripts, because this priceless blue pigment was so special it was only used to colour depictions of the Virgin Mary's robes. This led to the groundbreaking discovery that it was evidently not just men who had been skilled enough to create these manuscripts, as had previously been believed. Moreover, the women who worked on the manuscripts must have been extremely good at their jobs in order to have been permitted access to the precious lapis lazuli. However, when Drs Radini and Warinner asked art experts for assistance, they were initially met with disbelief at the notion a woman could have possibly been good enough to have painted such important manuscripts… because no existing history text told them this had been the case: "Art experts were still skeptical. Some dismissed the idea a woman could have been a painter skilled enough to work with ultramarine. One suggested to Warinner that this woman came into contact with ultramarine because she was simply the cleaning lady."[8] *The cleaning lady?!* Eventually, a female academic confirmed the lapis lazuli in the teeth did indeed mean the woman

7 Dr Naomi Paxton's books include: *The Methuen Drama Book of Suffrage Plays (2013), The Methuen Drama Book of Suffrage Plays: Taking the Stage (2018)* and *Stage Rights! The Actresses' Franchise League, Activism and Politics: 1908-1958 (2018).* She was a valued contributor to volume one of *The Women Who Built Bristol*. Her website is naomipaxton.co.uk

8 theatlantic.com/science/archive/2019/01/the-woman-with-lapis-lazuli-in-her-teeth/579760/

had been skilled enough to work on these manuscripts. What this depressing story demonstrates is that our understanding of what we have been told is always subject to change.

Here are a few more quickfire examples of history getting it wrong about women's abilities. Films such as *Gladiator* (2000, Ridley Scott) and other popular depictions of the Roman empire imply the fearless gladiators were exclusively male. Yet the *Journal of Combative Sport* has found there were actually rather a lot of female gladiators and the remains of one such woman are held at the Museum of London.[9] Similarly, the grave of Sweden's most famous Viking warrior, the Birka warrior, has for centuries been assumed to contain the body of a man because apparently Viking warriors were only men, but no! Recent DNA analysis of the bones reveals the Birka warrior was female.[10] Oh, and samurai fighters? Yes, you've guessed it, female samurai warriors were a lot more common than you have been led to believe. Women in ancient Japan were not always Geishas (decorative women who entertained the men with dance and song), instead some of them were killer fighters called Onna-Bugeisha who operated by exactly the same Bushido code as their male contemporaries: death before dishonour.[11]

The moral of these stories is simple: what you have read in old-fashioned history books is not always the definitive fact. We are still learning. New evidence is emerging all the time. Women are capable, equal human beings.

Now that we've established history is constantly evolving, back to the Bristol women...

9 ejmas.com/jcs/jcsart_murray_0703.htm

10 news.nationalgeographic.com/2017/09/viking-warrior-woman-archaeology-spd/

11 cracked.com/article_22142_5-badass-facts-about-women-that-history-books-leave-out.html

WHY DON'T WOMEN HAVE NAMES?

Of course, women *do* have names, it's just that often nobody bothered to write them down. Newspaper archives are full of stories about men doing stuff with little mention of the women who populated those men's lives and assisted them on their adventures. For instance, there is one woman in this book (**Mrs Beer**) for whom I have had to invent a name because the newspapers didn't bother to give her one, despite her story doing the Edwardian equivalent of going viral. And there are others (eg the **Landlady of the Jolly Sailor**) for whom no name was ever recorded, which is especially rude when you read their individual stories. This problem of women remaining nameless was emphasised by a tweet from **Amy Sherman**, an editor at a US publishing house. Amy was copyediting a history book and, frustrated with how the author had kept putting "and his wife" after a named man, she did a quick Google search and added in each woman's name, saying that if a woman was worth mentioning then she was worth naming. Amy added her research was "bare minimum stuff", making the point "anyone can do this".[12]

Tied to this business of referring to married women by their husband's names is the irritating habit of referring to women by their relationship to other people. Take for example **Mrs Johnson** in this volume, who achieved the astonishing feat of living to be 114 years old *and* of doing this as a working-class woman in a poor area of Bristol during the pre-NHS 18th century. Yet not only do we not know her actual name, but we also have to define her role simply as 'mother' because the scant records list her only as "mother of **Mrs Weymouth** from Post Office Bedminster" (which spirals into the problem of Mrs Weymouth

12 Amy Sherman, 23 August 2018, twitter.com/andcleverness/status/1032690089254707201

and why *she* is referred to only by *her* husband's name). Poor Mrs Johnson experiences a double whammy of indignities despite her astonishing feat of mortal endurance.

This remains the case today to a slightly lesser extent. Contemporary newspapers often only mention women as a protagonist if those women are either a victim or a mother; women are rarely featured in news stories for their business achievements or courageous triumphs, but the same cannot be said for men. We hear a lot about men and often we hear a lot about men which we really don't need to hear. We hear a lot of background noise about men which subconsciously informs us they are more dominant, but we don't have the same experience of women. We hear about men doing 'important stuff', and we see women looking pretty beside a man or having his babies. This needs to change. Because in 100 years, historians writing about women of the early 21st century will still struggle to find us among the miles and miles of column inches devoted to white, middle-class men in suits or white, working-class men in courts.

Let's illustrate this problem by using the example of this very basic news story which appeared in a Clifton newspaper in 1895. Allow me to type it in its entirety: "A woman, aged 67, fell downstairs in St Augustine's on Tuesday and broke her leg."[13] Admittedly, this is the Victorian equivalent of a NIB (News In Brief). However, as it stands, there's not really a story here. I mean, it's bad luck for the lady in question but without her name, her circumstances, her prognosis, there is no useful information for the reader whatsoever. We have her location and her age, but we don't have her name. Her name is surely the most crucial piece of absent information, and (with my journalist hat on) there is a lot of crucial information that's missing for this to even qualify

13 *Clifton and Redland Free Press*, 22 November 1895.

as a NIB. Without a name, she has no identity. And without an identity, she is impossible to trace, she becomes nobody and she is forgotten. Yet clearly somebody in 1895 thought it was in the public interest that this 67-year-old woman had fallen and broken her leg in St Augustine's on a Tuesday.

Another sticking point is the habit of referring to women as, for instance, '**Mrs Frederick William Rogers**' (this particular woman was a prominent suffrage campaigner in Bristol but it took me many, many months of digging to find her real name and this really stuck in my craw). The problems with calling a woman 'Mrs FW Rogers' are numerous. To start with: 1) These are her *husband's* first, second and third names, 2) *her* achievements are now being linked to her husband even though he probably had nothing to do with them, and 3) we still don't know what her name was and it's now really hard to find out on account of *his* name dominating the scant mentions of her that do survive. Alas, there are a handful of examples of this type of erasure in both volumes of *The Women Who Built Bristol*.[14]

Dr Naomi Paxton reinforces this idea of historians prioritising male stories: "Many published histories of famous or royal women, particularly in the first half of the 20th century, were by historians with their own interests and agendas, keen to capture a zeitgeist or add a new perspective to the life of a prominent male figure. This relationship to the male was therefore the underlying focus of the work because it was considered to have the broadest appeal, and the women described through the perceptions of contemporary men, rather than their female peers. Through these works, women are 're-discovered' as

14 I drafted this prior to finding out that Mrs FW Roger's name was Blanche Rogers (née Lyons), but I have decided to keep this paragraph reading largely as if we don't know her real name because it illustrates my point. I should not have had to spend months trying to find this woman's name, and I should not have had to find her name by accident due to the fact it had been misspelled on a census manuscript and only turned up by luck when I was researching an unrelated woman with the same surname.

domestic influencers, but often not portrayed as having their own creative or political agency. Criticism of their actions without an understanding of the conditions in which they were undertaken is therefore unfair and facile.

"The challenge is to rescue women in history from their auxiliary roles as wives, mothers and daughters, and clearly explain that their lack of political or economic agency was neither inevitable nor deserved but part of systemic and sexist inequality that actively prevented women and girls from having equal access, or sometimes *any* access, to formal education and employment opportunities. It's also important to state that the justification for this unequal treatment has often been based in the selective use of religious doctrine, medical terminology and perceptions of moral standards and sexuality."

Historian and writer **Naomi Clifford** supports this: "When thinking about women – who make up at least 50% of the population – and how they scarcely feature in 'serious' history books, one particular episode in my research stands out. In 1791, when **Mary Mills** confronted Richard Vining Perry on the Great North Road and asked to speak to Miss Clerke, the 14-year-old pupil Perry had abducted and forcibly married at Gretna Green, he scoffed and said **Clementina Clerke** no longer existed. She was Mrs Perry now. Marriage stripped Clementina not just of her recently inherited fortune – husbands then had a right to everything unless it was tied up in trusts – but also her name and therefore her identity. Arguably, it was worse for poor women who scarcely featured in the records except to be born, marry and die or if they transgressed in some way."

Although the example of Clementina Clerke (which you can read in full in volume one of *The Women Who Built Bristol*) is several centuries old, Naomi Clifford points out the problem of women losing their names to men is ongoing: "Until comparatively recently, men had total control of the official narrative on almost everything: politics, journalism, law, academia. Most of them viewed women's lives as primarily domestic, not worth recording. Their 'maiden' names were not even included on their children's birth certificates until 1911."[15]

THE IMPORTANCE OF EDUCATION

In the past, most schools didn't do a lot to help foster an interest or awareness in women's history either. Nor did they give much of a hint women even existed in history. The US suffragist Elizabeth Cady Stanton famously said: "I would have girls regard themselves not as adjectives, but as nouns."[16] And good goddess, that demand is as valid today as it was when first made in 1880. We need to teach girls that they can be history makers.

I attended three all-girls schools between the mid-1980s and mid-1990s, yet despite the fact the pupils were exclusively girls and the teachers were exclusively women, we were only taught history about men. This is baffling and illogical. This was in the era before the national curriculum was dictated by a central body and instead schools had a free rein to teach what the individual institutions and teachers wanted, which explains why one of my former history teachers devoted an entire term to sharing their passion for railways with a wholly uninterested class. Based on the fact my all-girls schools only taught history about men, is it any wonder I never pursued the subject at any academic level?

From speaking to contemporary teachers, I'm pleased to hear the situation has improved somewhat... but only in the sense

15 The language of 'maiden' names is problematic because the word 'maiden' has a lot of baggage. A maiden is historically an unmarried virgin or perhaps a 'maiden aunt', which has connotations of being celibate, unlovable and unwanted. The word 'maiden' also has implications of something happening for the first time (going back to the virgin idea): a ship or aircraft has its maiden voyage, a horse has a maiden race etc.

16 Elizabeth Cady Stanton, 1880, 'Our Girls' speech.

schools must teach what the national curriculum dictates. And to an extent, that does now include some women's history. I'm told the national curriculum states certain eras which schools are required to teach and there is some flexibility within this, so a school could choose to study what life was like for women in a particular period of history... but equally, they might not choose to do so. And it seems to be only a small handful of historical women who get taught on loop (eg social reformer **Florence Nightingale**, civil rights activist **Rosa Parks** and long-reigning **Queen Victoria**). What concerns me is that if schoolchildren are not given examples of women doing impressive stuff, how can they possibly either 1) know women are capable of doing impressive stuff or 2) have role models to inspire them to do impressive stuff themselves? Refreshingly, we can now see from Government figures that female students outnumber males in both uptake and grades for History classes at school and in further education, which can only have a positive impact on the types of histories which are researched and studied in the future.[17]

There are a few people who have gone above and beyond the call of duty to give historical women names. For example, in 2018, I interviewed suffrage historian **Elizabeth Crawford** for the online magazine *The Heroine Collective.*[18] Elizabeth (a generous contributor to volume one of *The Women Who Built Bristol*) has achieved many important and wonderful things in her decades of dedicated research. Perhaps her greatest gifts to future historians are her books *The Women's Suffrage Movement: A Reference Guide, 1866-1928* (1998) and *The Women's Suffrage Movement in Britain and Ireland: A Regional Survey* (2006), which painstakingly catalogue

17 Department for Education and Skills, 2007, *Gender and Education: The Evidence on Pupils in England.*

18 theheroinecollective.com/elizabeth-crawford/ In addition to those mentioned in the text, Elizabeth Crawford's other books include: *Campaigning for the Vote: Kate Parry Frye's Suffrage Diary (2013) and Art and Suffrage: A Biographical Dictionary of Suffrage Artists (2018).* Her website is: womanandhersphere.com

women from all over the UK who were involved with the movement. What is staggering is how Elizabeth wrote these books in the pre-internet age, relying on writing letters and making telephone calls to libraries and archives around the UK, and then visiting them in person to do the nitty gritty of her research. As is so often the case with women doing remarkable things, Elizabeth wasn't 'just' researching these books: she was also a mother to three children, a wife, a homemaker and a freelance editor. Oh, and she funded her research and travels from her own savings. Elizabeth told me: "I wrote to every library and archive in the country and they were very helpful, and I then methodically went and visited them all. I'm amazed now that I did it." On one hand, it *is* amazing Elizabeth did this. But on the other hand, it *isn't* amazing Elizabeth did this because she was simply doing what women have always done: the seemingly unimaginable.

One area which has proved enormously difficult to research is historical women of colour. Both volumes contain regrettably few stories about black and minority ethnic women, but this is certainly not for the want of research. I have spent a great deal of time questioning and discussing with others about why it may be that histories concerning non-white people have not been documented, and no good answer has been found. Although Bristol has a heavy slave history, the Bristolian slave traders rarely brought those slaves to work for them in Bristol, instead those enslaved people worked on tobacco and sugar plantations in the Americas. Of course, a few stories of slaves in Bristol have surfaced, such as **Fanny Coker** and manservant **Pero** (who are in volume one), but these are the exception. Most enslaved Africans, if they did make it to the UK, were recorded by an assumed first name and given the generic surname of 'Black' (eg **Dinah Black**, who is in volume one), and they largely exist as little more than an entry on a ship's log, which is insufficient to research their biography. Their stories did not make it into newspapers or legal documents, and while they may have been written about in letters by those who lived alongside them, accessing those letters (if they even survive) is another matter. Another suggestion is that many people of colour did not come to Bristol until the Windrush Generation (when approximately half a million people travelled to the UK from the Caribbean between 1948 and 1970) and they are still alive. There may be some truth to this. I have been asked several times if there were any black or minority ethnic suffragists or suffragettes in Bristol, and I wish I could find some but extensive research by myself and others repeatedly comes up blank. Indeed, the most notable suffragette of colour was **Princess Sophia Duleep Singh**, a London-born and -based woman of Indian descent who was **Queen Victoria**'s goddaughter and, more than likely, was only able to carry out suffragette campaigning because of her high social status and the fact she did not need to worry about money. This was very unusual at the turn of the last century: the majority of black and minority ethnic people in the UK at this time would not have had Princess Sophia's status or wealth to protect them from the law. There is certainly a big research project to be done concerning the untold stories of Bristolian women and men of colour.

SO WHERE DID THE WOMEN COME FROM FOR THIS BOOK?

When I was researching the women for volume two of *The Women Who Built Bristol*, there was very little reliance on existing books about Bristol and instead much more of a scattergun approach to finding women. Again, some (eg poet **UA Fanthorpe** and history writer **AJ Green-Armytage**) have been suggested to me by helpful people. But more often than not, I have had to overturn the mossiest of stones, remove the earwigs who had set up home underneath those stones, and dig a bit deeper still in order to find the women who now fill these pages. You could say that surely we have never heard of these women because they are uninteresting and unimportant. But I hope that once you have read their stories you are persuaded otherwise. These women are interesting and important and, in many ways, I consider them even more instrumental in building Bristol than the headliners.

The online British Newspaper Archive is a lot of fun once you get the hang of the search engine, and a one-month subscription is not too expensive if you just want to dip your toe in or have a concentrated period researching something you already know you want to find out more about. Similarly, there are a lot of small physical archives all over the place, although finding out they exist and getting to them are different – and often difficult – matters. With a full-time day job, this is not always practical or possible. So you need to accept there will be some limitations to your abilities to research while juggling a job, a family, a life and myriad other responsibilities.

For instance, I love the short entry about daredevil **Frances Holmes** in this volume. But I only found her story by chance while looking for something else in the newspaper archives. Her tale stood out to me as something so joyously madcap that I was itching to know more about her. Yet the fact I had stumbled upon her by mistake makes me wonder how many more women's stories and achievements are being overlooked.

Dr Naomi Paxton expands on this problem of needing to know who you are looking for before you can find her: "Archives are great places to look for women's stories but the trickiest part is finding the right search term. It's clear that the assumption that absence is indicative of insignificance is and has been persuasive. A good starting point is to think about who is or was collecting the data and papers, and what or who for. Absences in catalogues or finding aids can be because archivists and cataloguers have their own, and institutional, explicit and implicit biases. These apparent absences don't mean that the information isn't there, but they do require researchers to be creative and imaginative with search terms, to have a positive and open-minded approach to searching, and a working knowledge of related events, themes, people and networks.

"Where letters or diaries have been summarised rather than transcribed, key details and names may have not been considered worthy of inclusion, and the variables of OCR [optical character recognition] mean that online searches of digitised material won't always recognise misprints, spelling anomalies or certain fonts. Time and patience is therefore very important! Autobiographical writing in archives has most commonly been used to tell the stories of women's lives, but it was privileged women who had access to education, private incomes, leisure time and avenues to publication."

Written sources are not the only places to find forgotten women. Some women I found by accident just by going about my day-to-day life in Bristol. For instance, one morning I was walking through Quakers Friars and noticed a blue plaque for a woman called **Ellen King** which I had not spotted before. Who was she? Finding the answer to this question sent me down a fascinating rabbit hole and I could never have expected the answer would include almost 2,000 eggs. Similarly, I walked past the **Grace Reeves Study Centre** at the University of Bristol one afternoon, and ran past the **Amelia Nutt Clinic** in Withywood one rainy Sunday morning, and wondered who these women were who had buildings named in their honour. They must have been significant but finding out why wasn't as simple as asking the organisations in question because even they didn't know!

There are many street and place names in Bristol that also pose questions. For example, who was the grandmother who inspired **Granny's Lane** in Longwell Green, why does **Annie Scott** have a road named after her in Fishponds, and who was **Polly Barnes** and what did she do to have both a close and a hill named in her honour in Hanham? Annoyingly, I don't know the answers to these questions. Although I have found out a little about the origins of the **Seven Sisters** group of pine trees on Durdham Downs. They were planted by a doctor in 1871 to commemorate his seven daughters and, following storm damage, Bristol City Council has since planted a new group of seven pine trees on the Downs. Given the destruction of the Blathwayt family's Suffragette Woods near Bath in the mid-1960s, it is gratifying to see at least one example of West Country feminist landscape design surviving to some extent.[19]

Other places women in this book came from include: cemetery records (eg artist **Eliza Errington**), cathedral plaques (eg muse **Elizabeth Draper**), national newspaper obituaries (eg journalist **Mary Tisdall**), or as the writer of the foreword to a book I found in a junk shop (eg writer **Marguerite Fedden**). And from talking to people, although this tends to only unearth relatively recent women who can be recalled in somebody's living memory.

In some instances I looked at long-established businesses in the city and wondered who the women were who might have been involved behind the scenes. In this way I found the **Hort family** of restaurateurs whose name is brandished on Horts pub

19 The Suffragette Woods in Batheaston was a fascinating and unique project that was developed between 1909 and 1912 and saw more than 60 women plant a tree in the specially cultivated plot. Those who had undergone hunger strike and forced feeding were invited to plant a conifer, and non-militant suffragettes planted holly bushes. The planting of each was accompanied by a special ceremony in which the suffragette in question would dress in her finest clothes and her awarded suffrage jewellery. In the Edwardian era, ceremonial tree planting was not uncommon but has there ever been another collective work of feminist landscape design?

on Broad Street, while the story of **Louisa Wills** (who married into Bristol's tobacco dynasty and, like all women in this family, had been sidelined by historians in favour of the men) I found in an antique, suede-covered booklet wedged between lots of other old books on a shelf in my parents' spare bedroom in Somerset. She really was a chance discovery. Meaning there are limitless other chance discoveries still waiting to be found in dusty nooks in other people's houses all over the place.

There are, I have realised, a lot of women born in Bristol who went on to become television and film stars. They may not have been successful in that they did not become household names, but they were popular enough that they were continually in work, were highly praised by critics and peers, and were often in shows or films of which you will have heard. It would have been very repetitive for readers, however, if I had included all of these women, because by virtue of the evolution of film and television happening in a concentrated period of time, they were largely working in the same era and moving in the same circles as each other. So I have picked a handful of those whom I feel are the more novel stories to include in this book. But if you have a particular interest in actors with Bristol roots, then you could do a lot worse than investigating **Marjorie Avona** (1901-1978), **Nell Carter** (1984-1965), **Joyce Cummings** (1919-2002), **Jill Gregory** (1917-2010), **Margo Jenkins** (1934-1998), **Edna Maude** (1904-1996) or **Joan Seton** (1922-1985), to name but a few.

There are also women who I know would be fascinating if only I could find out more about them. The 1866 Women's Suffrage Petition was the one which kickstarted the suffrage movement as we know it.[20] The petition was signed by 1,521 people, of whom fewer than 20 give their address as being in Bristol. A handful

20 parliament.uk/documents/parliamentary-archives/1866SuffragePetitionNamesWebJune16.pdf

of these we know and have covered in volume one (**Ellen Drew Braysher** was the partner of **Amelia Blanford Edwards**, and **Florence Davenport Hill**, **Lady Anna Gore Langton**, **Agnes Beddoe** and **Catherine Norris** all have their own entries). But this still leaves a lot of women unaccounted for. Clearly, these women were pioneering, brave suffragists, prepared to stick their heads above the parapet in 1866 and lobby for votes for women. But we know precious little about them. The petition gives us a hint at their addresses but, given that many claim to share an address, it would seem some have fabricated this information. Many only put their initials rather than their first names, which makes it hard to track someone down with a fairly common surname. I would love to know more about these women, why they only lived in either Clifton or Stapleton, and what motivated them to take this bold step for the sisterhood.[21]

There are two women who signed the 1866 petition whom I was able to track down in the census reports, giving me a scant outline of their lives that I include here for completeness. **Mary Bengough** (born 1842) was from Surrey but lived as a widow at 5 Apsley Road, Clifton, with her two daughters and two servants at the time of the 1891 census. And single **Emily Maltby** (1806-1879), who had been born in London but was living at 2 Kensington Villas, Clifton, by the time of the 1861 census. Her occupation was 'fundholder', and she shared her home with two nephews and a niece (who were all school age) and three servants.

21 Here are the other unaccounted for women: EMT Brock of Heath House, Stapleton; Ann Hadfield of Clifton Park; E Ham of Clifton; Ellen Henley of Heath House, Stapleton; H Kortright of Stapleton; Sarah Solly of 11 West Mall; CE Stratton and M Stratton of Walls Court; Anna Thomas of 2 Great George Street; Elisabeth F Thomas of 2 Redland Parade; and Miss Winsas of Clifton.

THE EXTRAORDINARILY ORDINARY WOMEN

More than anything, in this book I want to tell the stories of 'real' women: women who you may not think did anything of interest but, wow, they really did. I truly celebrate the ordinary woman. After all, as the writer Virginia Woolf so eloquently pointed out: "The extraordinary woman depends on the ordinary woman. It is only when we know what were the conditions of the average woman's life ... it is only when we can measure the way of life and experience made possible to the ordinary woman that we can account for the success or failure of the extraordinary woman."[22]

One of my favourite extraordinary ordinary women in this book is **Harriet Lewis**. She initially presents as 'just' a working-class grocer from Bedminster, but her full story is fascinating, strong, inspiring and brave. Yes, she was a poorly educated, working-class woman from Bedminster who later ran a grocery shop in Easton. But the story of how she (a young widow with small children, all of whom were traumatised by the death of their husband and father in a mining accident) achieved this is remarkable. Harriet's story came to me via writer and historian **Mike Manson**, who recommended a book self-published by Harriet's granddaughter, **Sheila Hayward**. If Sheila hadn't written her book, then Harriet and her story would have been lost forever, so I am thankful Harriet will now be remembered and admired.

In many ways, 'real' women like Harriet speak to me more than obviously great women who built schools or invented machinery or wrote books etc. Because most of us are unlikely to achieve those sorts of things. We are too busy going to work, caring for others, running a home and worrying about our finances

22 Virginia Woolf, 1929, *A Room of One's Own.*

to have any time or money spare to open a specialist school for disadvantaged children, or to throw ourselves into a women's rights campaign full-time. The stories of women who created the smaller bricks that built Bristol are much more fascinating: they are more unusual, more revealing about what life was like for women in previous eras. We can learn a lot from them and we can see ourselves in them. Of course, I am not diminishing the achievements of women who had the time and funds to do more obviously notable things. I am immensely grateful to them.

Often, finding one woman will lead you to other women who helped that one woman achieve whatever it is she went on to achieve. For instance, when researching prima ballerina **Phyllis Bedells**, I came across choreographer **Edna Stacey**, pianist **Eileen Morley-Cooper** and the two women who founded the Bristol School of Dancing, **Mary Hoskyn** and **Muriel Carpenter**. Although following up on those leads is not always so straightforward, which is why none of those women are profiled in this book. Maybe in a future volume?

Genealogy websites such as Ancestry or FindMyPast are a good way to dig into people's backgrounds, explore the census reports and check the person you are looking up is definitely the one you want. For instance, while researching the aforementioned nursery school teacher **Ellen King**, I kept coming up with a Scottish swimmer from the same period also called Ellen King who was misleadingly being mentioned on Bristol heritage websites as the one on the blue plaque. There's also a third Ellen King, by the way, who was the landlady at the Bunch of Grapes pub on Denmark Street near the Hippodrome in 1878 (now the Smoke & Mirrors theatre pub). Doubtless, there are also many other Ellen Kings just waiting to be discovered.

WHY DO THESE WOMEN MATTER TO US?

I love (almost) all of the women in my books. But across both volumes, I have a particular fondness for the more unusual stories. While I obviously acknowledge the reformers, educators, suffragists and so on are hugely important women, it is in my nature to support the underdog. Which is why, for instance, from volume one it is the women such as centenarian fruit seller **Jane Martin**, grieving well watcher **Grandma Pugsley** or groundbreaking bus driver **Christine Preece** who most caught my imagination. And in this book, my favourites include **Frances Holmes** (who inexplicably climbed a church spire), **Anne Lutton** (who struggled with her social anxiety) and **Mary Griffiths** (who just did whatever the hell she wanted and, my word, I love her). These six women are examples of those you will almost definitely never have heard of before reading these two books and that is partly why they are so special to me. And because they, and those like them in *The Women Who Built Bristol* books, are now no longer hidden from history.

A-Z OF THE WOMEN WHO BUILT BRISTOL

ST CATHERINE OF ALEXANDRIA

c287-305, MARTYR

Where the massive Asda supermarket now stands in Bedminster, there used to sit St Catherine's Hospital, which explains why the shopping centre and flats opposite are called St Catherine's Place. This hospital was commissioned in 1207 by Robert de Berkeley[23], and the emblem for the hospital showed the martyr St Catherine carrying the spiked wheel on which she was tortured and crucified. Remember those Catherine Wheel fireworks you enjoyed as a child? They were called after our St Catherine, who met a gruesome and agonising end as a consequence of sticking true to her Christian beliefs.

In addition to looking after the sick, St Catherine's Hospital was a place of refuge for travelling pilgrims who would be offered a chunk of cheese, some bread and a mug of ale, as well as perhaps a place to rest, before continuing on their way to places of worship in St Ann's, Brislington or further away in Glastonbury. St Catherine's Hospital remained open until 1573. The site was later repurposed as a glass works and a tannery, before being demolished in 1887 to make way for a Wills tobacco factory and, more recently, the big branch of Asda we all recognise today.

However, St Catherine's wasn't the only hospital in the area because just around the corner on Philip Street there was the St Mary Magdalene Hospital, which was a women-only leper colony that operated until 1471. This was built in an era when people were so fearful of leprosy that those infected with the disease were required to carry and ring a bell, warning others they were approaching.

23 The Berkeley family were landowners who share a family tree with the Fitzharding family, who we meet in Eva Fitzharding's entry in the book.

And another thing... Fun fact: the area close to the former sites of both hospitals is now known as Windmill Hill and, once upon a time, there was a windmill on the hill. A farm stood on the side of the hill (now covered in rows of terraced housing) which had a windmill on its land, and this ground corn was sold to both hospitals, as well as many other homes and businesses.

Please also see: Eva Fitzharding (vol two).

LILLIAN ALLEN

1898-c1950, MOTORCYCLIST

Lillian Agnes Allen of 22 St John's Lane, Bedminster, was one of the very first female motorcyclists in Bristol and was also known to take her younger sister May Mullins out for a spin on her Douglas motorbike, which had been manufactured at the local Kingswood factory. Lillian's motorbike licence was issued on 27 April 1926 when she was 28, and she paid the handsome sum of £2 for her first ever motorbike, which was bought second-hand. Photos show Lillian enjoying her motorbikes throughout her whole life, as one particular picture of her in the sidecar of a motorbike driven by her husband George attests.[24] Lillian was also related to Archie Allen, who ran a motorbike dealership at 109 Redcliffe Hill, which survived until the 1960s before the wrecking ball came calling for the entire street.

Please also see: Lottie Cottrell (vol two), Rosina Douglas (vol two), Vera Hole (vol two).

24 flickr.com/photos/brizzlebornandbred/2060260315/in/album-72157603287015629/

MAY ALLEN
1835-1912, MISSIONARY NURSE

London-born nurse May Allen, who lived her final years in Bristol, devoted her life to treating freed slaves in East Africa, having become a missionary nurse in Zanzibar. After her father, the Archdeacon John Allen, was appointed to a church in Shropshire when May was ten years old, the family moved to the pretty village of Prees where the children had an idyllic upbringing and where their traditional education was supplemented by the many international visitors who came to see the Archdeacon. These visitors opened young May's eyes to the myriad problems affecting people all over the world, which were far removed from the sedate and privileged life she saw in Prees.

When she was 35, May decided to follow her younger sister Margaret and train to become a nurse and, once qualified, she took a post at the Convalescent Home for Ladies in Scarborough. While there, she was inspired to work as a missionary after hearing a lecture by Edward Steere, the Bishop of Central Africa, about the Universities' Mission to Central Africa and the slave trade.[25] So it was that at the age of 40, May travelled to East Africa to join Bishop Steere's mission.

When May arrived in Zanzibar in late 1875, she was stationed at the Universities' Mission, which was located on the former site of the region's slave market. Bishop Steere's primary role for his missionaries was that they should help convert the heathens to a Christian life, but as a female nurse May became invaluable in providing medical treatment to sick women and children who had been rescued from slave traders: although the British had

25 The Universities' Mission to Central Africa operated between 1857 and 1965, having been established as a missionary society by members of the Anglican church in response to a plea for help by the explorer David Livingstone, I presume, who returned from his travels and lectured widely in the UK about the crisis situation affecting freed slaves.

abolished the slave trade with West Africa in 1807, slavery had not been abolished between Amman (the capital city of Jordan) and Mozambique until 1873. In addition to nursing, May also translated the Bible into Swahili as part of her missionary work.

In an early letter to her father, May wrote: "I have already had a black patient in my hospital, a released slave girl, belonging to the mission, whose toe has been crushed. She is a very good patient and I hope is going on well. Today we have two black boys with bad legs, so we are beginning to work."[26] In total, May sent 66 letters to her father from Zanzibar during the 12 years she was stationed there and he passed these letters to the *Eddowes Journal* in Shropshire, which published them and as such they have provided a fascinating and rare insight into the life of a British nurse treating freed enslaved Africans in their home country.

Following a further 22 years working as a missionary nurse in Palestine, May returned to the UK in 1909 when she was 74. She chose to settle in Bristol for her retirement, although her retirement was short lived and, after just three years in Bristol, she died on 14 May 1912 following a short illness. May was buried at Arnos Vale Cemetery.

SVETLANA ALLILUYEVA

1926-2011, RUSSIAN DEFECTOR, DICTATOR'S DAUGHTER

Did you know Soviet dictator Joseph Stalin can claim a tenuous Bristol connection? His only daughter, favourite child and last surviving offspring was Svetlana Iosifovna Stalin (initially known as Stalina, later known as Lana Peters, for a time she also adopted

26 'Abolition: The May Allen Story' on BBC Shropshire, 10 April 2007.

her mother's family surname of Alliluyeva to distance herself from the Stalin connection). Svetlana defected to the West and lived quietly in Bristol for 15 years between 1992 and 2007, desperate to escape the shadow of her tyrannical father.

Born in Moscow, Russia, and raised by nannies, Svetlana was just six years old when her mother shot herself after incessant bullying from her husband. Yet Svetlana was told nothing of her mother's death until several days later when she was taken to see the body in its coffin. Svetlana was 16 before she learned her mother had died by suicide, after accidentally reading it in a Western newspaper. "Something in me was destroyed. I was no longer able to obey the word and will of my father," she said of the gut-wrenching moment of discovery.[27]

Yet Stalin gave the impression to the outside world that he was a great family man, and in 1942 British Prime Minister Winston Churchill, who was visiting the Kremlin, even noted in his diary he had met Svetlana and she was a "handsome red-haired girl, who kissed her father dutifully"[28]. Outsiders were often astonished at how such a brutal man could be so loving towards his daughter. However, once she grew older and wanted her independence, Stalin stood in the way of her happiness: he sentenced Svetlana's first boyfriend (a Jewish filmmaker who was 22 years her senior) to ten years in a labour camp and flatly refused to ever meet her first husband. Her second marriage was arranged by Stalin and the groom was one of his associates, although the marriage was later dissolved.

Following Stalin's death in 1953, Svetlana was a little more free to live how she wanted and she found work as a lecturer and translator (she was fluent in Russian, English, French and German) in Moscow, with history and politics begrudgingly

27 'Obituary: Lana Peters' in *The Telegraph*, 29 November 2011.

28 Ibid.

being her specialist subjects. 'Begrudgingly' because Stalin had forced Svetlana to study politics at university even though the subject did not interest her and she would have preferred to study literature and fine arts. Liberated from her father's grip, Svetlana grappled around to find a new identity. She experimented with a huge range of religions and roamed from continent to continent in search of somewhere that she could fit in. Seemingly, she never found the security she desperately craved.

Her third husband was an Indian Communist politician, and her fourth was an American architect. None of the four marriages lasted more than a few years each, although all but one marriage produced a child.

Desperate to shake off the stigma of her father, Svetlana approached the US and asked for political asylum: "On her arrival in New York in April 1967, she willingly became a propaganda tool in the Cold War, denouncing her father as a moral and spiritual monster, burning her Soviet passport in public, denouncing the Soviet regime."[29] She moved around the US under the watchful eye of the Central Intelligence Agency and working as a writer and lecturer, but she was effectively living in exile, unable to fully detach herself from the stigmatising label of 'Stalin's daughter'. Svetlana lost contact with her children, who had been left behind in the Soviet Union, and never felt settled in the US. However, her memoirs, *Twenty Letters to a Friend* (1967) and *Only One Year* (1969), were about her defection to the West and proved enormously popular. This brought in $2.5 million, which she desperately needed, having been left almost penniless after the fall of Stalin's empire.

It was around this time Svetlana married her fourth husband, US architect William Peters. She adopted the name of 'Lana

29 David Hearst, 'Lana Peters: Obituary' in *The Guardian*, 29 November 2011.

Peters', had another child and, in 1978, became a US citizen. After this marriage faltered, she moved with their daughter Olga (who is still alive but has now completely changed her identity) to the UK in 1982, became a British citizen in 1992 and settled in Canynge Square, Clifton. Little is known of Lana's time in Bristol because she tried her best to stay under the radar and not draw attention to herself. However, given how long she lived in Bristol and her family's significance to global politics, it feels important to include her here.

Lana stayed in Clifton until 2009, when she returned to the US where she died from cancer in 2011. Shortly before her death, she sadly told a journalist: "Wherever I go, here [the US], or Switzerland, or India, or wherever. Australia. Some island. I always will be a political prisoner of my father's name."[30]

And another thing... A play by David Lane entitled *Stalin's Daughter* was performed to a sell-out run at the Tobacco Factory Theatre, Southville, in 2014, before going on a national tour. Reviewing the play, which was about Svetlana's life during her 15 years in Bristol, *The Times* wrote: "It's often grotesque, always engrossing and in [director] Ed Viney's pin-sharp production, Kirsty Voc [playing Svetlana] is mesmeric ... Vivid, disturbing and utterly fascinating."[31]

RHODA AMINE

1919-2018, CODE BREAKER

Dying just two days before her 99th birthday, Fishponds-based war shero Rhoda Amine (née Connell) had lived a long and eventful

30 Rupert Cornwell, 'Lana Peters: Stalin's Daughter Whose Defection to the West did not bring Peace of Mind' in *The Independent*, 30 November 2011.

31 Sam Marlowe, 'Stalin's Daughter at the Tobacco Factory' in *The Times*, 1 August 2014.

life. Born in Edinburgh, Scotland, she was educated in China and spoke a number of languages, including Arabic and French. These linguistic skills helped her during World War Two when she worked for three years at the Government Communication Centre research labs in Wembley, London, in conjunction with Bletchley Park. As a member of the Women's Auxiliary Air Force, her role at Bletchley was to convert the frequency of German communications and to decipher Morse code messages.

After the war, Rhoda married an Egyptian man and went to live with him in Cairo. While there, she wrote the memoir *Seven Years In The Sun* (1959) about her claustrophobic domestic experiences as the Scottish wife of an Egyptian man, bringing up their children in a deeply patriarchal society. During her retirement, Rhoda came to live in Fishponds to be closer to family members and while here she was an active member of the Begbrook Retirement Club.[32]

Please also see: Mary Moore.

CATHERINE ANDRAS

1775-1860, WAX SCULPTOR

You will have heard of the famous waxworks in London named after the French sculptor Marie Tussaud, who started modelling with wax in 1777. Inspired by these popular creations was the Bristol-born sculptor Catherine Andras, who began making wax models while working in a toy shop and eventually progressed to become Modeller in Wax to Queen Charlotte: who knew royalty needed its own wax artist?

32 'War Heroine Rhoda Dies at 98' in *Fishponds Voice*, 29 June 2018.

Orphaned when they were very young, Catherine and her three sisters worked at a perfumery and toy shop in Bristol city centre. She taught herself how to model sculptures from pink wax and earned some extra income by supplying wax models to travelling fairs. After she turned 21, Catherine ventured to London where her talent was recognised by King George III's miniaturist painter Robert Bowyer. Indeed, Bowyer and his wife Mary were so enamoured by Catherine (and were grieving for their daughter Harriet who had recently died aged 19) they adopted her into their family.

Catherine's fortunes changed in 1802. Following a commission from Queen Charlotte (the wife of King George III) in 1801 to create a wax model of her five-year-old granddaughter Princess Charlotte, Catherine became Queen Charlotte's official Modeller in Wax. Blessed by this royal endorsement, she was commissioned by the great and good of society including Bristolian writer Hannah More, esteemed naval officer Lord Nelson, novelist Sir Walter Scott and statesman William Pitt the Younger.

The wax models Catherine and her contemporaries were creating were not like the mannequin-esque wax models we now see at attractions such as Madame Tussaud's, instead they were side-on miniature profiles of the head, similar to those featured on cameo brooches. These wax portraits were a respected form of art and were accepted by the prestigious Royal Academy of Arts in London's Piccadilly, where Catherine first exhibited in 1799.

Perhaps Catherine's most significant commission was in 1806 following the death of Lord Nelson, whom she had already modelled in silhouette. Westminster Abbey invited her to create a life-sized effigy of the navalman (to be dressed in his own uniform, medals and shoes) that would be displayed in the prestigious church. Nelson's mistress Emma Hamilton went so far as to praise Catherine's sculpture by saying "the likeness was so great it was impossible for anyone who had known him to doubt about or mistake it"[33].

Examples of Catherine's work are displayed in the British Museum and Westminster Abbey in London, and the Metropolitan Museum of Art in New York City, among many other places.

Please also see: Louisa (vol two), Hannah More (vol one).

EMILY ANDREWS

1851-1940, SUFFRAGE ARTIST

Having gained her initial education at Clifton Ladies' College, Emily Jane Harding went on to study at the Bristol School of Art from where she graduated in October 1868. Although her childhood and education had been in Bristol, the Harding family moved to London in 1871 and Emily continued with her art studies, exhibiting her portrait miniatures at the Royal Academy in Piccadilly, London, in 1877, 1897 and 1898, which was extremely flattering for the young painter.

She married fellow artist Edward Andrews in 1879 and the couple remained in London. Her biographer Elizabeth Crawford notes Emily reportedly scoffed at the idea of having a family, saying, "What? Have children? We haven't got time for children!" Emily carried on with her art and illustrated a number of children's books, working under her original name of Emily Harding. Her work shows her influences included the Pre-Raphaelites and the Victorian children's illustrator Kate Greenaway, who was a contemporary of Emily's.

By 1907, Emily had become a member of the Artists' Suffrage

33 collections.vam.ac.uk/item/O77802/lord-nelson-relief-andras-catherine/

League (ASL), and won second place after entering a poster in a competition organised jointly by the ASL and the National Union of Women's Suffrage Societies (NUWSS). Elizabeth Crawford suggests the most likely piece Emily submitted for this prize was a work called 'Convicts, Lunatics and Women! Have No Vote For Parliament', which was later published by the ASL in 1908. This poster became so popular it was reprinted numerous times throughout 1910 and is now a familiar design to those with an interest in suffrage history. 'Convicts, Lunatics and Women!' shows a dignified female graduate in her mortar board and gown, trapped behind a locked fence with a burly prisoner and a small 'lunatic' close beside her. However, re-evaluating the poster in 2003, *The New Statesman* was a little sniffy about the implications of the illustration, saying: "The text makes it clear that what connects these three is their inability to vote. Andrews's artistic execution may be deft, but her implicit argument is off-putting. There is something about the graduate's regular features compared with the puffy face of the lunatic and the sloping brow of the convict that suggests the educated woman's fitness to vote rests on nothing so much as her eugenic superiority."[34]

Emily maintained her links with the ASL and produced a number of other postcards, posters and works for them over the following years, although none would be as memorable as 'Convicts, Lunatics and Women!' Those printed in colour were affiliated to the NUWSS colours of red, white and green (rather than purple, white and green, which are better known and are the colours of the militant Women's Social and Political Union), which suggests Emily was committed to peaceful methods to secure votes for women.

Edward died in 1915 but, because being an artist was not a

34 Kathryn Hughes, 'A Stitch in Time' in *The New Statesman*, 13 October 2003.

lucrative profession, he left very little to his wife. However, because she was fluent in French and German, during World War One Emily was able to work as a decoder for the government. But it would seem she struggled financially once the war was over, because by 1931 she was living in "a private institution founded as a home for persons of gentle position brought to distress through genuine misfortune". In her mid 80s, Emily travelled by boat to Sydney, Australia, to join her younger sister Gertrude, who had also been widowed. It was in Australia that Emily died in 1940.[35]

MARY ATLAY

1757-1823, WORKHOUSE MATRON

From 1800 until her death in 1823, Mary Atlay was the much respected Matron of St Peter's Workhouse Hospital. Mary is particularly notable because she had the unusual distinction of being remembered for her kindness and compassion to the inmates, which sadly was a rare quality among workhouse staff.

The hospital was located behind St Peter's Church (of which the ruins survive) in Castle Park. There had been a hospital of sorts on the site since approximately 1400, always with the intention of providing healthcare to the poor. The original timbered, four-gabled mansion house was considered an architectural landmark and for a time in the late 1600s it was briefly used as the Bristol Mint. Although ostensibly a place where money was manufactured, the Bristol Mint was in reality another part of the workhouse system and occupied the labour of 100 boys. However, it wasn't long before the workhouse took over completely, the mint dissolved and it officially became the Mint Workhouse or

35 Elizabeth Crawford, 2018, *Art and Suffrage: A Biographical Dictionary of Suffrage Artists*, pp35-39.

— unpleasantly — The Purgatory, as it was known colloquially. By 1701, children, the aged, the infirm and 'lunatic patients' had been added to the list of inmates at St Peter's and there were up to 500 inmates at any one time; it was dangerously overcrowded, meaning infectious diseases were rife in the so-called sanitorium.

Widowed Mary was employed as Matron at St Peter's from 1800, when it was a workhouse hospital run by the Bristol Corporation of the Poor. In an enormous change from her predecessor, Mary was noted for her kindness to the inmates and consequently she was well respected by both her colleagues and charges. It was noted: "When [Mary] became too old and infirm for her arduous work, the [Poor Law] Guardians resolved to appoint a Sub-Matron to assist her. But their nominee respectfully declined to take this salaried post: she explained she had already been helping Mrs Atlay 'because of her kindness to me when I was bereaved', and she continued to do so without pay until Mrs Atlay's death in 1823."[36] Echoing this sentiment, the *Bristol Mirror* wrote in Mary's death notice that she was "matron of St Peter's Hospital, the duties of which situation she discharged with the greatest compassion and fidelity, and in every other respect was a devout and good Christian".[37]

The St Peter's Hospital Workhouse eventually closed in 1890 due to a much larger workhouse having been opened in Stapleton. However, the Board of Poor Law Guardians retained much of the stunning Castle Park building for offices, although some of the ground floor was turned over to become the Register Office in Bristol. With the complete demise of the workhouse system in 1930, the building instead became the home of the Social Welfare Committee in 1937. It was a popular location for weddings owing to its beautiful architecture and its scenic location beside the river

36 EE Butcher, [date unknown], *Bristol Corporation of the Poor 1696-1898*, pamphlet, p9.
37 'Deaths', in *Bristol Mirror*, on 22 November 1823.

and St Peter's Church, although the prospect of being married in a former workhouse seems rather macabre and distasteful to some sensibilities. Regrettably, the building and most of its records were destroyed by a German bomb on 24 November 1940.[38]

LORRAINE AYENSU

1962-2012, REFUGEE RIGHTS ACTIVIST, MUSICIAN

Acknowledging the important work done by Bristol-based refugee rights activist Lorraine Ayensu, June Burrough, the former chair of Bristol City of Sanctuary, said "without [Lorraine's] vision for Bristol, we would quite simply not be a City of Sanctuary.[39] After hearing about the movement at a conference in Brussels she returned to Bristol with an energy that enthused the Refugee Week Committee to initiate it ... Lorraine was a person with vision, determination, compassion and love, who made a real difference in this world."[40] Bristol was officially recognised as a City of Sanctuary in 2010, and the charity behind this recognition still works to ensure Bristol is an inclusive and welcoming city.

In addition to being a tireless campaigner, Lorraine, who was of Ghanaian and English descent, was also a social worker and talented jazz and blues musician who regularly performed at events including the famous Glastonbury and WOMAD festivals. With her music, she was influenced by British, African, Latin and American music, having performed for many years as a backing vocalist for Black Roots, which was a roots reggae band from St Paul's. Lorraine had also spent three years working as a singer and percussionist with Koko Kanyinda Mukala during the 1990s. Her

38 St Peter's Hospice, established in north Bristol in 1969, is named after St Peter's Hospital.
39 A City of Sanctuary is a city committed to being a welcoming and safe place for all people who are fleeing war, violence and persecution.
40 bristol.cityofsanctuary.org/2012/07/02/lorraine-ayensu

Lorraine Ayensu illustration by Rhi Lee

solo albums included *Last Conversation* (2006) and, posthumously, *Remembering* (2016). *Venue* magazine wrote of Lorraine: "Like most songwriters she can turn a good lyric, but what makes her music exceptional is her wealth of knowledge and insight that she brings to bear on the music. Steeped in African, Caribbean, Latin and American influences as well as jazz, each number has its own provenance as new world music from a global musician who respects her roots. It's a remarkable achievement."[41]

Lorraine died in 2012 following a two-year battle with brain cancer. The Lorraine Ayensu Refugee Arts fund has been set up by Bristol Refugee Rights in her memory and supports the art and music of asylum seekers and refugees living in Bristol.[42]

MIRIAM BADOCK

1832-1915, EDUCATIONAL INNOVATOR

Calling her a mere 'headteacher' feels like a disservice to Miriam Badock, who could better be called an educational innovator. In August 1858, Miriam founded the institution we now know as Badminton School with the express intention of offering girls the same standard of education their brothers enjoyed elsewhere. But back in 1858, hers was initially a modest dame school[43] based at Burlington Gardens, Clifton, with just four pupils. Miriam was married to a mahogany merchant called William, with whom she lived at the school. She would remain headteacher for 35 years and oversaw the growth of the school from four to 50+ pupils as well as the ensuing move to Badminton House, Clifton, before it moved to its current location at Westbury-on-Trym in 1924.

41 Tony Benjamin, 'Jazz World', *Venue*, January 2009.

42 With thanks to Edson Burton for the nomination of Lorraine Ayensu to this book.

43 A dame school was a small school run by older women from their homes. Miriam's school was a league above the standard dame school, though!

In her debut prospectus for the school, Miriam wrote that her aim was to "first secure [the girls'] affection and confidence and then, by a careful study of the character and mental capacities of each, to develop moral and religious principles and impart instruction in the manner best adapted to their individual tastes and dispositions".[44] As early as the 1860s, Miriam was encouraging her students to sit for their University of Cambridge entrance exams, even though women were not yet permitted to graduate, and the subjects the girls were taught ranged from botany to elementary physics and Ancient Greek.

By the time she retired in 1893 and handed the reins over to one of her former pupils, Miss Bartlett, Badminton School had grown from four to 58 girls. Miriam was described as "a lady of much learning and distinction and with a remarkable gift for inspiring young people … Mrs Badock was a lady with views almost in advance of her times, and her 'young ladies' wore gymnasium dresses and did gymnastics in a well-equipped gymnasium at a time when such exercises were considered by many as not quite suitable for girls."[45] After her retirement, Miriam moved to Bedford Villa on Richmond Hill, Clifton, where she lived as a widow with her granddaughter Mildred Badock.

Miriam's son Sir Stanley Badock was also a well-respected figure in the world of education. He was elected to the council of the newly formed University of Bristol in 1909 and by the time of his death in 1945 he had become Pro-Chancellor and Chairman of the University. Stanley called one of his daughters Miriam in honour of his mother, and he also established a scholarship in her name to enable a student from Bristol to progress to university.

Please also see: Beatrice Baker (vol two).

44 Cited in WAC Stewart et al, 1968, *The Educational Innovators: Volume II*, p46.

45 'Public School for Girls in Bristol' in *Western Daily Press*, 16 June 1931.

SARAH BAIRD-SMITH

1940-1994, PUBLISHER

Born in a Bristol air raid shelter in 1940, Sarah Hedley was a fighter from day one. Although her family lived in Bristol, Sarah attended Sherborne School for Girls, Dorset, and later read English at Somerville College, Oxford University. This fuelled her passion for literature and she graduated into a job with the publishers Longman Green, from where she worked her way up through a range of publishing houses and increasingly senior roles until she ran the religious imprint of Cassell; Sarah had converted to Roman Catholicism in adulthood.

She married fellow publisher Robin Baird-Smith with whom she had three children, and while bringing them up she continued to work for the religious imprints of various publishers. One of her key projects was to maintain promotion of the back catalogue of the Christian writer CS Lewis, and she commissioned writer and columnist AN Wilson to write a biography of Lewis in 1990.

Sarah took early retirement in order to focus on writing, and had completed her debut novel just days before she and her youngest son Archie were killed in a road traffic accident in 1994; *Hanging On* was published posthumously in 1995. Nicola Beauman, who would later set up the women's publishing house Persephone Books, reviewed *Hanging On* saying: "The novel is marvellously entertaining. The tragedy is that the author will never have the chance to go from strength to strength, as I am sure she would have done."[46]

46 Cited in Peter Stanford, ed, *The Death of a Child*, p92.

BEATRICE BAKER
1876-1973, HEADTEACHER

Hereford-born Beatrice May Baker (known as BMB) was always interested in learning and, after studying for a degree at London University in the late 1890s, she took up a range of teaching posts. One of these jobs was alongside the suffragist Mary Collin, who was headteacher of a girls' school in Cardiff and was a big influence on Beatrice: "[Mary's] personal style, which [Beatrice] adopted, combined carefully presented respectability with such overtly modern touches as the active encouragement of cycling."[47] Cycling (and the unladylike act of straddling something) was still a very daring activity for a respectable woman.

By 1911, Beatrice had moved to Bristol where she worked in Clifton at a private school for the daughters of gentlemen, Miss Bartlett's School for Young Ladies, which had been established in 1858. It was not long before she was both headteacher and proprietor of this school, and she duly appointed her life-long companion Lucy Rendall (whom she had met while working in Cardiff) as her deputy. Together, the two women transformed the Clifton school from a sedate place of education into an ambitious and socially aware school with a national reputation; they also renamed it Badminton School, after its one-time location at Badminton House in Clifton.

The majority of Mary's staff had studied at prestigious universities including Oxford, Cambridge and London, and she oversaw the setting up of societies for the girls to study archaeology, drama, reading and debating. Alongside the school, Beatrice and her staff set up a holiday cottage where families from the Bristol slums could go and get some fresh air. Beatrice

47 Christopher Watkins, 2007, 'Mary Beatrice Baker' in *Oxford Dictionary of National Biography*.

expected a lot of her students and insisted they be able to quote a line of poetry on demand. Parents (who included the publisher Victor Gollancz, painter Stanley Spencer and author Naomi Mitchison) largely found Beatrice's aspirational methods very appealing and places for students began to be in high demand.

By 1919, Badminton School had become so successful under Beatrice's guidance that it had outgrown its Clifton base and moved to its current location in Westbury-on-Trym. Beatrice continued to nurture the school and move it into the modern age, determined to create "forward looking citizens of a new world"[48]. She urged her pupils to take an interest in international affairs and to reject the staid ideas of nationalism that were being pushed by rival schools. She took the girls on annual trips to the League of Nations in Geneva, encouraged students to carry an excerpt from the covenant of the League in their pockets, and supported World War One conscientious objectors by organising peace conversion drives in the Bristol suburbs. She made it clear to her students that activism and political protest were vital parts of their education and essential tools for their futures.

Praising the school under Beatrice's guidance, in 1931 the *Western Daily Press* noted: "The school maintains a high standard of work, as may be seen both from the examination results and from the number of girls passing forward to the universities and other institutions preparing for the varied careers now open to girls."[49] After guiding Badminton School and its pupils through its temporary World War Two relocation to Dorset, Beatrice retired in 1946 but continued to exchange letters with former students for the rest of her life. She died at Greyfriars Nursing Home, Nailsea, in 1973.

48 Ibid.
49 'Public School For Girls in Bristol' in *Western Daily Press*, 16 June 1931.

And another thing... Notable former pupils from Badminton School include artist Mary Fedden, Indian Prime Minister Indira Ghandi and acclaimed writer **Iris Murdoch**. The latter of whom was so enamoured of Beatrice that she wrote an eponymous poem about her in 1938, kept up a lifelong correspondence with her *and*, in her 1954 novel *Under The Net*, Iris gave a horse the same name as Beatrice's house. If that's not the ultimate mark of respect, then I don't know what is.

Please also see: Miriam Badock (vol two), Mary Fedden (vol one), Indira Ghandi (vol two), Hannah Higgins (vol two).

BLANCHE BAKER

1844-1929, ARTIST

Born on Trenchard Street in the city centre, Blanche Baker was the middle child of nine for working-class Mary Baker and her builder husband William. When William inherited a large sum of money from his father in 1861, he bought a saw mill at Canon's Marsh and the family moved to live at Sneyd Park Villa, Ivywell Road, which was a significant step up from their run down Trenchard Street home (later demolished in slum clearance). Their new home boasted lush lawns, gardens, a conservatory, stables and even a small farm on adjoining land: it was a very dramatic change in circumstances.

This increase in fortunes meant the Baker children were able to benefit from a good education and Blanche chose to study at the Bristol School of Art, Queens Road (now part of the Royal West of England Academy), from where she graduated in 1864 and won a prize for a watercolour called 'Outline of Flowers'. However, her artistic education was cut short the following year when her mother Mary died suddenly and, aged 20, Blanche was called upon to help raise the younger children.

But Blanche didn't stop painting altogether and evidently returned to art with gusto by the end of the decade because in 1869 her watercolour drawing 'Greenfell Lane, Gloucester' was accepted by the Royal Academy, London, leading to her being given a one-woman show in Bristol in 1870, where 70 of her watercolours were exhibited; it is dispiriting to note that she often used the gender neutral 'BB' as the signature on her work to increase her appeal to buyers. When the Bristol Academy for the Promotion of Fine Arts opened a public exhibiting space in spring 1870, Blanche was one of the first to exhibit there and would continue doing so for the next 20 years. By 1876, Blanche was an Associate of the Bristol Academy (becoming a full member in 1901); she was also on the committee of the Bristol Boys' Home, as it was common for young women of social standing to be involved with good works.

The Baker family was hit by crisis in 1877 when Blanche's father William married a widow of dubious character called Gertrude Wilkinson, despite the opposition of his children who doubted the motives of the woman and believed she was only after William's fortune. Gertrude did nothing to prove the doubters wrong: she had affairs with her husband's coachman and carpenter, and she drank extremely heavily. By 1880, William had been classified as insane and placed in a 'lunatic asylum', so his children took the unusual step of filing for a divorce on behalf of their father, who was deemed incapable of representing himself. The marriage was dissolved in March 1881 and Gertrude received nothing.

It seems more than a coincidence that at the same time her father married Gertrude, Blanche moved out of the family's Sneyd Park home and left Bristol altogether, even resigning her post from the Bristol Boys' Home. However, once the marriage had been ended, Blanche returned and lived with her sister Laura on the farm adjacent to Sneyd Park Villa. In subsequent years, when her father was in a private asylum in London, Blanche moved to Ealing to be closer to him. While there, she worked as an art teacher at a school where two of her sisters also taught. Enterprisingly, Blanche also offered sketching tours for ladies along the banks of the River Thames during the summer months, which she advertised in *The Times* newspaper.

Blanche was one of the women whose work was exhibited at the Loan Exhibition of Women's Industries in Clifton in early 1885; a nationally significant and groundbreaking exhibition which was written about in the first volume of *The Women Who Built Bristol*. She also had 11 watercolours displayed at the Winter Exhibition at the Bristol Academy that year, which included pictures of Bristol landmarks Mary-le-Port Street and the Dutch House. Further pictures of Bristol scenes were exhibited in London the following year with the Society of Lady Artists.

However, despite her acclaim as an artist and having inherited a tidy sum upon the death of her father in 1884, neither Blanche nor her other unmarried sisters were financially well off. Artists simply didn't make much money from their work and teaching was not a lucrative profession. The Victorian philosopher Herbert Spencer (best remembered for having coined the phrase "survival of the fittest" after reading Charles Darwin's work about evolution) had been an inspiration to Blanche and she had met him through her London connections. He felt kindly about the struggling artist and in 1889 invited Blanche and her two unmarried sisters to live with him at 64 Avenue Road, St Johns Wood, London. This arrangement lasted until 1897, during which time Blanche was able to further her art career and exhibit more widely. She even travelled throughout Europe seeking inspiration for her work. After 1889, the three sisters remained living together in London and Blanche's career continued to flourish with the Royal Academy regularly exhibiting her work.

And another thing... Not only a talented artist, Blanche was also a good shot. In 1863, she took part in the Bristol Rifle Club's annual competition in Sneyd Park and won second prize in the Ladies' Rifle Match, firing with a Prussian needle rifle. The *Bristol Mercury* reported: "This match excited considerable interest and attracted numerous spectators, the ladies who entered into the competition firing with greater accuracy than had been expected. A target, only two feet in width, had been set up for their use in a meadow adjoining the range, upon which had been painted the figure of a man, having the bull's eye near the heart, and the whole of the body above the waist counting as centres."[50] As reward for her keen eye in the competition, Blanche won a photograph album.

ELIZA BALSUM
died 1821, KILLED BY STALKER

There is nothing new about women experiencing harassment from men, as Kingswood's Eliza Balsum could have testified... if only she had lived long enough. This young woman was obsessively stalked by an 18-year-old coal miner from Hanham called John Horwood, who became completely infatuated with her although she did not return his affection. This lack of interest didn't stop John from spending so much of his time following Eliza around (aka stalking her) that he eventually lost his job. In anger at her rejection, Horwood swore he would "mash her bones to pieces" if he ever saw her with another man.[51]

50 'The Ladies' Rifle Match' in *Bristol Mercury*, 1 August 1863.
51 thesteamcrane.co.uk/history-hanging/

One evening in January 1821, after seeing Eliza out with a group of friends including two men, an angered John threw a rock at Eliza's head and, although she managed to stagger home, she was in a huge amount of pain, bleeding from the wound and vomiting copiously as a result of the head injury. Her friends applied an ointment and bread poultice to the wound but it wasn't enough.[52] The injury caused Eliza agonising headaches and she was soon admitted to the Bristol Infirmary with a fever. Doctors found that Eliza's wound had become badly infected and, due to the rock causing a depressed fracture in her skull, she died in February 1821 of a brain abscess... having endured a horribly painful four weeks since Horwood's attack.

For the crime of Eliza's murder, Horwood was tried at the pub now known as the Steam Crane on North Street, Bedminster[53], and later hanged above the granite gatehouse at the New Gaol on Cumberland Road in April 1821; the original gatehouse of the gaol can still be seen amid a shiny new housing development. The crowd who attended to witness Horwood's death was so great that notices were issued warning people of their risk of being pushed into the New Cut by the seething throngs, long before any fences were erected on the river banks.

By the 2010s, new theories had emerged to suggest Horwood had not in fact killed Eliza and he had been wrongly convicted. Whether or not this is actually the case we cannot assert with any certainty but, using modern parlance, it is tempting to say #IBelieveHer and side with Eliza. Regardless, the facts are that Horwood was tried and convicted for Eliza's murder and for this he received the death penalty. Denied a burial at the time,

52 A home remedy thought to be good for curing infection.

53 It was standard practice to hold inquests and trials in pubs before the development of police courts because the pub was a large, indoor space that was easily accessible to many. The proceedings usually took place in a back room or upstairs, rather than in the main saloon. These inquests and trials were also a good source of extra income for the pub landlord.

Horwood's body was donated to medical science[54] and his skeleton was stored in a cupboard at the University of Bristol until 2011, when it was given what would have been a dignified funeral for Horwood's time.[55] A book covered in Horwood's skin and embossed with a gallows motif is kept at Bristol's M Shed Museum, and although there was a small campaign asking for the skin to be removed and buried with Horwood's skeleton, this did not come to pass.[56]

And another thing... At Horwood's trial on 11 April 1821, part of the prosecution against him rested on a phrenological report by **Mary Anne Schimmelpenninck**, which attempted to prove Horwood's guilt due to the shape of his skull. Phrenology is the scientific study into the lumps and bumps which make up an individual's skull and the belief these could determine the character and mental capacity of the individual. Phrenology has since been discredited as a science although it is still practised by some believers.

Please also see: Mary Anne Schimmelpenninck (vol one).

54 Prior to the Anatomy Act of 1832, it was common for the bodies of hanged felons to be used in this way.

55 I find this morally problematic; on one hand, I believe all human bodies should be treated with respect, including after death. On the other hand, Horwood was convicted and sentenced for murder and, while he should have been buried at the time, his life and death should not be retrospectively glorified.

56 A number of people who read advance copies of this book told me that while they had heard stories about John Horwood, they did not know anything about Eliza Balsum. This sadly tells us a lot about how history glorifies male violence against women but pays little attention to the female victim. The same scenario is repeated endlessly in history (as well as in contemporary news reports): books and films about real-life killers turn the violent man into a glamorous hero, while the woman/women he murdered are largely forgotten.

SAMUELLA and JOSEPHINE BARETTI
born 1872 and 1873, SISTER SUFFRAGISTS

These two sisters devoted their adult lives to campaigning for votes for women. Samuella and Josephine Baretti lived at 49 Royal York Crescent, Clifton, with their doctor father Thomas, who was supportive of his daughters' work to help secure equality for women.

Samuella became Secretary of the West of England Federation of the National Union of Women's Suffrage Societies (NUWSS), and was a regular speaker at public events for the organisation, including outdoors ones on the Durdham Downs and on the Horsefair in Broadmead. On one occasion in 1912, she even went head-to-head at a public debate in Clifton with a very vocal anti-suffragist called Mrs Solomon.[57] After 1928, when women had finally achieved the vote on the same terms as men, Samuella channelled her political energies into the relatively new Independent Labour Party.

Her sister Josephine was also a keen member of the NUWSS, as well as a playwright and poet; one volume of her poetry published in 1916 was dedicated to sister suffragist Sarah Jane Tanner[58]. Some academics have suggested the imagery in suffragist poetry can be likened to the martyrdom in Christian poetry, and women found a sense of freedom, adventure and self-achievement in their suffrage activities which had previously been denied to them due to strict Victorian and Edwardian morals. Jonathan Inkpin

57 Mrs Solomon is an interesting character but having no strong Bristol link she doesn't qualify for her own entry. However, she pops up in endless books and accounts of the suffrage movement, from Helen Pankhurst's 2018 book *Deeds Not Words* to the pages of many newspapers, writing stridently *against* granting the vote to herself and other women.

58 Sarah Jane Tanner was one of the very first prominent suffrage campaigners in the UK, and was one of the founding members of the Women's Liberal Association, which met at Bristol's Colston Hall in 1880. Her cousins were the Sturge sisters, who are profiled in volume one of *The Women Who Built Bristol*.

identifies that in one of Josephine's poems, 'Woman — The Christ', the representation of piety implies a kinship between the insults hurled at Christians and those thrown at suffrage campaigners: "Scorn'd, spat at, scourged, reviled, contemn'd, distress'd; A by-word, mock, the cynic world's great jest; Thou art the Christ, the one true saviour name."[59]

Like many suffragists, Josephine stepped back from her suffrage campaigning during World War One, favouring activities endorsed by the NUWSS such as working for the Scottish Women's Hospital and opening clubs for women and educational colleges for mothers, to further their opportunities in life. Once the war had ended in 1918, she returned to lobbying for women's rights and became Honorary Secretary of the Women's International League for Peace and Freedom.[60]

KATHLEEN BARKER
1925-1991, THEATRE HISTORIAN

Without Kathleen Mary Deborah Barker's decades of careful research, we would know a lot less about Bristol's colourful theatre history than we currently do. There are no fewer than 80 large lever-arch files (each containing 600-800 sheets of paper, many of which are double-sided) stored at the University of Bristol's Theatre Collection, and all of these were collated by Kathleen at her home at 21 St Matthew's Road, Cotham. She devoted her life to carefully researching regional theatre from the 18th and 19th centuries, and her passion for theatre shines through.

Kathleen began with a simple announcement in the *Western*

59 Jonathan Inkpin, 1996, 'Combating the Sin of Self-Sacrifice: Christian Feminism in the Women's Suffrage Struggle 1903-1918', PhD thesis, Durham University, p114.
60 Lucienne Boyce, Spring 2017, 'Suffrage City: Vote 100 – Women and Vote' in *Better Bristol* magazine, p22-23.

Kathleen Barker illustration by Rhi Lee

Daily Press stating she was looking for like-minded people with whom to establish a Society for Theatre Research, holding her group's inaugural meeting at the University of Bristol on 2 February 1950: "A cordial invitation is extended to all who are interested."[61] There was nothing theatrical that escaped Kathleen's attention: from a short newspaper announcement to a lengthier article in a theatre journal, Kathleen painstakingly retyped each piece of news coverage for posterity because the photocopier was yet to be widely available.

One of Kathleen's greatest gifts to contemporary theatre fans is her comprehensive history of the Theatre Royal on King Street (now called the Bristol Old Vic), which she documented from 1766 to 1966 and subsequently published as a book in 1974 called *Theatre Royal, Bristol*. Her research for this book filled 24 files and exceeds 16,000 pages. A further ten files document the dates and cast lists of every single production ever staged at the Theatre Royal from its opening night in 1766 right up until the launch of the Bristol Old Vic Theatre Company in 1946.

Kathleen's subsequent book was *Bristol at Play*, published in 1975, which looked at a wide range of popular entertainments spanning the 15th century to the 1970s and included fairs, circuses, travelling shows, music halls and much more besides. And her research was not just confined to Bristol: she also collated folders about 19th century entertainments in Nottingham, Sheffield, Newcastle and Brighton. There were few limits to her research and Kathleen was rewarded for her tireless efforts with a PhD in Victorian Studies from the University of Leicester in 1982.

In addition to written research, Kathleen lectured widely on her specialist subjects and, as you might expect, all of her lectures have been typed up and preserved. Along with the rest of her

61 'Society for Theatre Research' in *Western Daily Press*, 28 January 1950.

archive, they are available to visit at the University of Bristol's Theatre Collection.[62]

IRENE BASE
1897-1982, CALLIGRAPHER

The arts of calligraphy and illumination seem to be going out of fashion nowadays, but Edwardian artist Irene Esther Muriel Base was talented at both and respected globally for her work. Born in Norfolk to Esther and George Base, Irene had moved to 48 Station Road, Shirehampton, by 1939 where she worked as a calligrapher and illuminator. This meant she was skilled at creating manuscripts by hand using traditional calligraphic methods, and she illuminated the initial letters and edges of the pages: which is to say that, typically, vibrant ink colours and intricate patterns were created surrounding the initial letters of important documents. This was a traditional form of art that dates back to the Roman era but which declined in popularity following the rise of the printing press.

A local example of Irene's work can be seen in the Church of St Mary, Shirehampton, with *The Shirehampton Missal,* which is a gilded and painted complete order of service for Holy Communion in fine calligraphy on parchment. It took Irene a great number of years to finish this work, which resembles the illuminated books of medieval times.[63] She also created the lettering used on many war memorials in churches around England and contributed to a range of other tributes during her decades of work. Describing a piece that Irene had in an exhibition at the Clifton Arts Club in 1928, the *Western Daily Press* noted: "An unusually good piece

62 bristol.ac.uk/theatre-collection/explore/theatre/kathleen-barker-archive/
63 churchcrawler.co.uk/shiremar.htm

of engrossed illuminated work is the sonnet 'The Grasshopper and The Cricket' by Irene Base, which includes a mass of intricate detail handled with a considerable skill."[64]

After moving to Shirehampton, Irene lived for the rest of her life at first 48, and then 23, Station Road, before moving to the Elizabethan House on the High Street for her final years. She was a lifelong member of the Arts and Crafts Exhibition Society, and among the many places her work was exhibited was the prestigious Royal Academy of Arts on London's Piccadilly.

And another thing... One of the women honoured with a creation by Irene was **Catherine Court**, who had been a much-loved district nurse in Shirehampton between 1903 and 1937. When Catherine retired in 1937, the community was extremely sad to lose her and Irene was commissioned to record Shirehampton's appreciation of the ceaseless care and devotion the nurse had shown the parish with an illuminated address on calf's skin. At the top of this address is a golden depiction of Florence Nightingale holding a lit lamp.

AMELIA BAYNTUN
1919-1988, COMEDY ACTOR

Despite being born in Bristol, comedy actor Amelia Ellen Bayntun made a successful living playing Cockneys in a lifetime's worth of films and television roles, including with the popular *Carry On* movie franchise. She was described as "an artist of resource, originality and remarkable sensibility".[65]

Amelia's acting career began in 1937 when she joined the Bristol Unity Players led by Peggy Ann Wood, then during World

64 'Annual Autumn Sketch Exhibition Opened' in *Western Daily Press*, 15 October 1928.
65 'A Good Night At The Players" in *The Stage*, 16 November 1961.

War Two she toured abroad to entertain the troops, and by the 1960s she had moved to London and joined the well-regarded Joan Littlewood Theatre Workshop. With this company, she was cast as the grandmother in the popular new play *Sparrers Can't Sing* (fellow *Carry On* star Barbara Windsor would appear in the 1963 film of the play). *The Stage* reviewed her role saying: "Teamwork being such an essential feature of this production, there are no stars. However, in Amelia Bayntun who plays Granny Miggs, we see an actress giving a star performance which will be long remembered. Her voice, movements and gestures are absolutely true-to-life and the suggestion of an indomitable spirit bravely coping with an inner personal tragedy is skillfully portrayed."[66]

This acclaim led to Amelia being spotted by TV producers and she landed roles in such primetime shows as *Dixon of Dock Green* and *On The Buses*. Pop composer Lionel Bart cast Amelia as Mrs Blitzen in his 1962 West End musical *Blitz!* (about the Jewish community in the East End of London during World War Two), and she appeared in every single one of the 562 performances of this hit show. "There are nearly 60 named characters in *Blitz*! … but I doubt whether I shall remember anybody except Amelia Bayntun as the Cockney-Jewish mother of Petticoat Lane," enthused the *Illustrated London News*.[67]

Amelia featured in five *Carry On* films between 1969 and 1972, including *Carry On Camping* (1969, Gerald Thomas) for which Barbara Windsor would become so well known. She also had small parts in the James Bond film *Thunderball* (1965, Terence Young) and the family film *The Railway Children* (1970, Lionel Jeffries). She typically played Cockney ladies who were much older than Amelia herself, which was a trend that had begun with *Sparrers Can't Sing*. Amelia reflected: "No one else [but Joan Littlewood]

66 'Joan Littlewood's East-Enders Are Again Up West' in *The Stage*, 6 April 1961.
67 'The World of the Theatre' in *Illustrated London News*, 19 May 1962.

would have given me the chance of playing an old part. It was a wonderful opportunity, and all the more of a challenge because I was rather nervous about going to work at Theatre Workshop." Praising the faith Joan had put in her, Amelia added: "It is far more important than some people think, to have that sort of real faith placed in you. It can make a world of difference, not only to your work but to your whole professional outlook."[68]

In her personal life, Amelia married Ronald McCrindell in London in 1947. They managed the theatrical pub The Grapes on Great Marlborough Street, London (which closed in 1968 and was incorporated into the Liberty department store), and Amelia would help behind the bar when she wasn't engaged on acting jobs. However, the couple divorced in 1963 on the grounds of Ronald's infidelity and Amelia moved to Ireland, although she continued to act on stage into the 1970s.

Please also see: Peggy Ann Wood (vol one).

PHYLLIS BEDELLS

1893-1985, BALLERINA

The first British-born prima ballerina (the chief female dancer in a ballet company) was Bristolian Ethel Phyllis Bedells, who took the role at the prestigious Empire Theatre, Leicester Square, London, in 1914 after seven years with the company. She had come a long way since appearing as a cornflower in a production of *Alice in Wonderland* at London's Prince of Wales Theatre in 1906 aged 13, where a review of her performance presciently stated: "[Phyllis] dances on the tips of her toes like a future prima ballerina."[69]

68 'The Director With Faith Can Help The Actor' in *The Stage*, 2 February 1961.
69 'Alice in Wonderland', 21 December 1906, in *The Globe*.

When she was a little girl, Phyllis moved with her family from Barrow Gurney on the edge of Bristol to "a charming cottage" called Rose Mount in the then-new and then-leafy suburb of Knowle in south Bristol.[70] She attended the local Convent of St Agnes School in Knowle (the impressive buildings survive at the top of St Agnes Avenue), but once a week ventured up to Clifton for deportment lessons and "fancy dancing" classes, which were a form of ballroom dancing designed to give young ladies grace and social polish, both led by Edna Stacey, who was the choreographer and dancing mistress for the Bristol Amateur Operatic Society. "I can remember, step for step, some of the solo dances," Phyllis wrote in her autobiography. "We were never forced, always encouraged, and I adored [Edna]... Classes ended with a slow waltz round the room with us holding out our very full skirts, then we walked slowly and gracefully the length of the room to say goodbye to our teacher. No dashing about or chatting in class was permitted."[71]

In later years, thanks to Edna's encouragement and direction, Phyllis would go on to study with such greats of the dance world as Anna Pavlova (of whom she told an interviewer in 1914: "Pavlova is my very great friend. She is my ideal, the perfect artiste. I am indebted to her for a number of lessons"[72]). Phyllis was unusual among her contemporaries because she retained her English name rather than adopting a Russian moniker as many British dancers of the time did; the consensus being that good dancers apparently *only* came from Russia. Due to this national loyalty, Phyllis was clutched to the British heart even closer than she might otherwise have been: "Bedells, like everyone else, was under pressure to change her name. But she took it as a matter of

70 Phyllis Bedells, 1954, *My Dancing Days*, p7. The cottage has since been demolished.

71 Ibid. p10.

72 'Miss Phyllis Bedells Interviewed' in *The Western Daily Press*, 7 April 1914.

Phyllis Bedells illustration by Carrie Love

pride and principle to keep it, feeling that to be an 'openly English' dancer would increase the chances for British dance and dancers to be accepted on their own merits."[73]

After leaving the Empire Theatre in 1916, Phyllis became a popular dancer in West End musicals and at opera ballets in Covent Garden and was widely acknowledged as the finest dancer of her day. *The Dancing Times* credited Phyllis with single-handedly creating the dawn of the English ballet, and on her retirement in 1935 it wrote: "What a wonderful tonic the precept and example of Phyllis Bedells proved... We who are old enough to remember these things understand how much the present secure position of native ballet in England is due to the inspiring influence of [Phyllis]."[74] She also appeared in silent films such as the short fantasy movie *Fairyland* (1916) and the Russian drama *The Land of Mystery* (1920).

Phyllis married Lieutenant Ian MacBean in February 1918, keeping the wedding a secret after both felt overwhelmed by the publicity their engagement had generated. Ian, who was orphaned as a child, was a quiet person and it was his sadness which first drew Phyllis to him: "The loneliness of his life wrung my heart. I longed to be able to look after him."[75] The couple had two children, Jean and David, both of whom were taught to dance. In fact, Phyllis had been dancing until two days before she gave birth to Jean, leading her to claim that Jean was literally born to be a dancer.[76]

In 1920, the family moved to 12 Buckingham Vale, Clifton, and purchased the nearby 20 Vyvyan Terrace, which had previously been home to the Swedish Institute and gymnasium run by

73 Beth Genné, 1995, 'Openly English: Phyllis Bedells and the Birth of the British Ballet' in *Dance Chronicle*, p442.
74 Ibid, p437.
75 Phyllis Bedells, 1954, *My Dancing Days*, p83.
76 Ibid, p128.

Theodora Johnson. Phyllis established a ballet school there, named it the West of England Academy and a plaque remains above the door to commemorate this. Phyllis maintained that due to the lack of a ballet tradition in England, it was important for the next generation of ballerinas to have a more coherent education in their art than she had received: "I had to fight my way from the very beginning and to try to sift out what was best from the various schools and teachers. It is not so easy as going, as in Russia, straight into a school which everybody knows as a school with high traditions. You have to find it, and accept from it what it is that is good. Such a way will always be uphill until we have a national theatre for the ballet and a national school connected with it."[77] The Academy would put on week-long shows at the Bristol Hippodrome once the pupils were ready to perform in public.

In 1935, the Academy was granted the Royal Charter and became the Royal Academy of Dancing: "What great joy it gave us! After only 15 years of existence such an honour was intensely gratifying."[78] Phyllis, who also ran a dance school in London, would be delighted to know the Vyvyan Terrace space remains in use for ballet today as part of the Bristol School of Dancing.

After retiring from professional ballet performances in 1935, Phyllis devoted her time to teaching and working as an examiner for the Royal Academy of Dance. She also wrote her autobiography *My Dancing Days,* which was published in 1954. Portraits of her can be seen in London's National Portrait Gallery.[79]

And another thing... Phyllis and Ian's daughter **Jean Bedells** (who used her mother's surname professionally) was born in Bristol

77 'Miss Phyllis Bedells', in *Western Daily Press*, 15 March 1920.
78 Phyllis Bedells, 1954, *My Dancing Days*, p210.
79 With thanks to Lori Streich for the nomination of Phyllis Bedells to this book.

in 1924 and spent eight years being trained by Phyllis before joining the famous Sadler's Wells Ballet in London. She became an enormously well-respected dancer and examiner at the Royal Academy of Dance, having made her first appearance on stage at the age of two. Jean continued dancing professionally well into the 2000s despite being in her 70s. She died in April 2014 aged 89.[80]

Please also see: Theodora Johnson (vol one).

'MRS BEER'

born c1890 , BARTERED WIFE

Alas, we don't know the real name of this woman because it wasn't reported in the newspapers, so I have dubbed her 'Mrs Beer'. Why? Because this unlucky wife was bartered by her feckless husband in exchange for a pint of beer. He sounds like a truly terrible man: with the newspaper report adding that he was a workshy widower who expected his wife to keep not only him but also his five small children from his first marriage. The sad story gets worse, as Mrs Beer explained to Bristol Police Court in July 1914: "A week after our marriage he sold me to another man for a pint of beer. I wish I had stayed with the other man instead of returning to my husband, for the man who bought me worked and kept me."[81]

The story did the Edwardian version of going viral and appeared in regional newspapers all around the country in the following days. Whether or not it inspired several copycat incidences of husbands bartering brides for booze is unknown,

80 royalacademyofdance.org/news/jean-bedells-frad-arad

81 'Wife Sold For Beer: Deal With Week-Old Bride', *Daily Gazette for Middlesbrough*, 8 July 1914.

but in the following years similar cases of wives being sold for beer were reported in Sheffield, Ireland and even Romania.

EILEEN BELL

1907-2005, ARTIST

The eldest child of Clifton-based cellist Margaret Bowerbank and her bank manager husband John, Eileen Elizabeth Jefford Bowerbank was not encouraged by her parents to be an artist. Margaret and John felt there was no respectability in visual art and instead persuaded Eileen to study the piano. It was only after she married consultant surveyor Randall Bell (whom she affectionately called Badger) in 1937 that Eileen was able to express her previously quashed passion for art.

Eileen became a prolific natural artist who was still painting well into her ninth decade. She had joined the St John's Wood School of Art in 1939, where her classmates included the (future) esteemed artists Michael Ayrton and John Minton. She later studied at the Anglo-French Art Centre in 1947, where she learned from respected continental artists and in this way was able to exhibit in exhibitions across the UK.

During the 1950s, Eileen became an interior designer working with the Council of Industrial Design, and creating wallpaper and textile patterns for interior design companies including Elizabeth Eaton, Sanderson and many private clients. By the late 1960s, Eileen had expanded into working with clay and crocheting rugs, as well as writing books for children which were inspired by her son Sebastian. At the same time, she took in a young horticultural student called Alan Titchmarsh as a lodger for three years. He recalled Eileen supplied "wonderful soups and stews, and her own brand of moussaka, and wine — sometimes homemade (her oak leaf had a particularly detrimental effect on the legs) drunk from un-matching artful glasses"[82].

Eileen continued to create art into the 1990s, taking inspiration from landscapes and animals. She exhibited widely and it was only when her eyesight failed that she was forced to stop painting. A 2003 retrospective was held in Colchester which confirmed Eileen to be an adept colourist capable of producing still lifes with a very unique take.

FRANCES BELLERBY

1899-1975, WRITER

Born at St Aidan's House on Summerhill Road, St George, as a child Frances Mary Eirene Parker was a popular pupil at Mortimer House School in Clifton, where she excelled at both academic studies and sports. Feeling stifled by her parents' religious zeal, she sought refuge away from the home in paid work, and after leaving school she took jobs as varied as veterinary nurse, teacher, journalist and research assistant.

Her first books were published when she was in her late 20s and living independently in London: a volume of essays entitled *Perhaps?* in 1927 and a novella called *The Unspoiled* in 1928. Frances maintained her links to her home city by continuing to work as a drama critic for the *Bristol Times and Mirror* newspaper, which, in those glory days, still maintained a London office.

In December 1929, Frances married John Bellerby, who shared her passion for sports and physical activities. But their happiness was cut short when a fall on Lulworth cliffs in 1930 caused a spinal injury which left her a permanent invalid. The

82 Alan Titchmarsh, 2002, *Trowel and Error*, p165.

combined stress of this accident, and the emotional upset caused by her mother's suicide in 1932 (her only brother having already been killed in World War One in 1915), led the marriage to fail and Frances moved to Cornwall in 1940 without John. It was here she focussed on writing the poetry for which she would be best remembered, and she had five volumes of her poems published over the final decades of her life.

Frances' poetry deals with nature, memory and loss, as does her prose, and her best known novel was *Hath the Rain a Father?* (1946), which was concerned with the unimaginable scale of loss of life caused by World War One. Following a diagnosis of breast cancer in 1950, Frances became reclusive but fought the disease and lived until 1975, when the cancer returned and claimed her life. An obituary stated: "The death ... of Frances Bellerby ... has robbed contemporary poetry of a unique and distinguished voice. To read her is to be in the presence of a true original."[83]

'BLACKIE'

1912-1927, CAT

Author's note: I realise there will be some people who think animals should not be in this collection of Bristolian women. Those people will be pleased to know that although I initially wanted to include an entire section devoted to the wonderful female animals of Bristol, I eventually relented and handpicked only my favourites.

In his 1936 memoir *A Blind Musician Looks Back*, an organist from St Mary Redcliffe Church writes about how one evening he and fellow organist Ralph Morgan found a black kitten waiting for

83 Nathalie Blondel, 2013, 'Frances Bellerby' in *Oxford Dictionary of National Biography*.

them in the church. "Morgan told me that she had come about the church ever since he had been there," wrote Alfred Hollins of the cat who would live in the church for 15 years. "She was a very musical pussy, always waiting for him when he went to practise, ready to follow him in to church and, as soon as he got settled at the organ, jumped on to his knee and sat quietly the whole time. Realising that I was a stranger, instead of sitting on my knee, she sat beside me at the organ stool and I used often to leave off playing in order to stroke her."[84]

Some sources claim St Mary Redcliffe's cat was a male called Tom, others that it was a female named Blackie, while the cat's gravestone outside the south entrance to the church is enigmatically inscribed with 'The Church's Cat'. Given that I can find a greater number of sources which refer to the moggy as an unnamed lady cat, I'm going with the majority and presuming she was a female feline.

Blackie became a permanent fixture at St Mary Redcliffe and soon ventured indoors not only for organ practice but also for services (where she would often sit on the lap of somebody in the congregation, or follow the choir as they walked down the aisle to reach their pews), and was generally cared for by the verger Eli Richards. In return, Blackie kept on top of the church's mouse, rat and pigeon population, all of which were destructive to the church's architecture. When Blackie died, the much-loved cat was given a dignified funeral and burial service (including the playing of organ music, which she had enjoyed so much), before her final resting place was marked with the abovementioned tombstone.

84 Cited in Reece Winstone, Glyn Duggan, 1982, *Bristol Curiosities*, p15.

MISTRESS BLAKE

born c1660, SCORNED WOMAN

Deep under the old Bristol Castle walls was a wooden post which had been set up at the edge of the River Frome. Upon this post was a transverse beam that moved on a swivel and housed a chair upon the furthest end. This, dear reader, was Bristol's ducking stool and it had been in use since the 16th century as a punishment for women deemed to be 'immoral', 'nagging' or 'scolding', although there is a misconception the ducking stool was only used to identify so-called witches. With the ducking stool (which, quite literally, saw the victim ducked under the water three times), it was not uncommon for the poor woman to drown due to an overzealous operator who neglected to raise the stool in time. As academic Madge Dresser has observed: "The exercise of male control over women … could be manifested in many ways. One of the most chilling, perhaps, is the policing of female discourse through accusations of scolding, punishable by being ducked in the Frome in the ducking stool."[85]

The final occupant of the Bristol ducking stool was Mistress Blake in 1718. This woman was considered particularly obnoxious and sentenced by the Mayor of Bristol, Edmund Mountjoy… a man who lived to regret dishing out this particular punishment to this particular woman. It is said that while Mountjoy was respected and liked by the people of Bristol, he was belittled at home by his wife... and his citizens knew this all too well.

While walking in Hotwells one evening, Mountjoy overheard a high-pitched woman screaming at her husband from inside her house. She reportedly yelled: "You good for nothing, faint-hearted wretch," before pushing her husband onto the street and slamming

85 Madge Dresser, 2016, *Women and the City*, p38.

the door behind him. Attracting the attention of a passing police officer, Mountjoy ordered the woman to be arrested so he could teach her that it was a man who should be in charge of the home… not a woman. This was how he met Mistress Blake.

When Mistress Blake came before Mountjoy (for he was also magistrate) in the docks, her incessant shouting in the courtroom led the mayor to proclaim: "To the ducking stool with her. Give her three dips and see if that doesn't cool her body and quench her tongue."

A huge crowd gathered to watch the ducking and Mistress Blake accepted her fate with surprising calmness given her previous displays of hot headedness. While ducked into the freezing and fetid River Frome, she held her tongue while those in the crowd laughed and jeered, calling out "cold duck" and "soused tongue" in merriment. When Mistress Blake was finally unstrapped from the ducking stool, she ignored those around her and simply declared she would have the last laugh at Mountjoy… who she knew had ducked her in place of his own wife, the woman whom he really wanted to punish.

Biding her time, when Mountjoy's term as mayor came to an end, Mistress Blake sued the former mayor for assault and battery… and she won. Of course, this created a massive scandal with plentiful gossip and Mountjoy himself was subjected to a lot of dinner party invitations where the main course was always 'cold duck'. The result was that no other magistrate dared to give the Bristol ducking stool in punishment again, although the ducking stool was still used in some other places in the UK until as recently as the early 19th century.

And another thing… Many years after the Bristol ducking stool had been out of service, a local man bought the old stool and created snuff boxes from the wood. He claimed a pinch of snuff from one of these boxes would protect a man from ever encountering a scolding or domineering wife. But what would protect women from marrying the sort of fool who supported these notions?

DEBORAH BOWRING
1816-1902, SUFFRAGIST

Taking on the role of Vice-President of the Bristol and West of England Society for Women's Suffrage, Deborah Bowring (née Castle) made no secret of where she stood politically. As a Liberal, she regularly spoke on platforms all across the West Country in favour of votes for women, with her final speech before retirement being at the Exeter ice rink in May 1897.

As one of 14 siblings born to Clifton-based Mary and Thomas Castle, it would have been easy for young Deborah to have avoided attention from her preoccupied parents, but Deborah instead flourished in the company of their enlightened friends. As Unitarians, the Castle family moved in the same social circles as respected reformers such as Lant Carpenter (father of reformer Mary Carpenter) and John Bishop Estlin (father of abolitionist Mary Estlin), and their progressive attitudes to equality surely rubbed off on young Deborah.

In 1860, she married the politician Sir John Bowring and the couple moved to Exeter. Here, the new Lady Bowring immersed herself in philanthropy, with a particular interest in promoting the idea of a university education that was open to women as well as men. In 1871, she was named Vice President of the Bristol and West of England Society for Women's Suffrage and was described as an "apt and dignified speaker" who "blended a good deal of humour with her shrewd and graceful remarks"[86].

Please also see: Mary Carpenter (vol one), Mary Estlin (vol one).

JOAN BRACEY
1656-1685, DANDY HIGHWAYWOMAN

She's the dandy highwaywoman, who you're too scared to mention...[87]

What is a farmer's daughter to do when the love of her life is a highwayman? Why, rob her wealthy father and run off with her lover, of course! When Northampton-born Joan Phillips fell in love with Edward Bracey (although no records of a marriage exist, Joan assumed Edward's surname as her own), she could have had no idea of the adventures they would have. Hers was a short life (she died aged 29) but a full one.

For four years, Joan and Edward terrorised the highways of England, carrying out innumerable robberies and frauds. The authorities remained hot on their heels and the pair were often threatened by the gallows. It was this fear for their future which led them to settle in Bristol and try to assume a more honest life, which they established thanks to the large fortune they had amassed from their thefts.

This was how Joan and Edward came to be the landlords of an inn on the edge of Bristol, which they ran successfully and it became known for its fine wines and beautiful landlady. Joan was skilled in the art of flirting with her customers and persuading them to spend increasing amounts on drink. But when customers became too flirtatious or too infatuated by Joan, she had an

86 KD Reynolds, 2004, 'Lady Bowring' in *Oxford Dictionary of National Biography*.
87 With apologies to Adam and the Ants.

excellent ruse to dampen their ardour.

The tale goes that one suitor, a Mr Day, was excited by the prospect of Joan being home alone after hours one night while Edward was away. After last orders, Day hastened to the inn's door and was shown upstairs by a maid. The candle was out in Joan's bedroom so he scuttled into the darkness, calling out her name while stripping himself naked ready for an amorous encounter. Not hearing a response from Joan, Day carried on shuffling around the dark room looking for the bed until he suddenly fell down a flight of stairs, through a trapdoor and landed outside the inn... naked. At this point, Day realised Joan and her maid had set him up. He called out to them and knocked repeatedly at the door, anxious to retrieve his clothes, but the two women inside the house had bolted the doors and he was forced to make his way home: cold, naked and jeered at by all who saw him.

Despite the success of their inn, Joan and Edward were not well-received by everyone. And within a year, their inn had become a house of disrepute and they were forced out and back onto the highways with their tricks and robberies. One young man who had hoped to see the back of the couple was a Mr Rumbald, who had run up substantial bar debts with the Braceys. However, Rumbald was the heir to a large estate and the couple had their eyes on his land. First, Joan threatened him with prison on account of his huge debt to them. With Rumbald sufficiently nervous, Joan set up a faux-robbery that she persuaded him to assist with. Once the crime was committed (and Joan had returned the money to the stooge), she further threatened Rumbald by saying she would report him to the authorities for the robbery for which he would be hanged... unless he made over all of his estate to the Braceys. Rumbald did as he was bid. Not content to stop here, the couple kept Rumbald prisoner in their home until he had signed over his land *and* they had sold it on, so Rumbald could assure the future purchaser the sale was above board. Only once the Braceys had pocketed the money did they let Rumbald go free.

Following this perceived triumph, Joan began to dress in male highway robber clothing and return to a life roaming the roads with Edward. This was until April 1685, when Joan was finally seized by the authorities and sentenced to death by hanging. Edward escaped a similar fate by going into hiding before continuing his life of highway robbery, until he was fatally shot by a gang of men a few years after Joan's death.

BETTY BRYANT

1920-2005, ACTOR, HUMANITARIAN

Born in Bristol, Elizabeth 'Betty' Patterson was propelled to stardom after her recently-widowed mother emigrated the family to Australia when Betty was just four years old. Because her mother was a professional singer, she taught Betty how to sing and perform from a young age, which meant that by the time Betty was a teenager — and the family was living in Sydney — she was already achieving some success as a radio star in addition to acting in the theatre. Crediting her mother for supporting her, Betty said: "When I have given up heart in the past, Mother has said, 'Come on, keep your chin up.' I couldn't have got where I am without her."[88]

Hollywood scriptwriter Elsie Blake-Wilkins spotted Betty on Bondi Beach one day and the young woman was promptly cast as the lead in the 1941 war film *40,000 Horsemen*, which would go on to be the first ever international movie success for an Australian film. Betty's step-father said of the initial meeting: "Miss Wilkins

88 'Hollywood after Betty Bryant, "Forty" Lead', in *The Mail*, Adelaide, 18 January 1941.

visited Bondi on a Sunday, and just as she was passing our house a violent thunderstorm broke and she took shelter. We discovered that she was from Hollywood. Just at that moment, Betty, in a bathing suit, came running up from the beach. In spite of Betty's bedraggled appearance, the the scriptwriter was immediately impressed by her, told her she was a film type and urged her to become interested. She was so sure that Betty was a 'find' that she took her to Cinesound Studios for tests."[89] This was in 1938 and Betty's career galloped along afterwards.

The film *40,000 Horsemen* was directed by Charles Chauvel, who was enraptured by Betty's presence, telling *The Mail* newspaper in Adelaide in 1941 that Betty was "the most important film personality discovered in Australia since Errol Flynn"[90], which set her up for big things. Indeed, Betty became so popular after *40,000 Horsemen* that she was called on by the Red Cross to entertain the troops during World War Two, earning herself the nickname of The Red Cross Queen. This was to be the start of her lifelong work as a humanitarian.

Betty's marriage to film director Maurice Silverstein in August 1941 (he would ultimately become President of MGM International) and the subsequent arrival of their three children curtailed her acting career. By the time the children were older, Betty was also older… apparently *too* old to return to movies according to an industry which favours youth (her final film role was a small part as a café singer in the 1948 movie *Saigon*). So she resumed her humanitarian work and joined up with fellow actors Sophia Loren and Peter Ustinov in 1966 to launch the Foundation for the Peoples of the South Pacific (FSP), which was an organisation designed to support people in Melanesia and Polynesia by improving health, education, agriculture and

89 Ibid.
90 portrait.gov.au/magazines/59/the-life-of-bryant

business links. The organisation was a big success and remains a global network with organisations in more than 60 nations.

In 2000, Hillary Clinton awarded Betty with a humanitarian service award.[91] Stunning photos of Betty throughout her life can be viewed online at the Australian National Portrait Gallery.[92]

MARY BURDOCK
1805-1835, MURDERER

There is (sadly) no shortage of female murderers from Bristol and most of them do not warrant inclusion in this book. The murderers who are included in this book are those who were particularly unusual, whether in the scale of their crimes, the nature of their particular crimes or for other reasons that become apparent. And this is the category Mary Ann Burdock falls into: at the time of her execution on the roof of Bristol Gaol on Cumberland Road, she was the first woman to be hanged in Bristol in 33 years and it caused a national stir.

Born Mary Ann Williams in Herefordshire, when she was 19 years old Mary was employed as a maid by a Mr Plumley at St Nicholas Street in the city centre. This arrangement didn't last long: after 18 months Mary was sacked for petty theft and "other improper acts". Shortly after, she married a tailor named Charles Agar but this also didn't work out and he left her soon after the wedding. Mary then lived with (but in what capacity?) a married valet called Mr Thomas, before "forming a connection" (what kind of connection?) with a man called Mr Wade, who kept a lodging house at 17 Trinity Street, near Lawrence Hill. Around this time, Mary bore two children but it is not known who the

91 Tom Vallance, 'Betty Bryant' in *The Independent*, 14 October 2005.
92 portrait.gov.au/magazines/59/the-life-of-bryant

Mary Burdock illustration by Tina Altwegg

father was. However, what *is* known is that Mary was living by her wits.

While Mary was living at the Trinity Street house, Clara Smith, one of the other lodgers, suddenly died after experiencing severe stomach pains. Mary told people Clara was a pauper with no relations and this was why Mary arranged the burial herself. However, the truth was Clara was far from a pauper. In fact, she had hoarded as much as £3,000 in a locked box in her bedroom. Coincidentally, shortly after Clara's death, Mr Wade paid off his debts, bought £400 of stock to start a business and Mary herself seemed much more comfortable in her life... becoming still more comfortable after the sudden death of Mr Wade. Around this time, Mary bigamously married Paul Burdock, despite still being married to Charles Agar.

Life was not plain sailing. A few months later, relatives of the deceased Clara arrived in Bristol and started asking questions about what had happened to her estate. It didn't take long until their suspicions were aroused by Mary and the body was exhumed and sent to analytical chemist William Herapath at the Bristol Medical School, who found traces of arsenic in Clara's stomach. Mary's maid Mary Allen then confirmed she had seen her mistress buy and administer a yellow powder to Clara, and the finger of blame quickly pointed to Mary as the murderer.

Her trial began on 10 April 1835 and lasted three days, concluding with a definite verdict of guilty and the death sentence. On 15 April 1835, dressed entirely in black, Mary attended the condemned service in prison before being brought out for her execution at 1pm. An enormous crowd had been gathering for hours to see Mary's execution, despite the heavy rain, with the *Bristol Mirror* claiming an audience of 50,000 onlookers stretching the entire length of the Coronation Road: "The largest assemblage of human beings we ever beheld." It was reported to be a carnival atmosphere, with people seemingly enjoying the spectacle and camaraderie while forgetting the reason they had all gathered was to witness the sanctioned killing of a woman.[93]

The reasons that Mary's death drew such a crowd were several. First, there was the novelty of her being a woman; before Mary's execution in 1835, the last two women hanged in Bristol had been friends Maria Davis and Charlotte Bobbett in 1802 (who had left Davis' child to die of exposure). Second, at 30 years old, Mary was relatively young to be executed. Third, her crime had attracted a great deal of newspaper coverage and the public was deeply invested in what she had done and felt thoroughly vexed about a female killer.

After she had died, Mary's body was removed from the gallows and she was buried inside the prison walls. Bristol Gaol closed in 1883 and was replaced by the Horfield prison. The Cumberland Road site was then sold to the Great Western Railway but the buildings fell into ruin and now only the Grade II listed gatehouse survives. The remainder of the site has been levelled and, at the time of writing, luxury flats are being built on the land… for which the new entrance will be the old prison's original gates.[94]

VERA BURET

1908-2006, MUSIC LIBRARIAN

Although she is best remembered by those who knew her for having been a librarian in the Department of Music at the University of Bristol, Vera Ruth Buret had many other strings to her bow. Born in 1908 and growing up in Redland, as an only child Vera was given a musical education by her mother in the absence

93 georgianera.wordpress.com/2017/11/16/the-last-days-of-mary-ann-burdock/
94 georgianera.wordpress.com/tag/bristol-gaol/

of her father, who was often away due to his role as a sea captain. As a result, Vera was a Licentiate in piano and elocution from both the Royal Academy of Music and Trinity College of Music. These prestigious qualifications enabled her to earn an income teaching music and elocution during World War Two, which she did from her home at 30 Upper Cranbrook Road, Henleaze.

By 1928, Vera was a member of the Bristol and Clifton Dickens Society, which is the oldest society in the world dedicated to the works of the author Charles Dickens and still exists today. Among her involvements with the Society, Vera acted in productions of Dickens' works and played roles including Mrs Steerforth, Lavinia Spenlow, Miss Pross, Miss Havisham and Betsey Trotwood in amateur performances around Bristol, Somerset and Gloucestershire. For her performance as Lucy Manette in *A Tale of Two Cities* in 1938, one reviewer wrote she "played well" and gave a "charming" performance.[95] She even acted as Honorary Dramatic Secretary of the Society for several years and, towards the end of her life in 2003, she was involved with the annual International Dickens Fellowship conference, which that year Bristol had the honour of hosting at Clifton Hill House.

Vera was also a member of other amateur dramatics societies, including the Clifton Arts Club, for whom in 1932 she played Antigonus in a production of *The Winter's Tale*: "Miss Vera Buret has a stage voice worth cultivating, and in her smaller part as a lady-in-waiting her spontaneity and ease were a pleasure to watch."[96] She also competed in elocution competitions and in 1933 placed first in the professional ladies' class for the British Empire Shakespeare Society Preliminary Elocution Competition for Bristol, earning herself the Ellen Terry Trophy in the process.[97]

95 'Tale of Two Cities at Redland' in *Western Daily Press*, 14 April 1938.
96 'The Winter's Tale' in *Western Daily Press*, 19 May 1932.
97 'Elocution Success' in *Western Daily Press*, 17 July 1933.

Between 1964 and 1968, Vera was the Librarian for the University of Bristol's Department of Music, which was located in Royal Fort House. She also assisted colleagues with creating production notes for concerts which the department put on. Remembering Vera upon her death, colleagues at the university said: "Miss Buret had a long and active life ... She was greatly respected for her loyalty, her wry sense of humour, integrity, high standards, cheerfulness and charm of manner, and for her gift for friendship. She is greatly missed."[98]

Please also see: Ellen Terry (vol one), Alicia Tyndall (vol two).

JOAN BURTON

died 1467, MERCHANT'S WIFE

An effigy of Joan Burton can be found on the tomb she shares with her husband William Canynges in the church of St Mary Redcliffe. However, unusually, it is likely the tomb was made prior to Canynges' death in 1474 because, following Joan's death, Canynges took holy orders and was thereafter known as the Dean of Westbury-on-Trym College and has a monument in that parish church. So it is likely he commissioned the monument to his wife and himself prior to taking holy orders, and therefore the effigy of Joan on this tomb is a very rare example of an attempt to accurately portray the likeness of a medieval woman.[99]

98 bristol.ac.uk/news/2006/5146.html

99 Peter Fleming, 2016, 'Women and Funerary Commemoration c.1373-1660' in *Women and the City*, edited by Madge Dresser, p35.

ELIZA BUSH

born c1820, TRAVELLER

A little known female traveller from Bristol was Eliza Bush who published a book about her adventures in the Middle East, Greece and Turkey during the mid 1860s, in which she had attempted to follow the footsteps of Jesus in the Holy Land. *My Pilgrimage to Eastern Shrines* was published in 1867 but was sometimes rather acerbic about her experiences. For instance, she describes visiting a mosque in Turkey where she saw "howling dervishes" and met a Sultan who was a "plain, unpretending-looking man, more like a London banker than a luxurious Turk"[100]. And while travelling from Jerusalem to Jaffa in 1865, Eliza describes meeting "a large party coming from the Holy City, Americans, some of whom stopped me with characteristic questions, but amiable, in moving off, gave us information in return, intended to be useful". Which is somewhat dismissive! On her return trip from Jaffa to Jerusalem, Eliza expanded: "These Americans were worthy people, with few ideas between them all, except those of getting over the ground as quickly as they could, and giving an occasional guess or two as to the scenes they visited."[101]

BERTHA BUTLIN

1878-1934, FAIRGROUND BUSINESSWOMAN

Given her family had an interest in travelling fairs (her father had abandoned his career as a baker to become a fairground showman), Bedminster-born Bertha Cassandra Hill was often to be found enjoying herself at the rides and stalls. In fact, she spent so much

100 Cited in Madge Dresser, 2016, *Women and the City*, p130.
101 Cited in Lester Vogel, 1993, *To See A Promised Land*, p88.

time at the fairs that one night she ended up meeting the man she would marry: Gloucestershire-born William Butlin. After their marriage in December 1896, the young newly-weds emigrated to South Africa where they ran a bicycle shop... although it was Bertha who took on the lion's share of the work (including repairing the bicycles herself) as her workshy husband was much more interested in playing tennis. With discontent settling in, Bertha packed her things and took herself and their two sons back to Bristol, where she moved in with her elder brothers at Organs Yard, off Regent Road in Bedminster.[102] The Hill brothers were now running the family's travelling fair business, Marshall and Ernest Hill Entertainments, and Bertha ran the gingerbread stall for them.

One of Bertha's sons was called William but known as Billy. Born in 1899, he attended Bedminster Down School but also worked at the Hill family's travelling fairs with his mother and uncles and saw for himself the ways and means of the entertainment and leisure industry, which evidently struck a chord with him as he grew up to establish the popular Butlins holiday camps. Bertha's other son was Harry, who sadly contracted polio and died in 1907. By 1911, the family consisted of Bertha, her younger sister Lottie Coneley and Bertha's son Billy, and they were living in a horse-drawn caravan kept at Organs Yard while Billy continued his education at Bedminster Endowed Boys' School.

Bertha's second husband was Bristolian gas fitter Charles Robotham, with whom she emigrated to Canada for a number of years, persuading Billy to come and join her when he left school at 14. Bertha and Billy maintained a close relationship for the rest of her life, so much so that she managed his finances for him and therefore helped him to prudently build his business and

102 This location is now covered by Asda's car park.

become the success he was. In her later years, Bertha was back living with Lottie in Bedminster and their address was 25 Nelson Parade, close to Bedminster Bridge. This was a luxurious step up from being squashed into a caravan. She was immensely proud of Billy's triumphs with his fledgling holiday camp business, and he had already become a wealthy man by the time of Bertha's death while she was visiting his soon-to-be-opened camp in Skegness.[103]

ELIZA CANNINGFORD

died 1856, WORKHOUSE INMATE

The Bristol Lunatic Asylum opened in Fishponds in 1861 as a place where paupers with mental health needs could be sent if the workhouse was not suitable for them. Although the workhouses did – in theory – accommodate those with mental illnesses, it was far from an ideal place for them to seek appropriate care and support. So the Bristol Lunatic Asylum came about following a number of incidents in the workhouse which showed more specialist care was needed.

One such incident involved Eliza Canningford. In 1856, Eliza was an inmate at the Union of Clifton Workhouse on Church Lane, Cliftonwood, where she had been placed in the Female Imbecile Ward. While there, she found a knife, slit her own throat in the water closet and died. It was later found that neither of the two workhouse wardens had been on duty at the time and Eliza had been left unsupervised despite it being known she posed a danger to herself. Yet because Eliza was a pauper, there was no inquest. However, a report did discover the workhouse was keeping both

103 Paul Breedon, 'Genial Billy Butlin Founded a Holiday Empire' in *South Bristol Voice*, February 2019, pp29-33; Douglas A Reid, 2017, 'Sir William Butlin' in *Oxford Dictionary of National Biography*.

'imbeciles' and 'dangerous lunatics' in the same ward, due to the poor understanding of the differences between mental illness and criminality at the time. It was therefore tragedies such as this which led to the establishment of the Bristol Lunatic Asylum (later known as the Bristol Psychiatric Hospital).[104]

Please also see: Rosa Burden (vol one), Sarah Carpenter (vol two), Elizabeth Cox (vol two), Prudence Early (vol two), Kate Underwood (vol two), Hannah Wiltshire (vol one).

SARAH CAVILL

born c1790, BRIGHTSMITH

In today's metalworking terminology, a brightsmith is generally considered to be a jewellery maker. But in the mid 19th century, a brightsmith was someone who forged things out of brightly coloured metals such as copper, brass or tin, or someone who finished the work of an ironsmith. This was in contrast to a blacksmith, who forged items out of wrought iron or steel.

On 4 June 1842, an announcement appeared in the *Bristol Times and Mirror* affirming that the recently widowed Sarah Cavill would be carrying on her late husband John's "brightsmith, bell-hanger etc" business, which was located on Moon Street in Stokes Croft, close to where the Full Moon bar still stands. "It is her intention to carry on the business in all its branches, on behalf of her family, under the immediate inspection of an experienced Foreman, and begs to say all orders entrusted to her care shall be faithfully executed on the shortest notice and most moderate terms," wrote the paper.[105]

104 workhouses.org.uk/Bristol
105 'Sarah Cavill', in *Bristol Times & Mirror*, 4 June 1842.

In addition to brightsmith work and bell hanging, Sarah's business also promised to warm houses and offices thanks to an innovative new steam and hot water system: an early form of central heating.

MARY CHANDLER
born 1818, STATIONER

After the death of her husband, Bristol-born Mary Chandler worked hard — as was common for many widows — to maintain the stationers business which he had started. After all, she needed to keep a roof over the heads of herself and their son John. In the 1851 census, Mary and John (who was 14 at this time and working as a clerk) were living at 18 Welsh Back; they shared their home with a servant, which suggests they must have enjoyed some degree of success.

Mary is also listed as a rag merchant in some business directories for the 1850s, and it is likely she would have sourced these rags in order to pulp them into the paper which she sold through the stationery business. On one occasion in 1850, Mary was the victim of theft when three men with impressive criminal records stole the rags she had amassed. For this crime they were sentenced to "seven years transportation"[106] to the penal colonies in Australia, where they would be expected to work hard throughout their sentences.

106 'Bristol Quarter Session' in *Bristol Mercury*, 6 July 1850.

CONSTANCE CHAPMAN

1912-2003, ACTOR

A former pupil of Redland High School, Weston-super-Mare's Constance Chapman always knew her heart lay on the stage. After leaving school she went to a local drama college before making her professional debut in 1938 in *Hay Fever* at Weston's former Knightstone Theatre (now buried underneath a housing development). Constance stayed local and much of her early theatre work was in Bristol, appearing regularly for Peggy Ann Wood's Rapier Players at the Little Theatre between 1941 and 1953, and often with the Theatre Royal (now the Bristol Old Vic). She supplemented her theatre work with regular appearances in radio dramas which were broadcast from the BBC's studio on Whiteladies Road.

Constance was married to Travers Cousins but it was not a happy marriage and was eventually dissolved. Cousins reportedly had alcohol problems and perhaps Constance's frustrations at home helped fuel her convincing on-stage portrayals of women with difficult husbands. However, her marriage did lead her to become a mother to two sons whom she adored.

Constance's range was diverse and she could easily switch between comedy and serious drama as needed. She was a popular performer at the Theatre Royal on King Street and appeared there in roles including a musical version of Nancy Mitford's social comedy *The Pursuit of Love* (1967) and as the grandmother in *A Day in the Death of Joe Egg* (1968).

In 1969, when Constance was more than halfway through her career, she finally made her debut on the London stage when she played the matriarch of *In Celebration* at the Royal Court Theatre, directed by acclaimed film auteur Lindsay Anderson and co-starring Bill Owen as her stage husband (Bill would go on to become a household name thanks to his TV role in *Last of the Summer Wine*). Later the same year, she was again playing Bill's stage wife in another play directed by Anderson, *The Contractor,* which was performed at both the Royal Court and Fortune Theatres in London. Critics loved the chemistry between Constance and Bill, noting "the partnership ... was to be one of the most memorable onstage marriages in history. What it smacked of was the truth: misery and merriment, satisfaction and frustration, resignation and resentment".[107] For Constance's final major London theatre appearance, she was reunited with Bill and Anderson for *The March on Russia* at the National Theatre in 1989, which resurrected the type of characters Constance and Bill had played 20 years previously.

Constance's glowing reviews for her theatre work in London led to screen roles, such as the TV play *The Gorge* (1968, Christopher Morahan), the cinema drama *The Raging Moon* (1970, Bryan Forbes) and the John Cleese comedy film *Clockwise* (1986, Christopher Morahan).[108] Constance had a talent for comedy and was cast in television classics such as *Only Fools and Horses* as well as *Victoria Wood: As Seen on TV*. She continued to work on television and had roles in lots of popular shows including *Casualty, The Bill* and *The Ruth Rendell Mysteries* until as recently as the late 1990s. After retiring, Constance returned to Bristol where she lived to be 91 years old.

Please also see: Peggy Ann Wood (vol one).

107 Eric Shorter, 'Obituary: Constance Chapman' in *The Guardian*, 15 August 2003.
108 Fun fact: like Constance, John Cleese was born in Weston-super-Mare.

ELIZABETH CHEW

born c1730, ORGAN BUILDER

While we know Bristol has a long history of trades such as tobacco, shipbuilding and automotives, less well known is the city's history of manufacturing musical instruments. Elizabeth Chew was a Bristol-based organ builder and harpsichord maker, and she had a grand reputation for her instruments despite being a woman in a traditionally male industry. She appears in the 1775 edition of *Sketchley's Bristol Directory*, which is a useful book for confirming that in the Georgian era women's main places of work were related to the typically female industries of clothing, food and drink.

MARGARET CHILTON

1875-1962, STAINED GLASS ARTIST

Educated at Clifton High School and brought up in Westbury-on-Trym, Margaret Chilton had a good start to her life. Showing a flair for art, she studied at the Royal College of Art in London where she specialised in stained glass, before returning to Bristol in 1906 and setting herself up with a stained glass studio. During the next 12 years, Margaret became an Associate of the Royal College of Art in London as well as the Royal West of England Academy here in Bristol. She was living at 12 Cambridge Park, Redland, during this time.

Among her local commissions was a stained glass window for Pilton Church, Somerset, which she designed and executed herself. "The window ... reflects the greatest credit on the artist," wrote the *Western Daily Press*. It added that a tutor at the Royal College of Art praised "the exceptionally clever treatment of the subject"[109]. Another church which benefitted from a window designed and created by Margaret was St John's Church, Clifton (the window has since been relocated to the Ely Stained Glass Museum, Cambridgeshire) where, on Easter Day 1912, her three-light stained glass window was unveiled as a memorial to Jane Louise Appleton, the former headteacher of Ellenborough High School in Cheltenham who had died the previous year. "The window is a beautiful one in soft and delicate colouring," wrote the local paper, "as it was necessary to preserve as much light as possible."[110] A third local example of Margaret's work can be seen in the transept window of St Alban's Church, Westbury Park, which was the final part of the 1915 restoration of this building and shows various craftspeople working on the church. Margaret's window was paid for thanks to a donation from her father, Horace Chilton.

In 1918, Margaret moved to Glasgow where she taught at the Glasgow School of Art and later set up in partnership with one of her pupils, Marjorie Kemp. Margaret and Marjorie remained in Glasgow for their rest of the careers and continued to work together until Margaret's death in 1962.

And another thing... I beseech you to pay a visit to the Lady Chapel at St Mary Redcliffe Church. The stained glass windows in there are phenomenally beautiful and interesting. While the oldest stained glass windows in the church date back to the 14th century, those in the Lady Chapel were created in the 1960s. Designed by artist Harry Stammers, they depict ordinary women at work, rather than saints or angels as is more common for images of women in church windows. Stained glass enthusiast Jane Brocket describes the first time she saw Stammers' windows in the Lady Chapel: "I was amazed.

109 'Local Notes' in *Western Daily Press*, 13 September 1907.
110 'Local Notes' in *Western Daily Press*, 16 April 1912.

I'd never seen ordinary people in ordinary, contemporary clothes. Headscarves! Handbags! Court shoes! Aprons! On women who weren't saints or queens, but who probably scrubbed doorsteps and cleaned out stoves and swept floors, brought up children, and took them to Sunday school. Women who had a shampoo-and-set once a week, went shopping with baskets over their arms and wore sensible coats in winter. The kind of women I saw and knew when I was growing up: mothers, workers, wives, daughters."[111]

AGATHA CHRISTIE

1890-1976, AUTHOR

Does the best-selling novelist of all time have a link to Bristol? Of course she does.

Following the death of her father when she was just 11, Agatha Miller from Torquay, Devon, grew up quickly and became her mother's companion. Eager to secure a good future for them both, Mrs Miller was determined her daughter make a good match... and so the relentless mission to find Agatha a husband began. So focussed was this quest that Agatha entered into a number of relationships and one failed engagement before marrying army officer Archibald Christie in a hastily arranged ceremony on Christmas Eve 1914 at Emmanuel Church, Clifton College.[112] This was close to where Archibald's family lived and his stepfather was a schoolmaster at the college.

Archibald was stationed in France during World War One and during his first period of leave, he met with his fiancée Agatha in London on 23 December 1914. Fearing he might be killed at any

111 yarnstormpress.co.uk/glazed_expressions/2016/01/in-the-beginning-1.html

112 Emmanuel Church was deconsecrated in 1974 and largely demolished in 1977 to make way for a development of sheltered accommodation. However, the church's tower was retained as a feature of the new housing development and still exists today.

time, Agatha was anxious they marry as soon as possible but he was initially reluctant. However, as they travelled to Bristol that evening to visit his family, Archibald had a change of heart and decided they *must* marry the very next day. The morning of 24 December was spent applying for a marriage licence in Bristol based on Archibald's part-time home in Clifton and this cost the couple £8. There was no time for Agatha to find a wedding dress so she was married in her ordinary clothes. She didn't even have the chance to enlist a bridesmaid but by chance ran into her old friend Yvonne Bush near the church and roped her in as an immediate witness to the wedding.[113]

After the war, the London-based couple's daughter Rosalind was born in 1919 (the year before Agatha's debut novel was published) but Agatha and Archibald divorced in 1928 after he fell in love with another woman. The night Archibald announced the marriage was over, Agatha left their home leaving a letter for her secretary saying simply that she was going away. Later, Agatha's abandoned car was found by a chalk quarry, leading to fears she had taken her own life. A national hunt began for the missing novelist involving 15,000 volunteers, several aeroplanes and even a spirit medium employed by author Arthur Conan Doyle (Agatha was a massive fan of his *Sherlock Holmes* books). After ten days, Agatha was found in a Harrogate spa hotel where she had checked in under the surname of Archibald's mistress and was apparently experiencing amnesia and acute depression.

In 1930, Agatha married archaeologist Max Mallowan, with whom she remained happy until her death in 1976. She went on to write 85 books, which have collectively sold more than two billion copies all around the world. They have been adapted into countless film and television dramas as well as stage plays, and her

113 bristolmuseums.org.uk/blog/archives/desert-island-doc-agatha-christies-wartime-wedding/

Agatha Christie illustration by Carrie Love

murder mystery *The Mousetrap* has run continuously in London since 1952, making it the longest-running West End show ever.

And another thing... It was after visiting Agatha Christie in Devon, and struggling to find anything worth reading at the train station, that Allen Lane conceived the idea of mass market paperbacks to be sold from vending machines at train stations. In 1935, this idea became what we now know as Penguin Books, for which the archives are stored at the University of Bristol's library.

Please also see: Eva Longbottom (vol two).

ALICE CLARK

1874-1934, BUSINESS LEADER, SUFFRAGIST

Alice Clark was a leading member of the National Union of Women's Suffrage Societies (NUWSS) and, in the years before World War One broke out, tensions were building between the peaceful suffragists (of which Alice was one) and the increasingly militant suffragettes (the Women's Social and Political Union). Alice was also a respected community member owing to her vocal and monetary support for the temperance movement and other reform organisations, as well as being a significant local employer. Her parents Helen Priestman Bright and William Stephens Clark founded the Street-based shoe business which still exists today, and Alice was the only one of her siblings who showed an interest in the family firm, learning the manual roles as well as the managerial ones: Alice was one of the five original directors of Clarks Shoes.

Alice enjoyed a liberal and politically enlightened upbringing in a deeply pro-women's suffrage household. Her aunts Anna-Maria and Mary Priestman were significant figures in the movement locally, and her mother Helen had been lobbying for votes for women since the 1880s. Another great-aunt, Priscilla Bright McLaren, had been born on the anniversary of the emancipation of slaves and interpreted this as a sign she should spend her life lobbying for freedom. Given Alice lived with Priscilla for a while, it looks likely that Priscilla's determined attitude rubbed off on her great-niece. Via the well-connected maternal side of her family, Alice came to meet leading suffragists and reformers from both the UK and the US including Millicent Fawcett, Josephine Butler, Annie Besant and Elizabeth Cady Stanton.

Alice founded the Women's Liberal Association (WLA) in Somerset in 1890 when she was just 16 years old (she was Secretary for 11 years until her sister Hilda took over), and she carried out her first direct action for women's suffrage the same year when she began writing a regular column which collected together women's suffrage news from around the UK. The following year, Alice joined her first debate on women's suffrage and acted as a regional delegate for the WLA at national conferences, all very bold for a Victorian teenager. Following a stay in Bristol with her aunts Anna-Maria and Mary in 1893, Alice was so enraptured by the movement that she wrote home and asked her parents for permission to attend four imminent suffrage meetings. In the following years, her strident campaign for women's suffrage only escalated. For example, in 1907, Alice participated in the WSPU's first raid on the House of Commons although she never became an official member of the WSPU because, from 1908 onwards, she was resistant to its increasingly violent methods of campaigning for the vote. Instead, as a Quaker, Alice was in favour of passive resistance, civil disobedience and the refusal to pay taxes.

But then disaster struck... In 1909, Alice became gravely ill with tuberculosis of the throat and lungs, which came close to killing her. This illness left her bed-bound in a sanitorium for more than a year and house-bound for two further years. Alice's recovery was slow but, while the disease weakened her body, it strengthened her resolve to fight harder for women's rights, despite being rendered speechless by the tuberculosis until late 1910. Around that time, she wrote to Anna-Maria and Mary saying: "I rather long to go and break some windows. I am not sure whose but I think any liberal offices would serve the purpose."[114] A surprising sentiment given her allegiance to the non-militant NUWSS, but perhaps symptomatic of her frustrations at being cooped up sick for such a long time. It was the summer of 1911 before Alice was well enough to leave the house again.

Like many suffragists, Alice was initially sceptical about the Independent Labour Party (ILP) and what it could offer women, because there had been long-standing tensions between Labour and the NUWSS on the topic of votes for women. And it remained the case that some leading Labour politicians were still fiercely opposed to women's suffrage. Alice stated: "We must retain our freedom to be influenced by the suffragist actions of the Liberals,"[115] meaning that she was hesitant to firmly align herself to one party or the other. But she made it her business to be the go-between for the NUWSS and Labour on a central level.

In the years shortly before World War One, the NUWSS had identified East Bristol as a constituency they felt the ILP should fight for and take back from the sitting anti-suffrage Liberal MP, Charles Hobhouse. As such, Alice was recruited to join the London branch of the NUWSS to use her knowledge of the area to help them try to win the seat for the ILP. She had been a part of the Election Fighting Fund (EFF) for some time, and the formation

114 Sandra Stanley Holton, 'Suffrage Days: Stories from the Women's Suffrage Movement', p161

115 Ibid, p194.

of the East Bristol Society by the EFF was done to help Alice and her team push for ILP victory in the seat in 1913. It was a tough first year of campaigning but, in December 1913, Alice reported to comrade Catherine Marshall: "We coaxed them round... I wanted to help Labour if we possibly could."[116]

As a Quaker, Alice felt unable to take part in any war work during World War One but she continued to support NUWSS activities. She also took a prominent role in the Quaker-led Friends' War Victims Relief Committee, which provided support to refugees in France and organised post-war famine relief in Austria. After the war, and towards the end of her working life, Alice returned to the family business in Street where she became an innovator in marketing, staff training and personnel management, and promoted adult education among the employees of Clarks Shoes. Alice was buried at Arnos Vale Cemetery.[117]

And another thing... Following her illness in 1909, Alice was under doctor's orders to rest her voice and not strain it by speaking at suffrage meetings or rallies. During this period she researched and wrote her book *The Working Life of Women in the Seventeenth Century* (1919), in which she argued the advent of capitalism undermined the economic and social position of women. However, any hopes Alice might have had for developing her career as a historian and publishing further volumes was squashed by the hostility of university history departments to the presence of women in the historical canon.

Please also see: Josephine Butler, Anna-Maria Priestman, Mary Priestman, Helen Priestman Bright Clark (all vol one).

116 Ibid, p193.

117 With thanks to researchers at Arnos Vale Cemetery (including Marion Blackburn, Hildegard Dumper, Liz Johnson and Janine Marriott) for generously providing extra information for this entry.

ROTHA CLAY
1878-1961, HISTORIAN, SOCIAL WORKER

Rotha Mary Clay was named after the River Rothay in the Lake District, which had been a favourite spot of her great-grandfather and became a much loved place for Rotha herself in adulthood. Having been brought up in Middlesex, Rotha, her parents and 11 siblings moved to Bristol in 1893 when her father became the rector of St Michael's Church and the family set up home in Tyndall's Park. She would remain in Bristol for the rest of her life.

Although Rotha's education was largely informal, she developed a strong interest in medieval history and devoured as many books as she could find on the subject. She particularly focussed on medieval English hospitals, and her work was noticed by the scholar John Charles Cox who suggested she contribute to the series of history books he was editing for the publisher Methuen & Co. It was in this way that her debut book *The Medieval Hospitals of England* was published in 1909, followed by *The Hermits and Anchorites of England* in 1914. *The Oxford Dictionary of National Biography* noted: "Both books were well researched, using original records (chiefly printed ones), encompassing the whole of England, and combining clear and judicious exposition with detailed lists of hospitals, hermits, and anchorites throughout the country. They commanded their fields throughout the twentieth century, and are still valuable as surveys and inventories."[118]

By 1914, Rotha had become involved with social work at the Barton Hill University Settlement, before moving to Shirehampton in 1918 to set up a similar organisation there that would support people from poorer families to achieve an education and improve

118 Nicholas Orme, 2004, 'Rotha Mary Clay' in *Oxford Dictionary of National Biography*.

their circumstances; she eventually became Honorary Warden of the settlement. In Shirehampton, Rotha lived at Ilex Cottage on the High Street and remained there for the rest of her life, having chosen not to marry or have a family.

Rotha's interests evolved from medieval history to fine art, and in 1941 she published a history of an 18th-century artist entitled *Samuel Hieronymus Grimm of Burgdorf in Switzerland,* followed in 1948 by a book about the Yorkshire artist Julius Caesar Ibbetson. Her work as a historian was acknowledged by her election to the Royal Historical Society in 1943, and an honorary masters degree from the University of Bristol in 1954.

Please also see: Lucy de Newchurch (vol two).

EDITH CLAYPOLE and MARY MOODY

1870-1915 and 1870-1954,
PATHOLOGIST and ZOOLOGIST

Edith Jane Claypole and her twin sister Agnes Mary Claypole were born at 95 Pendennis Villa, Westbury-on-Trym, in sad circumstances, because their mother Jane died giving birth to them. The twins were raised by their scientist father Edward Claypole, who homeschooled the sisters. When Edith and Agnes were nine years old, Edward remarried and moved the family to Ohio, US, where both sisters would go on to study at Buchtel College (now the University of Akron) where their father taught, and both achieved Philosophy degrees in 1892.

Here the twins parted, and Edith went on to Cornell University to complete her Master of Science degree in 1893, writing her thesis on white blood cells. A range of university teaching posts followed alongside further studies, and Edith qualified as a doctor in 1904. She specialised in pathology and infectious diseases, and worked in hospitals in both Pasadena and Los Angeles. It was this work that would lead to her crucial gift to civilisation during World War One. With soldiers in the army succumbing to typhoid on a horribly regular basis, a cure was needed and Edith was one of the scientists tasked with creating an immunisation from the disease. It was this work that would kill her because, although Edith had been vaccinated against typhoid, her repeated exposure to the disease in her laboratory was too much and in 1915 she died in California of the very illness she was trying to prevent.

But what of her sister Agnes, who was known by her middle name of Mary? She also stayed in academia and continued her studies at the University of Chicago, from where she graduated in 1896 having completed her doctoral thesis on the digestive tracts of eels. In 1903, Mary married an anatomy professor called Robert Moody in Pasadena and the two remained together until his death in 1948.

Despite having a PhD, by virtue of being a woman Mary was relegated to the lowest academic rank at Cornell University where she worked and was employed only as an assistant rather than a researcher, which men with the same qualifications were able to be. Regardless, Mary's dogged determination would eventually see her become the first ever female lecturer in the medical department at Cornell. She lectured on zoology and natural science, and used her influence to become a valued spokesperson for the League of Women Voters at Berkeley, California, lobbying for votes for women in the US.

In addition, Mary did a great deal of work for the community as a local councillor and it was noted: "No woman of Alameda County has made a deeper impression on the educational and civil life of the community than Mrs Agnes Claypole Moody

... She is a woman of kindly and tactful manner, cordial and friendly in her social relations, and because of her attainments and helpful service she commands the respect and esteem of all who know her."[119]

LOUISE COLLARD

born 1875, BUTCHER

At the corner property of 57 North Street, Southville, you can still clearly see the Victorian tiling that reads 'A D Collard' outside the former butchers' shop which was run in its prime by Bedminster-born Louise Collard and her husband Aldred. However, the letters 'AD Collard' are actually for Aldred's father, Aldred Daw Collard, who had opened the shop in the 1850s. As was customary in the time before refrigeration, carcasses were displayed outside the property both for freshness and to entice potential customers. At one time, there were four butchers shops run by the Collard family in Bristol, with the other three being in Clifton, Old Market and on Redcliffe Hill.

Louise and Aldred, who lived above the shop, had taken over the running of the Collard family business following their marriage in the mid 1890s. Louise became a well-known and "strong-willed"[120] local figure who had grown-up in the trade because her parents, Mr and Mrs Woodhall, had run a butchers shop around the corner on East Street.

Louise continued to work at the North Street shop until the 1960s when she was well into her 90s. She was easily recognisable for always wearing her hair twisted up into a coil on the top of her head and securing it in place with tortoiseshell combs. She

119 Anon, 1928, *History of Alameda County: Volume 2*, pp247-248.
120 Will Musgrave, 2013, *South Bristol Through Time*, p60.

always wore a starched white coat but, in winter, added a black fur cape to keep herself warm.[121]

There remained a Collard butchers shop at 57 North Street for more than 130 years, until the business closed in the late 1980s when Louise and Aldred's son Alfred Henry Collard retired (the couple also had three daughters: Mercy, Audrey and Amy). However, having since seen a number of years as a bric-a-brac shop, the building is currently the Friendly Records Bar. Many original Victorian features have been restored in the interior of the property, as well as the glazed tiles and stained glass windows depicting cows and sheep.

And another thing... A bonus fact that is *not* about a woman who built Bristol but *is* about a woman's father-in-law and is charmingly odd. Aldred Daw Collard, who started the business, was known as both 'the worst poet in Bristol' and 'the poet butcher of Bristol'. The small and badly weathered gargoyle and sign for 'Poet's Corner, 1882' which can be seen opposite the shop on 57 North Street was a tender nod to his talents by his customers. Aldred was known for writing meat-themed poetry of a poor quality. Despite being bad, his poetry was popular and Aldred donated the profits of his pamphlets to the General Hospital. One poem was entitled 'The Redcliffe and Bedminster Christmas Meat Show of 1885' and namechecked all of the 26 butchers shops between North Street and Redcliffe Hill.

121 Anton Bantock, 1997, *Bedminster*, p62.

SARAH COLSTON

1608-1701, MERCHANT'S WIFE

As the wife of notorious politician and slave trader Edward Colston, Sarah Colston was arguably equally as culpable as her husband for condemning innumerable innocent people to a life of absolute hell. Born in Bristol as Sarah Batten, she had ten children with Colston (a tidy balance of five girls and five boys) and lived in Bristol her entire life.

The Colstons were an enormously wealthy family owing to their roles in the trade and exploitation of enslaved Africans, which was still legal at the time. They were deemed a generous family because they gave a lot of their money to Bristolian schools, almshouses, hospitals, churches etc, and as such many buildings and streets in the city retain the Colston name today, with a certain degree of controversy.

The Colston family memorial is in the now-closed All Saints Church, Corn Street, on the north aisle. It was erected by Sarah's son, also called Edward, and commemorates his parents. Given the horrors inflicted by the Colston family on so many enslaved people, I will not indulge Sarah with a lengthy entry in this book but I include her because her involvement in the slave trade alongside her husband should not be forgotten or overlooked.

BERYL COOK

1926-2008, ARTIST

Former boarding house landlady Beryl Cook was in her 40s before she turned to art but that didn't stop her from becoming a much-loved artist, favoured for her popular pictures of larger-figured ladies. However, due to the mass popularity of Beryl's work (her pictures have been bought by, among others, actor Whoopi Goldberg and novelist Jackie Collins) and the snobbish attitude of the art world to what is popular, she was largely discredited by the art industry which worked hard to keep her out of the traditional galleries. Despite this rebuff, Beryl's work has been seen on everything from postage stamps to greetings cards and adverts, ensuring she still reaches a huge audience.

Beryl Frances Lansley was born in Surrey, where she and her sisters were brought up single handedly by their mother after their father had walked out. Perhaps this matriarchal start to life instilled a belief in strong women in young Beryl. She left school aged 14 and trained as a typist, although during World War Two she performed as a showgirl… which was out of character for someone as neurotically shy as Beryl. She married merchant seaman John Cook in 1948 whom she had known since she was ten, but much of the first decade of their marriage was spent apart due to John being away at sea. After John left the merchant navy in 1958, the couple moved to southern Rhodesia and then Zambia in Africa with their son, also called John. It was in Zambia that Beryl began to paint "because there was nothing else to do"[122], although she discovered painting was not as easy as she had hoped it would be. But Beryl hated being away from home and within a year the family was back in England.

Initially they lived in Plymouth and took in lodgers, one of whom was so impressed by Beryl's paintings that he helped her secure an exhibition, which led to coverage in a national newspaper and propelled Beryl's artistic career forwards. This newfound success led the Cooks to stop taking in lodgers, employ a housemaid and live a much more comfortable life, which included travelling around seeking inspiration for Beryl's

122 Anon, 'Beryl Cook' in *The Daily Telegraph*, 28 May 2008.

Beryl Cook illustration by Rhi Lee

future works. In 1995 she was awarded an OBE, although Beryl's phobia of formal social situations prevented her from attending the ceremony and receiving her medal in person from the Queen.

In Beryl's own words, her paintings showed "ordinary people enjoying themselves"[123] and, drawing on her history as a seaside landlady, were in many ways reminiscent of the old-fashioned seaside postcards showing cartoons of larger women and men in slightly saucy poses. One obituary wrote: "She painted plump people in everyday and sometimes surreal situations, with special emphasis on bottoms and bosoms."[124] Beryl's focus was on recording the everyday life of real working-class people, regularly showing them in the pub, on a night out or at the beach.

In 1998, Beryl and John moved to a former coaching house on Camp Road near the Durdham Downs in Clifton, so as to be closer to their grandchildren and great-grandchildren. Beryl felt Bristol would be a good home for her and John, stating it had "leather and jazz pubs, and pubs for rockers"[125]. Bristol provided plentiful inspiration for Beryl. Her 2001 picture 'Jiving to Jazz' was inspired by a night out at the Tobacco Factory bar in Southville: "A whole night of jazz performed by Rod Mason's marvellous band. The sousaphone player, standing there with his instrument wrapped around him like a suit of armour fascinated me. He also played the trumpet very well and sang beautifully. The audience responded enthusiastically to every song and danced the night away. I of course just sat and watched (and sketched and made little notes about everyone's clothes)."[126]

While her 2003 picture 'In The Snug' is set in the Nova Scotia pub on Spike Island and shows four people enjoying a drink with their two dogs: "Although all the humans seem very

123 Ibid.
124 Ibid.
125 Veronica Horwell, 'Obituary: Beryl Cook' in *The Guardian*, 28 May 2008.
126 berylcookprints.co.uk/product/jiving-to-jazz/

jolly there does seem to be a little canine dispute over the seating arrangements, although I expect that calm will soon be restored and tails will soon start wagging."[127]

NORAH COOK

1909-2005, INSPIRATIONAL WRITER

Although she had been born in Dublin, Ireland, Norah Merrett moved to Bristol in 1960 after marrying sales rep Ron Cook. While in the city, she worked as a Latin and Greek teacher at Bristol Cathedral School and Henbury Comprehensive, and she remained in Bristol for the rest of her life.

At the age of 86, retired Norah co-wrote a book with her friend Vera Frampton which would end up transforming the lives of prison inmates up and down the country. *Hand on My Shoulder: True Stories of How God Communicates With Us Today* was written in 1995 to share stories of redemption and offer glimmers of hope to those in need. It secured an unexpected audience in the form of prisoners looking for inspiration, and prison chaplains found the simple stories of faith and personal discovery were having a positive impact on the prisoners with whom they had shared the book. Norah was surprised to find her doormat flooded with orders for the anthology, as well as letters of thanks from prison chaplains and prisoners. She spent her retirement responding kindly to the letters and posting packages of books to prisons and readers all over the UK.

However, *Hand on My Shoulder* was not Norah's first book. Her first inspirational volume, *We're All Looking for Something,* was published in 1970, followed by several others on a similar

127 berylcookprints.co.uk/product/in-the-snug/

theme in the following decades. Norah had also worked as editor of the Religious Education and Social Studies series for Blandford Press.[128]

VALERIE COOK

1924-2013, NUN, HEADTEACHER

Sister Valerie Cook was the Headteacher of the La Retraite High School on Clifton Hill from 1961 until its closure in 1982. She had come to Bristol from her home in Galway, Ireland, as a student to read History at the University of Bristol. While studying, she became interested in politics and often spent her weekends hiking in the countryside while debating political issues with her friends. It was around this time that she began to consider devoting her life to God, ultimately deciding her vocation lay with the Catholic order of the Sisters of La Retraite, whom she had known at school as a child.

After taking her vows in 1948, Valerie taught at La Retraite schools for girls in London and Salisbury before moving to Bristol in 1956 as Head of History, progressing to become Headteacher in the 1960s. As a member of the Clifton Diocesan Schools Commission, Valerie worked closely with teachers, clergy and education officials to secure the best possible futures for Bristolian Catholic secondary schools. And despite the heartbreak it caused her, she remained strong for her colleagues and pupils when her own school closed in 1982.

After the demise of the Clifton school, Valerie moved to Cork and then back to Galway, where she continued to work with the La Retraite sisters. When her health began in fail in 2002, she

128 Stan Hazell, 'Norah Cook' in *The Independent*, 10 May 2005.

returned to the UK and lived at a care home in Burnham-on-Sea. Sister Moira McDowall wrote: "Valerie will be remembered for many things, her wisdom and courage, her calm and her counsel, as well as her gift for friendship and love of life."[129]

Please also see: Pat Pilkington (vol one), Penny Brohn (vol one), Mary Delaney (vol two).

LOUISA COOPER

born 1868, DOMESTIC ABUSE SURVIVOR, ACCESSORY TO MURDER

Have you heard of the Brislington Villa Mystery of 1923? No? Well, buckle up and read on.

Just like the murder itself, this is a story that remained buried for a long time… until it resurfaced in 1984 when a surveyor went to visit an elderly man called George Cooper and heard the story first hand. In the early 1920s, George and his mother had been key figures in the Brislington Villa Mystery, as the newspapers dubbed the incident at the time.

By 1921, George's father (also called George, so let's call him George Snr) had been living at Croydon House on Montrose Avenue, Brislington, with his wife Louisa (née Blackburn) for some 20 years. They were a pleasant yet unremarkable couple and there was nothing about them which made them stand out to their neighbours, whose only comment about Louisa was that sometimes they could hear her singing as she did the housework. Father and son (let's call him George Jnr) were initially pattern makers at the scale manufacturing factory Bartletts of Brislington,

129 laretraite.ws/en/i_news/i1/i1_valerieObit.htm

and after this firm closed they found similar work at Sampson's Iron Foundry on Malago Road, Bedminster.

When George Jnr married in 1921, he and his new wife moved into Croydon House to live with his parents, which was common practice at the time. But by 1923, the younger couple had two little children and George Jnr's wife was largely staying with her own family in Cheddar so her mother could help with the kids. This took her out of the picture as a witness to what would transpire.

Not everything was as humdrum and suburban as this picture suggests. George Snr was an awful womaniser and Louisa was well aware of his flings with women from his workplaces; she had even confronted some of the women in person, as well as complaining to her husband's employers about his behaviour with colleagues. As if his philandering was not enough, it was later claimed by George Jnr that his father was physically abusive to Louisa, and he had not only knocked her to the ground on occasion but had also dragged her about by her feet or hair and then struck George Jnr when he tried to defend his mother.

Things came to a head in September 1923 when the neighbours eventually noticed they hadn't seen George Snr for a while. After numerous enquiries from acquaintances, Louisa was finally shamed into admitting he had left her for another woman. Given it seemed George Snr was gone for good, George Jnr was promoted into his father's now vacant job at Sampson's.

As the months wore on, things became more peaceful at Croydon House and, to celebrate the coming festivities, the Coopers invited friends and neighbours round for a pre-Christmas party, with George Jnr playing the piano and everyone gathering around to sing carols. But something was preying on George Jnr's mind and in January 1924 he felt he had to confess... choosing his maternal uncle George Blackburn as the person to share his burden. George Jnr's confession was that he had put his father "in a position that he won't come back again". When his uncle asked for clarification, George Jnr said: "We had a row with Father and it had to be him or me." When pushed further, George eventually admitted: "I killed my father."

Unsure what to do with this information, Blackburn asked the advice of a friend who was a retired policeman, who said the only option was to turn George Jnr in... and that night the police came to Croydon House and arrested him while Louisa was charged with being an accessory to the murder. The following morning, George Jnr and Louisa appeared at Keynsham Petty Sessional Court where newspaper reports stated Louisa was in floods of tears throughout the hearing. In the end, both mother and son were charged with murder because Louisa admitted she wasn't simply an accessory but she knew *exactly* what had happened. Louisa was taken to Cardiff Gaol and as she was led from the court, she shouted to her son: "Have I got to leave you? Let me share it. It is my fault. It is my fault."

At this point, the police visited Croydon House to thoroughly examine the property. They noticed some floorboards in the middle downstairs room had recently been replaced and, upon pulling them up, they found the decaying body of George Snr... inches underneath where Louisa, George Jnr and their friends had celebrated with a Christmas singsong just a few weeks before: the piano was directly above the decomposing body.

During the trial, which was held in Wells, George Jnr kept insisting he was innocent while Louisa, who had been released on bail, looked tearful and drained throughout. As details came to light, it emerged that one evening while Louisa was out, father and son had quarrelled over George Snr's threats to move out and live with another woman, which culminated in George Snr coming at his son with a hatchet and threatening to kill him. After the ensuing struggle, it was instead George Snr who was left dead on the ground with nine wounds to his head. When Louisa returned home, she helped her son bury the body under the floorboards.

But when the jury returned a guilty verdict, it was George Jnr who was sentenced to seven years' penal servitude and his mother returned to the house, where George Jnr himself would return once he was freed from prison and lived in silence... until, wanting to share his long-held secret, he finally told his story to that visiting surveyor in 1984.

ANNIE CORNALL

1867-1946, MISSIONARY DOCTOR

Along with sister Bristolians such as Elizabeth Blackwell and Florence Barrett, Dr Annie Cornall was one of the very first women to qualify as a doctor, although unlike them she carried out the bulk of her training at the Royal Free Hospital in London.

Annie was also an accomplished public speaker who was known for leading the sermon in church services and at Sunday School sessions, following in the footsteps of her father who had been the vicar of Emmanuel Church in St Philips for 45 years. Indeed, in February 1935 Annie was presented with a splendid bouquet of flowers in recognition of her 30 years spent volunteering with young people at her father's church and leading the Bible study classes there.

Annie's faith led her to work as a missionary in Lucknow, India, in 1901 as a part of the Zenana Bible and Medical Mission, which had an office at 1 Lansdown Place, Clifton. Zenana missions had been established in the mid-19th century with the aim of sending female missionaries into the homes of Indian women with the intention of converting them to Christianity; 'zenana' is an Indian word for the women's quarters in the home, in which women were isolated from men and therefore denied access to healthcare since Indian doctors were almost exclusively men. Annie was in charge of one of the mission's hospitals in Lucknow and it was said: "[Dr Cornall] spoke of the great number of Mohammedans in Lucknow, and said they were the hardest people to work among, as they thought themselves absolutely right, and everyone else wrong."[130] Annie would spend seven years in the 1930s as a missionary in Burma during a time of famine. Following her work in India, Annie returned to Bristol for the last 25 years of her life, living and working from Carnarvon Lodge on Redland Road.

Children were a key focus of Annie's care; she had been speaking and educating widely on the subject of healthcare for mothers and babies since the 1910s, and was on the board for the Bristol Asylum for Poor Orphan Girls (later known as the Blue Maids Orphanage). From this, Annie went on to join the board for the Victoria Gibbs Memorial Home for Babies, which was located in Kingsdown. Annie was the medical officer at the home and, in the years immediately following World War One, she was instrumental in reducing the infant mortality figures in Bristol.[131]

Although she was almost 80 at the time of her death, Annie had continued practising medicine and treating patients until only a few months before she died, when heart problems and a fractured hip forced her to take a rest. She was buried in Arnos Vale Cemetery.[132]

Please also see: Florence Barrett (vol one), Elizabeth Blackwell (vol one), Bethlehem Dawes (vol two), Victoria Gibbs (vol two).

130 'Zenana Bible and Medical Mission', 23 February 1904, *Western Daily Press*
131 'Caring For Babies: Splendid Work for Future Citizens', 2 May 1923, *Western Daily Press.*
132 'Bristol Lady Doctor: Death of Miss Annie Cornall', 11 September 1946, *Western Daily Press*

ELIZABETH COX and SARAH CARPENTER
born c1745, ASYLUM MATRONS

When their father Dr Joseph Mason died in 1779, his daughters Elizabeth Cox and Sarah Carpenter took over the running of the private lunatic asylum he had run in Fishponds (established in 1740 by Mason's own father, Dr Cox, long before the more well-known Bristol Lunatic Asylum was opened in nearby Glenside in 1861).

Mason (who had also run an asylum in Stapleton at the building which would later become the Stapleton Workhouse) promised to cure "hypochondriacs, mad and distracted people with great success"[133] at the institution known locally as 'Mason's Madhouse'. One of the most controversial ways he did this was via a swinging chair. This involved strapping the patient into a straightjacket, securing them to a chair which was suspended via a hook on the ceiling and having an attendant spin them around and around and around. Another 'treatment' Mason favoured was dunking the patient in icy cold water to shock the 'madness' out of them.

Privately run lunatic asylums were not uncommon, and Mason's asylum, which contained 25 bedrooms and a chapel, was housed in a property that no longer survives but would have been located on the large site now bordered by Manor Road, Oldbury Court Road, College Avenue and College Road in Fishponds.

In 1811, Elizabeth Cox applied to the Bristol Asylum for Poor Orphan Girls for one of its trained girls to come and work at her lunatic asylum as a servant but her request was denied because the orphanage stated that "we do not place orphans in such

133 H Temple Phillips, 1970, 'The Old Private Lunatic Asylum at Fishponds' in *The Bristol Medico-Chirurgical Journal*, Vol 85, p41.

places"[134], which showed a surprising degree of care for its girls from the orphanage and implies a degree of suspicion at the way the asylum was being run.

Please also see: Rosa Burden (vol one), Eliza Canningford (vol two), Bethlehem Dawes (vol two), Prudence Early (vol two).

SYLVIA CROWE, 1901-1997
LANDSCAPE ARCHITECT

Banbury-born Sylvia Crowe was a significant figure in the development of landscape architecture. She was home educated from the age of ten and her only further education was a practical horticultural course at Swanley Horticultural College. After World War Two, the landscape profession started to develop and Sylvia was one of the pioneering designers who was involved in the rebuilding and infrastructure expansion projects across the UK. She established her private practice in the offices of sister landscape architect Brenda Colvin. The scale of projects started to grow and mirrored the expansion of the Institute of Landscape Architects (now known as the Landscape Institute), of which Sylvia was the second female President between 1957 and 1959.

Meanwhile, in post-war Bristol, the City Corporation was planning the rebuilding of the fifth most bomb-damaged city in the country and used the opportunity of government-sponsored projects to modernise the city. In 1963, Sylvia Crowe and Associates was invited to produce a Landscape Report for the Cumberland Basin Bridges and Ashton Gate Junction and Sylvia was ultimately selected as the most suitable candidate. She

134 Mary Wright, 2009, *The Blue Maids Orphanage*, p11.

enlisted the landscape architect Wendy Powell to work on the project over the next three years and together they led the male-dominated design team.

The road scheme includes the Plimsoll Swing Bridge at the entrance lock, the Avon Bridge and the interchanges serving Hotwells, Cumberland Road and Clift House Road, extending nearly a mile south from Hotwells to the Ashton Gate Junction. The dynamic sculpture of the road scheme has the benefit of a dramatic and unique setting within sight of the Clifton Suspension Bridge and below the famous Clifton and Cliftonwood terraces. The functional landscape scheme provides the setting to the massive infrastructure and covers more than 36 acres.

Situated to the west of the city, Hotwells has an interesting history. It takes its name from a warm spring which emerged from the River Avon, and was always difficult to access until a carriage road was built in 1662 and Hotwells House was established as a place to visit for restorative vacations. This meant that by 1750 the area had become a fashionable summer spa resort with a pump room, hotels, assembly rooms, river gardens, elegant houses, shops, library and theatre. However, by the early 1800s, the popularity of the Hotwells spa was declining, as was the volume of trade to Bristol's port, owing to the difficulties of boats travelling up the river to the docks. This led to the creation of the New Cut and Floating Harbour in the early 1800s, and the conception of the Cumberland Basin as a place for larger ships to access the Floating Harbour via a network of locks. This gave Bristol a fresh lease of life, and new homes for the dock workers were created in hastily constructed tenement buildings in Hotwells. These tenements largely remained until a combination of 1930s' slum clearance and World War Two bombs razed them to the ground. Around the same time, trade to the Bristol docks was steadily decreasing in favour of ships going to the easier-to-access Avonmouth docks. During the 1950s and early 1960s, and a decade before the M5 Avonmouth Bridge crossing to the west was built, the rise in car ownership began to cause problems on the out-of-date road network in Bristol. Traffic between the north and south of the New Cut and Floating Harbour was becoming increasingly jammed. Something needed to change, and that change was a major infrastructure scheme to allow continuous traffic flow through an extensive system of elevated roads on a flyover, to ease the flow of north/south traffic.

Sylvia's 1964 Landscape Report outlined three main objectives of the scheme. First, to use 'ground shaping' and planting to connect the road and bridges into the wider landscape. Second, to provide a segregated safe route for pedestrians to travel from one end of the scheme to the other within the site boundaries. Third, to make recreational use of the area under the elevated roads.

The Cumberland Piazza in Hotwells consumed a large proportion of the budget and was designed as a modern urban park, complete with a nautical-themed playground, a modernist café, extravagant water feature, extensive mature trees and seating areas. The layout of the space employed dynamic shapes and elegant detailing, with a restrained modern palette of concrete slabs and coloured bitmac for the paving materials. The setting to this nationally important road scheme celebrated the dynamic excitement for people travelling in cars, while retaining care and attention to pedestrians and local people. In the landscape report, Sylvia said she hoped for the piazza to be "frequented and enjoyed by the people", and she envisaged open-air exhibitions, flower stalls and information points, as well as benches for "the interest of watching shipping coming into the docks" and enjoying views of the Clifton Suspension Bridge.

Despite the initial success and popularity of the award-winning scheme, over the decades the Cumberland Piazza became rundown with the playground being removed and the café shutting in the early-1970s, the fountain becoming grassed over in the early-1980s and the toilets closing in the early-1990s. Today, the scheme continues to undergo changes in response to transport and development pressures. To appreciate the national importance of the scheme, it is worth walking round to the 'look out' at the very western point of Spike Island. Here, a Brutalist sculptural concrete plinth displays three brass plaques commemorating the road scheme which was opened to much fanfare by the Minister for Transport.

Sylvia's career spanned six decades and covered an extensive range of work, including private gardens, new towns, power stations, hospitals and public parks. She wrote many influential books and articles, lectured widely and her projects extended overseas. An active member of many design and environmental organisations, in 1967 she was granted a CBE and in 1973 she was made a Dame (the first landscape architect to receive this honour). In 2004, on the 75th anniversary of the Landscape Institute, Sylvia was posthumously declared "The Landscape Architect who has made the greatest contribution to, or had the most significance on, the UK landscape in the last 25 years". In 2018, the Landscape Institute launched the inaugural Dame Sylvia Crowe Award for Outstanding International Contribution to People, Place and Nature. Poignantly, an extract from one of the hand drawn plans for the Cumberland Piazza illustrating the lost pond and fountain is used to promote the award.[135]

And another thing... In summer 2018, artist **Amy Hutchings** created a vibrant mural in the Cumberland Piazza featuring seven women

135 With grateful thanks to landscape architect Wendy Tippett for her assistance with this entry, which is based on research Wendy carried out for her MSc thesis: 'Unloved Landscapes: The Bristol Schemes of Sylvia Crowe'.

of Hotwells and Cliftonwood inspired by *The Women Who Built Bristol: Volume One* as well as Dame Sylvia. The mural was part of an ongoing regeneration project led by the Hotwells & Cliftonwood Community Association to breathe new life into the Basin.

MARYA CZAPLICKA
1884-1921, ANTHROPOLOGIST

"A lady of intellect and infinite courage is in England just now in the person of Miss M A Czaplicka, a Russian Pole of distinguished attainments," wrote the *Western Daily Press* in 1915.[136]

Polish geography teacher Marya Antonina Czaplicka initially worked in her home city of Warsaw before travelling to the UK in 1910 to study ethnology at the London School of Economics. This then took her to Somerville College, Oxford, where she obtained a diploma in anthropology the following year. Aided by academic grants, Marya was able to complete her first book *Aboriginal Siberia* in 1914, which documented the vanishing lifestyles of natives in Siberia. Buoyed by the warm reception her work received in academic circles, Marya was further funded to undertake additional research into native tribes elsewhere in eastern Europe.

By 1920, Marya had become a respected lecturer and a member of both the Royal Geographical Society and the Royal Anthropological Institution, and as such became a visiting lecturer in anthropology at the University of Bristol, where she was "quite the life of the university speleological society and the Clifton Ladies' Debating Society"[137].

136 'A Courageous Lady' in *Western Daily Press*, 22 September 1915.
137 David N Collins, 2004, 'Marya Antonina Czaplicka' in *Oxford Dictionary of National Biography.*

Marya Czaplicka illustration by Carrie Love

Consequently, her death in Bristol on 27 May 1921 was a shock and, while the official verdict was heart failure, the truth was that Marya had taken a deliberate overdose. "The sudden death of Miss Czaplicka ... has cast a deep gloom among those members of the University who came under her sphere of influence," moured the *Western Daily Press*. "As scholar, as teacher and as friend she had gained the appreciation, admiration and affection of all who came into contact with her."[138]

Considering reasons for why a Polish Catholic might have been desperate enough to take her own life, researchers have since suggested Marya, who had been unable to secure a permanent post with any British university, was troubled that as a foreign woman she would never be truly respected by her academic peers. In addition, she had more than £200 of debt but was earning such a small income she had little hope of repaying this. Marya, who never married, was honoured with a requiem mass at the Pro Cathedral on Park Place, Clifton. The Marya Antonina Czaplicka Fund was established in 1971 in her memory to assist future anthropologists at Somerville College with studying the ancient world.

PAT DALLIMORE

1937-2018, BROADCASTER, COMMUNITY CAMPAIGNER

Pat Dallimore was born in Knowle West and lived in Bristol her entire life, save for a few years during World War Two when she was evacuated to Cornwall. In acknowledgement of the kindness shown to her by her host family, Pat paid it forward by becoming a foster carer herself in adulthood. And although she eventually

138 'Weekly Diary of Events' in *Western Daily Press*, 2 June 1921.

moved to Redcliffe with her docker husband Jim, Pat always maintained strong links to Knowle West.

A founding member of Southwest Scriptwriters, Pat had her fingers in many pies. She was a writer of prose, poetry and plays, and during the 1970s and 1980s she was on the editorial board of the community publisher and social enterprise Bristol Broadsides, which also published some of her writing, such as *Up Knowle West* (1977). As a playwright, Pat's work attracted interest not just in Bristol but also further afield, such as at the Bush Theatre in London. Her plays included *Jane and Bill* and *The Book*.

Having been a presenter on Knowle West's community cable television station in the early-1970s, Pat progressed to a regular fortnightly appearance on *The Jon Turner Show* on BBC Radio Bristol in the 1980s, which she kept until 2007. In this spot, Pat would share stories from her life via her natural, easy and funny manner, which made her very popular with listeners.

However, Pat was more than just a broadcaster because she was also a campaigner. For example, along with other Knowle West residents, she tried to set up a co-operative food purchase scheme as a means of boycotting the disproportionately high food prices being charged by local shops on the estate. And in the mid-1990s, Pat worked with her friend Mary Smith on an anti-drugs campaign in the neighbourhood.[139]

Paying tribute to Pat, Father Richard McKay said on BBC Radio Bristol: "She was always full of fun. She'd always be ready with a remark. She could also be quite challenging at times as well – she'd certainly say what she thought in that wonderful voice. What I particularly remember her for is the fact that, I think, she was a great voice of Knowle West when Knowle West didn't really have a voice in the city, as it were. Publicly. And she was a great

139 Madge Dresser, 2016, *Women and the City*, p173.

advocate, really, for people who were put down by others. And that's one of the enduring things I remember about her. As well as her sense of humour, her sense of fun."[140]

JILL DANDO

1961-1999, BROADCASTER

Perhaps because her father and older brother already worked in newspapers, Jill Wendy Dando felt destined to follow them into the media. Born in Weston-super-Mare, Jill was educated locally and joined a nearby drama society, where she discovered a flair for performing and began dreaming of a job in television.

On her road to a television career, Jill found work as a junior reporter at the *Weston Mercury* in 1985 after writing an essay about 'My Thoughts on the Year 2000' for a competition the paper was running. Later the same year, she secured her first broadcasting job thanks to a position with BBC Radio Devon. This in turn led to a television break two years later via the BBC's news programme *Spotlight*. Jill was so comfortable in front of the cameras that when national BBC television was looking for a stand-in presenter for its flagship programme *Breakfast Time*, Jill was put up for the job. By 1988 she had become a full-time newsreader on *The Six O'Clock News* on BBC1.

In addition to *Breakfast Time* and *The Six O'Clock News*, Jill also presented the travel show *Holiday* and later *Crimewatch*, all for the BBC. Her relatable nature, empathy and professionalism helped to coax stories out of the members of the public whom she interviewed and Jill was a hit with viewers. However, her career was cut short one Monday morning in April 1999 when she was

140 southwestscriptwriters.uk/newsletter-april-2018/

shot dead on the doorstep of her home in Fulham, London.[141] Her body would later be cremated at Worle crematorium in Weston-super-Mare.

ELSIE DAVISON

1910-1940, PILOT

In a book such as this, where one of the criteria for inclusion is that the subject must no longer be alive, it still feels especially sad to be including a woman who is notable for, among other things, being the first woman to die in a particular way. And such is the case for Elsie Joy Davison (née Muntz).

The Canadian-born pilot moved to the UK as a baby, and she became fascinated by the big flying machines in the sky known as aeroplanes. Cocking a snook at the more traditional career expectations for a woman in the early 20th century (teacher, nurse, mother), Elsie determinedly became a pilot and gained her flying certificate at the age of 20. She would ultimately become the first British female pilot to die in World War Two.[142] She was also the first female director of an aircraft company in the UK, running Utility Airways with her husband Frank Davison.

When World War Two broke out, women pilots in the Air Transport Auxiliary (known as 'Atagirls') demanded they be allowed to play a part in the war effort and for the first time won the right to fly at equal pay and with the same aircraft as male pilots. As such, Elsie joined the Air Transport Auxiliary based at Whitchurch Aerodrome (the original location for Bristol Airport and currently Hengrove Park) and was one of the first women to do so. Alongside her sister Atagirls, Elsie was part of a group

141 Barry George was convicted of her murder in 2001 but acquitted in 2008 after a retrial.

142 In total, 15 British female pilots were killed during World War Two, including Elsie.

of determined and resourceful women who won the right to fly military aircraft alongside men, and at the same rate of pay as the men: this was very probably the first time in British history in which women achieved equal pay.

Shortly before her death, Elsie wrote in a letter to a cousin that her work was "extremely dangerous now and I don't know whether I will come out of it". Elsie was an experienced pilot and mechanic but at the age of 30 she was killed while on a training exercise at RAF Upavon in Wiltshire; her co-pilot also died. It is thought they were rendered unconscious due to a carbon monoxide leak in the Miles Master aircraft they were flying.

In her obituary, one of Elsie's uncles said: "She was always crazy about planes. Even as a little girl she could think of nothing but flying and puttering around motors."[143] Elsie was cremated at Arnos Vale Cemetery with her ashes scattered from an aircraft, although a memorial plaque remains at the south Bristol cemetery in her honour. She is one of just five servicewomen commemorated there. Two photographic portraits of Elsie can be viewed online at the National Portrait Gallery.[144]

Please also see: Princess Marina (vol two), Ann Wood Kelly (vol two).

143 bac2010.co.uk/air_transport_auxillary.php

144 With thanks to researchers at Arnos Vale Cemetery (including Marion Blackburn, Hildegard Dumper, Liz Johnson and Janine Marriott) for generously providing extra information for this entry.

BETHLEHEM DAWES

born 1784, WAIF & STRAY

An orphan spared the horror of the workhouse or transportation to the plantations[145], but without a generous relative to take her in as their ward, might have found their way into an orphanage. The Müller orphanage of Bristol is fairly well documented in other books but most of the smaller orphanages in the city have been forgotten. However, two of those small orphanages about which some information survives were the Church House and the Blue Maids Orphanage, both of which are linked to Bethlehem Dawes.

The Church House, which was part of St Andrew's Church at the end of Birdcage Walk in Clifton, had been open since at least 1720. It was created for sheltering the poor and homeless and came about following a 1696 Bill to introduce more workhouses to Bristol. The Church House was in one way a part of the workhouse system but in another way it operated independently.

In 1795, 11-year-old Bethlehem was recommended to the Church House because she experienced undiagnosed fits and had "an unsatisfactory father"; her mother had already died. It was recommended that Bethlehem be taken in by the parish and cared for there as her homelife was clearly unsuitable.[146] The Church House was a very useful and much-needed resource for the poorer residents of Bristol but it closed in 1819 when £800 was donated to improve the main St Andrew's Church building and

145 During the 17th century, homeless and wayward children were frequently shipped out to Barbados to work as slaves on the plantations. And until as recently as 1967, orphaned children could be sent to Australia to provide labour.

146 AJ Green-Armytage, 1922, *Concerning Clifton*, p31.

to extend the attached cemetery.[147]

Elsewhere in Bristol was the Blue Maids Orphanage. This was founded in 1795 and offered carefully selected working-class girls aged between nine and 15 years the opportunity to be trained to become domestic servants and 'useful members of society'; however, the Blue Maids refused admittance to illegitimate or non-white girls, or those with any kind of health concern.

Since 1791, Ashley Manor House on Ashley Hill had been home to a Magdalen Hospital for "deluded common women who will to reform"[148] although the nearby street name of Magdalen Place is now the only reminder of this past. The hospital was not profitable and in 1795 the property was repurposed as the Asylum for Poor Orphan Girls (sometimes called Hooke's Mill Orphanage, and officially becoming the Blue Maids Orphanage in 1916). All children at Blue Maids were brought up to be Protestants, regardless of any faith they may have had prior to entering the orphanage. As the name suggests, the Blue Maids was named in acknowledgement of the well-known Red Maids School in Bristol. Girls from the orphanage wore a dark blue dress, white apron and white cap when indoors. When outside, they had a white straw bonnet, white knitted gloves and a thick blue cape. Apart from the bonnets, the orphans made their uniforms themselves. Local historian AJ Green-Armytage romantically describes this uniform as "singularly picturesque and becoming,"[149] which perhaps paints a more charming picture of this rudimentary and no doubt scratchy outfit than reality presented.

147 The church itself was destroyed in a raid by the Luftwaffe in 1940, which struck on a Sunday evening while a service was taking place. Fortunately the congregation had heard the warnings and had taken shelter in the crypt so were unharmed. However, many of the tombstones remain in the areas to each side of Birdcage Walk. There had been a church of some kind on the site since the 12th century but now it is simply a place to walk and admire nature.

148 Mary Wright, 2009, *The Blue Maids Orphanage*, p6.

149 AJ Green-Armytage, 1914, *The Blue Maids of Hooke's Mills: History of the Institution*, p11.

Bethlehem is recorded as one of the first-ever girls who was admitted to the then-newly opened Asylum for Poor Orphan Girls in 1795: she would have been just 11 years old at the time.[150] However, in May 1797, Bethlehem (then 13) was sent from the Asylum to Somerset Square, Redcliffe, to work as a servant for Wilhelmenia and Daniel Wait, who would later become Mayor of Bristol; he was also a patron of the Asylum. But by January 1798, she was sent back to the Asylum due to her frequent fits. Unwilling to keep a child who was not well, the Asylum returned Bethlehem to her previously mentioned "unsatisfactory father" (it was unusual for the Asylum to have accepted a child with a living parent), who promptly handed her over to the Constable of Clifton who, in turn, returned her straight back to the Waits. The poor child was passed from one uncaring adult to another, all trying to shun responsibility for her welfare. Clearly the Waits kept her because, in March 1800, Bethlehem was presented to the committee at the Asylum with a complimentary letter from Mrs Wait stating that Bethlehem had been employed by her for 18 months and had "conducted herself with great propriety" and was "a very deserving girl".[151] At this point we sadly lose track of Bethlehem and what ultimately became of her.

Benefactors of Blue Maids included the writer Hannah More and her sister Martha More (who jointly subscribed the annual sum of £250), as well as respected local families including the Frys, Goldneys and Dightons. These benefactors gained from not only a glowing feeling of having contributed to a worthwhile charity but also a supply of well-trained servant girls to work in their households. Blue Maids favoured the businesses of its patrons for its consumables; for example, all groceries at the Asylum came from the business owned by benefactor Daniel Wait, and all soap

150 childrenshomes.org.uk/BristolBlueMaids/

151 Mary Wright, 2009, *The Blue Maids Orphanage*, p8.

and rope came from the business owned by benefactor Thomas Ware, whose enormous Victorian leather factory still operates on Coronation Road, Southville.

Blue Maids closed in 1927 when admissions and donations fell too low to be sustainable, and the conditions and training the girls experienced was called into question. In her pamphlet about the history of the orphanage which was published in 1914, AJ Green-Armytage blissfully described it as a "happy, home-like asylum"[152] which, given what else we know about the establishment in its final decades, feels optimistic at best.

And another thing... The first-ever patron of the Blue Maids Orphanage was a **Miss Gibbs**. She supported the orphanage for 46 years until her death in 1841 and followed her initial donation of £100 with an annual subscription of £5 5s. The minutes of 18 August 1795 note: "Ordered. That a letter from the Committee, signed by the Chairman, be sent to Miss Gibbs acknowledging the sense they entertain of the favour shown to this Institution by her genteel acquiescence in their request, and to express their sincere gratitude for her very liberal donation to the Charity."[153]

Please also see: AJ Green-Armytage (vol two), Mary Jeffries (vol one), Mary Milgrove (vol two), Hannah More (vol one).

MARY DELANEY

1961-1999, BARRISTER

With a lifelong passion for justice, Bristol-born Mary Delaney was motivated by her senses of fairness and compassion. The

152 AJ Green-Armytage, 1914, *The Blue Maids of Hooke's Mills: History of the Institution*, p4.
153 Ibid, p5.

eldest of four siblings, Mary was inspired to become a lawyer after watching the TV show *Crown Court* when she was seven. After finishing at the Catholic La Retraite High School on Clifton Hill, she graduated in law at University College London before being called to the bar at Gray's Inn, London, in 1984.

Once she had qualified, Mary built a solid reputation as a family barrister and also forged her path in an industry largely dominated by men. However, Mary defied the expectation that women in the law should behave like 'honorary men' and instead she treated others as she felt most appropriate and fair, without resorting to macho tactics. During her career, Mary channelled her experience and empathy into a number of significant campaigns. These included the Friends of John McCarthy pressure group (campaigning to release British hostages in Beirut), and Camden Women's Aid (providing accommodation for women escaping domestic violence).

Mary died in 1999 after developing an aggressive form of bone cancer. She married her long-term partner shortly before her death and is survived by their daughter.[154]

Please also see: Valerie Cook (vol two), Julie Exton (vol two), Angela Tuckett (vol one), Joan Tuckett (vol one).

EUGÉNIE DE MONTIJO

1826-1920, EMPRESS

If you visit 2 Royal York Crescent, Clifton, and look up, you will spot a green plaque on the building which commemorates the fact Eugénie De Montijo attended school here. But who was Eugénie?

154 Jill Morrell, 'Obituary: Mary Delaney' in *The Independent*, 1 February 1999.

In short, between 1853 and 1871 she was the last Empress Consort of the French, owing to her marriage to Napoleon III. Before this, Eugénie was largely educated at the Convent of the Sacré Cœur in Paris, but in 1837 she and her elder sister Paca spent a year at a boarding school for girls in Clifton to help them learn English. However, Eugénie didn't enjoy her time in Bristol: her red hair earned her the unkind nickname 'Carrots' and she attempted to run away to India, although did not get any further than the Bristol docks before she was collared and returned to the school. Recognising the unhappiness of their daughters, Eugénie and Paca's parents allowed them to resume their education in Paris.

LUCY de NEWCHURCH

born c1350, ANCHORITE

Beautiful Brandon Hill is a pleasure to visit, with arresting views across the city, carefully maintained paths to explore and the impressive Cabot Tower to climb. But it wasn't always this way. In medieval times, Brandon Hill was a heavily wooded wasteland that was fit for little more than grazing animals and it was considered an embarrassment to the city of Bristol, not least because by the 12th century — by virtue of its uninviting appearance — it had become home to an anchorite cell; an anchorite being someone of religious faith who has chosen to live as a recluse.

When the foundations were being dug to build the Cabot Tower in 1897, the builders were surprised to find the remains of the cell, information about which had previously been lost to time. Researchers have since been able to find out more about it and its most famous resident: Lucy de Newchurch, who was originally from Hereford.

Historian Rotha Clay found an anchorite cell had existed on

Brandon Hill since 1192. In the 14th century, Lucy ("tired of the world"[155]) was beseeching the Bishop of Worcester to permit her to be enclosed at the hermitage on Brandon Hill and her application was endorsed with letters from notable men, one of whom was already an anchorite at the site.

Rotha records the Bishop of Worcester writing in support of Lucy's application: "Lucy de Newchirche [sic] has approached us many times with earnest and humble devotion, as was clear to us from her appearance and demeanour, asking to be enclosed in the hermitage of St Brandan [sic] at Bristol in our diocese. But as we have no knowledge of the life and conversation of the said Lucy, we commit to you in whose trustiness, diligence and caution we have full confidence, an enquiry from men and women worthy of credit with regard to the conversation of this Lucy, and whether you would consider her to be of pure and praiseworthy life, and whether she excels in those notable virtues which ought to prevail in persons who give up the life of the world."[156]

Thanks to this endorsement from the bishop, Lucy was successfully enclosed at the hermitage in 1351 and "had a piece of ground walled in and a croft nearby"[157].

And another thing... On the theme of Brandon Hill: **Queen Elizabeth I** visited Bristol in 1574 and was reportedly in a right huff because her royal ruffs had become dirty on the journey. The Mayor of Bristol gave the ruffs to the washerwomen at Jacob's Wells, and Her Majesty was so delighted with the cleanliness of them that she decreed that from this point onwards the washerwomen had the right to wash their own linen in the pure waters of Jacob's Wells

155 gutenberg.org/files/45273/45273-h/45273-h.htm
156 brisray.com/bristol/hermits.htm
157 In different sources the year varies from 1251 to 1351, but because 1351 appears more frequently I am going with that one as correct. Marguerite Fedden, 1950, *Bristol Bypaths: Stray Sketches*, p33-34.

and then hang them out to dry on the south slope of Brandon Hill.[158]

And another other thing... This second postscript about Brandon Hill is a sad one: in 1753, destitute **Sarah Gallop** gave birth alone on the slopes of the hill. Unfortunately, her baby was stillborn. This opens up (currently unanswered) questions about why a woman would be reduced to delivering her own baby alone and in public, as well as what happened to poor Sarah afterwards.

Please also see: Rotha Clay (vol two), Joan Young (vol two).

MARY DISRAELI
1792-1872, SOCIALITE

Following the death of her first husband, in 1839 Clifton-dwelling Mary Anne Lewis married a man 15 years her junior who had been a close friend of her late husband. That man was Benjamin Disraeli, who would go on to become Prime Minister on two separate occasions.[159] Because Mary had an income of £5,000 a year, many cynics felt Disraeli's intentions for marrying her were mercenary but this seems to have been far from the truth. Disraeli said of his wife: "She has never given me a dull moment." The couple were happily married for 33 years and enjoyed "unclouded domestic happiness", indeed Disraeli was known to be absolutely furious with anyone who dared to criticise Mary; which, given her outspoken and sometimes confrontational character, might have been fairly often.

Reigning Queen Victoria was so impressed by Disraeli's skills as Prime Minister that in 1868 she wanted to ennoble him but,

158 *Washing In The Well: Bathing in the Past*, 2018, booklet, p6.
159 Benjamin Disraeli was Prime Minister in 1868 and again from 1874-1880.

as he wished to remain in the House of Commons, Mary took the title instead, becoming Viscountess Beaconsfield in the process; following her death, Disraeli assumed the title of Earl of Beaconsfield. After Mary died in 1872, a grieving Disraeli wrote to his colleague (and fellow Prime Minister) William Gladstone: "Marriage is the highest earthly happiness when founded on complete sympathy. That hallowed lot was mine."[160]

And another thing... Mary is immortalised in numerous feature films including *Disraeli* (1929, Alfred E Green), *The Prime Minister* (1941, Thorold Dickinson) and *Mrs Brown* (1997, John Madden). Most bizarrely, she is also a character in the 2015 video game *Assassin's Creed: Syndicate* as part of a storyline which features a plot to kill her husband. Given Mary's eccentric character, I think this would have greatly amused her.

MAY DIXON

born c1890, CANTEEN OWNER

Just seven days after World War Two was declared, enterprising minister's wife May Dixon opened the gates of the vicarage of St Mary's at The Priory, High Street, Shirehampton, set up a trestle table and began offering teas and sandwiches to the many drivers and other servicewomen and men who passed by her home on their way to the docks at Avonmouth, from where they would be sent to France.

Before long, the demand for May's catering outstripped what she could supply from her table so, thanks to a community whip round, funds were raised to build a large wooden hut which she

160 AJ Green-Armytage, 1922, *Concerning Clifton*, p63.

could use as a canteen. This was built on empty land opposite the vicarage (and is now the site of The Lawn bungalows). There was a second hut next door which was used as a games and recreation room for the servicewomen and men. In this manner, May's canteen — known as St Mary's Canteen because of the church next door — operated from the very start to the very end of World War Two and, unlike other canteens that followed in its wake, St Mary's was unique in staying open all day, every day.

The canteen was staffed entirely by female volunteers from St Mary's Mother's Union and the prices were kept as low as possible so as to remain affordable. One of the most popular dishes was a simple cheese on toast, although "oft-times the ladies were hard put to keep pace with orders". By January 1945, it was reported that St Mary's Canteen had served an astonishing 1,183,221 snack meals to servicewomen and men, and the profits from these meals were donated to the Soldiers, Sailors and Airmen's Families Association.[161]

ROSINA DOUGLAS

1913-2000, MOTORCYCLIST

The sight of Rosina 'Rosie' Douglas standing on the saddle of her motorbike and speeding down Kingswood High Street was enough to make even the most composed of bystanders feel nervous. But if they considered her pedigree, it should have come as no surprise.

The Douglas Engineering Company was started near Bristol's Old Market in the mid-1860s by Newcastle-born John Douglas; although at this point it was a firm which manufactured boot

161 Ethel Thomas, 1989, *War Story*, p107-108.

Rosina Douglas illustration by Carrie Love

and shoe machinery. In 1880, when John died, his wife Jane ran the business until their son William was old enough to take over in 1885. In time, they expanded into the 12-acre Douglas Motorcycles site in Kingswood (now a housing estate) employing more than 5,000 people after they began manufacturing motorbikes in 1907, including those used for the popular new sport of speedway racing. A big opportunity for the firm came with the outbreak of World War One in 1914, when the Ministry of Defence commissioned Douglas Motorcycles to manufacture 36,000 motorbikes for military use during the war. This deal made the Kingswood site the largest manufacturer of motorbikes in Europe and the Douglas family became extremely wealthy.[162]

William lived at The Woodlands on Court Road, Kingswood (now a retirement home). His daughter Rosie had been educated at home by a governess before attending Colston's Girls' School. However, no amount of 'good' education could dampen her passion for motorbikes. Photos survive of Rosie with her Duggies, as the bikes were affectionately called. Although promotional postcards from the 1910s and 1920s exclusively show men riding astride their Duggies, sometimes with women delicately perched side-saddle on the back, Rosie showed no such restraint and straddled her bike in exactly the same way as a male rider. Sometimes she even stood on the saddle and rode in the most showy manner possible.

Although motorcycling was largely a male-dominated scene, Rosie, her sister Irene and cousin Margaret were excellent motorcyclists and competed successfully in competitions as the Douglas Motorbikes' Women's Team in the years leading up to World War Two, winning hill climbs, trail and other events. In 1927, the team won the International Vase against men's

162 bbc.co.uk/programmes/p01q9pnx

teams from all over Europe. In this way, they were an excellent advertisement for the family business showing the Duggies to be not only reliable but also winning machines.

Production of Douglas motorbikes in Kingswood ceased in 1957 after the business experienced a number of financial difficulties and was sold.

And another thing... Rosie's cousin **Mary Douglas** (born 1887, Australia) is shown in the 1901 census to be living in Kingswood with her extended family. Like many in the Douglas family, she loved motorbikes and photographs show her as a well-dressed, smart woman sitting astride her Duggie while wearing a floor-length fur coat, which cannot have been very practical... or safe.

Please also see: Lillian Allen (vol two), Lottie Cottrell (vol two), Vera Hole (vol two).

ELIZA DRAPER

1744-1778, MUSE

Elizabeth Draper's father was in the employ of the East India Company, which explains why his daughter, known as Eliza, was born in Anjengo (now Anchuthengu), India. At the age of ten, Eliza and her sisters were sent to a boarding school in England until Eliza was returned to India in 1757 to be married to Daniel Draper: she was 14 and he was 32. Together, they had two children and the family moved to England so the children could benefit from a British education.

When Daniel opted to return to India in 1766, Eliza remained in the UK with the children and set up home in Soho, London. It was here she met the writer Laurence Sterne, who had achieved success with his nine-volume novel *Tristram Shandy* (1759). When Eliza was obliged to visit Daniel in India, a bereft Laurence comforted himself by writing about her in his 1768 novel *A Sentimental Journey Through France and Italy* and, despite the chaste nature of their friendship, Sterne's writing caused tongues to wag. His follow up, the fictionalised diary and letters which comprised *Journal to Eliza*, did nothing to quiet the scurrilous rumours. When Sterne died in 1768, Eliza fought hard to have *Journal to Eliza* suppressed and to prevent it being published and further ruining her reputation: she succeeded, the book was unpublished until 1904. Depressingly, Eliza has since been immortalised as 'Sterne's Eliza' thanks to a book of the same name by Arnold Wright and William Lutley Sclater (1922), which claims Eliza is only famous for her friendship with Sterne and, judging by the title, that she belonged to him.

However, Eliza wasn't the only one casting shadows upon the Drapers' marriage. Her husband Daniel was not only having an affair with his wife's maid, he was also 'keeping' a number of Indian women. Unsurprisingly, the marriage broke down and in January 1773 Eliza fled their Indian home, taking their daughter Elizabeth with her, and she never saw Daniel again. Eliza returned to London, where she had previously enjoyed being a part of the literary scene and became a muse to writers including Abbé Raynal, John Wilkes and others. Yet she fell ill in May 1777 and travelled to Bristol to benefit from the healing waters at Hotwells spa. She stayed with her brother-in-law General Sir William Draper at his Clifton home, Manilla Hall: Draper had commissioned his enormous property to be built on the edge of the Durdham Downs in honour of his perceived triumph at having captured Manila City in the Philippines in 1762.[163] It was at Manilla Hall that Eliza died on 3 August 1778 aged just 35, having contracted consumption.

Eliza was buried at Bristol Cathedral and a diamond-shaped floor plaque declaring her "genius and benevolence" remains in her honour, as does a monument in the cloisters sculpted by the respected artist John Bacon: these were commissioned by William, who was known to be a generous and ostentatious man. The Bacon monument consists of a plain base supporting a pointed arch of Siena marble, under which is a pedestal bearing an urn which is flanked by two female figures in white marble.

MAUD DUNCAN and MABEL CROSS
born 1866 and 1872, SISTER SUFFRAGISTS

The redoubtable Duncan sisters were loyal supporters of the national votes for women campaign, regularly attending peaceful National Union of Women's Suffrage Society (NUWSS) meetings in the South West. In the 1871 census, their parents Adelaide and Edward Duncan were living with their daughters on Berkeley Road, Redland, and there were two other siblings, named Adelaide and Edward after their parents.

Maud and Mabel Duncan then lived with their parents (although their mother died in 1906) at 16 West Mall, Clifton, and hosted NUWSS meetings in their front room, which were attended by Bristol's great and good who similarly felt a peaceful approach was what would win women the vote. Mabel was

163 A note on spellings: the Philippines city is spelled 'Manila' but the Bristol property is 'Manilla'. Manilla Hall was demolished in the 1880s, however the obelisk and memorial that Sir William had commissioned as tributes to the men who died during the capture of Manila City — and which had stood in the grounds of Manilla Hall — were relocated to Clifton village, where they still remain on the green opposite Christ Church on Clifton Down Road.

Honorary Secretary of the Women's Reform Union (WRU), which Anna-Maria Priestman had founded in 1905 to focus on women's suffrage and other reforms that prioritised women. One goal of the WRU was to centralise working-class women in the campaign while recognising working women did not have the luxury of time or money to attend meetings in Clifton. In this way, the WRU took itself to working women and, as such, weekly meetings were held outdoors in east Bristol, as well as in the kitchens of women who were tied to the home looking after family members. In 1909, the WRU merged with the Bristol Women's Suffrage Society and Mabel retained the role of Honorary Secretary.

After marrying a local solicitor in 1908 and becoming Mrs Cross, Mabel and her husband William moved to 9 Beaufort Road, Clifton, and Maud came to live with them. The sisters carried on their suffrage campaigning with the support of Mabel's sympathetic husband, and in 1910 Mabel and William had a daughter, Mary. Interestingly, in the 1911 census, Mabel simply lists her occupation as "wife" yet Maud throws caution to the wind and lists her job as "women's suffrage worker". This disparity opens up a lot of questions about why Mabel would have chosen a conservative entry, especially given the support she clearly had from William.

Following the start of World War One and the cessation of suffrage activities in the name of the war effort, Mabel continued to prioritise working-class women by becoming the Superintendent of the Bedminster Maternity Centre and School for Mothers in December 1914. In this capacity, she was organising protests in 1919 about the high price of milk and arranging a boycott of local farmers who she felt were exploiting mothers who depended on the milk for their infants. In the 1920s, after the war had ended, Mabel joined the Bristol Women's Liberal Foundation and in the 1930s she began speaking out about birth control and offering advice to women as to how to avoid pregnancy: an absolutely radical topic for the time.

Please also see: Anna-Maria Priestman (vol one), Blanche Rogers (vol two).

ADALIZA DUNSCOMBE
1867-1943, OPTICIAN

Located at 5 St Augustines Parade in the city centre, Dunscombe's Opticians was a long-established Bristol family business for more than 100 years. It was instantly recognisable by the enormous mural of the company's name displayed as if in an eye-examination chart painted onto the side of the large, white, corner building.

The fantastically named Adaliza Amelia Clara Mary Elizabeth Emma Frances Dunscombe (wow!) was born in Clerkenwell, London, but her family had relocated to 17 St Augustines Parade, Bristol, by the time she was just four years old in 1871. Adaliza was the eldest of eight children and the only daughter, although she bore enough names for seven girls. Her father Matthew, who had grown up in Bristol, was already a practising optician and he set up his business near the family home.

By the time of the 1901 census, Adaliza, now 33, was living at 54 Woodstock Road, Redland, with her family and her occupation was listed as 'refractionist and optician'. In this way, she was not only the first female optician in Bristol but she was also the first female optician anywhere in the UK. It would be 2005 before the number of female opticians in the UK equalled the number of males in the profession, so Adaliza made huge pioneering steps.

The British Optical Association (BOA) finally permitted women to take its ophthalmic optic examination in 1895, and

Adaliza was the very first woman to sit and pass the exam when she did so in February 1899; she consequently became the very first female member of the BOA. At this time, only female relatives of male BOA members were considered eligible to sit the exams, so Adaliza was fortunate that her father was already an established and respected optician... indeed, he had been a founding member of the BOA.

Adaliza never married or had children, and continued to work as an optician at Dunscombe's for the remainder of her career.[164]

AMELIA DYER

1837-1896, SERIAL KILLER

One of the most prolific serial killers in Victorian England, Amelia Dyer of Old Market reportedly murdered up to 400 infants in her care during a 20-year timeframe.

The daughter of a shoemaker living in Pile Marsh, Redfield, as a child Amelia benefitted from a good education and developed a love for literature. However, hers was not a happy childhood because her mother Sarah became mentally unwell due to typhus and was prone to violent fits until her death in 1848. This was understandably a lot for 11-year-old Amelia to take in, not least because she had been her mother's primary carer during her illness. Following Sarah's death, Amelia went to live with an aunt in central Bristol and was apprenticed to a corset maker. And after her father's death in 1859, Amelia joined the family shoemaking business which her brother Thomas had inherited and went to live at Trinity Street, Old Market. It was here that she met George Thomas whom she quickly married despite a significant age gap:

164 With thanks to Mark Small for the nomination of Adaliza Dunscombe to this book.

he was 59 and she was just 24.

With the support of Thomas, Amelia pursued a new career as a nurse in a mental asylum, and on the side she offered her home as a place for expectant mothers of illegitimate babies... for a fee, of course. The unmarried mothers-to-be had little choice but to accept Amelia's 'help' because, due to the 1834 Poor Law Amendment Act, fathers of illegitimate children were not obliged to provide financial support and the stigma of being an unmarried mother was ruinous.

In 1869, Thomas died, leaving Amelia a single mother to their young daughter Ellen. Unable to continue her work as a nurse and needing to support herself and Ellen, Amelia developed her 'help' for unmarried mothers-to-be by becoming a fully fledged baby farmer. As was common for other baby farmers, she did this in return for a substantial lump sum and clothing for the child, which would be immediately taken to a pawnbroker and Amelia would keep the money herself. Long before any kind of social welfare system existed, the practice of baby farming was not uncommon and was often felt to be the only option for unmarried expectant mothers. Once they had given birth, the mothers would hand their babies over to a baby farmer such as Amelia to be housed with a foster family, and the mother would be expected to pay regular money to the foster family to help bring the baby up. The money was paid to the baby farmer to hand on but it usually never reached the foster family; often because the baby farmer had starved the child to death before it had been fostered, yet had told the mother the child was living happily with a kind family, meaning the baby farmer could pocket the money. The fee was anywhere from £5 (for a woman with no income) to £80 (for a society woman who needed to keep the baby's existence secret to protect her reputation).

While this was going on, in 1872 Amelia re-married. Her new

husband was a brewer's labourer called William Dyer with whom she had two more children: Mary Ann and William. Although she later left Dyer, Amelia remained a mother to her three children.

The police first became suspicious about Amelia in 1879, after a doctor raised concerns about the number of infant deaths he was called upon to certify at Amelia's address. But cleared of murder or manslaughter, Amelia simply received a six-month sentence for neglect. Her period in prison had a terrible effect on her mental health and after she was released Amelia was confined to a mental hospital due to her suicidal thoughts; a place she began to voluntarily admit herself to on occasion. It was later noted that Amelia's admissions to the mental hospital always coincided with a time when it would be convenient for her to have a low profile, such as when the police were asking too many difficult questions. Drawing on her experience as a nurse in a mental asylum, Amelia knew how to behave so as to convince the staff that she was troubled enough to warrant admission, but also to ensure she did not behave in such an unstable manner that she was badly treated. However, she did come to abuse the alcohol and opiates which she was prescribed as a patient and this continued long after she was released to her Old Market home. Indeed, alcohol and drugs were both substances which were also linked to the deaths of some of the infants in her care.

Alert to the problems created by involving the authorities when a baby died in her care, Amelia simply began disposing of the bodies herself, either by throwing them in rivers or burying them in the gardens of her rented homes. She also began the habit of moving house and city every so often so as to escape suspicion, and to restart her business in a new place where nobody knew of her reputation or history. Amelia became known as 'Mother' in front of potential new clients in order to present herself as warm and trustworthy.

On 30 March 1896, police in Reading discovered a package that had been thrown into the River Thames. It contained the body of a baby girl called Helena Fry. By forensically examining the paper wrapped around the body, police could detect faint writing for 'Mrs Thomas' and 'Temple Meads Station'.[165] It wasn't long before they made the link to Amelia Dyer, although they were still lacking strong enough evidence to convict her. So officers set a young woman up as a decoy to approach Amelia for help, claiming she was pregnant and unmarried. Having arranged to meet Amelia at her home on 3 April 1896, it was not actually the young woman who presented herself on Amelia's doorstep but the police.

The officers were confronted by an overpowering stench of human decomposition at the property but could find no bodily remains. However, there was plenty of other evidence linking Amelia to the crime of baby farming and infanticide: telegrams concerning adoptions, white tape (which matched that found wrapped around Helena Fry), pawn tickets for children's clothing and letters from women asking how their babies were doing. Police estimates place the number of children murdered by Amelia Dyer as being up to 400.

Amelia was arrested on 4 April 1896 and charged with murder. Later the same month, the River Thames was dredged and six more infant bodies were found. When Amelia appeared in court on 22 May 1896 she pleaded guilty to just one count of murder, but her family and associates testified they had become increasingly suspicious about her behaviour. In the end, it was the testimony of Amelia's daughter Mary which sealed her fate and the jury took just four-and-a-half minutes to find Amelia guilty.

165 A box containing the brown paper, string and white tape that had been wrapped around Helena Fry, and an evidence tag, was uncovered in a loft in March 2017. It had been stored by a relative of DC James Beattie Anderson, who was the arresting officer in the case, and has subsequently been donated to a museum in Berkshire.

She was hanged on 10 June 1896 aged 57. As a result of Amelia Dyer's case, the laws concerning baby farming and adoption became much tighter with the intention of eradicating this type of abuse.

PRUDENCE EARLY

1918-2017, MENTAL HEALTH PIONEER

Alongside her husband Dr Donal Early, Dr Prudence Early worked to treat patients with mental illnesses at the Bristol Psychiatric Hospital[166] in Fishponds, where Donal began work in 1944. The Irish-born couple would go on to pioneer radical new treatments for mental health patients in Bristol during the 1960s. At the time of his training, Donal had been taught mental health patients were hopeless cases but he rejected this thinking and was horrified at the disgraceful way patients with mental illnesses were treated.

Following the birth of her two children in the late 1940s, Prudence returned to the medical studies which she had begun prior to marriage and she soon passed her exams. With her mother helping to look after the children, Prudence worked part-time in the Observation Ward at Manor Park Hospital, before becoming a clinical assistant at the rather rundown Bristol Psychiatric Hospital.

During this time, Donal was also working at the Bristol Psychiatric Hospital, which had been founded in 1861 as a mental asylum for patients who had been rejected by the workhouses. In those days, admission to a mental asylum wasn't just for those

166 NB: The Bristol Psychiatric Hospital was known by a range of names at different times, however I am consistently using this one name throughout because this is how the Glenside Hospital Museum refers to it.

with conditions we now understand to be mental illnesses but also for anyone from alcoholics to epileptics. In short, people whom society found difficult to manage.

Under Prudence and Donal's guidance, by the 1950s the Bristol Psychiatric Hospital had become a pioneering centre for mental health research and they often worked in conjunction with the Burden Neurological Institute at Stoke Park Hospital. Thanks to the introduction of the National Health Service in 1948, Donal was able to introduce a radical new system of 'industrial rehabilitation' whereby he kept patients gainfully occupied in making items such as ballpoint pens which were useful to the outside world, or working at tasks such as car washing.

In 1984, after they had both retired, Prudence and Donal founded the nationally important Glenside Hospital Museum, which is a fascinating resource exploring the history of mental health treatment in the UK during the 20th century. A visit to this museum is an excellent use of your time.

Please also see: Rosa Burden (vol one), Sarah Carpenter (vol two), Elizabeth Cox (vol two), Kate Underwood (vol two).

EMILY EBERLE

1858-1908, DOCTOR

"The late Dr Emily Eberle ... [was] one of the most energetic and devoted women that Bristol has ever known, and it is stated that for 20 years she exerted a charming and helpful influence among the women and children of St Augustine's ... She was well known and highly esteemed by the rich, and was much sought after for her skill and medical ability. But she loved the poor and preferred working among them ... Her best work was done in connection with the Read Dispensary in St George's Road. The women and children of St Augustine's and Clifton Ward have lost in her one of their best and truest friends. She was generous, unassuming, large hearted, tender and beautifully patient. Dr Eberle treated poor women as if they were her sisters and they knew it and felt it. She called them 'dear' and they were dear to her. No skill was too great, no medicine was too costly, no time was too precious, no effort was too exacting, for the women who sought her and whom she delighted to help."[167] What an obituary!

Dr Emily Elizabeth Eberle was born in London as the fifth child to Hannah and Jacob Eberle. Moravian minister Jacob was born and grew up in Greenland and he moved to the UK in his 30s when he married Bristolian Hannah Fuller (although how they came to meet is sadly unknown). Emily was educated at the Fulneck School, West Yorkshire, which was a Moravian institution that she attended as a boarder. After Jacob died in 1876, Emily went to Dublin to live with her older brother Samuel who had already moved there for work, and she studied at Trinity College, Dublin, where she achieved a string of qualifications: Master of Arts in Mathematics, Bachelor of Medicine and Fellow of the Royal College of Surgeons. She would go on to achieve many more qualifications throughout her life; she would ultimately be an MA, MB, BAORUI, FRCS and IM. And sources imply this is a limited list!

Upon qualification and the death of Samuel in 1894, Emily had no further reason to stay in Dublin so she moved to Bristol to swell the number of women doctors practising in the city. Another brother, Birtill, was already established in Bristol having found work at the Fuller Coachworks (remember that Emily's father married a Bristolian called Hannah Fuller) on Limekiln

167 'Dr Eberle' in *Western Daily Press*, 6 October 1908.

Lane, which was run by their uncle James Eberle Fuller, a Bristol city councillor who was later granted the Freedom of the City of Bristol. The Eberle family was well respected in the city and some of their ancestors still live and work in Bristol today.

In the 1901 census, the Eberle family was living at 17 Oakfield Road, Clifton, with Birtill being the head of house and Emily having "surgeon" listed as her profession. Their younger sister Clara and one servant completed the household.

In Bristol, Emily worked tirelessly for the benefit of sick children and it was this work which led her to join the team at the Read Dispensary for Women and Children in Hotwells. She was also the Assistant House Surgeon and the only gynaecologist at the Bristol Children's Hospital, Surgeon at the Private Hospital for Women at 34 Berkeley Square, and she even briefly established her own dispensary in Bedminster. However, the more her private practice work increased, the more Emily had to step back from her unpaid public service and she eventually resigned her post at the Bristol Children's Hospital and lowered her commitments to the Read Dispensary and Berkeley Square hospital to mere visiting days.

Emily, who never married, died while visiting relations in Dublin in 1908 aged just 50. She had been undergoing an abdominal operation and died 15 days later having contracted tetanus during the procedure. One colleague mourned: "Dr Eberle was truly a noble woman and, like her Lord, she found her truest happiness in healing the sick and spending her life doing good." Another said: "Today we mourn the loss of one of the most devoted and energetic women that Bristol has ever known … The rich and poor alike valued her professional talent and her extreme kindness."[168]

168 Cited in James Eberle, 2007, *From Greenland's Icy Shore*, p84.

An obituary for Emily said: "Dr Eberle brought to her medical practice quick intelligence, uncommon energy, a power of lively sympathy and good business ability. She concentrated all her powers upon her professions, and passed laborious days devoted to it alone, knowing little or nothing of pleasures outside those of the family circle. Her sympathy and interest in the sick never flagged, and ailing women of all classes and from a wide area availed themselves in a large number of her medical help, given with ungrudging expenditure of time, thought and warm sympathy. Her colleagues at the Read Dispensary and Private Hospital for Women lament the loss of the single-eyed devotion and alert intelligence which she brought to her work, and know that their loss will not be easily repaired."[169]

Following her untimely death, a fund was set up in Emily's name to enable a woman who had attended the Read Dispensary and was deemed to be needing a hospital stay, but who could not afford it, to have a bed at the Private Hospital on Berkeley Square. This was known as the 'Dr Emily Eberle Bed' and it was felt by those who knew her to be a fitting way to pay tribute to her work and memory. The cost of the bed was £500 per year and paid for by a fund managed in her name.[170]

And another thing... Remember Emily's uncle James Eberle Fuller, who is mentioned above and who ran the Fuller Coachworks? He was brought up as an unofficial adopted son by **Clara Fedden** (sister of Marguerite Fedden, who is profiled in this book), who had married John Fuller. It was this John Fuller who had set up the Fuller Coachworks where James later worked. James subsequently added Fuller to his name in acknowledgment of the kindness of Clara and John. The Eberle and Fedden families remained closely

169 pdfs.semanticscholar.org/a790/25a083f26dcab8c5ce27bd95ba804609fe67.pdf
170 'Clifton Notes' in *Western Daily Press*, 14 October 1908.

entwined for many, many years and both families retain a presence in Bristol today.

Please also see: Eliza Dunbar Walker (vol one), Mary Fedden (vol one), Marguerite Fedden (vol two), Marion Linton (vol two), Lucy Read (vol two).

PADDI EDWARDS

1931-1999, VOICE ACTOR

You know in the Hollywood blockbuster *Ghostbusters* (1984, Ivan Reitman) when our four spooktacular heroes encounter the demonic deity of Gozer? Well, Gozer was voiced by Bristol-born actor Paddi Edwards. As far as Bristolian sci-fi movie legends go, attention is always given to Southmead's Dave Prowse who played Darth Vader in the original *Star Wars* trilogy but, given the legacy and love showered on the *Ghostbusters* franchise, it seems unfair to exclude Paddi from this glory.

Born Patricia Mary Ursula Edwards and raised in Wotton-under-Edge, Paddi's fortunes turned when her family emigrated to the US in the early 1950s. She found regular roles on TV as well as doing voiceover work for Disney, and she voices Flotsam and Jetsam in *The Little Mermaid* animated franchise (1989, Clements & Musker), and also voiced Atropos in Disney's *Hercules* movie (1997, Clements & Musker) among others.

ROSALIND ELLICOTT

1857-1924, COMPOSER

Born to the Bishop of Gloucester & Bristol (Charles Ellicott) and his wife, Rosalind Frances Ellicott became one of the leading female composers of her generation.

In her younger days, her mother Constantina Ellicott had been a singer and shunned the conventional expectations for a clergyman's wife by performing publicly and socialising in bohemian circles; among her musical achievements was founding the Handel Society's choir. Once she became a mother, Constantina shared her love for music with her young daughter, in whom she spotted a talent for singing and recital from an early age. Constantina's own mother had been musical and was delighted in her granddaughter's talent, as Rosalind modestly observed: "[She] was wild with joy when I showed a musical talent, thinking that I was going to be something wonderful. My juvenile efforts caused such great expectations that I ought to have done much better than I have."[171] Alas, despite his wife and daughter being gifted singers and musicians (and his cathedrals being filled with melodious sounds), the Bishop himself maintained a lifelong lack of interest in music.

A determined and ambitious young woman, Rosalind began taking music lessons from Gloucester Cathedral's organist at the age of 12, and by 16 had progressed to writing her own music and her first sonata. In 1874, she moved to London to study piano at the Royal Academy of Music for several years, where Constantina was so respected that she was called upon to present prizes at awards ceremonies. As a member of both the Incorporated Society of Musicians (it was no mean feat to join this prestigious

171 Sarah A Tooley, 1896, 'Ladies of Bristol and Clifton', in *The Woman at Home*, p449.

organisation) and the National Society of Professional Musicians, Rosalind received every encouragement and she was constantly composing music and working on new pieces.

Rosalind was initially known for her ambitious choral and orchestral pieces but later turned to chamber music, which was decidedly more popular with audiences and generated a better income. Following in her unconventional mother's footsteps, Rosalind similarly rejected the idea a young woman must be restrained and dignified in her behaviour. She made no secret of her ambition to be a successful and respected musician, which was an extremely unusual career choice for a young woman born into a family of high social standing. Because she was so unusual as a society woman forging a career in a man's world, coupled with her much-admired beauty, Rosalind was the subject of a number of magazine interviews and photographs. She said in 1896: "It was my wish from my earliest years to be a great composer, but I had no faith in myself. About ten years ago a celebrated teacher of singing came to visit us, and after seeing some of my work urged me strongly to devote myself to musical composition."[172]

Rosalind's first great success came in 1883, when her song 'To The Immortals' was performed at the Gloucester Festival and later published. She described the process of writing music, which involved mentally composing the piece before committing it to manuscript, saying: "In scoring for orchestra, I can hear all the different instruments playing, and when the performance takes place it sounds exactly as I have heard it in my mind."[173]

In addition to composing, Rosalind performed as a soprano soloist at concerts throughout Bristol, Gloucester and London, where she was also a member of the Handel Society's choir which Constantina had founded. And it was in Bristol in 1886

172 Ibid, p449.
173 Ibid, p448.

that her first major orchestral work, 'To Spring', was debuted before transferring to St James' Hall, London. She was repeatedly commissioned to compose pieces for the annual Ladies' Night of the Bristol Madrigals and was pleased to maintain her connection to her home city.

In later years, pieces by Rosalind would be heard at venues in the US as well as in the UK, and her 'Dramatic Overture' was performed at the opening ceremony for the Women's Building at the Chicago World's Columbian Exposition in the US in 1893, which was enormously flattering. In 1896, Rosalind gave a series of concerts of her own music at the Queen's Hall, London, and later established a series of her chamber music in Gloucester.

However, at the same time in which she was being celebrated for her unique talent, there were certain areas of society that were criticising Rosalind for being "unfeminine" or, worse, "disconcertingly masculine". And by virtue of being a woman, she found it very hard to shake off the "amateur" label, despite her repeated self-declaration as "professional". Some reviews of her compositions complained about how "manly" they were, while others berated them for not being masculine enough: this must have been exasperating for Rosalind, who knew her talent was "above the average of lady musicians".[174] Rosalind believed she was not rare as a female composer but that she had been fortunate to have been granted an audience in an era that did not support women in music, and she felt "women's work was not taken seriously enough and it was difficult for them to get a hearing, but [I believe] that there were many women who would come forward with excellent work if only they had an opening".[175]

Regrettably little of Rosalind's work has survived into the 21st century, aside from a handful of songs and instrumental pieces,

174 Cited in Paula Gillett, 2000, *Musical Women in England: 1870-1914*, p16.
175 Sarah A Tooley, 1896, 'Ladies of Bristol and Clifton', in *The Woman at Home*, p449.

and this is because so little of it was formally published. In her later years, as an unmarried daughter, she was called upon to assist her parents as they grew old, and she seems to have retired from professional life in 1900 in order to prioritise caring for her parents. She said in the early 1900s: "Lately, through various family reasons, there have been so many calls on my time that I have not done anything in the way of composition. I am practically secretary to my father and my mother's delicate health makes me her constant companion."[176]

LESLEY ELLIOTT

1958-1994, CANCER CAMPAIGNER

"I have good days and bad days but above all I have busy days. Each night I pray that I don't die tomorrow because I have too much to do."[177] These words were written by Bristol-born Lesley Elliott a few months before her death from breast cancer: a disease she devoted her final years to raising awareness of and funds to tackle.

Lesley's diagnosis came when she was just 33. As a happily married woman with three children under five, this was especially devastating news. She underwent a mastectomy, and endured chemotherapy and radiotherapy, but still the cancer spread into her lungs. Lesley was horrified to discover how prevalent cancer diagnoses were in young women, so she teamed up with the charity Breakthrough Breast Cancer to fundraise for a breast cancer research centre in London (the Lesley Elliott & People of Dorset Laboratory opened in May 2001). She also wrote articles campaigning for the establishment of walk-in breast cancer

176 Cited in Paula Gillett, 2000, *Musical Women in England: 1870-1914*, p16.

177 Lesley Elliott, 'Tomorrow For Me is a Luxury' in *The Independent*, 9 December 1993.

screening centres, the first of which was opened in Dorchester, Dorset, in May 1994, a few months before her death.

Lesley wrote an anthology of poems, *The Longest Journey*, which was published in 1993 and dealt with the themes of being terminally ill; the proceeds from the book were donated to the hospice that cared for her. As well as countless interviews talking about her experiences of cancer, Lesley was the subject of a Channel 4 documentary (*Living with Lesley*), and she spent time answering phones on a cancer helpline that was set up following the documentary's broadcast: "I wouldn't want people to think I made a film and then just walked away."[178]

ELIZABETH ELTON

1696-1775, QUAKER, LANDOWNER

Bath-born Elizabeth Marchant came to be a prominent Bristol landowner via a sad path. Her first husband was the Quaker and distiller George Bridges, whom she had married in 1717 and with whom she had four children. In 1731, Bridges had bought 200 acres of land in east Bristol which had previously belonged to the Hooke family. Although largely fields, the land also included a number of farm buildings, mills and houses, and was only part of the estate owned by Bridges, who also had property and land in Glastonbury, Keynsham, Bedminster and Redcliffe (including the Seven Stars pub, which still stands). However, by 1734 Bridges had died, which left his widow Elizabeth a very wealthy woman.

Eight years later, in April 1739, Elizabeth married again, to the widowed Jacob Elton, who had three children from his first wife. However, Elton was not a Quaker, which makes this union very

178 Clare Walmsley, 'Obituary: Lesley Elliott' in *The Independent*, 12 August 1994.

unusual, given how strongly Elizabeth felt about her faith. The number of bequests in her will to Quaker causes, and her own children's marriages into respected Quaker families, suggests she remained true to her faith throughout her life. In addition to not sharing her faith, Elton had also been a prominent player in the transatlantic slave trade and had a stake in at least two of Bristol's sugar houses.[179] Given how vehemently opposed Quakers were to the slave trade, Elizabeth's alliance to him seems incredibly strange. The couple's home had been at Ashley Court, which Elizabeth's first husband had built in 1746 and was an elegant house surrounded by a wall and balustrades, with a formal garden as well as orchards and fields. Unfortunately, the house was pulled down in the 19th century although the gate piers on Ashley Court Road, Montpelier, still remain. However, their decision to live in the house built by Elizabeth's first husband is itself odd, given Elton owned considerable property himself in Bristol. Regardless, the marriage lasted until Elton's death in 1765.

Elizabeth had a further ten years of life as a widow, and in her will she strangely left no bequests to any members of her second husband's family although she did make many bequests to members of her own extended family. And she was very generous in her bequests to her servants. She also left very substantial sums of money to be administered by her executors, including £1,000 to be put in trust and shared annually among "18 named poor women", £1,000 each to the husbands of two of her grandchildren and a further £1,000 to her three grandchildren.

179 Alongside tobacco, sugar was one of the most lucrative imports for Bristolian merchants who owned plantations in the Americas that were run by enslaved Africans. For example, John Pinney (who 'owned' the enslaved woman Fanny Coker: profiled in volume one of *The Women Who Built Bristol*) was a slave trader who ran a sugar trading company from his Great George Street property (the Georgian House is now a museum). Echoes of Bristol's sugar houses (where sugar would be processed from raw cane into an edible substance) remain in Bristol. For example, the Sugar House on Lewins Mead was constructed in 1728 and operated until 1831; it is now a luxury hotel. Similarly, the Three Sugar Loaves pub nearby opened in 1714 but has more recently been regenerated into a fashionable pub called the Christmas Steps.

Empress Matilda illustration by Rhi Lee

Most of her substantial landed estate was split equally between the three grandchildren and it remained in the families until at least 1823. However, according to Mary Wright in *Montpelier, A Bristol Suburb:* "Within two years most of the Ashley lands had been sold: the change from agricultural to residential use was under way."

It is very confusing as to why a staunch Quaker married so far outside her faith that she was able to align with someone so deeply involved with the slave trade, especially given that two of her sons-in-law were leading members of Bristol's abolition committee which had been set up in 1788. Although we don't have the answers to these questions at the moment, these are certainly issues that should be given thought considering how unusual it all was. Perhaps there was more going on behind the scenes than the history records show us?[180]

EMPRESS MATILDA
1102-1167, SMITED QUEEN

The only legitimate daughter of King Henry I of England, Matilda became the claimant to the throne during the civil war known as the Anarchy. In 1114, at the age of 12, Matilda was married to the German Holy Roman Emperor Henry V, but following her husband's death in 1125 the German crown was taken by one of Henry's enemies. Back in England, Matilda's male siblings were dying (or being killed) at a rapid pace. Fearing a succession crisis, Matilda's father ordered her to marry Geoffrey of Anjou, to strengthen the border alliances and hopefully produce a male heir. In the meantime, King Henry nominated Matilda to be his

180 With very grateful thanks to Ruth Hecht for nominating Elizabeth Elton to this book and for providing the information that enabled this entry.

successor to the English crown. He went so far as to order his court to swear an oath of loyalty to her. Yet when King Henry died in 1135, Matilda and Geoffrey were fought down by the Normans and Matilda's cousin Stephen of Blois instead took the throne.

Support for Matilda came from her half-brother Robert of Gloucester (known to be King Henry's favourite of his illegitimate children) who, in 1138, rebelled against Stephen and was determined to see Matilda crowned. This triggered a war across the entire South West of England. Bristol became caught up in this civil war and, owing to its position being surrounded on most sides by water (this was before the River Frome beneath what is now Broadmead shopping centre had been covered up), Bristol Castle (in what is now Castle Park) proved a very safe and sturdy retreat.

After a lengthy battle, Matilda had captured Stephen and locked him up in Bristol Castle. With her pesky cousin out of the way, Matilda took steps to begin her coronation at the Palace of Westminster, but the London crowds were too fierce in opposition and she remained uncrowned. Matilda never became Queen of England as her father intended, and instead was given the title Lady of the English. She maintained her ties to Bristol, and particularly Bristol Castle and its security, by sending her son Henry to live at the castle and be educated in safety there.

And another thing... If we learned only one thing from the BBC1 series *Danny Dyer's Right Royal Family*, broadcast in January 2019, let that be the humbling fact that, as well as calling King Edward III his 22-times great-grandfather, the actor can also claim our own Empress Matilda as his 28-times great-grandmother.

MARY ENGLISH

1919-2009, MYCOLOGIST

For those who do not know, mycology is the biological study of fungi and its use by humans as medicine, food and more. And the world's foremost mycologist of the 20th century was a woman from Bristol named Mary Phyllis English... and what she did was pretty important for all of us.

Born in Malaya (now Malaysia) as the eldest child of a rubber planter, Mary was sent to school in England when she was seven, before moving to London to study botany at King's College in 1937. During World War Two, she and her fellow students were evacuated to Bristol to complete their studies and she graduated with honours in 1941. This enabled Mary to work as a chemist for the War Agricultural Advisory Centre in Bristol, while spending her spare time studying for an MSc in mycology from the University of London, which she completed in 1943. "My career was shaped by the war," Mary said. "The war meant it became acceptable for women to take scientific jobs."[181]

A range of mycology research posts around the UK ensued, as well as publication in scientific journals, before Mary was head hunted to help set up a laboratory specialising in the fungal diseases of humans at the United Bristol Hospitals. As head of the laboratory located at the Bristol General Hospital, Mary was catapulted to a new league of respect within her male-dominated field... although she faced opposition from some men who felt threatened by a woman 'stealing' a 'man's job'. Despite some men treating Mary as a mere laboratory technician and thinking her inferior, she insisted on using the men-only dining and common rooms set aside for the hospital's medical staff as a point of

181 Barbara Mellor, 'Mary English Obituary' in *The Guardian*, 25 January 2010.

principle. Mary was also a member of the British Mycological Society for more than 60 years, twice serving on its council.

The diagnostic service which Mary's team provided would eventually serve many of the hospitals across the entire south of England and in 1970 she was given the title of Consultant Mycologist, which was a wholly unique honour for a clinical scientist at that time. In 1972, the unit was absorbed into the pathology department of the Bristol Royal Infirmary and Mary moved there until her retirement in 1980, when she was praised for her consistently high standard of scientific excellence. Not that her retirement was peaceful, because Mary used her so-called twilight years to start researching and writing books about medical mycology as well as indulging a previously untapped passion for social history.

ELIZA ERRINGTON

1808-1869, ARTIST

Born in Plymouth, Eliza Loudon was always destined to travel. Along with her sister Charlotte, she attended a finishing school in Paris, France, and it was here she really explored her passion and talent for drawing, where she would make excellent copies of pictures she admired. In Paris, the sisters became acquainted with the composer Franz Liszt and among Eliza's belongings was piano sheet music presented to her with an inscription from Liszt himself, as well as a portrait given to Eliza by Liszt's mother.

Once back in Plymouth, Eliza married Captain Arnold Errington in 1838 with whom she had a son, John. In 1843, the young family sailed to Hobart Town, Tasmania, on the convict ship Duchess of Northumberland and, once docked, Arnold was appointed the Commanding Officer of the 51st Light

Infantry Regiment. For the three years they lived in Tasmania, Eliza furthered her passion for painting and sketching, with the lithographer John Skinner Proust being an influence on her work.

From Tasmania, the couple moved to Bangalore, India, and then Cape Town, South Africa, before returning to the UK and settling at Lansdown Place, Clifton. It was here that they were living at the time of Eliza's death in 1869 and she was subsequently buried at Arnos Vale Cemetery.

MARY EVANS

1761-1861, CENTENARIAN

When Mary Evans died on Christmas Day in 1861, she did so having reached the grand age of 100 years. Mary was a resident at Colston's Almshouses on St Michael's Hill (the Grade I listed building remains in use as an almshouse today although has been renovated internally), where she enjoyed her independence and declined any assistance from friends or family. Right up until the last, Mary was described as being "able to walk around and attend to her usual occupations". However, when she took to her room for a rest at 6pm on 25 December 1861, this was to be the last time that anybody saw Mary alive. Complaining of a cold, she had given her apologies for the evening church service (it was expected that the almshouse residents would attend church twice a day) and retired for a rest. But by 7.30pm a smell of smoke coming from her room alerted people to a problem and, after breaking into Mary's room, they found her dead on the floor with a smouldering candlestick beside her, which she must have knocked over when she collapsed.

Please also see: Mrs Johnson (vol two), Jane Martin (vol one).

FLORENCE EXTEN-HANN

1891-1973, SUFFRAGIST, SOCIALIST, TRADE UNIONIST

Born into a socialist family in Southampton, Florence Exten was aware of class agitation from a young age through helping her father (one of the first socialists to be elected to Southampton Council) with his campaigning in the backstreets of Southampton's docklands. Alongside her mother, Florence would cycle around the rural and urban areas as a Clarion cyclist, helping to spread socialist views. She told historian Sheila Rowbotham in 1973: "Mother and I rode bicycles and wore bloomers, but had to carry a skirt to put on when riding in a town for fear of being mobbed."[182]

Unsurprisingly, given their socialist attitudes, Florence's parents treated their daughters the same as their sons with regard to their education yet, despite this, her father didn't take Florence's plans for a career very seriously. Although he did assume she would earn her keep as soon as possible; the family was not wealthy and there was no room for anybody to coast along. It was for this reason that Florence didn't follow her heart into education and instead became an office clerk in the mid-1900s. In 1908, at the age of 17, she joined a union with the support of her parents, lobbying for better pay and conditions for clerks. She recalled in 1973: "It is difficult now to recall that when I was a teenager one could not walk the streets alone; it was not done. I was considered fast and loose because I used to travel to London alone at this time to attend the Women's Advisory Council of the Shop Assistants Union at least once a month arriving home at 1.30am in the morning. I had an extremely bad reputation among the neighbours and my parents were told how wrong they were to allow it, fortunately my parents were understanding."[183]

182 brh.org.uk/site/articles/two-rebel-women/
183 Ibid.

Inspired by fellow working-class woman Annie Kenney, who was a key figure in the militant Women's Social and Political Union (WSPU), Florence gravitated towards the suffrage campaign, which in 1908 maintained good links to the socialist movement as well as the Independent Labour Party. Still living in Southampton, Florence became involved in suffragette activity such as chalking pavements with the slogan 'Votes for Women', secretly pasting posters up at night and helping to organise meetings, as well as being press secretary for the Southampton branch of the WSPU. She told Sheila Rowbotham: "Most meetings were the butt of students who threw stones, eggs or tomatoes, and many an indoor meeting had to be abandoned because of floating pepper thrown by the opposition."[184] Still just 17, it was Florence who carried the Southampton WSPU banner during the suffragettes' enormous march in London's Hyde Park in June 1908, where her youthful pigtails made her look even younger than she actually was.

In 1910, the Exten family relocated to Bristol and Florence remained a member of the WSPU, although the increasing militancy of the group unnerved her. She felt the methods of violence and assault were too much and she broke away from the suffragettes in favour of a more peaceful method of campaigning. As such, during 1911 and 1912 she worked with a range of women's organisations to try and achieve votes for women via pressure tactics. Throughout everything, Florence was driven by a desire to improve the situation for women and girls.

By 1911, Florence was working as a clerk at a brush making factory in Bristol (possibly Greenslades on Thomas Street) and she remained brutally aware of the injustices experienced by lowly staff. She recalled: "In 1911, I earned eight shillings per week at what was grandiloquently described as a 'departmental section

184 Ibid.

clerk'."[185] As humble as this pay was, as a clerk Florence was on a better wage than the manual workers at the brush factory, who were making the brushes in the most unpleasant and unsafe environments and only being paid for finished brushes which passed an inspection. It was experiences like this that prompted Florence to retain her involvement in the trades union movement after moving to Bristol, and in 1911 she told the Shop Workers' Conference: "The differences between man's work and woman's is no more than a cherished trade union phantom. This was proved during the two world wars." She added: "One found that a woman is required to be more experienced and better equipped than a man in order to obtain a post; then to work harder and obtain 25% less salary."[186]

Given she spent so much time at trades union meetings, it is not surprising that eventually Florence would fall in love at one and this is what happened after she met grocer's assistant Maurice Hann, who was on the executive committee of the trades union. The two married in 1913, despite a feeling among some socialists and anarchists that marriage should be rejected in favour of defying the system and living freely.

By the time World War One had begun, the couple had moved to London, where they were active members of the Independent Labour Party. Florence was a staunch pacifist and remained opposed to the war on moral grounds. It was in this way that she came to work alongside Sylvia Pankhurst, who was also anti-war. Throughout World War One, Florence worked for a low wage to visit and support conscientious objectors in prison, which was dangerous work at a time when everyone was supposed to be seen to support their country in the battle.

Throughout the following decades, Florence and Maurice

185 Ibid.
186 Ibid.

supported the peace movement and trade unionism, working for a variety of socialist organisations and often favouring those with a feminist slant. Florence died in 1973 but had remained engaged in the movement right up until the end of her life, always lobbying for change in a peaceful manner.

Please also see: Annie Kenney (vol one).

JULIE EXTON

1958-2017, BARRISTER

Gloucestershire-born Julie Exton took after her mother, a legal secretary, by studying law at Leicester University. After graduation, Julie moved to Bristol as an articled clerk to Burges Salmon LLP and, once qualified, she joined Veale Wasbrough Vizards LLP, where she became a partner in 1988. In addition to her work, Julie was appointed a deputy district judge in 1993 and a district judge in 1999, and she sat at the Bristol Civil and Family Justice Centre on Redcliff Street. By 2014, she had become President of the Association of Her Majesty's District Judges.

Julie's proudest achievement was creating and presiding over Gloucester's Family Drug and Alcohol Court (FDAC), which was only the second of its kind in the UK and enabled parents with drug and alcohol problems to keep custody of their children so long as they could stay sober. Her brother Tim Exton said: "Julie's priority was to keep families together whenever it was in the best interest of the children, but she also believed in giving the parents another chance to get their lives on track. She hated bureaucracy and waste and could never understand why there were not more FDACs in the UK, as they not only keep families together but are more cost-effective than putting children into care."[187]

Fellow Bristolian and lawyer Beverley Watkins said of Julie: "She was wonderful in every way. She was always very hard working, but also had a sense of humour and was very encouraging to women lawyers. She made a huge contribution to the Bristol judicial scene."[188]

To unwind from the pressures of the legal world, Julie sang with the Cabot Choir and was a keen birdwatcher. She had two children and two step-children from her two marriages. However, Julie also lived with Motor Neurone Disease for the final few months of her life and it was from this that she died when she was just 59 years old.

Please also see: Mary Delaney (vol two), Angela Tuckett (vol one), Joan Tuckett (vol one).

UA FANTHORPE
1929-2009, POET

Kentish-born Ursula Askham Fanthorpe preferred the snappier moniker of UA for her published poems, some of which were inspired by the students she had taught for 16 years at Cheltenham Ladies' College (a post she acquired thanks to her first-class degree in English from Oxford University). Her friends described her as "a wise, gentle, wry but definite person, too often pulled down by ill-health, though uncomplaining".[189]

However, teaching was not where UA's heart lay. After deciding that the "power" associated with her recent promotion to Head of Department at Cheltenham didn't suit her, she became a self-

187 Tim Exton, 'Julie Exton Obituary' in *The Guardian*, 17 December 2017.
188 Michael Cross, 'Tributes Paid to Julie Exton' in *The Law Gazette*, 16 October 2017.
189 Anthony Brownjohn et al, 'Obituary: UA Fanthorpe' in *The Guardian*, 2 May 2009.

styled "middle-aged drop out"[190]. This initially involved moving to Bristol and finding work variously as a secretary, receptionist and hospital clerk at the Burden Neurological Institute.

As she states very precisely in the introduction to her *Collected Poems*, it was in Bristol on 18 April 1974 that UA began writing. Some of her early poems recall the patients whose records she had taken care of and she often sided with the patients instead of the doctors – perhaps because she experienced episodes of depression herself, so saw how fragile the line between them was. She said: "At once I'd found the subject that I'd been looking for all my life: the strangeness of other people, particularly neurological patients, and how it felt to be them, and to use their words."[191] *The Independent* noted: "She observed the gallery of characters who passed before her en route to the doctors and made poetry from their raw troubles."[192]

UA was also concerned with themes of England and Englishness, although if the reader digs a little deeper (for example, in the poem 'Driving South') they will see she was also debunking some of the traditional myths concerning the sceptered isle. In a 1994 interview, UA said: "I'm particularly involved with people who have no voice: the dead, the dispossessed, or the inarticulate in various ways. I'm not carrying on a campaign on their behalf but this is the theme I recognise as having a call on me: people at the edge of things."[193]

Her first volume of poetry, *Side Effects*, was published in 1978 when she was 50 and the book was influenced by her time at the Burden Neurological Institute. She later told *The Poetry Archive*: "Poetry is important because it reaches the places that other

190 Ibid.

191 Tom Wilkinson, 'UA Fanthorpe: Poet Who Championed the Underdog' in *The Independent*, 2 May 2009.

192 Ibid.

193 Ibid.

kinds of writing can't reach. I became aware of this myself when I was working as a receptionist in a hospital, and saw how much the doctors and nurses had to leave out of the queernesses and sadnesses of the patients because they were confined to prose."[194]

UA would go on to publish nine volumes of poetry and in her obituary *The Guardian* described her writing by saying: "Qualities of sly wit and an incisiveness of statement that [are] invariably gentle began to surface in her well-crafted and accessible verse"[195]. A theme in her work when being read aloud was to use two voices, because she saw a poem as "a conversation between the poet and the reader". The other voice frequently belonged to her partner of 44 years, the academic and teacher Dr Rosie Bailey. The 2007 volume *From Me To You: Love Poems* was jointly written by the couple, who lived their final years in Wotton-under-Edge and were united by a Civil Partnership in March 2006. Rosie said at the time: "It's a shame the registration is completely non-religious as we are both committed Christians, but it is important that minority groups are all recognised as equal humans."[196]

Despite being courted by the monolithic international publisher Penguin, UA preferred to give her support to the smaller Peterloo Poets, which sadly ceased to operate in 2009. She was a Fellow of the Royal Society of Literature; the first woman in 315 years to be nominated as Professor of Poetry at Oxford University; and in 2001 UA was made CBE for her services to poetry. During her career she won countless awards, most notably becoming only the fifth woman in 70 years to win the Queen's Gold Medal for Poetry, which she did in 2003. She even featured as a castaway on BBC Radio 4's *Desert Island Discs* in 2001, when she surprised everyone who knew her by choosing

194 poetryfoundation.org/poets/ua-fanthorpe
195 Anthony Brownjohn et al, 'Obituary: UA Fanthorpe' in *The Guardian*, 2 May 2009.
196 Anon, 'Poetic Pair Embark Upon Relationship' in *The Gazette*, 17 February 2006.

Cilla Black's version of 'Anyone Who Had A Heart' as one of her favourite songs.[197]

And another thing... UA's best-known poem, despite its unromantic view of love, is a 1995 piece called 'Atlas', and writer Jeanette Winterson maintains 'Atlas' is one of her all-time favourite poems. Another prestigious admirer of UA's work is Carol Ann Duffy, who was Poet Laureate at the time of UA's death and would dedicate some of her own writing to UA's memory. Carol wrote: "Along with all the writers and readers who adored her, I am grief-stricken to hear of the death of the poet UA Fanthorpe, an unofficial, deeply loved laureate for so many people for so many years."[198]

Please also see: Rosa Burden (vol one).

BARBARA FAULKS

1929-1987, MARSH RESIDENT

Born Barbara Gillett and becoming Barbara Faulks after marriage, this was one St Philip's Marsh resident who well understood the workings of the area's famous cattle market on Feeder Road. Not that she was a fan of it.

Describing the Thursday livestock market, Barbara recalled how cows and bulls were herded up Albert Road to the Feeder Road, or sometimes to the market that was held near the railway and behind St Silas Infants' School. "It was terrifying to hear the herdsmen shouting and hitting these maddened cows, and the bulls had rings through their noses with men pulling them along on huge ropes. Blood would be running down from their faces

197 With thanks to Lori Streich for the nomination of UA Fanthorpe to this book.
198 peterloopoets.com/html/u_a__fanthorpe.html

where the rings had cut into their nostrils. Sometimes the men would put a sack over the bull's head to quieten them down," she said. "Once a bull put his backside against my auntie's front door and broke it down, and then one of the cows ran into the house."

Barbara remembered how the housewives would always be sure to do their shopping on a Wednesday so that by the time the cattle filled the streets on a Thursday they could be safely inside their homes, away from the chaos outside: "I used to go to school along by the Cattle Market and if I heard the cows coming I would jump down onto the river bank and hide, and to this day I am terrified of cows."[199]

Please also see: Maggie Simmons (vol two).

ROSA FEAR
1875-1967, MATRIARCH

Author's note: Rosa Fear was my great-grandmother and Leonard Fear was my great-uncle, so I hope you will indulge me including their story in this book. My family has a long history in Bristol and I wanted to include one of the women who is still fondly remembered today by family members. PS: I proudly wear a Fears watch.

Born on Watling Street (now Watling Way) in Hotwells, Rosa Ellen Amelia Blann married into Bristol's watch and clock-making Fear family when she wed Samuel Fear in October 1896. The Fear family business had been founded on Redcliff Street in 1846 by Edwin Fear and over the decades progressed to a large store on the corner of Bristol Bridge (known colloquially

199 Bristol Broadsides, 1986, *St Philips Marsh: The Story of an Island and its People*, p39.

as Fear's Corner but brutally destroyed during World War Two) among others; Fears remains one of the UK's oldest family-run watch companies.

In the early years of their marriage, Rosa and Samuel lived in Ashley Down, where the first of their five children was born in 1897, who was a daughter called Marjorie. By 1931, the family was living at 14 Trelawney Road, Cotham, and Samuel was working as a travelling clock salesman. His brother Daniel came to visit that summer and wrote in his diary: "[Samuel] travels over a large portion of England chiefly in the West and in Wales in a large motor van fitted up as a clock shop and carries 600 clocks with him. He is a very successful salesman and is highly recommended by his numerous band of customers."[200]

However, Samuel died in 1940, meaning Rosa had to face the bulk of World War Two on her own. By this time, she was living at 27 Salisbury Road, Redland, and her adult children had spread out around the UK with their own families. Most notably, her eldest son Leonard was a particular cause for concern. Before the war, Leonard and his wife Vera had moved to Guernsey and, after the island was occupied by the Nazis in June 1940, the couple decided to remain even when many islanders chose to leave.

The Nazis imposed many restrictions on the remaining islanders. They were not allowed to travel, own a car or listen to the radio. And on 20 December 1941, the death penalty was announced for anyone found keeping pigeons, which could be used for sending messages. Although the islanders were not technically prisoners, the Nazis could shoot anyone trying to leave Guernsey. In addition, everyone had to keep to a curfew and food became scarce; by the end of the war, islanders and Nazis alike were close to starvation.

200 Daniel Fear's diary is kept in family archives.

All communication with the outside world was cut off except for a monthly 25-word Red Cross message, which Leonard and Vera took it in turns to use. Knowing her eldest son was living in such a hostile and dangerous environment would have been very stressful for Rosa, who was living alone in Bristol and barely getting any news of her son so far away. These bimonthly Red Cross telegrams provided a lifeline and the complete collection of messages sent between Rosa and Leonard during the war survive in family archives. Although superficially dull in their lack of information and repetitive phrases, closer readings reveal a claustrophobic, panicked and tense exchange of bare-bones information at a time when very little could be said because of Nazi interception.

Red Cross messages were subject to censorship in both England and Guernsey. The Nazis not only examined the hand-printed or typewritten texts, but also brushed a chemical on the paper to reveal any 'invisible' messages that may have been smuggled on. Most message forms include multiple stamps indicating that the contents had been censored, including ones in the jackboot font used by the Nazis. It took Red Cross messages an average of four months to reach the Channel Islands from the UK and be returned to the sender.

"Hope you are well. We are. Love from all, Mother," was all Rosa's first message said in September 1940. Five months later in February 1941, Leonard's reply arrived: "Delighted to have message. We are both well and happy. Please convey tidings to all concerned. Would like to have news of Vera's people." A further four months later, in June 1941, Rosa's answer reached him: "Delighted to have news of you. All still safe and well. K [another son] soon to join up. Much love, Mother."

And so it continues, with brief, scrappy implorations for news of family members and promises that everyone is well...

when they must have been stressed to high heaven: it turned out Leonard and Vera, as Brits, were living under the radar in Guernsey and were not in any record books, having taken a spare room with a Guernsian family and were living secretly so as to escape the attention of the Nazis. The phrases "longing to see you" and "so anxious to know the latest news" were frantically repeated, as were the beseeching repetitions they had had "no messages in your hand". Read one after the other, these telegrams make a very tense and stressful collection.

In October 1941, while sending Christmas wishes to her son, Rosa mentioned she was intending to take "a congenial job soon", which was news to her family who don't think Rosa ever worked (as was the way for women of her generation and class). It may have simply been that Rosa meant she was volunteering for the war effort. Finally, Guernsey was liberated in May 1945 and World War Two ended in September 1945.

Leonard and Vera survived the Nazi occupation and continued to live on Guernsey until their deaths in the late 1970s. Rosa remained living in Bristol, although she was delighted to reunite with all her children once the war was over, and to see them and her grandchildren growing up. She died peacefully in June 1967.

JEMIMA FEDDEN

1806-1876, WITNESS TO BRISTOL RIOTS

The Bristol Riots of 1831 in Queen Square lasted three days from October 29 to October 31, and were the culmination of unease about the proposed reform of the electoral franchise (at this time, less than 10% of British men had the vote and no women had the vote at all). Local magistrate Sir Charles Wetherell had claimed in Parliament that Bristolians did *not* want a reform of the electoral franchise but this was a complete lie. When this got out and the people of Bristol realised they would not be any closer to having a say in how their country was run, there was uproar. Wetherell's carriage was pelted with stones and he took refuge in the Mansion House on Queen Square, prompting three days of rioting, looting and arson which was the bloodiest battle on mainland Britain since the Battle of Culloden in 1746.[201]

Jemima Fedden (née Maggs) of 41 Queen Square was a witness to the riots, and prudently squirreled away her precious wine coolers in the cellar to keep them safe from looters: very wise considering the wine cellars of many neighbours were plundered. She had married into the wealthy and long-established Fedden family in Bristol, who still have a presence in the city and whose notable female ancestors include the writer Marguerite Fedden (who was Jemima's granddaughter) and artist Mary Fedden.

What follows is an extract from a letter Jemima wrote on 5 November 1831 to her sister Marianne Maggs: "Thank God Almighty, we are all safe; amid the wrack and ruin around us, we are comparatively saved. Oh, my beloved Marianne, the horrors of Sunday evening and night can never be effaced from my memory; the scene from our bedroom and drawing-room windows baffles description; our city fired in seven different parts at one time ... Then came Queen Square, which I must fail in attempting to describe, the flames towering to the skies, and the long volume of smoke which the wind blew this way, curling in a thousand varied forms; now and then balls of fire would be blown into the air and carried to a considerable distance, while the reflection of the light on the surrounding trees, various steeples and distant landscapes formed a scene terrific indeed, but at the same time beautifully awful."

201 Steve Mills, 'The Bristol Reform Riots' in *The Bristol Cable*, 27 October 2017. Tristram Hunt, 'I Predict a Riot' in *The Guardian*, 21 August 2006.

Later in the letter, Jemima writes: "The shouts and hurrahs of the rioters, which we could distinctly hear, the falling of the burning roofs and the crackling of the stone, which sounded like the quick succession of distant shots, altogether formed a scene scarcely to be conceived! You may imagine my feelings, my little ones clinging round me and asking a thousand questions, and my husband [William Fedden, a colonial broker] out to ascertain the fate of his mother [Sarah Fedden, née Gittoe] and sisters."

The description of the rioters breaking into her mother-in-law Sarah Fedden's house is certainly alarming: "At three o'clock, two sides of [Queen] Square and Prince Street were in flames and they appeared to have commenced on the third side where Mrs [Sarah] Fedden's house is: when to assuage his mother's agonised feelings William went to see what had become of her sister Mary; he found the rioters had entire possession of the corner house on the third side of the Square and within one door of his mother's; they commenced by dashing in every window and had actually fired it in several places; one bed is fired to ashes."

She continues: "At this critical moment, part of the mob being already in Mrs Fedden's house, the soldiers rode up and cut and slew all before them and thus saved that side of the Square and indeed prevented further conflagration; indeed the principal rioters were lying dead drunk about the Square and the incendiaries were dwindled down to about 40 or 50 — principally boys."[202]

As a consequence of the 1831 Bristol Riots, four rioters died and 86 were wounded, and the number of innocent lives lost in the fires in properties on Queen Square has never been confirmed but is estimated to be 250. In January 1832, around 100 rioters were tried for their roles in the riot, with four men sentenced to

202 Marguerite Fedden, 1950, *Bristol Bypaths: Stray Sketches*, p97-99.

hang and another 88 either sent to prison or the colonies. The coward Wetherall, whose fault all of this had been, had escaped in disguise from the Mansion House where he had been hiding; the building itself was destroyed by arsonists. A new reform bill was proposed and passed in June 1832, which increased the vote to include one in seven men from middle-class and upwards households.[203]

And another thing... Another woman who experienced the terror of the 1831 Bristol Riots first hand was **Mary Canning**, who was one of the approximately 250 civilians who died during the riots when the house she was staying in on Queen Square was destroyed by rioters and she burned to death.

Please also see: Marguerite Fedden (vol two), Mary Fedden (vol one).

MARGUERITE FEDDEN

1879-1962, AUTHOR, SUFFRAGIST

Considering how much there is written *by* Marguerite Fedden, it is surprising how little there is written *about* her. Born and baptised in Clifton, raised in Saltford, educated in Bath and linked to the prominent Fedden family in Bristol (renowned artist Mary Fedden was her great-niece, while disability campaigner Ada Vachell was a cousin), Constance Marguerite Fedden spent the bulk of her adulthood in Clifton.

"My childhood days were spent at Saltford and I received my early education in Bath," she wrote in a nostalgic column for the *Bath Chronicle and Weekly Gazette*. "First of all, in 1886 or 1887, I

203 Tristram Hunt, 'I Predict a Riot' in *The Guardian*, 21 August 2006.

was brought into Bath from Saltford by my mother or big sister to attend Miss Axten's Kindergarten in Brock Street. There I learnt fascinating weaving of prayer mats with coloured shiny paper, basket-making and how to pass a parcel when sitting in a row. I liked Miss Axten, but not the little fellow pupil, a boy, who pinched my arm till it was black and blue." Marguerite continued: "Before this school, I had had lessons at home from my big sisters, from a wonderful book called *The Child's Instructor* (I wish I could get a copy of it now), and whenever I think of the sovereigns of England I see their portraits on a particular page of that book. It also taught me how to draw a cat's back view!"[204]

After this, Marguerite moved to the Ladies' College at 27 The Circus, Bath. This education for a lady included violin lessons, dancing classes, presentation, cookery and, of all things, bookbinding.[205] However, these skills clearly came in useful, because Marguerite would later became the Principal of the College of Housecraft and Domestic Science at 4 Chichester Street, Pimlico, London. At the same time, in the 1910s, Marguerite wrote a series of instructional books aimed at the new generation of housewife who no longer had a maid and had to run her home without help. With titles such as *How to Cook a Simple Meal* (1910), *How to Do your Own Upholstery and Machining* (1912) and *How To Do the Weekly Wash* (1914), these were published by the Women's Industrial Council in London.[206] By 1941, while living at 6 Wetherell Place, Clifton, Marguerite drew upon her

204 Marguerite Fedden, 'Bath Dame Schools' in *Bath Chronicle and Weekly Gazette*, 5 January 1946.

205 Marguerite Fedden, 'Bath Dame Schools' in *Bath Chronicle and Weekly Gazette*, 19 January 1946.

206 The Women's Industrial Council was founded in 1889 and was intended as a federation of women's trade unions and, as such, represented more than 100 women's trades and the vast majority of its members were suffragists (the Council worked closely with both the National Union of Women's Suffrage Societies led by Millicent Fawcett and the Women's Freedom League led by Charlotte Despard). The Council folded in 1917 due to the looming shadow of World War One.

considerable experience as a writer of housecraft to give talks to women's groups all over Bristol about how to make their World War Two food rations go further.[207]

Marguerite had worked as a cook in a Red Cross unit for the Voluntary Aid Detachment at the 42nd General Hospital in Salonika (now Thessaloniki), Greece, during World War One, and in 1922 her book *Sisters' Quarters: Salonika* was published. It was a "fresh and cheerful account" of her experiences, wrote a review in the suffrage journal *Common Cause,* adding "it is impossible not to admire [Marguerite's] spirit and her keen interest in the whole of life"[208]. Meanwhile, *The Vote* called it "a chatty little volume of nursing reminiscences during the Great War ... The writer of these reminiscences was not a nurse, but was sent out to Salonika to take charge of one of the Red Cross Invalid Kitchens".[209] Marguerite was honoured with two medals for her role in World War One: the British War Medal and the Victory Medal.

After Salonika, Marguerite was stationed at the Relatives' Hostel in Abbeville, France, at the end of World War One, and this was documented in her book *From An Abbeville Window*. In a review, the *Western Daily Press* wrote: "Her account throws an interesting light on a phase of war work that has largely eluded public recognition ... It is clear her duties brought her in tender contact with the bereaved, the sacredness of whose sorrow she knows how to respect."[210]

In addition to reflective histories, Marguerite was a regular contributor to the suffrage newspaper *The Vote* (the newspaper of the Women's Freedom League), as well as *The Sphere* newspaper and *Common Cause* (the newspaper of the National Union of

207 'Evening Meetings Again" in *Western Daily Press*, 10 March 1941.

208 IB O'Malley, 'Women's Adventures in Three Continents' in *Common Cause*, 20 January 1922.

209 DMN, 'Book Reviews' in *The Vote*, 23 December 1921.

210 'Recent Publications' in *Western Daily Press*, 16 September 1922.

Women's Suffrage Societies). She was an active member of a little-known suffrage society called St Joan's Social and Political Alliance[211], and would speak at suffrage events in her capacity as a St Joan's member. An example is when sister suffragist Kate Parry Frye met Marguerite at a talk held at 49 Claverton Street, London, and noted in her diary: "[I] had to take the Chair and as Miss Fedden had not turned up by 8.15 I went on as long as I could as Miss D'Oyly was the only other speaker. But Miss Fedden arrived and held the crowd for a long time. [Miss Fedden] is a nice woman but overwrought with militancy. The things that are going on are too awful. It is enough to wring anyone's heart and mind."[212]

After the war had ended, and long after some women had been given the vote (but not on equal terms to men), Marguerite continued campaigning for equal suffrage. For instance, she spoke at a Women's Freedom League meeting on The Strand, London, on 27 March 1924 (fun fact: that meeting was chaired by a woman named Mrs Mustard). At the meeting, Marguerite spoke about the courage and bravery of women during World War One and how this proved they deserved to be able to vote on the same terms as men: "She remembered seeing seven little graves, in Abbeville of young WAACs [Women's Army Auxiliary Corp], all under 30, who were killed on duty when the town was bombed. The young women of this country were courageous and capable of self-sacrifice, and they should have a say in the affairs of their country."[213]

Via her journalism, Marguerite lobbied for improvements in the lot of working women. For instance, in one *Common Cause*

211 St Joan's Social and Political Alliance is a Catholic feminist organisation founded in 1911 to enhance women's equality, which exists today as St Joan's International Alliance. It is named after Joan of Arc.

212 Elizabeth Crawford, ed, 2013, *Campaigning For the Vote: Kate Parry Frye's Suffrage Diary*, p192.

213 'Votes For Women Meeting' in *The Vote*, 4 April 1924.

article from January 1921 she put forward the suggestion that pregnant working-class women be loaned "maternity bags" by "young wives", to save them from having to find the money for the expensive but necessary clothing items they would need for only the first few months of a baby's life.[214] In another *Common Cause* article she spoke about the problem for young, uneducated women of finding work in the contemporary age, now that being a governess or companion was out of vogue and becoming a chorus girl was the fall back option: "The life [of a chorus girl] is not one that would be acceptable to many girls. Late hours are kept, so rising is the rule in the untidy theatrical lodgings, crowded out with knick-knacks, photos of 'pros', paper flowers and other dust traps. The rooms are generally crowded. In one place I know of, the landlady and her husband slept in the combined lavatory and bathroom, and the child in the kitchen."[215] As such, Marguerite was lobbying for better pay and better conditions for young women pushed into work as a chorus girl, and the establishment of "theatrical girls' hostels" where they could safely stay and be looked after.

During the 1940s, Marguerite focused on novels and published prolifically. These included *Myrtle Among Thorns* in 1948 (covering a 'mixed marriage' between a couple of different faiths); and *Dark Extremity* in 1949 (about the horrors inflicted on Bath by the Blitz). She also wrote a romantic novel set in South Africa, *Coral On The Reef* (1946), in which she attempted to challenge the issue of racism.

Later in her career, Marguerite indulged her enormous love for Bristol by writing an astonishing number of books documenting the city, and she also wrote regularly to the local papers pleading with the town planners to make wise decisions

214 Marguerite Fedden, 'Glorified Old Clothes' in *Common Cause*, 7 January 1921.
215 Marguerite Fedden, 'Chorus Girls' in *Common Cause*, 25 November 1921.

as they rebuilt the city after the Blitz. These Bristol book were all beautifully illustrated, such as *Bristol Vignettes* (1958) and *Bristol Bypaths — Stray Sketches* (1950), both of which in some ways could be seen as an influence on *The Women Who Built Bristol*, given they focus on interesting and influential figures from Bristol's past and there is even some crossover with the people included.

Marguerite remained unmarried and child-free throughout her life. At the time of her death in 1962, she was living at 9 Great George Street, just off Park Street, and she was buried in Clifton. Marguerite was remembered fondly by her nieces and nephews, who affectionately called her 'Aunty Mardi' and who organised her funeral and memorial service.

Please also see: Jemima Fedden (vol two), Mary Fedden (vol one), Ada Vachell (vol one).

LOUISA FERRIS

1817-1854, MAID, MURDERER

Lots of people celebrate their birthdays by going a bit wild. Housemaid and seamstress Louisa Ferris of Lion Street, St Philip's, took this to the extreme.

Louisa, who had been separated from her husband William Ferris for a year, was left as a single mother to two young children and so she took in Irish policeman Patrick White as a lodger to bring in some extra money. However, "there is reason to fear that an intimacy of an improper kind had subsisted between them"[216].

In November 1846, on the afternoon of her 29th birthday, she fatally slashed White's throat in her house. The couple had

216 'Appalling Murder of a Policeman', in *Bristol Mercury*, 7 November 1846.

been drinking for most of the day and were joined by a number of friends including Jessie Jones. But when Jessie went into a bedroom and White followed her, Louisa burst in and erupted with a fit of jealousy. With any hint of romance between Jessie and White now dampened, White followed Louisa back downstairs and was preparing to light his pipe... and it was then that Jessie saw Louisa grab a knife and slit his throat from ear to ear.

"The unfortunate man contrived to crawl out of the room into the street," reported *The London Illustrated News*, "where he was picked up by a person who was passing, and a surgeon was instantly sent for, but the poor fellow gradually faded and expired shortly after being taken into the house." While this was going on, Louisa took herself to the nearest police station (where her father-in-law was one of the sergeants) and handed herself in saying: "Take me into custody. Take me into custody."[217]

Reporting on the ensuing court case, *The Spectator* wrote in April 1847: "[Ferris] cut White's throat in a fit of jealousy, while he was sitting at her lodgings. Both had been drinking. The counsel for the defence contended the provocation and also the excitement under which the prisoner was labouring, reduced the crime to manslaughter."[218] In punishment, Louisa was "transported for life" to Tasmania on the convict ship Cadet. However, in 1852 her sentence was reduced for "exemplary behaviour". Which was a mistake because she promptly slashed the throat of a man in Melbourne, Australia, and was sentenced to death in 1854.

217 *The Illustrated London News*, 7 November 1846, Volume 9, p302.
218 *The Spectator*, 10 April 1847, Volume 20, p340.

CELIA FIENNES

1662-1741, TRAVEL WRITER

Intrepid Celia Fiennes was born in Wiltshire to a parliamentarian colonel in 1662. Remaining unattached for her entire life, she was free to do exactly as she pleased… within the social confines of the day.

In 1691, Celia moved to London to live with a married sister having begun several years previously, in 1684, to travel around the UK on horseback (side saddle, obviously), exploring as she went. This was in an age when travel for the fun of it was unusual and people typically only travelled out of necessity. Between 1684 and 1712, Celia travelled on horseback around the UK, sometimes taking one or two servants with her but often going solo.

In 1702, she wrote a memoir of her adventures, although it was intended only to be read by family members and was not published in her lifetime. In 1812, long after her death, Robert Southey issued extracts of Celia's writing, with a complete edition being issued in 1888 under the title *Travels Through England on a Side Saddle.* The book has remained in print ever since. Celia was plain spoken and straightforward in her writing style; she was not interested in florid or dramatic prose, despite living through a time of social and political revolution. However, she was a very curious person and was eager to find out more about everything.

Her travels took her across almost all of the country, including to Bristol in 1698. Arriving from Bath, Celia came in via Kingswood and observes she passed a great many horses laden with coal on her way into Bristol. Of her entrance to the city, she noted: "Bristol Lyes Low in a bottom the Greatest part of the town, tho' one End of it you have a pretty rise of ground." She went on to discuss the churches and the cathedral in detail, although of the latter she was rather damning, writing that it "has nothing fine or Curious in it. … There are some few monuments in this Church with good Carvings of stone round ye tombs and some Effigies, there are eight bells in this Church, there is two men goes to ye ringing ye biggest bell."[219]

Yet of Bristol generally, she said: "The Buildings of ye town are pretty high, most of timber work, the streetes are narrow and something Darkish because the roomes on ye upper storys are more jutting out, soe Contracts ye streete and the Light. The Suburbs are better buildings and more spacious streetes." Recalling the original Bristol Bridge, which used to have property built all along it, she said: "The bridge is built over with houses just as London bridge is, but it's not so bigg or Long — there are four arches here."[220]

The Bristol Diamond also came under Celia's inspection[221], which she said was bright and sparkling and "in their native Rudeness have a great Lustre and are pointed and Like ye Diamond Cutting; I had a piece just as it Came out of ye Rock wth ye Rock on ye back side and it appeared to me as a Cluster of Diamonds polish'd and irregularly Cut."[222]

What interested Celia was the new and the unusual. She visited fashionable spa towns such as Bath and Harrogate, she anticipated the boom in the tourism industry and she particularly pre-empted the rise in people wanting to travel within a certain budget. On her travels, she visited a great number of the English stately homes, many of which were still under construction at the time and her descriptions of these lavish properties are truly stunning. Indeed, Celia's writing about the UK during the period

219 visionofbritain.org.uk/travellers/Fiennes/26

220 Ibid.

221 Bristol Diamonds are quartz crystals found in the Avon Gorge that are between 200 and 250 million years old. They were a popular novelty for visitors to the Hotwells spa during the 18th and 19th centuries. Despite being called diamonds, they are worthless apart from their aesthetic charm.

222 visionofbritain.org.uk/travellers/Fiennes/26

of her travels is an important historical document providing valuable insights into how the country looked and behaved at the time, which might otherwise not be available to historians now.

And another thing... With explorer and travel writer Celia Fiennes as an ancestor, of course Ranulph Fiennes would go on to be the world's greatest living explorer himself (according to no lesser authority than the *Guinness Book of World Records*).

Please also see: Sarah Goldsmith (vol two).

ANNE FISH

1890-1964, ILLUSTRATOR

Born in Horfield towards the end of the Victorian era, Anne Harriet Fish was a wholly unusual character in an absolutely wonderful way. This creative and gifted woman became a respected cartoonist and illustrator, and her images accompanying the popular 'Letters of Eve' series which featured in *Tatler* magazine were so impressive they inspired a number of plays, books and movies; in 1918 alone there are 12 'Eve' short films credited to 'Miss Fish' as writer on the IMDb.[223] However, Anne was typically known professionally by the mononym 'Fish'.

Although Anne's childhood was spent in Bristol, the Fish family later moved to London and it was here that Anne trained with acclaimed illustrators including George Belcher and John Hassall before securing work with the publisher John Lane, who published her debut work, which was an illustrated edition of Stephen Leacock's humorous book *Behind the Beyond* (1913).

223 imdb.com/name/nm0279296/

However, it was the illustrations which accompanied the 'Letters of Eve' series written by Mrs Maitland Davies in *Tatler* that really made Anne's name: the costumes for the character of Eve, as worn by actor Phyllis Dare at London's Adelphi Theatre, were inspired by Anne's cartoons. Eve was a spoof of the social butterfly or flapper girl of the 1920s and the series chronicled her adventures with dashing but useless men. However, when fellow artist Gladys Peto created a series of drawings which were strikingly similar to Anne's, a court case ensued. Anne continued to illustrate the 'Eve' series in *Tatler* until 1920, when sister Bristolian illustrator Dolly Tree picked up her pen.

Anne's illustrations also appeared in – and on the covers of – international magazines including *Vanity Fair, Harper's Bazaar* and *Vogue,* and her illustrations accompanied an advice column in *Tatler,* among others. Her style was typically solid blacks and fine lines, and her characters often had neither background nor shadow. She later married a man called Walter Sefton and the couple retired to St Ives, Cornwall, which is where Anne saw out her final years painting pictures of landscapes and cats.

Please also see: Dolly Tree (vol two).

EVA FITZHARDING

1099-1170, PRIORESS

The St Mary Magdalene Nunnery in Kingsdown (the derelict King David Hotel on the lower corner of St Michael's Hill is on the former site of the Benedictine nunnery, and some medieval stonework from it has been found within the inn's foundations) was founded in 1170 by Eva Fitzharding and it remained active until it was dissolved in 1536. St Mary Magdalene remains one of

Anne Fish illustration by Tina Altwegg

the least understood monastic sites in Bristol.

As well as founding St Mary Magdalene, Eva was also (briefly, owing to her death the same year) the first Prioress of the nunnery and as such she also appears in records as both 'Eva of Bristol' and 'Prioress Eva of Bristol'. Her husband was Robert 'The Devout' Fitzharding, who also died in 1170 having committed his life to religious duty: as a wealthy burgess of Bristol, he had become the Lord of Berkeley and founded St Augustine's Abbey (now known as Bristol Cathedral), of which he became a canon.

Born Eva FitzEstmond in 1099 in Normandy, France, her parents were Godiva Normandie and Estmond FitzEstmond, and she had three siblings. She married Robert in 1119 when she was 20 and the couple had nine children. We do not know many other facts about Eva but the legacy of her nunnery endured for several centuries. Eva was buried alongside Robert in St Augustine's Abbey and the couple are commemorated with a large stained glass window that shows them with King Henry I (although she is only captioned as 'Eva his wife', which is a sign of the times but still dismissive of her achievements).[224]

By 1480, there were only three nuns at St Mary Magdalene and their church was measured as being just 27 steps long during a national survey of religious buildings. There was also a small burial ground beside the nunnery. By 1535, the number of nuns at St Mary Magdalene had dropped to just two with a combined annual income of £21 (by contrast, in the same survey, there were 19 nuns at St Augustine's Abbey with a combined annual income of £670). So it seemed inevitable that by the time of the Dissolution of Monasteries Act in 1536, which seized the "lesser religious houses", St Mary Magdalene would be forced to close. Despite its small size, at the time of its closure the nunnery was found to be

224 Eva and Robert's eldest son Maurice FitzRobert 'The Make Peace' FitzHarding was also buried at St Augustine's Abbey.

free from debt and in good condition but with possessions worth just a few pounds. The two nuns living at St Mary Magdalene at the time it was closed were an unnamed young novice and an elder nun called Eleanor Gaunt, who had been Prioress since 1521. It is not known what became of these two women, although Maudlin Street is so named because of the former nunnery.

LETTICE FLOYD

1865-1934, SUFFRAGETTE, REFORMER

After Birmingham-born Lettice Floyd's father died when she was just 14 years old, he left her the collosal-for-the-time sum of £3,000, which meant she never needed to worry about work. But a life of leisure didn't suit Lettice and she quickly grew bored, so she found satisfaction by working as a nurse for a children's hospital. When she realised the problems she was seeing again and again in the children were largely born out of poverty and unsanitary conditions, Lettice resolved to make a positive change for these young people. She later said: "I was there some years, but as most of the cases seemed to be due to bad housing, bad feeding or immorality, it was not entirely satisfactory work and it did not go to the root of the matter."[225]

In response, Lettice and her sister Mary strongly believed that if women had the vote, then they would be in a solid position to make the necessary changes to prevent the sort of crippling poverty they were witnessing in the hospital wards, and so they threw themselves into campaigning for women's suffrage. It was in this way that they set up the Birmingham Women's Suffrage Society in 1907 and began politely lobbying for the vote. Within

225 sussexpast.co.uk/wp-content/uploads/2011/08/Priest-House-suffragette-handkerchief.pdf

a year they tired of asking nicely and instead teamed up with Emmeline and Christabel Pankhurst to join the militant Women's Social and Political Union (WSPU), aka the suffragettes.

Lettice became a paid organiser for the WSPU and soon began a romantic relationship with Cornish teacher and sister suffragette Annie Williams (who had been holidaying in Bristol), whom she met while stationed in Bristol helping Annie Kenney, who was leading the WSPU's operation in the South West. The couple divided their time between Bristol or Newcastle, depending on what their work demanded, and as part of their campaigning both women were variously arrested, went on hunger strike and were forcibly fed. Lettice was also one of the many suffragettes who was assaulted and arrested on the notorious Black Friday demonstration in London on 18 November 1910.

Following the cessation of suffrage militancy during World War One, Lettice and Annie moved to Birmingham and campaigned for peace, something for which they continued to strive until the end of their lives. When Lettice died following an operation in 1934, Annie was right beside her until the very end.

Please also see: Violet Bland (vol one), Annie Kenney (vol one).

EDITH LONG FOX

died 1928, ANTI-SUFFRAGIST

Woman at Home was a monthly magazine published between 1893 and 1920. It was one of a new genre of domestic magazines which was designed to appeal to a broad readership that included middle-class women, as well as some working-class readers with lofty aspirations. These were chatty magazines but they were also instructional. You were, after all, a woman at home, so you needed an informative friend to help you keep things nice for hubby and to occupy you until he came home from work. *Woman at Home* was also a place to find out more about genteel women of the day, people whom it was OK to look up to and feel inspired by knowing there was no risk of your getting into trouble by doing anything unladylike. In this way, we find Sarah A Tooley writing a series of polite profiles for *Woman at Home* about 'Ladies of Bristol and Clifton' in 1896 and it is in this article that we meet Edith Long Fox. Remember her name because you will meet her again in Winifred Parry's entry: Edith is Winifred's nemesis because she is a member of the Bristol Branch of the National League for *Opposing* Woman Suffrage (NLOWS) and suffragist Winifred is fully prepared to energetically discredit Edith's every statement.

Before becoming consumed by her work with the NLOWS, reverend's daughter Edith was "fond of scribbling"[226] and her first book of short stories was published in 1895 and called *The Coombe Park Tragedy*. These were gentle detective stories set in the shadows of grand country houses and occasionally they included remarkably chaste romantic subplots. Rather witheringly, the *Western Daily Press* wrote upon publication of *The Coombe Park Tragedy*: "Her sketchy, pleasant manner just suits these little fictions in which it is only needed to give outline portraits, and not to develop character at the length required in more elaborate productions."[227] Which strikes me as a passive aggressive way of saying Edith's stories and characters lacked depth and development. Despite this, the first print run sold out in three days and a second run was immediately commissioned.

Another reviewer was even more scathing. "The title has its attractions for a certain class of readers, and the entire improbability of the plot has apparently ensured it some success,"

226 Sarah A Tooley, 1896, 'Ladies of Bristol and Clifton', in *The Woman at Home*, p447.
227 'Miss Fox Writes', in *Western Daily Press*, 12 December 1895.

began the review. "We use the term 'improbability' in lieu of stronger language, and we can only surmise that the authoress of the story is labouring under the disadvantages of want of any literary experience."[228] Again, a rather sly way of saying Edith's writing style was a little naïve. These reviews seem to have dampened Edith's enthusiasm for creative writing as I can find no other evidence of her pursuing fiction.

However, *The Coombe Park Tragedy* was not Edith's first foray into writing, whatever her unimpressed reviewers may have thought. In 1894 and 1895, Edith had been busy penning a series of articles in *The Young Woman* magazine which went under the heading of 'A Girl's Mistakes and How to Avoid Them'. We need to remember that Edith remained unmarried and pious throughout her life, so quite how well placed she was to impart useful advice to girls on the brink of womanhood is unclear. In an 1894 interview about her short story *A New Woman's Idol*, Edith reveals what she perceives a 'good' young woman to be: "A girl educated at a high school of good tone, where she is trained to play as well as to study, and who at a university acquires, through contact with her superiors, a sense of proportion which makes her humble. She is honest and unaffected, and has attained that power of self-control which enables her to meet all the vicissitudes of life with a sweet reasonableness."[229] In later years she turned to the safer subject of horticulture (gardening having been a lifelong enthusiasm), as evidenced by her 1919 book *My Weekend Garden*.

Edith was a member of a Quaker family and in keeping with the charitable nature of her faith she spent a great deal of time doing good deeds. This included spending six years teaching boys at a Bristol evening school and setting up a dining-room for 100

228 'The Book World for Women and Nurses', in *The Hospital Nursing Supplement*, 16 May 1896, p4.
229 Sarah A Tooley, 1896, 'Ladies of Bristol and Clifton', in *The Woman at Home*, p447-448.

Edith Long Fox illustration by Tina Altwegg

factory girls. In this way she was able to exert her moral influence on working-class and underprivileged boys and girls. Her belief was that everybody needed to be trained for a particular role: "It is so sad to see the number of 'incapables' who are trying to earn their living, and who have to learn through sad experience that amateur work finds no market."[230]

In the later decades of her life, Edith threw herself into opposing women's suffrage, which was in contrast to many other Quaker women in Bristol (and elsewhere) who were passionately fighting to *achieve* the vote. Edith filled the role of Honorary Secretary of the Bristol Branch of the NLOWS and was an Executive Committee Member of the central organisation. She was adamant that votes for women would be A Terrible Thing. Indeed, researcher Julia Bush notes of Edith's dogmatism: "Bristol provided even more impressive evidence of local support for the Women's League, apparently mobilised through the organisational skills of the honorary secretary, Edith Long Fox, rather than as an outcome of social deference or wealthy patronage."[231]

As a busy letter writer to the local papers, given her involvement with the NLOWS, Edith centered her correspondence on opposing women's suffrage and decrying the behaviour of the suffragettes. For instance, when Teresa Garnett attacked Winston Churchill with a whip at Temple Meads Station in 1909, Edith wrote to *Clifton Society* to say the attack was "a slur cast upon Bristol women and that many must read of the incident with shame ... [the incident] produced a most painful impression in the city and ... any self-respecting women should make their influence felt by joining the Anti-Suffrage League."[232]

230 Ibid, p448

231 Julia Bush, 2007, *Women Against The Vote: Female Anti-Suffragism in Britain*, p186.

232 Edith Long Fox, 'Women's Anti-Suffrage League' in *Clifton Society*, 18 November 1909. See volume one of *The Women Who Built Bristol* for the full story about Teresa Garnett's attack on Churchill.

Following her death in 1928, Edith was buried at Arnos Vale Cemetery. This was the year that women were granted the vote on the same terms as men. She would have been livid.

Please also see: Teresa Garnett (vol one), Winifred Parry (vol two).

FRANCIS
born c1600, DISSENTER

In volume one of *The Women Who Built Bristol* we met Dorothy Hazzard, a dissident and non-conformist who – with the assistance of around 200 Bristolian women, girls and children – attempted to resist the surrender of Bristol to Parliamentarian leaders in 1643. When they were overcome on 27 July, Dorothy and a group of her closest allies fled to London and we now know they were joined by an African maid from Welsh Back known only as Francis, who was one of the first two women of colour in Bristol to be recorded with a name.

Francis is described as a "servant, Blackymore, sister and Baptist" and she went on to become one of the leaders of Dorothy's religious sect. In her role as a leader, Francis attended the Putney Debates in 1647. These were a key moment in English history when the New Model Army was discussing its own future and that of the nation. This was an extremely radical organisation which, among its many tenets for liberation, held firm the belief that slavery of Africans must end. This would have been of particular interest for a woman of colour such as Francis.

And another thing... One earlier mention of a woman of colour has been found in Bristol, which is for **Katherine**, a woman who died in 1612 having worked at the Horsehead Tavern on Christmas Street, which is recorded in Madge Dresser and Peter Fleming's book *Bristol: Ethnic Minorities and the City 1000-2001*.[233]

Please also see: Dorothy Hazzard (vol one).

MAITA FRANK
1919-2009, TOY MAKER

Although born in Finland and educated in Czechoslovakia, Maita Frank always maintained strong family links to Russia owing to the fact her father had worked as a professor in St Petersburg for many years and her two elder sisters had been born there. In 1938, she spent a year in Cambridge, learning English and working as an au pair for historian and academic Walter Adams. However, in 1939, back in Finland, Maita met a British man called Sir Charles Frank who had come over to help raise relief funds for Finland, which at that time was being invaded by Russia. The couple fell in love, were married in 1940 and moved to Bristol in 1946 when Charles was appointed as a physics lecturer – and later head of department – at the University of Bristol; Maita and Charles Frank were good friends with Isobel and Cecil Powell, who also feature in this volume. In 1950, Maita and Charles bought Orchard Cottage behind Blaise Castle and this remained their home for the rest of their lives.

Settling in to life in Bristol, Maita became friends with a woman named Mary Horder, with whom she set up a successful toy-making business in Hotwells; Mary had previously made jigsaw puzzles and wooden toys on a small scale. The business was called Mary Horder Toys and Mary would design the playthings

233 With thanks to Mark Steeds for the nominations of and information about Francis and Katherine.

and Maita then made them, having taught herself how to use a lathe and other tools with the aid of a book, becoming an excellent woodworker in the process. A third friend, Diana Murray Hill, helped with the painting of the toys. At one point, Maita, Mary and Diana were supplying toys to the prestigious Heals department store in London, although they quickly realised that large-scale toy manufacture was beyond their capabilities. The toys were also displayed at the influential Ideal Home Exhibition in 1947 and the Festival of Britain in 1951, both in London. The business lasted until 1952, when Mary married and moved to France. However, examples of some of the toys they made can be seen at the Victoria & Albert Museum of Childhood in London.

Needing a new project, Maita became aware of the problems faced by the wives of foreign research students who had come to Bristol but had little to occupy them while their husbands were at the university. She established the Newcomers Club in 1952, which was a place for these women to socialise and improve their English language skills. The club was very successful and in 1973 was absorbed into the University of Bristol's Women's Club.[234]

Please also see: Isobel Powell (vol two).

ELIZA GARDNER

1814-1897, PRISON MATRON

Born in Bedminster on 28 August 1814, Eliza Stokes was just 15 when she married Captain James Gardner in 1830: he was seven years her senior. Within a year, Eliza had become a mother to

234 bristol.ac.uk/news/2009/6297.html

their only child, a son who was also called James. The family had moved to live at Bristol New Gaol on Cumberland Road by the time of the 1841 census, where Eliza was the prison matron and James the prison governor. They maintained these posts for at least 30 years, as evidenced by the fact that on the 1871 census both are still listed as resident and working at the prison.

In the Victorian era, the prison matron would be expected to live at the prison, to take full responsibility for the female inmates (which involved making sure she had seen each inmate at least once during any 24-hour period) and to check they adhered to the prison's rules. She would also be expected to oversee all meals in the prison, and confirm that their clothing and bedding were in a satisfactory order. The prison matron reported directly to the prison governor, who in Eliza's case was her husband James. He was also expected to live in the prison and could not have even one night's absence without written permission from a Visiting Justice. The governor had a great number of responsibilities and it would seem logical that this was a job for a married couple, given the intensity of the job and the restriction on where they could live and on not leaving the prison. As such, it was not uncommon for Victorian prison matrons and governors to be a married couple.

The couple sadly had to endure the early death of their son James, who was a Lieutenant in the army and had been posted to India. He accidentally drowned while bathing in 1861: he was just 30 at the time of his death and, while initially buried in India, James' body was returned to the UK in 1862 and he is now buried at Arnos Vale Cemetery.

An 1878 report was published concerning the future of Bristol's New Gaol on Cumberland Road, which had previously been run by the Corporation of Bristol but had just been taken over by the Secretary of State following the Prison Act 1877 (when it was decided that all regional prisons now fell under the rule of the government). The Cumberland Road prison had fallen into a state of disrepair and land had been bought at Horfield on which to build a new prison, but at the time of the 1878 report there were suggestions this land be sold and the new prison relocated elsewhere[235]; we know this did not come to pass because HM Prison Bristol remains in Horfield today. As an aside, here's an ironic fact about HM Prison Bristol in Horfield: the site was previously a pleasure garden for Bristolians to enjoy spending their free time in.

By the time of her husband James' death in 1872, the Gardners had retired and were living at The Bourne in Burrington, Somerset, although Eliza clearly preferred to be closer to friends and family because soon after his death she returned to Bristol and lived on Ravenswood Road, Redland. This is where Eliza was at the time of the 1891 census, where she lived with her companion, Sarah Adey. Eliza was also buried at Arnos Vale Cemetery.

INDIRA GHANDI

1917-1984, POLITICIAN

Why would the former Prime Minister (PM) of India be featured in *The Women Who Built Bristol*? Because Indira Ghandi attended what is now called Badminton School in Westbury-on-Trym, which set her up to then attend Somerville College at the University of Oxford. Given the many astonishing things Indira achieved in her life (the first — and, to date, only — female PM of India, second longest-serving PM of India, member of the Indian National Congress, committed politician and statesperson), it is

235 'Prisons Committee' in *Bristol Mercury*, 6 November 1878.

interesting and gratifying to know that a chunk of her formative years were spent here in Bristol.

She was born Indira Nehru in Allahabad, India. As her parents' only surviving child, young Indira spent a lot of time alone with her sick mother and her early education came from governesses, so she felt rather isolated from the world while growing up. She rarely saw her father, who was frequently away with his political work; he became the first PM of India in 1947 when his daughter was 30. At the age of 17, Indira was sent to formal schools in India and Switzerland and, following the death of her mother in 1936, Indira attended Badminton School in Bristol between 1936 and 1937 to give her the grounding she needed to pass the entrance exams to Somerville College.

During her studies at Oxford, Indira was recuperating in Switzerland following an illness at the same time that World War Two was declared. She tried to make her way back to India via England, although it was a slow process due to the disruption of war, but she finally got home to India in 1941... without completing her Oxford degree, although she was later awarded an honorary degree. In 1942, she married the Indian politician Feroze Ghandi with whom she had two children, although the marriage ended in 1960 with his untimely death from a heart attack.

Indira had begun working for her father as his assistant during the 1950s. In her own right, she became President of the Indian National Congress and, after her father's death in 1964, she was appointed to his successor's cabinet as Minister of Information and Broadcasting. By 1966, Indira was the third PM of India, a post she held until 1977, and again from 1980 to 1984. Shockingly, she was assassinated in India on 31 October 1984 by two of her own bodyguards. However, during her time in office she achieved an extraordinary number of things for the betterment of her people, including agricultural improvements to enable India to become

Indira Ghandi illustration by Tina Altwegg

more self-sufficient; guiding India through the war with Pakistan that led to the liberation of Bangladesh; rejecting pressure from the US to join the war in Vietnam; and overseeing the sending of the first Indian into space. Although it should be noted she also received a fair amount of criticism, such as for promoting her sons to positions of power (one of whom led a forced mass-sterilisation campaign to limit population growth); suppressing dissent among her citizens; and controversially declaring a state of emergency in India between 1975 and 1977 because she believed there were internal and external threats to her country. This was in response to unrest against her government and it curbed civil liberties, saw many of her political opponents imprisoned and demanded a censorship of the press.

BLANCHE GIBBS

1817-1887, PHILANTHROPIST

If you visit the National Trust's property at Tyntesfield, you will learn about the Gibbs family, headed by William Gibbs. But lest we forget his wife, Matilda Blanche Gibbs is included here in acknowledgement of her plentiful good deeds.

Born into the Crawley-Boevey family in Gloucester, Blanche was married to William on 1 August 1839 and the couple had seven children, three of whom would lead long lives but four of whom died in their 20s. Alongside her husband, Blanche was known to be a philanthropist.

William died in 1875 and Blanche divided her final years between Tyntesfield and their home at 16 Hyde Park Gardens, London. And in memory of William, Blanche continued his philanthropic work. For instance, she commissioned the St Michael's Free Home for Consumptives at Axbridge; had the chancel at St Michael's church in Exeter (which William had built) redecorated; and endowed Keble College, Oxford, with a scholarship fund to assist students in need. Other philanthropic endeavours included building and maintaining the St John's Lodge convalescent home in Wraxall, where she also built the village club and a row of seven almshouses, known as the Jubilee Cottages. In line with her support of the temperance movement, Blanche took on the Battleaxes Inn and arranged for it to be run on temperance lines as somewhere for Tyntesfield estate workers to socialise without the temptation of booze.[236] In gratitude for Blanche donating the cost of 33 beds, a ward at the Weston-super-Mare Convalescent Home was named in her honour.

Blanche is remembered with a memorial inscription at Wraxall churchyard and church, and further memorials in the chapels at Tyntesfield, Barrow Gurney, Flaxley, Barrow Court and Keble College, all of which had benefited from her generosity.[237]

Please also see: Victoria Gibbs (vol two).

VICTORIA GIBBS

1880-1920, PHILANTHROPIST

Tucked away inside an unassuming residential house at 14 Somerset Street, Kingsdown, was the Victoria Gibbs Memorial Home for Babies, which was opened on 25 January 1921 by the Waifs and Strays Society. The property had previously been the Bristol Industrial School for Girls and the new organisation was named in honour of a woman who had been devoted to

236 The Battleaxes Inn is still open today, although it now permits its' customers to drink alcohol.
237 gibbsfamilytree.com/tng/getperson.php?personID=I1628&tree=gft1

fundraising for baby care facilities in Bristol.

But who exactly was Victoria Florence de Burgh Gibbs? Born in London as Victoria Long, in 1901 she married into the Gibbs family who were linked to the Tyntesfield estate in Wraxall, with her husband being George Gibbs MP. The couple lived in Tyntesfield with their three servants. Know to her friends as Via, she had three children with George although two of them died tragically young (one on the day he was born and another when he was just five days old), so it is not a wild leap to assume these awful losses led Victoria to fundraise so passionately for better healthcare for babies. Her surviving child was Doreen Albinia de Burgh Gibbs, who lived a long life and died in 2008.

During World War One, Victoria directed the Bristol Soldiers' and Sailors' Help Society, was the Chair of the Ladies' House and Social Committee for the Bristol branch of the Royal Colonial Institute, and she was an active member of the Bristol Women's Unionist Association. She was made a CBE in 1918 in recognition of her work with the British Red Cross.

Victoria died at the age of 39, having contracted the Spanish Flu that was sweeping the UK at the time. She is commemorated with an oil painting by Albert Collings which hangs at Tyntesfield, as well as by a simple cross in the house's chapel; because the UK was experiencing a financial depression, it was felt by the wealthy Gibbs family that it would be tactless of them to spend money on a lavish memorial for Victoria at this time.

At the opening ceremony for the Victoria Gibbs Memorial Home for Babies, the ribbon was cut by her sister-in-law Lady Helena Gibbs and the very first matron was one Mrs Clive Gibbs. During World War Two, Bristol was badly bombed and so in 1940 the Somerset Street property was closed and the 29 infants (all aged under two years old) were evacuated to a property in Chippenham for the duration. In 1943, the children were again moved, this time to Bath. The Somerset Street property had been so badly damaged that new permanent premises needed to be found and these were to be on Durdham Park; it boasted a nursery ceiling with "a fresco of very fat cherubs playing musical instruments" which had been painted by an Italian artist.[238] The new site could house 31 children and welcomed infants up to the age of five years. The Victoria Gibbs Memorial Home for Babies finally closed in 1970 and the Durdham Park property has since been converted into flats.

Please also see: Blanche Gibbs (vol two).

MARGARET GILES
1868-1949, SCULPTOR

A painter, medallist and modeller as well as a sculptor, Clifton-born Margaret May Giles was gifted in many disciplines. Initially educated at home at 4 Kings Parade, Clifton, she later studied at the National Art Training School in London under the prominent French sculptor and medallist Édouard Lantéri. Margaret earned a clutch of prizes for her work in the 1890s, including for her statuette 'Hero' in 1895, which won the Sir Frederick Leighton Award from the Art Union of London — giving her the sum of £150 and, err, praise for her father in the local paper: "Miss Margaret Giles is the very accomplished daughter of Mr R W Giles of Clifton," wrote the *Bristol Mercury*[239], although it remains unclear what part Richard Giles played in the artistic creation of Margaret's award-winning statuette.

Margaret also had her works exhibited at London's Royal

238 hiddenlives.org.uk/homes/BRISTO2.html
239 'The Talk of Bristol' in *Bristol Mercury*, 20 November 1895.

Academy consistently between 1895 and 1900, and was written about very favourably in *The Times* newspaper. Based on this acclaim, she was commissioned by a number of architectural companies to create friezes, including one for a house on Newgate Street, London (now demolished). When Margaret was appointed as Associate of the Bristol Academy in 1905, she donated a statuette called 'With Wallet and Script' to the institution. In 1898, she married the civil engineer Bernard Jenkin and from this point onwards she worked under her married name of Margaret Jenkin.

MOLLY and DOBBY GILES

born 1749 and 1754, POSSESSED SISTERS

A 1736 act repealed the 1604 Witchcraft Act (which had made the raising of spirits illegal) but there was still widespread belief in the existence of witches. Richard Giles, the landlord of the Lamb Inn near Lawford's Gate on West Street, Old Market[240], was believed to have two daughters who had been cursed by the Witch of Mangotsfield. His pub had been built in 1651 and it was in 1761 that the terrifying events apparently took place.

Molly, 13, and Dobby, eight, experienced unexplained fits and stated that they could hear voices. Each night, something was pricking their necks and arms with pins, and furniture flew around their bedroom. Eventually, the malevolent forces behind these activities began throwing the girls out of their beds at night and even four stout men could not hold each girl down, such was the strength of the spirits. Clergymen attended the Lamb Inn and tried to reason with the spirits possessing the girls and, although conversations were held with the spirits, the forces

240 The Lamb Inn, built in 1651, was demolished in 1905. It was sited close to where Lawfords Gate still stands, near the top of Pennywell Road.

showed no signs of leaving. Henry Durbin, a pharmacist from Redcliff Street, came to take a look and claimed he witnessed several manifestations himself, which he about in his 1800 book *Witchcraft at the Lamb Inn, Bristol*. Durbin wrote that as well as observing furniture flying in the girls' room and seeing the pin pricks on their bodies, he also witnessed a wine glass being thrown by an unseen force from the table straight into a nearby woman. He also saw Molly's cap rise four feet above her head, followed by the sound of someone hitting the headboard of the bed as if it was a drum.

It was believed the truth lay in witchcraft. Richard Giles had recently started a flying wagon service (a fast-paced horse-drawn coach) between Bristol and London and one woman to whom he had given a lift was a witch from Mangotsfield, who had been paid by a rival wagon driver to torment Richard and ruin his business. It was believed that in addition to cursing his daughters, the witch conjured up a spirit who not only spooked Richard's 18 horses so badly that the coach was overturned in Hanham, but also cast a spell on Richard causing him to become so ill that he died on 16 May 1762. From the moment of his death, his daughters were freed from their mysterious possession. Perhaps they had suffered enough?

However, Molly and Dobby began to be possessed again in July and the behaviour became so bad that the Lamb Inn was given a wide berth by customers. Their mother sought the help of a white witch living in Bedminster, who claimed that for a few shillings she could free the girls of the curse. The price was paid and the girls were liberated.

Many people believed the whole thing was conjured up by trickery but so much of what happened could not be easily explained and remains clouded in mystery. The Lamb Inn was demolished in 1905 and shops on Old Market now occupy the former site. No plausible explanation for the events that overtook Molly and Dobby has ever been found.[241]

EDITH GILLIARD, 1884-1981
PIANO TEACHER

The number of children introduced to the joy of playing the piano by Edith Ethel Gilliard would easily spiral into the hundreds.

Known affectionately as 'Miss Gilly' by her pupils, Edith taught piano (initially from the family home at 21 West Shrubbery and later from her own home at 12 Exeter Buildings, both in Redland) for more than 70 years. She had qualified as a piano teacher at the end of 1908 after studying at the Royal Academy of Music in London.

For her pupils, having lessons with Edith was about much more than just learning to play the piano. Because, without a great deal of persuasion, she would launch into engaging stories about her childhood, thereby opening a window onto a bygone world. Edith was one of ten children born to Mary and Robert Gilliard, and the young family initially lived at 9 Ashley View, Stapleton. Theirs was a household filled with music, art and conversation, and Robert was a Christian socialist who had been involved with the strikes at the Great Western Cotton Factory during the 1880s.[242] Of course, the family never forgot their youngest daughter, Elsie Grace Gilliard, who died of tuberculosis in 1908 at the age of just 19. Former pupil Elizabeth Gould recalls: "Edith described winding Elsie's waist-length golden hair in rags

241 Valerie Pitt, 2015, *Bloody British History: Bristol*. p63-64.

242 For more information about the strikes at the Great Western Cotton Factory, and other Bristolian factories, please refer to the 'Women's Work' section in volume one of *The Women Who Built Bristol*. The Bristol Radical History Group also has a number of interesting pamphlets on this subject.

to create waves, and Elsie's faded sepia photograph had pride of place in the music room in Miss Gilly's home in Exeter Buildings."

For decades, the local newspapers were filled to bursting with regular lists of Edith's former students who had excelled at their music exams thanks to her tutelage. One of her better known pupils was the blind singer and poet Eva Longbottom, whom Edith coached for the theory element of her exams to become an Associate of the Royal College of Music in the spring of 1913: "It is interesting to learn that in her examination she had to sing a 'sight reading' from braille, besides singing songs in Latin, Italian, German and English."[243] In her memoirs, Eva recalled: "Although I took my braille frame into the [examination] room, it was never used, even for taking notes. As Miss Gilliard knew nothing of braille, I had grown accustomed to working all answers mentally."[244]

Anyone who had had the pleasure of meeting Edith would be unlikely to forget her. She was "a tiny, birdlike figure with twinkling eyes and the merriest of laughs, she patiently instructed her pupils over the years, delighting in their progress". And when pupils received the results of their piano exams there was always a jolly letter from Edith to accompany them. Sometimes it would say: "Well done!" Other times: "More practice next time".[245]

Please also see: Eva Longbottom (vol two).

243 'Miss Eva Longbottom' in *Western Daily Press*, 26 April 1913.

244 Eva Longbottom, 1933, *The Silver Bells of Memory*, pp43-47.

245 With very grateful thanks to Elizabeth Gould for nominating Edith Gilliard to this book and for providing much of the information that enabled this entry. Elizabeth and her sister Susan were both taught piano by Edith.

ETHEL GLAZEBROOK
1856-1926, PHILANTHROPIST

As seems to be common for women of Ethel Glazebrook's era and class, among her other pursuits she also tried her hand at writing a novel. Oxford-born Ethel's husband Michael Glazebrook had been the headmaster of Clifton College since 1890, which was where they both lived. In lieu of having any children, Ethel cared for the boys at her husband's school as if they were her own and "likes to be in a measure a mother to the large family of boys who reside in the headmaster's house"[246]. She was praised for taking a "wise, active and warm interest in the affairs of the school, her work being invaluable to the interests of the establishment"[247].

Ethel's novel *The Dower of Earth* was published in 1891. This three volume book is a sprawling work of romantic fiction and an exercise in character studies. One reviewer observed: "The author's knowledge of the world may not be great, but she is evidently a sympathetic student of human character."[248] While another noted: "It is a hectic sort of story altogether, but there is ample reason for expecting better things hereafter from Ethel Glazebrook's pen."[249] However, those better things never came because Ethel found her life as a headmaster's wife so consuming that she had no further opportunity for fiction, saying in 1894: "I have really no time for it now; my chief work lies in the College, and if one is to take a real interest in the boys and make them your friends, watch over them if they are ill and be ready to sympathise with their little troubles, there is no time for literature, and I really enjoy my present work very much."[250]

246 Sarah A Tooley, 1896, 'Ladies of Bristol and Clifton', in *The Woman at Home*, p445.
247 News, in *Clifton Society*, 26 October 1905.
248 'The Dower of Earth' in *Glasgow Herald*, 26 March 1891.
249 'The Dower of Earth' in *Graphic*, 27 June 1891.
250 Sarah A Tooley, 1896, 'Ladies of Bristol and Clifton', in *The Woman at Home*, p445.

In addition to her devotion to the boys at the college, Ethel occupied herself by volunteering for a variety of charitable organisations. For example, she was the first treasurer of the new Bristol Private Hospital for Women and Children, which Eliza Walker Dunbar had launched in 1895, and she opened an endless amount of charity fêtes and galas across Bristol.

After Michael retired from Clifton College in 1905, he and Ethel moved to Cambridge for their final years. When the couple died within 17 days of each other in 1926, the *Western Daily Press* remembered them both kindly, remarking about Edith's "devotion to [Clifton College] and the memorable influence of her refined and artistic personality upon the whole life of the school."[251]

Please also see: Eliza Walker Dunbar (vol one).

SARAH GOLDSMITH
born c1700, PENITENT QUAKER

The history of Quakers in Bristol is plentiful and long reaching. A notable feature of many of the women in volume one of *The Women Who Built Bristol* was how many were Quakers or linked to Quaker families. The same trend can be noticed in this volume.

One most repentant Quaker was Bristol's Sarah Goldsmith, who – dressed only in a sackcloth, her hair smeared with ashes and generally being "sufficiently nasty"[252] – held a silent vigil in front of the highly ornate market cross in Bristol.[253] Her vigil was a demonstration against the perceived self-satisfaction of the

251 'The Late Canon and Mrs Glazebrook' in *Western Daily Press*, 31 March 1927.
252 Gerardus Croese, 1696, *The General History of the Quakers*, p116.
253 The cross was erected in 1373 at the centremost point of Bristol and had a foot each on Broad Street, Wine Street, Corn Street and High Street. It was moved to College Green in 1733, and to its current home at the Stourhead estate (now owned by the National Trust) in 1780.

city. But the fact Sarah protected her modesty with a sackcloth showed a degree of pride in herself. Some penitent early Quakers were known to protest completely in the nude to "symbolise the spiritual nakedness of the unconverted".[254]

But let's not do Sarah's vigil a disservice. She didn't simply smother herself in sackcloth and ashes and stand before the market cross. She also passed through every gate in Bristol on the way to the market cross, in full view of everyone, so "that the Truth might be publick and made known there, and the true and real cause of the full and certain wrath of God, and an Example be given all People for the appeasing thereof, and this for the space of six whole Days".[255] Yes, her vigil lasted for six full days.

As Sarah stood silent and motionless by the market cross, dressed as she was, she attracted quite a crowd: "All sorts of Men, especially Boys, flock to her, and every one according to his Judgment, wonders, conjectures, enquires, what Woman was there, what new Habit that was, what she meant and would have by standing there ... Every one together with their tongues use their hands, and did so jeer and entertain this Spectacle, that was thus adorned and furnished to receive the shock, that she did not know what to do, or which way to turn her self."[256]

Eventually, the authorities were called and they took Sarah to the courthouse where the alderman demanded to know what she meant by her behaviour. She told them "she obeyed the Light of her Conscience; and seeing that she seemed without all doubt to be Mad, and out of her Senses, and not fit to walk about in the Streets, they commanded her to be shut up in Prison"[257]. Yes, she was sent to prison for her silent and peaceful protest. However,

254 Rebecca Larson, 2000, *Daughters of Light: Quaker Women Preaching and Prophesying in the Colonies and Abroad 1700-1775*, p24.
255 Gerardus Croese, 1696, *The General History of the Quakers*, p116.
256 Ibid, p116-117.
257 Ibid, p117.

Sarah's fellow Quakers defended her actions and stated she was simply following the examples of the saints in the Old Testament.

And another thing... When travel writer **Celia Fiennes** visited Bristol in 1698, she wrote of the market cross: "There is a very high and magnificent Cross built all of ye stone or sort of Marble of ye Country, it's in the manner of Coventry Cross a Piramedy form running up of a great height, with severall divisions in nitches where is King John's Effigy and several other, adorned with armes and figures of Beasts and birds and flowers. Great part of it Gilt and painted and soe terminates in a spire on ye top, the Lower part is white Like Marble."[258]

Please also see: Celia Fiennes (vol two).

BRIDGET GOOD

1948-1984, QUADRUPLET

The world's first ever quadruplets delivered by Caesarean Section were the Good quads, who were born at Southmead Hospital on 12 June 1948. Bridget, Elizabeth, Frances and Jennifer Good were born to Margaret and Charles and delivered by Beryl Corner, who had created a pioneering special baby unit at the hospital. Astonishingly, Margaret only found out the day before the birth that she was going to have four babies. Despite her very large pregnancy bump arousing her doctor's suspicions, previous x-rays had suggested she was simply expecting twins.

Consultant Paediatrician Beryl later said: "We knew that we had to have four cots ready, four Queen Charlotte boxes, which

258 visionofbritain.org.uk/travellers/Fiennes/26

were the sort of tents we put over the cots. We had got to have them all heated up with hot water bottles. Each cot had four hot water bottles in it and a thermometer in the corner to tell the temperature. And then at 2pm we were all assembled in the operating theatre."[259]

The birth of these four babies was extraordinary and attracted huge nationwide interest. "When we were delivered the theatre was chock-a-block and people were climbing on chairs outside to see through the windows," said Frances. "Neonatal surgeries have come a long way since then, with babies nowadays being incubated in state-of-the-art ventilation."[260]

They Good quads were six months old before they were strong enough to leave the hospital and go to their home in Westerleigh, near Yate, which consisted of two semi-detached council houses which had been knocked into one. Their arrival was greeted with national excitement: a marching band, huge crowd, banners in the streets and TV crews following them around. The square where they lived was renamed The Quadrangle.

Luxuries were bestowed upon the family: complimentary shoes from Clarks, their nannies paid for by Cow & Gate and free holidays at Butlins. But these perks came with a price and Jennifer admitted all the attention made the four sisters feel as though they were a circus attraction: "The other children just did not like the thought of the special treatment. They thought we were making money, which we weren't." While Frances added: "Mummy said she could very rarely take us shopping because she never got any shopping done. Everybody used to stop her to talk to her and to us. So she gave up taking us."[261]

The four quads and their elder sister Susan remained very

259 Anon, 'Quads Celebrate 50 Years of Firsts' on *BBC News*, 1 June 1998.
260 Anon, 'The Good Sisters: World's First Quads Born by Caesarean Section Celebrate their 60th Birthday' in *The Daily Mail*, 13 June 2008.
261 Anon, 'Quads Celebrate 50 Years of Firsts' on *BBC News*, 1 June 1998.

close throughout their lives. And although Bridget sadly died of a brain haemorrhage in 1984 at the age of 36, her surviving sisters remain living in Bristol and the South West.

And another thing... On the subject of multiple births, spare a thought for **Mary Stanfast** (1602-1636). Mary was married to Richard Stanfast, who was 44 years her senior, and in May 1636 she gave birth to triplets. All three baby boys survived and were named Abraham, Isaac and Joseph. However, their poor mother died two weeks after the birth, leaving the boys to be raised by their 78-year-old father. More than likely, he would have offloaded the babies to a wet nurse and foster family.

Please also see: Beryl Corner (vol one).

MARTHA GRACE

1812-1884, DAREDEVIL

If your dad had invented the box-kite, there's a strong chance you'd have wanted to have a play with it as well. And that's exactly what Martha Pocock did when she became the first woman to travel by kite-drawn carriage... prior to becoming the grand dame of a cricketing dynasty. One biographer described her as "a spirited girl from a decidedly eccentric background", which seems to be putting things mildly.[262]

Bristolian schoolteacher George Pocock ran a boys' academy in Prospect Place, Easton, but when he wasn't there he was forever tinkering with his inventions. One of which was the charvolant: a kite-drawn carriage. George had always been fascinated by kites

262 Robert Low, 2004, *WG Grace: An Intimate Biography*, p17.

and had experimented with all kinds of methods of using kites to pull loads along, often enlisting the boys he taught to help with his experiments. In 1824 he finally solved the puzzle and this time invited his young daughter Martha along for the ride.

With the aid of a nine-metre long kite attached to a rigged kitchen chair, George was able to strap Martha in and lift his 12-year-old daughter more than 82 metres into the air above the chasm of the Avon Gorge: the spectacle was watched by a huge crowd which had gathered on the Durdham Downs, long before the Clifton Suspension Bridge had been built. In the process, Martha became the very first woman anywhere in the world to travel by charvolant, or to be carried by the power of wind. Having proved – with Martha's assistance – that his invention worked and that kites could indeed transport humans, George set his sights to working out how kites could move vehicles including, in 1826, a carriage containing passengers, and in later years George, Martha and his other children travelled from Bristol to London in a kite-drawn carriage. On the same theme, George also invented a kite-powered boat.

In 1831, barely 19, Martha married a young doctor called Henry Grace and the couple set up home in Downend, where they remained for the rest of their lives. To cut a long story short, one of her nine children was William Gilbert Grace, born 1848: aka the future international cricket superstar WG Grace. Several of her other children were also very keen on the game and more than a century after her death Martha remains one of the most influential women ever involved in the world of cricket. Victorian cricketer Richard Daft said of Martha: "She knew ten times more about cricket than any lady I ever met."[263]

Martha's brother Alfred was a keen cricket player and

263 Robert Low, 2004, *WG Grace: An Intimate Biography*, p18.

his enthusiasm may have rubbed off on his young nephews. Alongside Martha, Alfred was certainly involved with training and encouraging her sons, including WG, and she used to bowl at her sons so they could practice batting. Biographer Robert Low wrote: "She watched [her sons] play whenever she could and was forthright in her criticisms ... In her old age she regularly attended Gloucestershire matches and was noted for her pithy comments on play and the players. Indeed, it appears to have been part of a Gloucestershire batsman's duties, once dismissed, to pay his respects to Mrs Grace as she sat in the stand and to listen attentively as she told him just where he had gone wrong."[264]

JANE GREEN

c1680-c1745, ROPE MAKER

When Jane Green's husband Francis died in the early 1700s, she had no choice but to throw herself into running his ropemaking business on Tower Lane (now demolished) in the area of Temple Parish (now called Temple Back), close to the River Avon, which offered good opportunities for trading and transporting the manufactured rope.

The process of making rope was not an easy one and remains a tough ask to this day, despite the invention of machinery to assist. So for a woman in the rope making business, life was particularly hard. This was seen as a man's job. To make rope, you initially needed a length of twine which was at least a third as long as the desired finished strand of rope. And this would be repeatedly twisted, tighter and tighter, with further strands added until it reached the required thickness and tightness. Due to the volume

264 Robert Low, 2004, *WG Grace: An Intimate Biography*, p18. With thanks to John Cooper for nominating Martha Grace for this book.

of rope produced for the rigging of ships, rope makers were often situated — as Jane was — close to the harbour, meaning the finished rope could easily be delivered to its new owner on the docks via a handcart.

In 1975, a "roping house" site in the former Temple Parish was excavated and evidence confirms the site as a place of rope making dating back to 1639, when a man called Thomas Taylor initially took it up. By 1745, ropemaking appears to have ceased at this site and a 1750 map describes the area as "formerly a rope walk"[265], suggesting that Jane's business died when she did.[266]

AJ GREEN-ARMYTAGE

1854-1922, HISTORIAN

This little-remembered Bristolian, historian and public speaker wrote under the name 'AJ Green-Armytage' throughout her time as a historian of Bristol's great and good, although her full name was Amy Julia Green-Armytage. Perhaps the saddest story of all is that she died in June 1922 on the very day she handed in the manuscript for what would, obviously, be her final book: a small work entitled *Concerning Clifton*, which is, as you might expect, all about Clifton, where she had been born and where she lived throughout her life. This was a pocket-sized volume which largely covers the churches of Clifton and the nearby areas as well as a few notable residents. Most charmingly, the book also includes a section about the etymology of the word 'hedgehogs', with which Clifton was apparently infested during the 18th century.

265 A rope walk is the name for the long stretch of land required to stretch out the cord so it can be twisted into the rope. The Ropewalk pub on Bedminster Parade is presumably sited on a former rope walk, which would make sense as it is also located close to the harbour and the Bristol docks extended out to Bedminster at this time.

266 b-i-a-s.org.uk/BIAS_Journal10_ROPEWALKS_AND_ROPEMAKERS.pdf

AJ Green-Armytage illustration by Carrie Love

Reporting on a talk she had given about the olden days of Bristol, the *Western Daily Press* wrote in 1912: "Mrs Green-Armytage, at the outset of her lecture, reminded the assemblage that [poet Robert] Southey, writing to a friend, 80 years ago, said that he did not think there was any city in England that compared to Bristol in singularity and beauty, and that nobody loved his native city more than he. She agreed with Southey's sentiments, and they were her qualifications for giving this lecture. Probably there were present people who knew more than she did about the city, but no one loved it more ardently or was prouder of it and of being by birth and residence a Bristolian."[267]

By way of introduction to Amy, here are some key facts about our proud Bristolian. Her parents were Catherine Dayrell from Shirehampton and Robert Bartley from London, and Amy was the middle of their five children. On 8 June 1876, aged 22, she married solicitor Alfred Green-Armytage at St Paul's Church, Clifton and, in the 1881 census, she was living at 1 Kensington Villa with Alfred and their four children. By the 1891 census, they were still in Clifton but now at 16 Apsley Road and with five children. This would remain their home for the rest of their lives.

Once her children were well into adulthood, Amy turned to writing. Her most easy-to-find book is the 1906 volume *Maids of Honour: Twelve Descriptive Sketches of Single Women Who Have Distinguished Themselves in Philanthropy, Nursing, Poetry, Travel, Science, Prose*. *The Spectator* wrote: "This somewhat eccentric title ... is a book well worthy of attention; possibly the biographer may now and then look at things from a standpoint different from the reader's. But it is written with sympathy, even enthusiasm, and, indeed, a book of this kind cannot be written to any good purpose without them."[268]

267 'Lecture At The Museum Hall' in the *Western Daily Press*, 13 March 1912.
268 Anon, 'Maids of Honour' in *The Spectator*, 29 December 1906.

In 1914, Amy wrote various pamphlets about specific areas of Bristol's history. However, these books were not always well received or well respected. A letter writer called Jane Baker sniped in the *Bristol Magpie*: "The *Western Daily Press* is serving up a *réchauffé*[269] of alleged Bristol History under the title of 'Rosemary's Papers' by Mrs Green-Armytage. Part 1 appeared on Sept 9th, and the day following an editorial note called attention to a 'typographical mistake'... As only one misquotation has been put right, I presume that all the other literary errors with which this article bristles are still unknown to its author. I will, therefore, briefly draw attention to some others, which, by the way, will not exhaust the entire list."[270] And so Ms Baker goes on. I feel rather sorry for Mrs Green-Armytage.

Undeterred, Amy's passion for local history endured and as well as writing about Bristol's past she also lectured about it, usually at one of the many ladies' clubs of which she was a member: such as when she gave a lecture entitled 'Bits of Old Bristol' to the Clifton Ladies' Club in November 1911. Amy's public speaking received a much warmer response than Ms Baker felt her writing deserved. "It was evident that the lecturer had studied her subject with great care," wrote *Clifton Society*. "For besides speaking of all the better known bits of old Bristol, she pointed out a number of others with which the ordinary person has a very slight acquaintance, if any at all. Her knowledge of the historical associations of the city was not the least interesting part of the lecture and was considerable."[271] Evidently buoyed by this review, Amy repeated the talk at the Museum Lecture Hall on Queen's Road in March 1912, with all the proceeds going to the Bristol Female Penitentiary. Her interest in Bristol's history was widespread but had a definite

269 '*Réchauffé*': "A dish of warmed-up food left over from a previous meal." Ouch! Poor Mrs Green-Armytage.

270 Jane Baker, 'Slip Shod History' in *Bristol Magpie*, 19 September 1907.

271 'Barbara's Budget' in *Clifton Society*, 2 November 1911

leaning towards women's social inclusion. So it should come as no surprise (although it *did* pleasantly surprise me, based on the rather stiff, God-fearing, Victorian figure I found in her writing) that Amy was pro-women's suffrage, and spoke on platforms in support of votes for women on occasion. On 12 February 1910, Amy was a speaker at the first annual meeting of the Bristol Branch of the Conservative and Unionist Women's Franchise Association at the Victoria Rooms in Clifton. By 1914, we find her with the same society, proposing it "requests the Conservative party favourably to consider the granting of the Parliamentary franchise to those women who pay rates and tax".[272]

In 1916, mid-World War One, she was still going strong, chairing a meeting at Hamilton's Rooms at 40 Park Street (now the Folk House) for the National Union of Women's Suffrage Societies where she stoutly "contradicted the impression which some few people seemed to be under that women's suffrage was a dead letter, that their political enthusiasm had died out, and that automatically the movement had ceased to exist. If they needed the vote two years ago they needed it a great deal more today, and would feel it even more as time went on. When the war was over the difficulties of reconstruction would be enormous and they claimed most insistently that they should have a voice in that work of reconstruction."[273]

And another thing... Amy's eldest granddaughter **Vivienne Dayrell-Browning** followed in her grandmother's footsteps when, aged 13 in 1921, she published her first volume of prose and poetry with *The Little Wings*. The *Western Daily Press* wrote: "The young author... is neither silly nor incoherent. That she has many friends

272 'Conservative Women's Franchise Association' in *Western Daily Press*, 15 January 1914.
273 'Women's Suffrage Meeting' in *Western Daily Press*, 21 October 2016. With thanks to Mike Manson for nominating AJ Green-Armytage to this book.

here gives the volume a local interest, but we do not ask readers to procure and examine this book because of this local association but because of its intrinsic merits."[274] Vivienne later said of her precocious publication: "I felt as if I should go up in flames."[275] Her husband was the novelist Graham Greene, whom she married in 1927 and had two children with, although the couple separated in 1947 due to his many affairs. In addition, Vivienne was considered the world's foremost expert on dolls' houses, with which she had been fascinated since girlhood and about which she wrote a number of books.[276] Vivienne died in 2003 aged 99.

ALICE GRENFELL

1842-1917, SUFFRAGIST

While visiting the US in 1888, Alice Grenfell (née Pyne) met the prominent American suffragist Susan B Anthony in Washington at the inaugural meeting of the International Council of Women, a global organisation which still exists today and seeks to advance the human rights of women. Inspired by this meeting, when she returned to the UK Alice became Honorary Secretary of the Women's Progressive Society in 1890, in which politically active women lobbied men in politics to support the notion of votes for women.

It was in this manner that Alice contacted the novelist Thomas Hardy in 1892 and asked if he would support women's suffrage. Initially Hardy declined Alice's request but by 1906 he had changed his mind, writing to Millicent Fawcett that "the tendency of the women's vote will be to break up the present pernicious

274 'The Little Wings', in Western Daily Press, 17 January 1921.
275 Anon, 'Vivien Greene' in *The Daily Telegraph*, 22 August 2003. NB: Vivienne changed the spelling of her first name to Vivien during her lifetime.
276 Ibid.

convention in respect of manners, customs, religion, illegitimacy, the stereotyped household (that it must be the unit of society), the father of a woman's child (that it is anybody's business but the woman's own except in cases of disease or insanity)".[277]

Alice was married to John Grenville, a teacher at Clifton College, which their son Bernard attended following the family's move to Bristol from Birmingham. Alice was also on the school's board for three years around 1883. Following John's death in 1897, Alice moved to live with her now-adult son and through him she developed an interest in ancient Egyptian scarabs, taught herself to read hieroglyphics and wrote widely on the subject.

MARY GRIFFITHS

1843-1936, DAREDEVIL

When the brand-new Clifton Suspension Bridge was opened to the public on 8 December 1864, the very first member of the public to cross it on foot was Mary Griffiths, 21, who had been born in Chipping Sodbury but now lived in Hanham. Her father was the landlord of the Robin Hood Inn on St Michael's Hill, which was where the young barmaid worked.

Determined to be the very first civilian to make it over the Clifton Suspension Bridge[278], Mary pushed through the crowd of 100,000 just before it was officially opened. However, a young man had had the same idea, and the two raced each other from the Clifton side to the Leigh Woods side, with Mary's uncle shouting words of encouragement behind her. "When the gate opened I

277 Thomas Hardy cited in Penelope Ann Boumelha, 1981, 'Female Sexuality, Marriage and Divorce in the Fiction of Thomas Hardy, with Special Reference to the Period 1887-1896', PhD thesis, University of Oxford.

278 Prior to its official opening, a number of cars had driven over the Clifton Suspension Bridge, including one that was carrying the famous explorer David Livingstone, who somehow manages to get two mentions in this book (see also the entry for May Allen).

began to run," she recalled. "I heard my uncle shout, 'Run, Mary, run!', and I turned round and saw a young man some yards behind me, running as fast as he could. I could see he was trying to beat me across, so I tucked up my long dress and ran for dear life." Mary beat the young man by a few yards and paid her one penny toll with pleasure when she reached the other side.[279]

Some 69 years later, on 3 February 1933, Mary (who now lived in Redfield) made her radio debut at the age of 91 in a BBC show presented by the future Poet Laureate John Betjeman. Still in excellent health in her tenth decade, Mary kept radio audiences thoroughly entertained with the thrilling story of her mischievous bridge run, which she and Betjeman broadcast live from Clifton Suspension Bridge as he recreated the daring run on her behalf. So popular was Mary's story that she was called back to repeat her tale in August of the same year (tape recordings not being a thing back then). Despite her advanced years, Mary was still a regular volunteer at the bazaars at St Patrick's Church near her home in Redfield, where she held court over the bran tub. And evidencing the fact that she was no shrinking violet, in 1929, aged 87, Mary took her first ever aeroplane flight "when she expressed a desire to fly to London and back" — at a time when it was far from common for any civilian to fly, never mind an elderly lady from Bristol who simply fancied a jolly in a flying machine.

It is with a heavy heart that I have to tell you that, despite her youthful spirit and immense sense of fun, Mary died at her home in 1936 at the age of 93. If she was still alive today, despite being almost 200 years old, I strongly suspect she would still be enjoying herself enormously. Bravo, Mary! I think of you every time I run across the Clifton Suspension Bridge and, each time, I do so in your memory.

279 cliftonbridge.org.uk/visit/history/timeline

And another thing... Here's a bonus fact about the Clifton Suspension Bridge. The foundation stone was laid on 21 June 1831 by **Lady Elton** of Clevedon Court, whose husband Sir Abraham Elton was a major investor in the new bridge. Lady Elton's stone, which was passed to her by Isambard Kingdom Brunel himself, is at St Vincent's Rocks and marks the site of the Clifton abutment.[280]

CATHERINE GULLEY
1908-1962, ARTIST

Watercolour artist Catherine Gulley lived and worked from Bristol throughout her whole life and was primarily based at Westbury-on-Trym. Alongside exhibiting her work, Catherine qualified and worked as an art teacher, having trained at the Bristol School of Science and Art. As a lifelong member of the Royal West of England Academy, Catherine was able to use the letters 'RWA' after her name to denote her pedigree and she regularly exhibited at the gallery on Queens Road. Her watercolours were typically scenes of refined Edwardian living and could be described as somewhat sentimental in style.

Catherine worked from a small studio at the top of a house in Arlington Villas, St Paul's Road, Clifton, accessed via a steep, winding staircase and opening into a bright room. Describing a visit here, the *Western Daily Press* wrote: "This talented artist is very well known in Bristol and always has a number of delightful paintings in the Royal West of England Academy Exhibition. For some years Miss Gulley limited her work almost entirely to miniatures, but so many demanded that she should do real portrait

280 cliftonbridge.org.uk/visit/history

painting, that now her time is amply filled by that branch of work, and any spare moments in studies of still life the colouring of the latter being a joy to the eye."[281]

Gushing further over the qualities of Catherine's portraits, the same paper described a painting she had been commissioned to do of a little boy called Colin saying: "Miss Gulley has made it appear so amazingly real and natural that one almost feels able to talk to the blue-eyed baby lying snugly in his shawl, his head resting on a little pillow beautifully embroidered with sprays of flowers."[282]

SARAH HABERFIELD
c1800-1874, PHILANTHROPIST

Born Sarah Dupont, by the time of her death as Dame Sarah Haberfield in 1874, this woman had proved herself to be an extremely generous person who would leave a mark on Bristol which endures to this day, because her legacy continues to support older women in need.

Sarah lived at 31 Royal York Crescent, Clifton, and became a widow following the death of her husband, Sir John Kerle Haberfield, who had been an alderman, magistrate, town councillor and six-times mayor of Bristol. Perhaps her greatest gifts to Bristol are the Lady Haberfield Almshouses in Hotwells, which overlook Cabot Way, close to the Floating Harbour and the Cumberland Basin. The 35 almshouses were completed in 1891 and, in addition to their home, residents of the almshouses received the weekly sum of ten shillings, plus 224lbs of coal at Christmas. Oh, and matron Harriet Biggs wielded a bottle of medicinal brandy that she would pour hearty doses from in an

281 'Barbara's Budget' in *Western Daily Press*, 18 February 1933.
282 'Barbara's Budget' in *Western Daily Press*, 3 February 1934.

effort to cure most minor ailments. The almshouses still operate today and benefitted from a thorough renovation in 1977.

After Sarah's death in 1874 (she was buried in the Anglican Crypt of Arnos Vale Cemetery), the Dame Sarah Haberfield Charity was established. This provided a £12 10s annuity to a married but poor woman who was over the age of 50 and whose husband remained alive, meaning the family did not qualify for poor law relief. This charity still exists today, although — along with many other small and long-established charities — it has been absorbed into the wider Bristol Charities pot, which administers the endowment funds of a number of local charities. Sarah's will also contained bequests to organisations including the Bristol Royal Infirmary and Müller Orphanage, as well as the sum of £640 to be used for the purchase of a lifeboat ('The Lady Haberfield'), to be stationed "on such part of the Coast of England, between Anglesea and the Land's End, as the Institution may deem fit".

In line with Sarah's support for older women in need, Bristol Charities spearheaded a project to build an £8m three-storey development in Hollway Road, Stockwood, for older residents, which was completed in the summer of 2018 and is named Haberfield House in honour of Sarah.[283]

MARY HAMILTON

born 1721, FEMALE HUSBAND

It was only in 2004 that same-sex civil partnerships became legal in the UK and it was 2014 before same-sex marriage became legal.

283 bristolcharities.org.uk/housing/stockwood With thanks to researchers at Arnos Vale Cemetery (including Marion Blackburn, Hildegard Dumper, Liz Johnson and Janine Marriott) for generously providing extra information for this entry.

But this didn't stop Mary Hamilton from marrying 14 different women during the 18th century. As such, she was dubbed 'a female husband' thanks to the fictionalised portrayal of her experiences in the 1813 short story of the same name by Henry Fielding.

The true details of Mary's story are rather muddy, due to limited and unsympathetic contemporary news coverage and the fact that, because of Fielding's fictionalised version of events, the story has become distorted with each retelling. However, to the best of my understanding, this is Mary's story:

Born in Somerset, Mary had been dressing in her brother's clothes since she was 14 and had passed as a boy ever since. Her first same-sex relationship was with an older neighbour called Anne when Mary was 14 years old. The couple moved to Bristol to live together but Anne broke Mary's heart by falling in love with someone else... worse, a man! As a consequence, Mary claimed she had become sexually attracted to women in "Bristol with my Methodistical sisters".[284]

Due to her gender nonconformity, Mary successfully convinced two doctors in Northumberland that she was male, so they would take her on as their apprentice (a job which a woman would never have been able to do at the time). By the age of 18, Mary was travelling widely around the UK as a man, which enabled her to court various women... several of whom she married without them having any previous idea that she was really a woman.

In Wells, Somerset, Mary introduced herself as 'Charles Hamilton' and in July 1746 she was married again, this time to a relative of her landlady, and the newly married couple worked as travelling salespeople selling medicines. It was two months before Mary's young wife realised her 'husband' was actually

284 outstoriesbristol.org.uk/people/biographies/hamilton-mary/

a woman, reported Mary to the authorities and this time Mary was arrested. In her deposition, the duped wife said that Mary had "entered her body several times, which made this examinant believe, at first, that the said Hamilton was a real man, but soon had reason to judge that the said Hamilton was not a man but a woman".[285]

Mary's trial was held in Taunton and she was found guilty of fraud. Her punishment involved being stripped to the waist and whipped in Taunton, Glastonbury, Wells and Shepton Mallet, before facing a prison sentence of six months.

Her story was never forgotten. Almost a century after the events, the *Bristol Mirror* wrote: "In the apportionment of punishment to crime, a correspondent thinks it was either fortunate for the Princess Caraboo[286], or indicative of the more indulgent spirit of jurisprudence in the present times, that the following unique precedent was not referred to in her case. At a quarter session of the peace held at Taunton in November 1746, Mary Hamilton, otherwise Charles, otherwise George Hamilton, was tried for pretending herself a man, and marrying 14 wives! After debate of the nature of the crime and what to call it, it was agreed that she was an uncommon notorious cheat, and sentenced to be publicly whipped in Taunton, Glastonbury, Wells and Shepton Mallet, to be imprisoned for six months, and to find security for her good behaviour for as long time as the justices at the next quarter sessions should think fit."[287]

Please also see: Princess Caraboo (vol one).

285 Sheridan Baker (1959), "Henry Fielding's the Female Husband: Fact and Fiction", *PMLA*, Vol 74, No 3, 213-224.

286 Princess Caraboo was a character created by beggar Mary Wilcocks. She became an international sensation after 'washing up' on the shores of Bristol having apparently been captured by pirates. Her reality was a much sadder story, however, and involved a dead son, mental illness and leeches. Her full story is in volume one of *The Women Who Built Bristol*.

287 'To The Editor', in the *Bristol Mirror*, 1 October 1825.

EDITH HANNAM

1878-1951, OLYMPIAN

The very first Bristolian, female or male, to win an Olympic gold medal was tennis ace Edith Hannam. And to really make her point, she won not one but two Olympic gold medals during her career. Take that, patriarchy![288]

Born in Long Ashton into a pharmaceutical family which ran a chemist shop on Union Street, central Bristol, Edith Boucher had six siblings, many of whom were also excellent sports players and with whom she practised tennis, a game she learned and practised at Clifton Tennis Club under the guidance of her brother John.

Edith was 29 before she began to see real success as a tennis player, although it was common in this era for tennis players to emerge as stars in their late 20s and early 30s. Similarly, it was usual for elite tennis players to continue competing into their 40s and 50s. Indeed, Edith was still winning tournaments when she was well into her 40s.

After marrying Bristolian timber merchant and cricket player Francis Hannam in Nailsea in May 1909, Edith gave up tennis for a while when the couple relocated to Toronto, Canada. But they decided life overseas was not for them and returned to the UK where Edith picked up her racquet and became an outstanding figure at the Welsh Championships, winning ten titles between 1912 and 1923. By this time, the couple were living in Nailsea.

When the 1912 Olympics in Stockholm, Sweden, came around it clashed with Wimbledon, so Great Britain was not represented in the outdoor lawn tennis events in Sweden. However, there was a strong GB tennis team for the indoor Olympic events in May

288 Bristol's men had had four previous modern Olympics in which to try and win a gold medal, but they apparently needed Edith to come along and show them how it was done. Indeed, in 1912 when Edith competed in the Olympics, out of the 2,409 athletes competing across all disciplines, only 47 were women. Well done, Edith!

Edith Hannam illustration by Tina Altwegg

of that year. Edith was the most successful member of the team, winning two gold medals. It should be noted that the two events she won medals for were the only two events open to female players. Perhaps she would have won even more medals if she had been allowed to compete in other events.

Edith never enjoyed similar success at Wimbledon, however, with her two best years there being 1911 and 1914. Two years later, in July 1916, Edith was widowed after Francis was killed in action during World War One. She then moved from Nailsea to live in a house in Leigh Woods with her unmarried sister Helen, although she continued playing tennis for a long time to follow.[289]

And another thing... Not content with being a superstar tennis player, Edith was also a whizz at ping pong. She and her brother John were the county table tennis winners when the first ever Gloucester Table Tennis Championships were held at the Victoria Rooms in Clifton in 1902.

JULIA HARRIS and JULIA PILLINGER

1797-1880 and 1823-1876, PROFESSORS OF MUSIC

Londoner Julia Bartlett married her sweetheart George Pillinger in Bath and their daughter Julia Maria Pillinger was born the following year. But their happiness was not to last because apothecary George died in 1829 when he was only 29. In order to keep herself and her daughter, widowed Julia, who had aspirations to be a singer, trained to become a music teacher and relocated to 6 Queen Square, Bristol, in 1839 where she set up a music school and titled herself a professor of music.

289 tennisforum.com/59-blast-past/679482-edith-boucher-hannam-early-english-lawn-tennis-player.html

In 1840, she married for a second time, to carver and gilder Richard Harris. Their wedding was at St John's Church in Bedminster and, afterwards, the family lived at Julia's home and music school on Queen Square. As she grew older, daughter Julia took after her musical mother and trained at the Royal Academy of Music in London under no lesser a tutor than Madame Dulcken, who was pianist to Queen Victoria. She then returned to Bristol where she became a piano teacher at her mother's school. Daughter Julia worked under her father's surname of Pillinger: presumably to avoid the confusion of having exactly the same name as her mother.[290] Pupils from the school of music were regularly involved in putting on concerts throughout Bristol to showcase their newly honed talents, and this continued throughout the decades in which the school was in business.

Things became a little confusing in the 1861 census, however. This was because both Julias were still living at 6 Queen Square but Richard was no longer there. It may simply have been that he was away from home the night the census was taken and his absence could be explained this easily, because he was definitely still alive in 1861. However, clearly the family's circumstances had been reduced because the head of the house at 6 Queen Square was now a widow named Harriet Page whose profession was 'boarding house keeper'. Both Julias were lodgers in what was once their family home and place of business, but where had Richard gone? (NB: He resurfaced on the 1871 census when he and wife Julia, still a professor of music, had moved up the hill to Clifton and were lodging at 9 West Clifton Terrace.)

Given their musical connections and location on Queen Square, it should not come as a big surprise that the Harris/

290 Daughter Julia applied for a passport in 1855 but did she ever have occasion to use it? I cannot find any evidence of her on ship passenger records but I would like to think she had the chance to see some of the world if that is what she aspired to do.

Pillinger family forged strong connections with the nearby Theatre Royal on King Street (now the Bristol Old Vic). Richard was a carver and gilder, which suggests he may well have been involved with set building and decoration at the theatre. And daughter Julia, who never married or had her own family, became such good friends with the Macready-Chute family who ran the theatre that she moved in to live with them for a number of years before her death in 1876. Her mother must have had a great deal in common with theatre manager Sarah Macready, who was herself a musical woman and also a widow. It also seems the connections between the Harris and Pillinger women and the Macready-Chute family lasted for several further decades.[291]

Please also see: Sarah Macready (vol one).

LILY HARRIS

1886-1978, GOOD TEMPLAR

Lily Elisabeth Harvey of Stillhouse Lane, Bedminster, met William Harris at the Redcliffe Crescent Methodist Chapel, where they were both members of the International Order of Good Templars: which embraced the values of a pure and sober life that avoided temptations offered by alcohol or drugs. Ironically, William was a cigarette-machine operator at the nearby HO Wills factory. With his waxed moustache and smart uniform, William immediately turned Lily's head; he was six years her senior and she thought: "He looks the sort of man my mother always warned me against." She married him in September 1909 at the church where they had met and the newlyweds lived at 14 Southville Place, Southville.

291 bristolfamilyhistoryblog.wordpress.com/2010/08/23/macready-chute-pillinger/

However, when World War One was declared, William was called up to serve as a rifleman and was sent to France, where he fought in the 1914 Battle of Mons before being captured and ending up a prisoner of war. He wrote to Lily asking her to "send golden syrup", a message which she interpreted as "send gold in syrup" and swiftly sent him a tin of treacle containing a gold sovereign that she hoped would somehow help him escape. For the rest of his life, William wore Lily's sovereign on his watchchain as a good luck charm.[292]

By 1939, Lily and William were retired and happily living in one of the new houses at 29 Durnford Avenue, Southville, with their two daughters Nora and Winifred. This was a definite step up from the three-room house that they had previously shared on Southville Place.

MARY HART

1807-1883, MOURNER

Unlucky in love, Mary Hart was considered to be an eccentric character because, for her remaining 50 years on earth following the death of her fiancé, she spent her spare time visiting all of the places where they had gone in their courtship and only wearing clothes which she had worn while her former partner was still alive. Mary, who worked as a cook, lived with her parents Ann and John Hart at Iron Acton, which was where she died having outlived them both. Mary's was a life of sadness and grief, and in some ways her eternal commitment to her deceased partner is reminiscent of the lifelong devotion Gammer Pugsley (who we met in volume one of *The Women Who Built Bristol)* displayed for

292 Anton Bantock, 1997, *Bedminster*, p112.

her young husband who was killed at war. There are also hints of Miss Havisham about her and, given Charles Dickens wrote *Great Expectations* in 1861, maybe in some way Mary was an influence on his leading lady?[293]

Please also see: Gammer Pugsley (vol one).

CAROLINE HASLETT
1895-1957, ELECTRICAL ENGINEER

Caroline Haslett saw World War Two as the moment for women to seize the day and strive for equality. "The war has given us the day of the middle-aged woman," she declared to a meeting of female engineers in 1943. "No longer are we out of fashion. No longer are we behind the times. We are on the front line. Every woman of 45 must do a part-time job of war work outside the home." And the key to empowering women to take up this work? Men doing their fair share at home! "I have been in homes recently where the husband realises he can help with the washing-up and the chores occasionally. If we get more husbands interested in doing their share of the domestic work, we will be able to have far more effective work from the women." She added: "It is greatly unfair to expect a woman to do all the jobs she is expected to do as a wife and mother, also to do a job outside the home, and for the man to expect to come home and find his meals ready. Why shouldn't he take his share in running the home?"[294]

Why indeed? This was radical talk from the Director of the

293 If this turns out to be true, I will eat my typewriter. It is suggested the real influence for Miss Havisham was an Australian woman called Eliza Donnithorne, who was jilted on her wedding day and lived the rest of her life in a dark house, wedding cake rotting on the table and the front door left open in case her husband-to-be should deign to come back.
294 'Man Must Help Run The Home', 4 June 1943, *Western Daily Press*

Electrical Association for Women. Especially at a time when women were asked to assist their brave menfolk who were out fighting for king and country. But it was to be expected from a woman as bold and radical as Caroline Haslett, a woman who had been striving to free women from domestic drudgery for years… and who would continue to do so for the rest of her life. One of her most unique projects was based in Bristol.

Caroline was elected President of the Women's Engineering Society (WES) in 1939 and remained so until 1956. She had previously been its first ever Secretary and the editor of its journal *The Woman Engineer*. Caroline had also been a proud member of the Women's Social and Political Union, campaigning for votes for women. Given the WES was formed as a result of women's work done in World War One, it seemed only appropriate that during World War Two it was Caroline who was again inspiring women to ask for more. She had already been instrumental in setting up new careers for women in the field of 'domestic electrification' (ie using new machines to make domestic tasks, such as cleaning clothes, less laborious for the user).

Part of this electrical liberation for women came via Caroline's conception of the All-Electric House in Stoke Bishop in 1935 (not to be confused with Electricity House opposite the cenotaph). The purpose of the All-Electric House was to showcase how women's lives could be made less miserable by the invention of newfangled electrical devices such as an electric fridge, cooker, clock, drying cupboard and warming plates. The design of the house assumes the homeowners no longer have a maid or domestic staff to undertake household chores for them, and acknowledges that in the modern age many wives are charged with keeping their own houses themselves.

Led by the chair*man* (ouch!) of the Bristol Branch, one Mrs AJ Newman, the All-Electric House followed the classic Modernist

Caroline Haslett illustration by Tina Altwegg

mould externally with clean lines and few flourishes, and is an interesting experimental design concept lurking in the Bristol suburbs. Commissioned by the Bristol Branch of the Electrical Association for Women, it was designed by local architect Adrian Powell (who was a man) based on the results of a questionnaire asking women what they would find most revolutionary in a modern home. After all, "in house planning there is a crying need for the expression of a woman's point of view"[295].

The All-Electric House is a four-bedroom house with a long sitting area, and a small dining room with a hatch through to the electrical built-in kitchen. All of the light fittings were electrical tubes, and there were power points in useful places… as opposed to the useless places they were often retrospectively fitted in older properties. In a paper about the labour-saving home, the University of Westminster wrote: "The house was planned to be 'labour-saving', so the housewife would 'not have to carry wood and coal, clean dirty grates with the resultant dust on floors and furnishings, wind any clocks, clean any metal used in the construction, buy any material for pelmets, clean windows frequently or have any chimney swept, and her cleaning, washing and decorating bills will correspondingly diminish'."[296]

Once the completed house was unveiled at a lavish ceremony by Catherine, Countess of Westmorland (Vice-President of the Women's Engineering Society), it was put on the market. The house sold for £1,000 within one week and was deemed a huge success.[297] Pleasingly, the house still stands and the current owners have maintained the house and garden in a manner sympathetic to its 1935 origins. Less good news is the fact that buoyed by the

295 'An All-Electric House for Housewife's Needs', 30 September 1935, *Western Daily Press*
296 sites.google.com/a/staff.westminster.ac.uk/electricity-for-women/home/the-labour-saving-home#TOC-The-All-Electric-House
297 By contrast, the average price paid for a house in Stoke Bishop in 2019 is £725,000, according to Zoopla.

success of the Stoke Bishop property, the Bristol Branch of the Electrical Association for Women commissioned a second All-Electric House nearby in Sneyd Park, which has fared less well over the decades and could use some TLC.

The Stoke Bishop house was described as one of the first all-electric homes in the UK, and although there had been a few others elsewhere none were as successful as this example. The houses had a novelty value and therefore were good publicity machines for the architects and engineers involved in designing and building them. The goal was to encourage women to think about electricity and how it could improve their quality of life, and to prove to builders and architects the valuable role women could play in the planning of a house.

Throughout the remaining decades of her buzzing career, Caroline Haslett would achieve so much more, including being the only woman delegate at the World Power Conference in Berlin in 1930; being the only woman on a 20-person committee during World War Two to consider electrical installation in post-war Britain; writing several books inspiring women and girls to work with electricity; being president of innumerable societies promoting women in electrical engineering; being made a Dame in 1947; and having both a road and a school named after her.

KIM HASTINGS

1954-2016, ART THERAPIST

Kim Hastings, who spent the last few decades of her life living in Montpelier, Bristol, helped to set up the Bath Counselling and Psychotherapy Asylum Project to work with refugees and asylum seekers who had been abused and tortured. This empathy was doubtless born after spending her teenage years with her family in South Africa, where she worked on anti-apartheid and feminist campaigns.

After returning to the UK, Kim married Jon Hastings and the couple lived in Cardiff where they had two daughters, Shelley and Abbie. Concerned about bringing up children in London (where they were living by this time), the family moved to a commune in Bristol and settled there. Although the marriage broke down after a few years, Kim trained as a humanistic psychologist and art therapist before joining the Bath Counselling and Psychotherapy Asylum Project (now the Trauma Centre).

Kim experienced hearing loss from her mid-20s onwards, eventually becoming completely deaf, but she felt this gave her a unique insight into her work with refugees. In addition to the above, Kim was also involved with the Greenham Women's Peace Camp, the Campaign Against Nuclear Disarmament, the socialist walking group Red Rope, and she was a volunteer at the Amnesty International bookshop on Gloucester Road.

ETHEL HAWKINS

born 1882, SHEROIC NURSEMAID

We do not have a definite name for this woman, which is scandalous when you learn what she went through, but the census reports suggest she may well have been Bedminster-born Ethel May Hawkins, so that is what I am going with.

In the late 1890s, Rock Cottage (now repurposed for business use) at 240-248 West Street, Bedminster, was the grand home of the Bennett family. John Bennett had made his fortune as a colliery owner and was a very affluent man. With his wife Florence, he had seven daughters and three sons.

The story goes that toddler Henry Bennett was causing so

much noise and disturbance one afternoon that his nursemaid, Ethel, took him out into the garden so his elder siblings would not be disturbed during their school lessons. While sitting on the side of the old well at the bottom of the garden and holding Henry in her arms, Ethel was terrified when the wall gave way beneath her and both she and Henry tumbled to the bottom of the well. Ethel had wrapped herself around the young boy to protect him, meaning that it was she alone who became agonisingly impaled on a rusty pipe at the bottom of the well.

Ethel called for help for more than an hour before her cries were finally heard and she was rescued. But never once during her ordeal did she let go of young Henry or allow any harm to come to him. Both Ethel and the boy made a full recovery and the brave nursemaid would go on to marry the Bennett family's gardener. However, young Henry was tragically killed in action during World War One.

MARY HAYS

1760-1824, WRITER

It was unusual in the 1790s for a woman to publicly be a radical feminist yet that is exactly what writer and philosopher Mary Hays was, and she became notorious for her beliefs.

Born into a dissenting family in Southwark, London, as a teenager Mary Hays fell in love with a fellow dissenter named John Eccles but their marriage was forbidden by her family, who felt Eccles was from a lesser family. Undeterred, the couple still met in secret for walks and exchanged hundreds of love letters. In a heartbreaking twist, once Mary's parents had been persuaded the marriage could go ahead, Eccles died of a fever in 1780, leaving his 20-year-old fiancée devastated. She wrote to Eccles' sister saying: "The best beloved of my soul! All my pleasures and every opening prospect are buried with him."[298] Mary vowed she would never marry and instead turned to writing to find fulfilment.

Through her writing, Mary spoke out against the slave trade and began to attend public lectures on the topic. She also sometimes wrote under the pseudonym Eusebia[299], including the 1791 pamphlet *Cursory Remarks on An Enquiry into the Expediency and Propriety of Public or Social Worship,* which condemned the social aspects of worship and the established church. She received favourable reviews for this but it was after being given a copy of Mary Wollstonecraft's *A Vindication of the Rights of Woman* in 1792 that her writing really changed direction.

The book made a huge impression upon Mary and she sought out its author, who was a member of a group of radical Jacobin intellectuals. Mary promptly joined the group and asked Wollstonecraft to comment on her own volume of feminist writing, 1793's *Letters and Essays, Moral and Miscellaneous* (Mary expresses her admiration for Wollstonecraft on several occasions in this book, most notably saying: "The rights of woman, and the name of Wollstonecraft, will go down to posterity with reverence, when the pointless sarcasms of witlings are forgotten."[300])

Her next book was the novel *The Memoirs of Emma Courtney* in 1796, which was semi-autobiographical and partly based on her own love letters to William Frend, who had not returned her affection; clearly her vow to remain pure to Eccles' memory had worn thin. But what shocked readers and critics was the celebration of female sexuality and passion in the book, particularly when the heroine offers herself to a man to whom she is not married… and who spurns her advances. While the response to the book was

298 chawtonhouse.org/wp-content/uploads/2012/06/Mary-Hays.pdf

299 Eusebia was the second wife of Roman Emperor Constantius II. It is also the name of the Greek philosophical concept of piety.

300 Ibid.

largely positive, critics were cautious about Mary's claims that women should be independent of men for their happiness.

She followed this with what seems to be a response to *A Vindication of the Rights of Women* in her (initially) anonymously published 1798 book *Appeal to the Men of Great Britain on Behalf of Women*. In this volume, she sets out a demand for better education for women and states quite categorically that women are in no way inferior to men. In quick succession, her 1799 novel *The Victim of Prejudice* challenged the patriarchy and ridiculed it. However, due to a change in attitudes in society towards radicals and Jacobins, the novel was unfairly badly reviewed.

Undeterred, Mary continued to write with the goal of improving the lives of women, and spent three years working on the six volumes which comprised her 1803 tome *Female Biography: or Memoirs of Illustrious and Celebrated Women of All Ages and Countries*, which highlighted the lives of 294 previously overlooked women.

Mary wrote for all of her life, defying the critics who felt her views were too radical for contemporary society. However, she was unable to earn a good living from her writing and was constantly moving house and city to try and find a more affordable way of life. It was for this reason that in 1814 she came to live in Hotwells, Bristol, where she spent the final ten years of her life as a lodger with Penelope and William Pennington, became friends with influential Bristolian women such as Hannah More and wrote evangelical tracts to educate the poor. It would seem from her letters, however, that Mary was not happy living in Bristol, although perhaps this was less to do with her hosts and more to do with the unfavourable response to her writing which she was receiving at the time. Mary's final wish was for a simple tombstone which said nothing more than her name, and this is what she was granted as if she wished to fade into obscurity.

Her tombstone can be visited in Abney Park Cemetery, Stoke Newington, London.

And another thing... Mary's landlady **Penelope Pennington** is herself an interesting character. In 1791, she married William Pennington, who was Master of Ceremonies at the Hotwell Spa and presided over all public events there. This was around the time that the 'milkmaid poet' Ann Yearsley opened her library at the Colonnade in Hotwells and, via his friendship with Ann, William met her troubled acquaintance Penelope Weston. Owing to her brother's bad behaviour, Penelope had been brought into financial ruin so William proposed marriage to make her life easier. Penelope accepted and the couple lived happily at Dowry Square for the next three decades until her death in 1828. Penelope and William were honoured with memorial plaques in the Dowry Chapel, although the building was demolished in 1872.

Please also see: Hannah More (vol one), Mary Wollstonecraft (vol one), Ann Yearsley (vol one).

GERTRUDE HERMES

1901-1983, ARTIST

At long last there is a reason to reference David Bowie in *The Women Who Built Bristol*. I feared this moment would never come (largely because he was a man with no particular connection to Bristol beyond having performed here a few times). The reason we can mention Bowie is because his private art collection included a 1926 bronze door knocker of a swallow by the feminist sculptor, printmaker and wood engraver Gertrude Hermes, who lived out her final years at 5 Sion Hill, Clifton.

Born in Kent to German parents, Gertrude (or Gerty to her friends) first attended Beckenham School of Art and then Leon Underwood's Brook Green School of Painting and Sculpture — where her contemporaries included the sculptor Henry Moore, Surrealist painter and photographer Eileen Agar (who described Gertrude's work as having "a sort of womb magic"[301]) and Gertrude's future husband, wood engraver Blair Hughes-Stanton. They married in 1926 and spent their honeymoon in a tent at the end of Moore's garden. The couple worked together on wood engravings for the 1926 edition of John Bunyan's famous book *The Pilgrim's Progress*. However, the marriage was not a happy one and the couple divorced in 1933, although not before children Judith and Simon had been born. In her new role as a single mother, Gertrude was not afforded the luxury of a private studio to work from, so made her prints at the kitchen table and carved sculptures in the spare bedroom upstairs.

Gertrude's work was somewhat austere in style but she was not prepared to compromise. In a series of engravings made between 1933 and 1953, she tied modernist language to psychological concerns, revealing an intense series of work which earned her a good reputation. Gertrude was a regular exhibitor at the prestigious Royal Academy in London, and in 1939 had the honour of being shown at the Venice International Exhibition. Along with exhibitions, Gertrude supplemented her income by teaching wood engraving and lino-cutting at the Central School of Art in London during the 1940s and 1950s, from where she would sometimes take her students to the nearby London Zoo to make images of the animals. However, during World War Two she escaped the UK to live in Canada.

By 1963, Gertrude was as Associate of the Royal Academy,

301 Matilda Bathurst, 'Gertrude Hermes Gets a Room of Her Own' in *Apollo*, 26 November 2015.

becoming a full Royal Academician in 1971. But she stuck two fingers up to the patriarchal Academy by kicking up a stink at the fact that no women were allowed to attend the dinner following the Annual General Meeting of Academicians. Such was the impact of her protest that the following year both Gertrude and her lifelong-friend Barbara Hepworth, herself an extraordinary sculptor and artist, took their places at the dinner table alongside all the men.[302]

It was 2015, some 32 years after her death and 33 years after she had been given an OBE, before Gertrude finally received the solo exhibition which her work demanded and this was 'Wild Girl: Gertrude Hermes' at the Hepworth Wakefield Gallery.[303] It achieved excellent reviews, with *AnOther Magazine* writing: "Everything exudes the joy apparent that Hermes found in making her work, and that joy is infectious."[304]

Linking back to Bowie's appreciation of Gertrude's swallow knocker, the 'Wild Girl' exhibition came about after her frog knocker was discovered on someone's front door by an eagle-eyed gallery curator (wildlife was a significant feature of her work). Captivated by the frog, the curator began a mission to celebrate Gertrude's work. The exhibition included 120 pieces, covering pictures as well as sculptures, although Gertrude herself had never exhibited the two together in her lifetime.

302 Harry Seymour, 'Wild Girl: The Artistic Rebellion of Gertrude Hermes' in *AnOther*, 18 November 2015.
303 hepworthwakefield.org/whats-on/wild-girl-gertrude-hermes/
304 Harry Seymour, 'Wild Girl: The Artistic Rebellion of Gertrude Hermes' in *AnOther*, 18 November 2015.

HANNAH HIGGINS

born c1890, PEACE CAMPAIGNER

A socialist, suffragist and member of the Bristol Independent Labour Party (ILP), Hannah Higgins was committed to campaigning for peace in the face of World War One. Alongside her trades unionist husband Tommy and activists Mabel Tothill and Annie Townley, Hannah was part of a closely knit Bristolian group which was determined to combine socialism, women's suffrage and peaceful ideals to bring about a better future for the UK. They would continue to campaign until well into the 1920s and Hannah urged other women to recognise the importance of politics in their own lives.

Hannah demanded: "Let us tell the men that we will not bring babies into the world to be killed … they should tell the conscriptionists that unless they could have free born babies they would not have them born slaves."[305] Hannah's argument was that because women were not entitled to vote, they should shoulder no responsibility for the fact England had ended up at war and therefore they should not have to fight nor see their men called up to fight.

Hannah was Vice President of the Bristol Women's Labour League and acted as a delegate from the ILP to the South West Federation. She also worked with Annie Townley in the newly formed East Bristol Women's Suffrage Society, carrying out propaganda and electioneering work to support Mabel Tothill when she stood as the prospective Labour candidate for East Bristol in 1912. In 1914, Hannah formed a women's committee to support Bristol's locked out and striking tramway workers and she called on women to support the men in their fight.

305 'Stop The War' in *Western Daily Press*, 26 January 1916.

When so many ILP men (including her husband Tommy) were imprisoned during World War One for being conscientious objectors, Hannah and her sister socialists took on the work which had previously been done by those men. This needed to be done in addition to caring single-handedly for any children they may have and Hannah was the mother of two young daughters. This work included representing the Bristol branch of the ILP at national conferences and being delegates at affiliated organisations. In the built up to the 1918 general election, Hannah was also chairing public meetings alongside Annie Townley.

Please also see: Beatrice Baker (vol two), Mabel Tothill (vol one), Annie Townley (vol one).

GERALDINE HODGSON

1865-1937, LECTURER

Brighton-born Geraldine Hodgson studied for an undergraduate degree from Newnham College at the University of Cambridge (graduating in 1889) before becoming head of the women's secondary teaching training department at Bristol University College[306] in 1902... where she didn't stand for any patriarchal nonsense whatsoever.

In 1911, Geraldine was among a group of female graduates who formed the first Bristol branch of the British Federation of University Women (that lasted until 1992), which campaigned to see women's achievements in the workplace treated equally to men's. Some 26 women attended the inaugural meeting in Bristol, which was held at Clifton Hill House on Lower Clifton Hill at 5pm

306 Bristol University College is now the University of Bristol.

with business conducted in a civilised manner over tea and cakes. The Bristol branch had a number of goals including wanting a Bristol woman to serve on the Bristol Education Committee, although this was a slow process and they were still pushing for this four years later in 1915. The branch was also concerned with private schools, women's suffrage and improving the lot of working-class women in east Bristol (via work with the National Union of Women Workers). Until 1916, an average of 25 women attended the regular meetings, although there were recurring problems of financially sustaining the group and of maintaining membership.[307]

Aside from education, Geraldine was a key committee member of the Bristol and West of England Suffrage Society, and in February 1908 she chaired a Society meeting which deplored the torture of militant suffragettes in the prison system. She also wrote a series of informative pamphlets for the National Union of Women's Suffrage Societies. However, once the Women's Social and Political Union increased its levels of militancy and violence, Geraldine withdrew her support from the suffragette organisation, going so far as to step down from a suffrage meeting at the Victoria Rooms because the guest speaker (Forbes Robertson) was known to be a supporter of militant tactics.

Her dismissal from the university in 1916 appears to have been due to strained relationships with colleagues, the fact she was unhappy about the education department being removed from the Faculty of Arts and protracted disagreements with the university about salary levels. She was justified in this because, in 1911, Geraldine's annual salary as Lecturer in Education was £200, while a Mr T Foster with the same job title at the same university in the same year was being paid £400, despite not even

307 Brenda Bardgett, 2004, 'Bristol Association of University Women: The Early Years 1911-1928' in *The Regional Historian*, p28-32.

having the doctorate that Geraldine did.[308] In 1913, she had also complained about "certain unnamed persons" at the University of Bristol who wanted to "undermine her position and make it impossible"[309], which appears to have been an instigating factor in her downfall.

Such was her influence that when Geraldine was sacked, 37 of her former students wrote to the press to defend her, stating: "Under her inspiring direction, our period of training became, to a degree unique in our experience, a time of mental quickening, of intellectual growth. Her wide knowledge, her sound judgment, her inflexible logic, stimulated and energised us all."[310] As if this wasn't endorsement enough, Geraldine was also considered "one of the most distinguished of the teacher trainers appointed to universities before the First World War"[311], so the fact she had been sacked was truly shocking.

In addition to writing widely on the subject of education, Geraldine was the author of four novels plus a great number of books on religious studies. She died at home at 17 Sion Hill, Clifton, in 1937.

Please also see: Helen Wodehouse (vol two).

308 Claire Davey, 2012, 'Teacher Training in Bristol, 1892-1930: A Comparison Across Gender and Through Time'. Undergraduate dissertation at the University of Bristol, p21.

309 Carol Dyhouse, 1995, *No Distinction of Sex?: Women in British Universities, 1870-1939*, p156.

310 Geraldine Hodgson, 'To The Editor' in *The Spectator*, 29 July 1916.

311 Carol Dyhouse, 1995, *No Distinction of Sex?: Women in British Universities, 1870-1939*, p155.

VERA HOLE and LOTTIE COTTRELL
born 1909 (Vera) and born c1905 (Lottie), SPEEDWAY STARS

In the 1920s, the relatively new sport of speedway, or dirt-track motorbike racing, was, like most things, a male-dominated area. That was until Irish woman Fay Taylour came along and became the most successful female speedway rider of the day; she also devoted her time to changing the perception of women in the activity. Speedway was an exciting and dramatic spectator sport, with these daring new machines racing laps at thrilling speeds around dirt tracks... and occasionally bursting into flames.

Following in Fay's inspiring path were two local speedway riders: Vera Hole (also known as 'Sunny Somerset') from Watchet and Lottie Cottrell from Bristol. With the respected Douglas motorbike company — which manufactured bikes specifically for speedway, most notably the Dirt Track Douglas — being located in Kingswood from 1907 to 1957, Bristol was in a good position to support its residents who wanted to take up this new and exciting sport... including female ones.

Finding detailed information about Lottie or Vera is tricky. The *Western Daily Press* reports that on 8 May 1928, Vera — who was the better known of the two — was out with the newly-formed Exmoor and District Motor Club when she swerved to avoid a dog and crashed, sustaining injuries so bad that she needed medical attention.[312] Then, in April 1930, Vera took part in a women's speedway event at Wembley, London, were she was thrown over her handlebars and broke her collarbone. The English Motor Union chalked this accident up on its list of reasons why women should be banned from the sport, and on 30 May 1930

312 'Injured in the Motor Club Trial', 8 May 1928, *Western Daily Press*

it once and for all prohibited women from participating in dirt-track racing claiming — bafflingly — the activity posed a risk to women's fertility. This sexist ban remained in place until the late 1960s, despite fevered opposition from female riders including the ever-vociferous Fay Taylour.[313]

Vera and other female speedway stars may have been banned from the sport in 1930 but that didn't stop Vera's male relatives, Bristolians Derek and Johnnie Hole, from being influenced by her and becoming speedway stars in their own rights. Vera also had three brothers, including the well-remembered Billy Hole, who were speedway riders, so the sport is clearly in the family genes… although Vera was the only female dirt-track rider in the Hole family about whom we know.

Bristol had two speedway stadiums in its time. One was the Knowle Stadium on the Wells Road, which was home to the Bristol Bulldogs speedway team. This was demolished in 1961 and the residential streets of Long Eaton Drive and Ravenhead Drive now occupy the site. After this, the Bulldogs moved to Bristol Rovers' stadium at Eastville for the 1977 and 1978 seasons. There are currently no speedway stadiums in the city although a committed groups of fans are campaigning to find a suitable location and return the sport to Bristol.

And another thing... One woman who was a confirmed fan of the Bristol Bulldogs was Knowle's **Louise Brown**, who in 1978 made history as the first-ever baby to be born via IVF. Louise was sometimes spotted at the Eastville speedway stadium with her parents. She still lives in Bristol.

Please also see: Lillian Allen (vol two), Rosina Douglas (vol two).

313 speedwaylife.com/miss-eva/

FRANCES HOLMES

born c1885, DAREDEVIL

Here are a few things that were happening on Monday 9 September 1912: Winston Churchill was Prime Minister, women still didn't have the vote and (randomly) a new comet was discovered. Someone who might have had a good chance of seeing the new comet was young Ms Frances Holmes… owing to the fact she had taken it upon herself that day to ascend the spire of St Nicholas Church (which still stands on the corner of High Street and Bristol Bridge, opposite Castle Park). Repairs were being undertaken to the church roof, which meant there was a steeplejack's sling already in place: Frances hopped in and hoisted herself up to the top of the spire. Was it a protest? A dare? An impulse? A cry for help? Fun? Alas, we know nothing more about who Frances was or why she did this, but we are assured "a large crowd witnessed the incident".[314] It seems wrong that such a bold and adventurous move for a young lady should be overlooked by the history books, hence Frances' inclusion here.

ETHEL HOOK

1884-1975, SINGER

From Bedminster slum to regular concert contralto and occasional movie singer, Bertha Beatrice Butt showed great potential but lived her life in the shadows of her big sister. I'll be honest, she didn't achieve any grand fame but the story of Bertha Butt (who chose the stage name of Ethel Hook: Hook being her mother's family name) is one which charms me and so I am sharing her

314 'Local Happenings', 13 September 1912, *Clifton and Redland Free Press*

with you. NB: You will almost definitely have heard of her older sister, the singer Clara Butt who became a national treasure. With a sister whose star was this bright, poor Ethel was sentenced to a life in permanent second place.

Ethel was born at 1 Sidney Terrace, Bedminster, as the tenth child (of 11) to Clara and Henry Butt. By 1901, the family had moved to 94 Coronation Road but they remained in south Bristol. A number of the Butt children were encouraged on to the stage, and alongside Ethel and Clara, sisters Pauline (who also adopted the surname 'Hook' for professional purposes) and Hazel joined them for music lessons.

By 1903, Clara's star was shining bright and the lesser known sisters were regularly singing together in Bristol and Bath, receiving polite reports in the local press. In a 1904 concert headlined by superstar Clara at the Colston Hall, Ethel and Pauline were one of the support acts: "Much interest centres in the first appearance of Madame Butt's sisters, the Misses Pauline and Ethel Hook, in our city. Their duets have been spoken very highly of in other music centres, and Bristolians are anxious to hear these two young artistes for themselves."[315]

Clearly they were a hit: "The Misses Pauline and Ethel Hook … were warmly welcomed. The excerpt was effectively rendered, and manifested that the young ladies possess vocal organs that have been judiciously trained, their effort being far more finished than when some time ago they appeared at Bedminster Town Hall. They were twice re-called." This is far more glowing than for the poor man who graced the stage before them and received simply "a tame reception"[316]. Ethel continued performing locally with Pauline for the next few years, always to a warm but muted reception, and always being reported in the press with the fact

315 'The Clara Butt Concert' in *Clifton and Redland Free Press*, 18 March 1904.
316 'Madame Clara Butt's Concert' in *Western Daily Press*, 22 March 1904.

Ethel Hook illustration by Rhi Lee

they were "Madame Clara Butt's sisters" following their names, which must have stung.

In 1909, Ethel married David Hastings-Wilson in Hampstead, London, although she still seemed to be living and performing in Bristol, now without Pauline. A report of a 1911 concert in Bath said: "It is gratifying to observe that her style has matured. That she is a thoroughly accomplished artist, nobody could hear her sing ... and deny. It was a fine effort."[317] So fine there was not even a mention of her celebrated elder sister!

During World War One, Ethel embarked on a tour of military hospitals, singing to entertain the wounded troops. The tour was organised in Clara's name, so once again Ethel was cast in her sister's shadow. "The whole of the wounded soldiers at the Bristol Royal Infirmary ... had a rare treat yesterday afternoon in the shape of a concert by artistes well known in the musical world. Madame Clara Butt, who has already done splendid work on behalf of soldiers, is sending an excellent company of artistes – including her sister, Miss Ethel Hook – upon a tour of military hospitals and yesterday it was the Infirmary's turn to enjoy the privilege."[318]

There was excitement for Ethel during the 1920s when, post war, her own career showed signs of rising without Clara's assistance. She made several records, sang regularly on the radio, performed at venues in London and even toured in the US. However, the clouds closed in when her husband David filed for divorce in 1925 on the basis that she had had an affair with a man called Cyril Baker. Her second marriage was to actor Arthur Argent in 1927, with whom she lived at 2A Belvedere Road, Redland. In 1928 and 1929, Bertha sang on a number of short film reels, which were largely promotional tools showing off the

317 'Miss Ethel Hook' in *Clifton Society*, 27 April 1911.
318 'Mdme Clara Butt Delights Wounded Soldiers' in *Western Daily Press*, 17 December 1914.

ability to record sound in this new-fangled age. Her last known recording was a 1971 broadcast on BBC Radio 4 which celebrated her sister Clara, and Ethel spoke proudly about her elder sibling. Ethel died in 1975 while staying in Norfolk. She had outlived Arthur by 15 years and was the last surviving Butt sibling.

Please also see: Clara Butt (vol one).

HENRIETTA HOPE and WILLIELMA CAMPBELL

1750-1786 and 1741-1786, BENEFACTORS

There is a beautiful building known as Hope Chapel located on what is now called Hope Chapel Hill (just off Granby Hill in Clifton), which was founded in 1784 by the Scottish friends Lady Henrietta Hope and Willielma Campbell (Viscountess Glenorchy), who had met in 1772. The two devoutly religious women had visited the health resort of the Hotwells Spa in 1780 in search of a tonic to revive Henrietta, who was not at all well. Both were struck by the beauty of the area and decided to stay put.

The two women fell in love with Hotwells and, frustrated that the only places of worship at the time were up a steep hill, they were united in their desire to build a chapel there, working hard to find a suitable location. Henrietta donated £2,500 to the construction of the chapel and, owing to the fact she died shortly before it was completed, Willielma decided to name the building in her honour (Willielma had previously built a number of chapels and already had at least one named in her own honour in her native Scotland). In February 1786, a month after Henrietta's death, Willielma wrote to a friend to say: "A neat place of worship, plain but elegant, will be a suitable monument for my dear friend Lady Henrietta, which I mean to call Hope Chapel. It is to be finished this summer and will be opened next spring."[319] As it transpired, Willielma herself died just five months later and also never saw the finished chapel, although her executor Lady Maxwell ensured the chapel was completed in a manner that would be agreeable to the two recently departed friends.

The chapel was a great success and regularly welcomed up to 800 people through its doors for each service, although over the decades the numbers dwindled. It belonged to the Congregational Federation, which, when the congregation fell to single figures in 1975, applied for permission to demolish the Grade II listed building. This plan was strongly opposed by the community, which put in a planning application to convert it to a community centre, allowing the congregation to continue to meet there on a Sunday morning. The transformed building was reopened in June 1977 as the Hope Centre and it ran on a lease from the Congregational Federation as a successful arts centre and community centre for 25 years. In 2013, the crypt was converted into a public space following a lengthy programme overseen by Bristol and Regional Archaeological Services.[320]

KATE HORNER

1873-1957, CHOCOLATE FACTORY WORKER

While JS Fry & Sons was the biggest of Bristol's chocolatiers, the HJ Packer & Company Limited chocolate factory was giving it a run for its money and became the second largest. The business, which focused on the cheaper end of the market, was founded on Stapleton Road in 1881 by Edward Packer, who was a former employee of Fry's. Just nine years later in January 1890, his newest

319 AJ Green-Armytage, 1922, *Concerning Clifton*, p50-51.
320 With thanks to Katherine Martin for extra information about the regenerated Hope Chapel.

member of staff was a woman named Kate Elizabeth Horner, who was employed to hand-cover chocolate creams.

With Easton running through her veins, Kate was typical of many of Packers' staff. Her father Henry was a railway porter and the family initially lived at 7 Weston Avenue, close to Packers. Kate, who never married, remained living with family members for her whole life and, following the deaths of their parents, she and her younger brother Albert stayed at the family's subsequent home at 54 Roseberry Park until their own deaths. The modest two-storey house with one bay window still stands today.

At the time Kate joined the business, Packers was based in a house on St Paul's Street, where she worked from 8am until 6pm and earned 4s 6d per week, which was considered a good wage. She was still with the firm by the time Packer built his huge factory on Carlyle Road, Greenbank, in 1903, and she hadn't gone anywhere by 1922 when Packers had grown to be the fourth-largest chocolate manufacturer in the UK. In fact, such was her longevity with the firm that Kate was still with Packers in 1925 when her lengthy career with the business justified an article in the factory's staff magazine *HJP*. The following text is based on what Kate wrote in that piece.

"My first work (as far as I can remember) was hand covering creams in a small room fitted with two tables and domes for heating our chocolate," wrote Kate in 1925. "In one corner of the room we had a small copper to keep the chocolate in, and outside the window we had a lift, and when we wanted work sent up we shook the ropes and called out for what we wanted … I often think of the many happy days I spent in the old factory."

Talking about later developments with machinery at the firm, Kate went on to say: "The business still improved, and we had one machine installed for coating Packer's two-ounces-a-penny chocolates … It was placed in one corner of the room and I well remember the speed of it (how irregular it was), but what a wonderful machine it was to us! The girls from the other rooms, knowing when Mr Cole[321] was gone to lunch, would come down to see one line of work coated. This machine, being successful, others were soon added, and from that time I have super-intended in the machine rooms. I think we had about 38 of those coating machines before we left St Paul's."

As mentioned above, Kate was one of the early staff members who was still with Packers when the factory moved to Greenbank, as she explained: "I was sent to Greenbank with a few girls and machines in 1902. What a change it was for us after such small rooms to go into large and lofty ones! We found it terribly cold and had to return to St Paul's until the factory was properly heated. It must have been in 1903 when we really started work in the new factory. I am still in the same room, which has 50 coating machines, super-intended by Miss Barrett and myself ... Needless to say, working with one firm for so many years, I have seen many changes and improvements. The conditions under which we work today are far in advance of what they were when I first started."[322]

Unfortunately, Packer's struggled financially in the economic climate following World War Two and, by 1960, had been divested and became Carsons Ltd in 1962. Carsons would go on to buy up a number of struggling confectionery firms, including Elizabeth Shaw in 1968. The large Greenbank factory finally closed its doors in 2006 and the site has remained empty ever

321 Charles Bruce Cole was a confectionary salesman who, in 1886, invested £950 in Packer's then-ailing business to save it. From this point on, he took an active interest in the day-to-day running of the chocolate factory and, under his guidance, Packer's became the major player that it was at the time Kate Horner worked there. Following his death in 1912, the Bruce Cole Institute was opened beside the playing fields on Johnson's Lane to house the social and recreational activities of the Packer's employees. The building was sold to Bristol City Council in the 1930s when Packer's needed to generate some money and it is now known as the Whitehall Pavillion. It is currently in desperate need of regeneration.

322 cems.uwe.ac.uk/~rstephen/livingeaston/local_history/katehorner.html

since, with debate rumbling on about the best way to regenerate the neglected property.

Please also see: Elizabeth Fry (vol one), Elsie Griffin (vol one), Elizabeth Shaw (vol two).

ANNIE HORT and CLARA HORT
1866-1933 and 1872-1946, RESTAURATEURS

The Horts pub on Broad Street in the city centre is so named thanks to the siblings who ran a restaurant on the site: Annie and Clara (known as Bessie) Hort plus their brother Richard. The Hort family had long been involved with the catering trade and their mother Eliza (alongside her own mother) initially ran the Exchange Dining Rooms on nearby Wine Street.[323] In the 1901 census, the Hort family lived at 23 Small Street: father William, mother Elizabeth, daughters Annie, Clara and Edith, as well as four servants. In the 1911 census, the Horts are at the same address but by this time Annie is listed as head of the household as well as "restaurant keeper". The 1911 census also shows two cooks and two waiters from the restaurant to be living with them.

The Exchange was considered Bristol's premier restaurant and it is claimed that the first-ever cocktails mixed in Bristol were created there. Despite being run by women, like many upper-class restaurants of the day, female customers were only allowed into certain parts of the establishment. Indeed, the entire business was men-only until the outbreak of World War One, when the male soldiers began to complain they couldn't bring their wives and girlfriends for a nice meal out. Due to expansion, in 1922 the

323 Their father, William Hort, was not in the catering industry and instead was Bristol's chief rates collector.

Exchange was moved to a property on Broad Street where the signature dishes were oyster soup and Dover sole.

When Annie died in 1933, she left a fortune worth £12,617 14s 7d, which is equivalent to £500,000 in contemporary money. In 1939, Clara, now aged 71, was company director and she was living at 32 Pembroke Road, Clifton, with Richard. They had three domestic servants, which is rather grand for this time as most households were finding it hard to secure and maintain domestic staff after the changes wrought on society by the inter-war economy. In 1943, as the last surviving sibling, Clara sold the business to Frank and Aldo Berni, who a few decades later would establish the Berni Inns chain.[324]

FANNY HUNT

died 1822, BROKEN-HEARTED FIANCÉE

In volume one of *The Women Who Built Bristol,* we met Sarah Henley, the heartbroken barmaid from Easton who jumped off the Clifton Suspension Bridge after her lover broke off their engagement… but miraculously lived to tell the tale. In this volume, we meet Fanny Hunt, who was also left desperate and distraught after her fiancée broke her heart.

Fanny was engaged to a sailor whom she loved very much and she expected to marry him in July 1822 as soon as he returned to Bristol from his voyage to the West Indies. She was so determined to marry him that she completely spurned the advances of another man who tried to court her, insisting she was betrothed

324 In 1956, The Rummer in St Nicholas Market became the first Berni Inn, offering steak and chips dinners and starting the biggest restaurant chain outside the US. With thanks to researchers at Arnos Vale Cemetery (including Marion Blackburn, Hildegard Dumper, Liz Johnson and Janine Marriott) for generously providing extra information for this entry. eugenebyrne.wordpress.com/2010/12/21/what-i-did-today-berni-inns/

to her sailor and would not be tempted. Out of spite, the spurned would-be suitor wrote to Fanny's sailor claiming he had had a lusty affair with her which, of course, prompted the sailor to end his relationship with Fanny as soon as he returned to Bristol. Fanny was left so heartbroken that she vowed to take her own life.

Which was why, on 29 July 1822, Fanny was seen pacing up and down the harbourside in Broad Quay. When she realised her unusual behaviour had caught the attention of a concerned onlooker, William Gregory, she rushed away from him and jumped onboard a nearby moored boat. Gregory tried to follow her but Fanny jumped from boat to boat across the harbourside before throwing herself into the water. Gregory had been calling out for help and a nearby sailor dived straight in after Fanny, but he was too late and poor Fanny drowned in the River Avon.

Please also see: Sarah Henley (vol one).

ELLEN JEFFERIES

1837-1917, ENTREPRENEUR

It is probably not something you have ever given thought to, but the business of providing refreshments to people travelling by train had to begin somewhere. And in mid-Victorian Bristol, it was given a head start by Ellen Jefferies (née Sainsbury). She was so successful in her business that, by the time of her death in 1917, her estate was valued at £58,000, equivalent to almost £3.5 million today.

Ellen lived at Harefield Hall on Bath Road, Willsbridge, a grand estate near Longwell Green which she had been able to afford thanks to her own hard work, because she had certainly not inherited any money from her modest family. Harefield Hall was a plush 14-room property with more than 250 acres of land, and was a fitting home for a self-made success story who had built herself up via a railway catering enterprise.

Ellen grew up in Easton, where her parents Elizabeth and William Sainsbury ran The Three Blackbirds pub on Stapleton Road. As an enterprising young woman, Ellen had initially worked as a maid for a wine and spirit merchant at 7 Bath Parade, Redcliffe, and she was evidently inspired by both her boss and her father to find employment in the refreshment trade. By the early 1870s, Ellen was the Manager of the refreshment room at Cheddar train station and, by 1881, she was the "keeper of Refreshment Rooms" at Bristol Joint Station (BJS), where she managed a staff of 12 people and provided high-quality catering for travellers.

The BJS was a reinvigoration of Temple Meads Station, which, when it opened in 1840, was simply a hub known as Bristol Old Station for the Great Western Railway (GWR) to oversee the departure of trains from Bristol. By 1841, trains were also running to Exeter (operated not by GWR but by the Bristol and Exeter Railway service) on a new line which was added onto the existing Temple Meads track structure. With the addition of the Midland Railway in 1844 and its associated platforms and tracks, there was a need for a radical overhaul of the original station's design and this became the Bristol Joint Station in 1874. A contract Ellen held with GWR enabled her to cater on, for instance, all of the luncheon cars between Bristol and Liverpool, which was no small job, and by 1890 she was running refreshment rooms at Temple Meads on the first- and second-class platforms as well as onboard some routes. It is interesting to note that, based on advertisements placed in newspapers, she largely employed women in all roles, whether as waiters, secretaries or in management positions.

During the 1880s, Ellen had been living as a lodger with David Jefferies and his family in St George's and, following the death of his first wife, Ellen and David were married in 1887. The 1891 census reports the couple were living at Harefield Hall. Ellen also employed a companion in the form of 22-year-old Florence Maggs and there were a number of domestic servants.

When David died in 1900, it was observed that he "was well known in commercial and trading circles in Bristol and the neighbouring counties, and especially amongst those travelling on the Great Western Railway"[325], which implies he was also involved in the Royal Refreshments Rooms business, although he had previously been the Station Master at Axbridge, Somerset. His death made Ellen the official head of the household and the 1901 census records her profession as both "railway refreshment contractor" and "employer". She was now living at Harefield Hall with her unmarried younger sister Maria Sainsbury, who had become her new companion after David's death. Ellen and David had not had any children of their own, although Ellen was step-mother to David's adult children from his first marriage. Ellen defied convention and continued to work following her marriage and she ran refreshment rooms at Chippenham, Cheddar and Weston-super-Mare alongside her cafe at Temple Meads.

Recording Ellen's death in 1917, the *Western Daily Press* commented she "had been in indifferent health for some time, but up to the middle of the present week she was able to attend to her many philanthropic works"[326]. Most of Ellen's fortune went to her nephews, nieces and cousins. However, acknowledging the great debt she owed to many with whom she had worked on the railway canteens, Ellen's will also left a number of generous bequests to former employees as well as to hospitals and other good works. She had been a religious woman and donated regularly to the churches around Harefield Hall, including paying for a stained

325 'The Talk of Bristol' in *Bristol Mercury*, 8 May 1900.
326 'Death of Mrs Jefferies of Harefield Hall' in *Western Daily Press*, 19 May 1917.

glass window at St Anne's Church and being a bountiful donor to the building fund for All Saints Church, both in Longwell Green. She also left a Belgian centrepiece of a large metal Argonaut and Cupid which could be filled with flowers or fruit to the Bristol Museum and Art Gallery.[327]

There is a substantial and ornate Jefferies monument at Arnos Vale Cemetery remembering David and Ellen. And as for Harefield Hall, despite parcels of land belonging to the estate being auctioned off in September 1917, Harefield Hall itself clearly stayed in the Jefferies family for many decades because the records show a Margaret Jefferies who died there in 1981.[328] The property subsequently became a residential care home but, at the time of writing, sits empty.

And another thing... Ellen was a longstanding member of the Longwell Green Parish Council and, upon hearing many complaints from residents about how hazardous the evening walk between Hanham and Longwell Green was, she paid for oil lamps to be erected on the route. On another occasion, Ellen donated the trees that now stand on Bath Road, Longwell Green, which became known as the Coronation Trees.[329]

327 'Art Treasures for Bristol' in *Western Daily Press*, 23 July 1917.
328 Although Ellen had no children of her own, David had had children from his first marriage so Margaret is likely to be a descendant from this line.
329 With thanks to researchers at Arnos Vale Cemetery (including Marion Blackburn, Hildegard Dumper, Liz Johnson and Janine Marriott) for generously providing extra information for this entry.

JEMIMA
BARRAGE BALLOON

A barrage balloon is an enormous rubber or cotton silver-coloured balloon filled with hydrogen which can be used to defend against low-level enemy aircraft attacks by holding aloft cables that can cause a collision with anything that flies too close to it; when 'friendly' aircraft were flying, the balloons were lowered so as not to cause a risk. Bristol, Avonmouth and Shirehampton saw barrage balloons fill the sky from the very outset of World War Two, with about 12 of the massive structures being positioned to form a defensive 'roof' over the area. However, because of the aerodrome at Filton, it was not practical to cover the whole of the city with barrage balloons.

The balloons were each 63 feet in length, 31 feet tall and weighed 550lbs. Manoeuvring them and maintaining them required team work, skill and strength; not least because the balloons would need to be raised and lowered according to the perceived threat from enemy aircraft at any particular time. In addition, a 24-hour guard was required to monitor the balloons for signs of damage, as well as to ensure the wind was not blowing them in the wrong direction… or completely away, as occasionally happened in particularly strong winds.

So it was no small feat when, from January 1941, the Women's Auxiliary Air Force was permitted to take over the monitoring of the barrage balloons and relieve the men for other war work; the large No 11 Balloon Centre in Pucklechurch employed 880 women. Historian Ethel Thomas noted: "At first this suggestion was met with some dismay, but any doubt of the capability of women for such a strenuous task was soon dispelled. After training the girls proved equally as efficient as the men as balloon operators, although it was one of the hardest jobs undertaken by women in the war."[330] One of the Avonmouth barrage balloons was nicknamed Jemima by the women who operated her and on one occasion, in strong weather, Jemima broke free of her tethering and drifted away before crashing into electricity cables, inadvertently cutting off the electricity supply to the area.

Please also see: Ethel Thomas (vol one), Paule Vézelay (vol one).

MRS JOHNSON

1700-1814, CENTENARIAN

Described merely as "the mother of Mrs Weymouth of Post Office Bedminster", Mrs Johnson was an astounding 114 years old when she died on 24 January 1814. She reportedly "enjoyed her faculties to the last and was confined to her bed for only three weeks"[331]. Sadly, this is as much information as we can muster for Mrs Johnson, but it is so astonishing that a working-class woman living in the (then) squalours of Bedminster could achieve such a fine age in 1814 that she is crying out to be remembered.

Please also see: Mary Evans (vol two), Jane Martin (vol one).

ROSINA JONES

1908-1984, CANTEEN WORKER

When Rosina Agnes Jones took on a job in the canteen of the Bristol Aeroplane Company in 1936, she took on a tough role. During World War Two, hundreds of workers were kept fed

330 Ethel Thomas, 1989, *War Story*, p89.
331 *New Monthly Journal*, 1814, London

thanks to Rosina and her colleagues, who often worked shifts up to 12 hours in length. The staff at the Bristol Aeroplane Company depended on the canteen for sustenance, so readying the food and keeping the dining rooms clean was no small task. All food was prepared by hand, and surfaces were cleaned by scalding them with boiling water and scrubbing the floor with highly corrosive caustic soda, which can't have been good for the lungs or skin. However, Rosina was not merely confined to the staff canteen because she was also called upon to serve food in the management dining rooms, at events and even onboard during promotional flights for the Britannia aircraft.[332] In March 1943, Rosina married Frank Hipken and the couple enjoyed a long marriage.

Please also see: Dorothy Stanleick (vol two).

SARAH KANE

1971-1999, DRAMATIST

Throughout her short life, Sarah Marie Kane was plagued by depression. However, as seems to be so often the way, those most troubled by poor mental health are often among the most creative and Sarah was no exception. Playwright Mark Ravenhill wrote: "Kane's plays have almost certainly achieved canonical status. All over the world, they are seen and admired. Almost since the arrival of *Blasted* [in 1995], she has been regarded as the most important of the new British dramatists."[333]

The Essex-born playwright studied drama at the University of Bristol and remains linked to the city via her work with

332 Built by the Bristol Aeroplane Company in 1952, the Bristol Type 175 Britannia was designed to fly across the British Empire. Only 85 were built before production ended in 1960. However, it was popular with passengers for its smooth journey and quiet engines.
333 Mark Ravenhill, 'Suicide Art? She's Better Than That' in *The Guardian*, 12 October 2005.

the Bristol Old Vic, because the theatre periodically stages productions of her work. Inspired by Modernist writers such as TS Eliot and Samuel Beckett, Sarah sought inspiration for her writing from the claustrophobic horrors of history such as Nazi concentration camps and wartorn Serbia. During her brief career, Sarah wrote five plays and one short film (*Skin*, which was televised by Channel 4 in 1997), and her plays continue to be performed to critical acclaim around the world. More locally, for example, *Phaedra's Love* was produced at the Bristol Old Vic in 2005, followed by *Crave* at The Wardrobe Theatre on Old Market in 2017. Sarah took her own life in 1999.

MARYANNE KEMPF

1967-2018, CAMPAIGNER

Author's note: This entry was the hardest one to write in the whole book because Mas was a friend and colleague of mine.

Maryanne 'Mas' Kempf was a fierce advocate for women's rights throughout her life, and a particular champion and expert with regard to addressing violence against women and girls. Based in St Paul's, she dedicated an enormous amount of her time and energy to supporting women directly and to working on projects which looked at longer-term prevention and culture change in terms of violence against women and girls.

A former tattoo artist who had managed the Pierced Up tattoo parlour off Park Row, Mas was easily recognisable for her wild dreadlocks and head-to-toe tattoos. She was also a long-term trustee of Bristol Women's Voice, and gave up innumerable hours over the years to improving the work done by this charity. Mas regularly compèred Bristol Women's Voice events and brought

Maryanne Kempf illustration by Carrie Love

them to life with her vivacious personality. She was particularly determined to see the Bristol Zero Tolerance project developed as a model which could be rolled out to other cities across the UK, and was working on this even while fighting cancer.

In addition to working with Bristol Women's Voice, Mas volunteered with other Bristol projects including the charity One25, St Paul's Unlimited (a community partnership which aims to reduce crime) and her local Neighbourhood Partnership. She prioritised work that supported women, those in the sex trade, drug users and victims of crime. She also had a full-time job working for the domestic violence charity Survive in Kingswood and was a qualified Independent Domestic and Sexual Violence advisor. Where Mas found all of her energy is a mystery.

Mas' passion for the women's sector included the understanding that women needed to support and encourage one another. Her wit, energy, courage and determination are much missed by everyone who had the joy of knowing her. Mas was an activist whose impact on all of the communities and people she worked with was inspiring and profound. She is survived by her husband Ben, daughter Tilly and Steve the stripey dog.[334]

ELLEN KING

1896-1968, NURSERY SUPERINTENDENT

When a blue plaque was erected for Ellen King MBE in the Quakers Friars shopping area of central Bristol, it is probable that not many passers-by had any idea who Ellen was or why she was deserving of a plaque. However, Ellen was the resident superintendent (akin to a headteacher) of the Friars' Nursery School, which was Bristol's

334 Adapted with kind permission from bristolwomensvoice.org.uk/tribute-to-our-sister-maryanne-kempf/

first-ever nursery school and was located on Philadelphia Street. She was supported by 18 volunteers. The school was set up to assist "the needy child, the child who is delicate and whose home conditions make healthy, happy development impossible"[335]. In the school's 1931 annual report, Ellen wrote that it was "full to its utmost capacity, and the health record is unique in a school dealing with such small children. This is proof that these little ones are building a sound foundation which will enable them to face the elementary school."[336]

In 1925, Ellen and her colleagues at the nearby Friars' Play Centre on Rosemary Street[337] (which had a clinic set up by the Quakers to provide healthcare to children from poor families, as well as to add "sunlight, wisdom and knowledge" to the children's lives[338]) were fundraising to send 100 impoverished children to a holiday camp by the sea. Getting behind the campaign, the *Western Daily Press* wrote: "This is so good a cause that one does not hesitate in asking our readers to consider the claims of these children and to help them spend a week in the bracing air of Brean Down and Sandford."[339]

Tireless in her campaigning for children, Ellen was a regular speaker at public events to promote her school and to generate donations to keep it afloat. For example, she spoke to the Saltford Women's Institute (WI) about how the "school was much appreciated by mothers who were able to earn money, which they could not do if the babies were at home"[340]. Ellen's talk clearly had a big impact on her audience because, by the following April, the Saltford WI had conducted a successful door-to-door appeal

335 'Help Needed', 22 May 1930, *Western Daily Press*

336 'Good Work of the Friars' Nursery School', 6 March 1931, *Western Daily Press*

337 The Friars' Play Centre lives on in the form of Rosemary Nursery School and Children's Centre, which is now based at Haviland House, St Jude's.

338 'Infant Welfare', 13 June 1927, *Western Daily Press*

339 'Help Needed', 22 May 1930, *Western Daily Press*

340 'Infant School', 19 March 1937, *Western Daily Press*

asking for donations of eggs to, among other places, the Friars' Nursery School and a grand total of 1,955 eggs were donated.[341]

Ellen's philanthropic interests were not restricted to helping children from poor families to have a better life. She was also concerned with supporting families from the rundown areas surrounding Philadelphia Street. In early November 1934, she wrote a plaintive letter to the *Western Daily Press* imploring readers not to put unwanted furniture on their bonfires, pointing out that "a great many people are moving away from slum areas to the new estates — many of them have very little furniture to take with them", and offering her nursery school as a place to receive the donations to pass on.[342]

IRIS KNIGHT

1908-1985, COUNCILLOR

This Bristol councillor, who was born Iris Mae Lobb, worked hard in order to gain a position of power and to achieve some semblance of change for the future women of this city.

Iris' father George Lobb ran a cycle and engineering business on Stapleton Road, Easton, and Iris was the eldest of his five children, with the family living at 28 Warden Road, Southville. She was the only one of her siblings to go to private school but any hopes she had of attending university were dashed when her father's business was hit by the great depression of the 1920s and Iris was required to take a job as a clerk with a railway company to help support the family. "The depression was beginning to affect my father's business and from 1928 to 1930 he was unemployed," Iris remembered. "I was the only wage-earner for a family of six.

341 '1,955 Eggs For Hospitals', 29 April 1938, *Western Daily Press*
342 'Bonfires', 5 November 1934, *Western Daily Press*

My father, self-employed, did not qualify for the dole, so apart from the odd jobs he did we all lived on the 35 shillings a week I brought home ... Those two years turned me into a socialist."[343]

Iris' mother Bertha became so desperate for food to feed her family during the depression that she joined a demonstration at the Council House on College Green. This women-only procession was dominated by the repeated chant of "Bread for our children".[344] But despite this time of hardship, Iris recalled how the community spirit fostered by the need to club together for survival led to some good times: "The girls made their own clothes but they took the work round to friends' houses and all sewed together and gossiped or had a sing-song. Our brothers brought their friends as well, so we had great fun. We went to the cinema or the theatre by saving up for it. I walked to work every day to save 6d on tram fares and that paid for a cinema seat or a balcony seat at the Prince's Theatre."[345]

When she became a Socialist and a Bristol councillor, one area Iris was involved with was supporting the striking miners in the 1980s and she was an active member of the pressure group Women Against Pit Closures (WAPC), speaking at rallies and joining marches to support the men whose jobs were threatened by Prime Minister Margaret Thatcher's intention to shut down the British coal industry. WAPC was formed in May 1984 to defend the miners and Iris dedicated the final 18 months of her life to campaigning for the rights of those miners.

343 Helen Reid in David Harrison, ed, 1984, *Bristol Between the Wars*, p69-70.
344 Ibid, p73.
345 Ibid, p77.

LANDLADY OF THE JOLLY SAILOR
died 1751, SHOT BY SAILORS

There was once a pub and lodging house called The Jolly Sailor on Marsh Street in the city centre. As the name suggests, this pub was often frequented by naval men but not all of them were particularly jolly... as the luckless landlady found to her cost one day, when a fight ensued in the pub and she was shot dead after a bullet struck her in the throat.

When Bristol men were impressed (aka press-ganged) to sign up to work on the boats against their will, this inevitably led to desperate fights. And an article from 12 May 1751 explained there were a number of privateers hiding in a pub in Long Ashton and a press-gang was sent out to find them and force them to sign up. However, the privateers put up a strong fight and accidentally killed the leader of the press-gang. The following day, some of the same privateers were drinking in The Jolly Sailor when they were surrounded by the same press gang, which led to an extremely violent fight during which the pub's landlady was shot dead. At least one of the privateers also died during the fight.[346]

Since she was an innocent bystander to the fight *and* its cause, it is a double injustice that this poor woman lost not only her life but also her identity, given her name has been forgotten over the years. However, we will remember her in some small way today on this page. The Jolly Sailor survived well into the 19th century but is now long since demolished.[347]

346 texts.wishful-thinking.org.uk/Latimer1800/Annals1751.html
347 With thanks to Mark Steeds for bringing this story to my attention.

HARRIET LEWIS
1885-1967, GROCER

On the face of it, the life of Bedminster-born Harriet Bolt seems unremarkable. She was born into a working-class family in Whitehouse Lane, married at 19, bore children and ran a small but prosperous grocery shop in Easton. She didn't start a school or enter politics or invent something which changed the world. But what makes Harriet's story unusual is that her granddaughter Sheila Hayward researched her life and recorded it in the fascinating local history book *Harriet's Family.*[348] And in this biography we learn so much about Harriet's family, living conditions and what life was like for an everyday woman living in south Bristol through two world wars, the great depression and into an era of consumerism. The stories of ordinary women are so rarely recorded in this much detail and that is what makes Harriet's story so important.

As a child, Harriet saw her parents struggle to keep a roof over their heads and feed their children. But despite her father's alcoholism and the domestic abuse he rained on her mother (Sheila records it was common for wives to walk around sporting bruises and injuries with no attempt at hiding them, such was the ubiquity of the assaulted woman), Harriet grew into a fair and caring woman. Harriet's parents had run a successful grocery shop on North Street, Southville, when she had been a child, meaning Harriet and her siblings had grown up learning to help in the shop, with Harriet showing an aptitude for balancing the books. Unlike many of her peers, Harriet was able to read and write well, and she was particularly adept with numbers. She married her first husband at the age of 19. He was miner William

348 Sheila Hayward, 2008, *Harriet's Family*.

Fricker, with whom she had daughters Alice and Lilian, although they were yearning for a son to complete their family. Harriet was devoted to her husband who was a wonderful father, and was distraught when he was killed in an explosion at the mines in April 1911. The shock caused Harriet, who was only 26 when she was widowed, to miscarry the baby she was pregnant with at the time, and her elder daughter Alice (five years old at the time) was struck dumb for months by her grief. As a child, Harriet had been taught to sew by her mother and drew on this skill to bring in enough work to keep her daughters and herself going. She also successfully petitioned the mining board to provide an income for her daughters, since their father had been killed at work. However, this was far from a sexism-free experience.

Describing her experience petitioning the Miners' Board for financial support, Sheila writes that Harriet struggled to persuade the Board to take her seriously as an intelligent young woman: "The Board, all men, conferred, and decided that Harriet did have a case, she should be awarded a lump sum, to be paid out to her at no more than five shillings a week." But Harriet had wanted all the money upfront so she could buy a grocery shop and earn enough money to look after her daughters independent of handouts. The Board had other ideas: "They saw in Harriet a young, attractive woman who might conceivably squander all the money and then become destitute, in spite of their generosity." They declined Harriet's request for financial independence, assuming her to be irresponsible and predicting she would end up penniless and in the workhouse. The injustice of this to an intelligent and sensible woman like Harriet was infuriating; she simply wanted to draw on her experience of the grocery trade and her skills with bookkeeping to provide for her family.

Leaving the Board meeting, Sheila writes: "'Can't manage my money!' Harriet thought indignantly, but she was too dispirited

Harriet Lewis illustration by Rhi Lee

to take issue with the Board. 'If I had been a man of 26 they wouldn't have said that. Why are we women so looked down on? We do as much if not more than men to hold a family together.'"[349] This was neither the first nor last time Harriet would express her frustrations at the way women were treated as lesser beings than men. It was 1911 and women were lobbying the government for the right to vote and to be treated as equal citizens, although this was not a cause Harriet had time to engage in: she was too busy being a working single mother to her young, grieving children.

Eighteen months later, Harriet married again, to carpenter Fred Lewis, who was besotted with his new wife and treated her daughters as if they were his own. The family moved to Easton and bought a small grocery shop on Bloy Street. Harriet borrowed the money and defied the naysayers at the Miners' Board by making a huge success of the business. When Fred was sent away to fight in World War One, Harriet kept her shop and daughters going while grieving for two of her brothers who had been killed in the war and fearing the news that her second husband had also been killed... fears which were close to realisation when he was hospitalised with diptheria. In the era before antibiotics, diphtheria was often a death sentence but thankfully Fred survived.

In World War One, women all over Britain pulled together to keep the country running while so many men were away fighting. And in 1918, some women were granted the right to vote provided they met certain criteria: if they were over 30, owned property, were married to a property owner, or were a university graduate. Needless to say, many of the women who had campaigned so hard before the war for the vote were still unable to do so as they didn't meet these strict criteria and Harriet was one of those for whom the 1918 Act made no difference. Although she had not

349 Ibid, p68.

been directly involved in the suffrage campaign, Harriet still felt frustrated that women of her class were being ignored by the government: "'Looks as though poor women are being excluded again,' thought Harriet. 'Suppose they don't count still.'"[350]

In September 1920, Harriet, now in her mid-30s, gave birth to Fred's daughter Edna and the couple were delighted to have a child of their own. Resourceful as ever, Harriet juggled looking after a newborn baby with running the shop, but eventually tired of the hard physical labour and, in the late 1920s, now in her 40s, Harriet and Fred sold the Bloy Street shop. They bought a house on Heath Road, Eastville, in a newly-built area which was part of the expanding Bristol suburbs. It was a real sign of things changing: "The house was a brick-built pebble dashed semi, with bay windows upstairs and down, making the house much lighter than the Victorian and Edwardian houses Harriet had previously occupied," writes Sheila. "She loved her new house; the windows opened easily, compared to the old sash windows, and all the plumbing and wiring was neatly concealed in the walls."[351] The house was the envy of all her family and still stands today.

Harriet lived at Heath Road until she died in 1967 at the age of 83. Fred had died a few years earlier of lung cancer and, just as she always had, Harriet devoted her time and energy to looking after her extended family of children, grandchildren and great-grandchildren. Sheila's book *Harriet's Family* is a wonderful testament to the legacy of this strong and resourceful Bristolian woman who lived through an extraordinary period of history, seeing fast changes in every aspect of society.[352]

Please also see... Harriett Plaster (vol two).

350 Ibid, p108.
351 Ibid, p124.
352 With thanks to Mike Manson for the nomination of Harriet Lewis to this book.

MARION LINTON

1867-1952, DOCTOR, TEMPERANCE ACTIVIST

Marion Sanford Linton was born in Dorset as the third of six children to Catherine Linton and her solicitor husband Robert. The family had relocated to Cairns Villa, Westbury-on-Trym, by the time baby Marion was just one year old and she remained in the city until her retirement. She studied Biology at the University College in Bristol and sat the first of her exams in 1892. By 1906, Marion had qualified and established herself as a respected doctor and she would soon have the honour of becoming the third female doctor (with Eliza Dunbar Walker and Emily Eberle) to work at the Read Dispensary in Hotwells. She was also involved with the Bristol Refuge Society, for whom she offered advice and support on improving the hygiene and sanitary conditions of the women there, and later helped establish the Hotwells Day Nursery and School for Mothers, for which she was also the medical officer.

Marion was a woman of strict Christian faith (she and Emily Eberle were active members of the Bristol Free Church Girls' Guild) who, along with Eliza Dunbar Walker, subscribed throughout her entire life to the temperance movement, a subject about which she regularly extolled the virtues. As such, she was a member of the British Temperance Association and, for example, on one occasion in Fishponds in 1907, spoke to a meeting to dispel a few myths about the drink being a nutritious substance: "Some people said that [alcohol] was an excellent food but it was not so. Alcohol has very few food properties and if taken as food it was an extremely wasteful food." She also debunked the suggestion that alcohol kept you warm on a cold night by pointing out that the great explorers who went to search for the North Pole spent their days "amongst the icebergs but not alcohol".[353] Marion concluded in 1933 (although one hopes she took a break at some point in the intervening 26 years): "Total abstinence and temperance used to be the subject of people regarded as fanatics with bees in their bonnets, but within the last few years a great change has come over the scientific opinion on that subject ... It has been decided that alcohol was not a stimulant but a narcotic."[354]

As part of her commitment to bettering the living conditions of women and girls, Marion, who was a member of the Bristol branch of the Royal Sanitary Institute, gave talks on the topic around the South West. For example, in November 1911 she addressed a meeting organised by the Nurses' Social Union in Taunton on the subject of 'moral hygiene and eugenics'. The aim was to teach nurses and schoolteachers what they could do to improve the understanding of hygiene and cleanliness in children who came from poor and possibly unhygienic slum homes. "Dr Marion Linton's earnest address was of great practical utility, explaining how mothers of her acquaintance had dealt with the question of imparting knowledge to their children gradually from a very tender age, and had taught them, through the care of domestic animals, some of the vital truths of life, the sacredness of motherhood and the cherishing thereof."[355]

Surprisingly, given some of her above attitudes to topics such as alcohol and morality, Marion was a supporter of votes for women. More than this, she didn't simply support the peaceful National Union of Women's Suffrage Societies (NUWSS, of which she was a member of the Bristol branch) but she also supported the militant activities of the Women's Social and Political Union. In 1912, at the height of suffragette militancy and when suffragettes

353 'British Temperance Association' in *Western Daily Press*, 23 January 1907.
354 'Scientific Opinion' in *Western Daily Press*, 31 March 1933.
355 'Moral Hygiene and Eugenics' in *The British Journal of Nursing*, 25 November 1911, p432.

were hunger striking and being force fed in prisons, Marion spoke at a women's meeting in Clifton. She "considered that the suffragettes were justified in the hunger strike ... She thought the Government made a great mistake in continuing to feed them forcibly when they found it was so ineffectual. It was a disgrace on their part to continue to do so ... She had the greatest respect and the most wholehearted admiration for the women who had undergone [hunger strike and force feeding]."[356]

A few years later in 1917, Marion is reported as attending the annual general meeting of the Bristol branch of the NUWSS at the Hamilton Rooms on Park Street, which was presided over by Mabel Cross. It is good to know she was still involved with the suffrage campaign, and also that the NUWSS was still lobbying for votes for women despite other organisations, such as the WSPU, standing down during World War One.[357]

Marion remained unmarried and died in Weston-super-Mare in 1952 aged 84.

Please also see: Mabel Cross (vol two), Eliza Dunbar Walker (vol one), Emily Eberle (vol two), Lily Harris (vol two), Mary Milgrove (vol two), Lucy Read (vol two).

ROTHA LINTORN-ORMAN

1895-1935, FASCIST

It was while living at Upper Langford Court on the edge of south Bristol that, inspired by the Italian dictator Benito Mussolini, Rotha Beryl Linton-Orman began Britain's first fascist party in the

356 'Barbara's Budget' in *Clifton Society*, 28 November 1912.
357 'Women's Suffrage: Bristol Society's Annual Meeting' in *Western Daily Press*, 28 February 1917.

1920s. Born into a military family in London, as a girl Rotha kicked up a storm when she and a girl friend demanded to be allowed to join the Boy Scouts and it was this action which ultimately led to the creation of the Girl Guides in 1908. Consequently, in 1911, Rotha became one of the very first girls to receive a Silver Fish Award from the Guides, which was in acknowledgement of her outstanding service to the organisation.[358]

During World War One, Rotha trained to become an ambulance driver and by 1918 she was the head of the British Red Cross Motor School, training other drivers to work in the battlefields. It was during the war that she developed her strong sense of nationalism. When the war ended and while based at Upper Langford Court, Rotha advertised in the right-wing journal *The Patriot* for fellow anti-communists and, once she found them, she set up the British Fascisti (which would later become the British Fascists) in 1923. This was in direct response to the Independent Labour Party (ILP), which she felt stirred up class conflict and encouraged internationalism. Thankfully, the British Fascists never achieved as much as Rotha had hoped, largely because it was too closely linked in ethos to the Conservatives. Meanwhile, her hatred for communism meant Rotha was unable to align to Oswald Mosley's British Union of Fascists, because she felt Mosley was effectively a communist and his former alliance to the ILP appalled her.

Please also see: Beatrice Wise (vol two).

358 Silver Fish awards are still given in rare circumstances. Girlguiding (as the organisation is now known) explains on its website: "The award is for an exceptional contribution to a wide section of Girlguiding ... This award may be given to an active adult member of Girlguiding or one of the Branch Associations. Only a small number of these awards are granted."

LITTLETON WHALE
died 1885, SEA MAMMAL

When an enormous whale washed up near the brick and tile works at Littleton-upon-Severn on 5 January 1885, she caused quite a splash. Bella Durnell (whose husband was the foreman at the works) found the whale while out walking early in the morning and she was the first to alert the community to what she had seen. The whale was still just about alive when she was discovered but was moving feebly on the shore while the tide ebbed further and further away from her. But rather than try and drag the whale back into the water where she needed to be to stand any chance of survival, local fishermen used their boats to pull the ailing and frightened mammal even further away from the water. Inevitably, it wasn't long before she died.

The poor creature's carcass was displayed at Littleton for two weeks and later towed to St Philip's Marsh where she was displayed for a further two weeks. Curious folk could come and view her body in both locations for the price of 6d, and people were itching to have their photo taken while standing beside her. The Midland Railway even put on a special train from London Paddington to Thornbury (the closest train station to Littleton, but which closed in 1966) to take people to see her.

Most extraordinarily, the entrepreneurial Victorians — not content with charging people just to look at the whale or pose for a snapshot — set up a barber's shop inside the whale's mouth... so you could go inside and have a haircut (but only if you were male). A man of six foot was apparently able to stand upright inside her mouth without stooping.[359] Who on earth conceived of this idea and however did it progress from being an idea to

359 Lyn Carnaby, A Forgotten Landscape, 'Whale Wharf' short film, vimeo.com/177207667

an actual thing that happened? Extraordinary! A local fisherman called Hector Knapp wrote in his diary: "There was a whale come ashore at Littleton Pill and bid there a fortnight. [She] was 68 feet long. [Her] mouth was 12 feet. The queen claimed it at last and sold it for £40. There were supposed to be 40,000 people who saw it from all parts of the county and far and near."[360] While *The Dursley Gazette* reported on 31 January 1885: "Those who stood to leeward, and into whose faces the spicy breeze from the monster blew, held their noses and manifested in a very demonstrative manner that their olfactory organs were in no way delightfully tickled."[361] Which is a polite way of saying, almost a month after her death, the decomposing whale understandably stank.

Her remains were later turned into fertiliser and her bones were donated to the British Museum, London. The section of the shore where she was found in Littleton-upon-Severn is now called Whale Wharf in her memory and a stone plaque honours her story.

ALICE LOANE

1863-1922, AUTHOR

Given her education was at the Royal Naval School for Females, it should be little surprise that Alice Eliza Loane's first — and only — novel published under her own name was 1912's *Shipmates*. However, other work was published under the more ambiguous 'M Loane'. By the end of 1912, Alice — who lived at 22 Elmdale Road, Clifton — had become an active member of the Bristol Civil League and worked with them to try and address the prevalent issue of poverty in the city.

360 aforgottenlandscape.org.uk/projects/whale-wharf/
361 thornburyroots.co.uk/other/whale/

MARY LOBEL

1900-1993, HISTORIAN, EDITOR

Known to her friends as Roddy, Mary Jane Lobel was a redoubtable historian who was born into Bristol's staunchly pro-suffrage Rogers family at the end of the Victorian era. Living with her progressive family at 4 Avon Street, Temple Meads, it probably seemed inevitable to her relatives that young Mary would go on to achieve great things. And she did.

Mary attended Clifton Girls' High School and spent her school holidays working in Westbury-on-Trym with the Scottish linguist Walter Crum on several volumes of his *A Coptic Dictionary* (1929-1939), which was a study of ancient languages. It was via Crum that she met the eminent papyrologist Edgar Lobel, and despite his being in the army and several years older than schoolgirl Mary, the couple fell in love and Edgar referred to Mary fondly as "my lamb". The couple's marriage lasted more than 50 years and only ended when Edgar died in 1982.

After leaving school, Mary attended St Hugh's College at Oxford University where she wrote a history of the town of Bury for her thesis, which was to be her first published book in the early 1920s. Mary also developed a passion and skill for cricket while at university.

After graduation, Mary spent a short time in Norwich working as a teacher before she and Edgar moved to Oxford, living in a medieval house on Merton Street. The couple enjoyed walks and bicycle rides together, as well as countryside holidays in England and Wales. As a gesture of kindness to his busy wife, Edgar often chose to eat at the university where he worked to save Mary the trouble of having to cook for him. However, Oxford University was not the sole domain of Edgar because Mary worked as a librarian at Somerville College, which was a position she enjoyed enormously. This job afforded her the time and resources to carry on her local history research and she always donated a copy of her latest book to the library.

Following Edgar's death, Mary concentrated on producing three volumes of *The Atlas of Historic Towns,* which was responsible for her being awarded an OBE in 1990. By the time of her death in 1993, Mary had worked on more than ten voluminous editions of local history guides which spanned the entire UK.[362]

DENNY LONG

1944-2018, ARTIST

The multi-media artist Denise 'Denny' Long was popular throughout Bristol and Cornwall for her pictures which were galvanised by the elements of nature. Having been born in Bristol, she attended Redland High School for Girls and then the West of England College of Art (now the University of the West of England) to study 3D ceramics, from where she graduated in 1967. As part of her course, Denny was inspired by visiting art tutor Janet Leach to visit the ceramics village of Mashiko, Japan, where she developed her belief in Zen Buddhism. This time in Japan would influence Denny's work for the rest of her life.

Denny created art in a range of media, from painting and collage to etching and printing, and she shared this enthusiasm via her role as Head of Art at the Whitefield Fishponds Community School (now Bristol Metropolitan Academy). Denny's daughter Tamsin Costigan said: "She felt such joy in teaching that she started a children's Saturday art class at Hotwells Primary School which ran for 22 years, took on supply teaching at Colston's Girls'

362 Brian McGuinness, 'Obituary: Mary Lobel' in *The Independent*, 16 December 1993.

School and Redland High School for Girls, and ran evening adult learning art classes."[363]

Denny was also a busy member of the local art scene, being a member of Royal West of England Academy (RWA) on Queens Road, Clifton, as well as co-founding the group Women's Art Works in 1981. The RWA said: "Denny's etchings manifest a minimal approach to the medium, employing fine linear techniques combined with aquatint, Chine-collé and collagraph ... The overall effect of her work is one of calm, order and simplicity."[364] She exhibited widely in the South West, including frequently at the RWA as well as regularly in Cornwall.

In 1969, Denny married fellow Bristolian artist Sir Richard Long (he won the prestigious Turner Prize in 1989), with whom she had daughters Tamsin and Betsy. Following their divorce in 1995, Denny moved to live on a Dutch barge moored in Bristol, and then sailed it to Cornwall where she undertook further art courses and achieved greater success as a professional artist. She eventually settled in Zennor, near St Ives, where alongside her art she was the UK representative of the Tibetan Refugee Nuns Project, having been a practicing Buddhist for many years.

EVA LONGBOTTOM

1892-1957, SINGER, POET

Despite having been born blind, the singer and poet Eva Hannah Longbottom (the pronunciation of 'long-bo-tham' was encouraged by her upwardly mobile father so as to create an air of sophistication) was certain she had seen fairies. She told *Sherlock Holmes* writer — and spirit believer — Sir Arthur Conan Doyle: "I

363 Tamsin Costigan, 'Denny Long Obituary' in *The Guardian*, 10 August 2018.
364 rwa.org.uk/artists/denny-long

have seen many fairies with my mind's eye, that is, clairvoyantly. They are of various kinds, the ones I see. The music fairies are very beautiful."[365] Conan Doyle was fascinated by fairies and the supernatural, so this revelation from Eva enchanted him. And given Eva sometimes spoke at the Bristol Theosophical Society on Tyndalls Park Road, Clifton, this allusion to fairies is not out of character for her.

Born in Halifax, Eva spent most of her life at 19 Chandos Road, Redland, where she lived with her parents. Her devotion to Bristol was fervent and she wrote in 1933: "We have resided here now for more than a quarter of a century, and have learned to love Bristol very, very much indeed, so much so that we should be truly sorry were we obliged to leave the city of our adoption."[366]

Aged 17, Eva wrote an ode in honour of King Edward's birthday called 'The Message of the Birthday Bells', which she sent to him typed in braille. She received the following reply from the King's secretary: "Sir Arthur Davidson is commanded by the King to thank Miss Eva Longbottom for her congratulations and good wishes, written in braille, on the occasion of his birthday, and also to thank her for her photograph, which His Majesty has been pleased to accept."[367] A keen royalist, a few years later Eva sent a gift and a specially composed verse to the King's sister, Princess Mary, for her wedding and received this reply: "The Princess sends her grateful thanks both for the good wishes offered to her and for the pretty table napkin rings, which she has much pleasure in accepting. Her Royal Highness is much touched by the kindness and goodwill that have prompted Miss Longbottom's verses and gift, and is much interested to see how little Miss Longbottom's blindness has affected her ability to do good work."[368]

365 Arthur Conan Doyle, 1921, *The Coming of The Fairies*, p168-169.
366 Eva Longbottom, 1933, *The Silver Bells of Memory*, p53.
367 News in *Clifton Society*, 14 November 1907.
368 'Bristol Lady's Gift' in *Western Daily Press*, 17 January 1922.

Following her studies at the Royal Academy of Music in London, Eva was thought to be the first blind person to graduate from there when she did so in 1913. She performed endlessly in Bristol throughout the 1910s and 1920s, often at the Victoria Rooms in Clifton, and the local newspapers were filled with articles either announcing a forthcoming appearance or declaring how delightful a recent performance had been. Eva was clearly much loved in Bristol as well as elsewhere in the UK: "Although I have done a great deal of public work, my engagements had been confined to Bristol. But now [1908] a change came, and, during the next two years, I made several tours of the north, which were helpful financially as well as musically. The first of these began soon after my 16th birthday and a delightful time I had, making many new friends, which, to me at any rate, are one of the most precious things in life."[369]

After World War One, Eva wrote a number of poems in an effort to try and make sense of the countless losses of life and she felt her best effort was a piece called 'When Will My Spring Come?' She said of the poem: "The title was suggested by an article from the pen of Mr James Douglas, in which he said that when he listened to a certain thrush, it seemed all the time to be singing the words, 'When will my spring come?' It is only the title I owe to Mr Douglas, however. The thoughts in the poem itself are mine and mine alone."[370]

In 1933, Eva's memoirs *The Silver Bells of Memory: A Brief Account of My Life, Views and Interests* were published and, while I have not thoroughly read this book myself (although I have skimmed a copy and, at 388 pages, it is not nearly as brief as she claims), Eva's relative Richard Bartle has and he is not entirely complimentary: "Reading through this from cover to cover was

369 Eva Longbottom, 1933, *The Silver Bells of Memory*, p122.
370 Ibid, p201.

one of the most boring things I have ever done. Eva may have been a celebrated musician, but she was not the most exciting author in the world, and the number of times she stresses that she isn't bitter about being blind and continually professes gratitude to God leads me to conclude that she was trying to persuade herself as much as anyone else."[371]

Returning to the fairies, Eva concluded: "When I was young I had it so much impressed on me that fairies were imaginary beings that I would not believe in them, but when I was about 14 I began to realise them and now I love them. Perhaps it was the deeper study of the arts that brought them to me. I have felt a sympathetic vibration for them and they have made me feel that we are friends. I have had a great deal of happiness and good fortune in my life, and perhaps I can attribute some of that to the fairies."[372] Therefore it should come as no surprise that in Eva's book *Dreamtime Stories*, every single one of the stories within it includes a fairy or some other supernatural creature.

And another thing... The Bristol Lodge of the Theosophical Society has been located at 14 Tyndalls Park Road, Clifton, since the late Victorian era. The Theosophical Society was founded in 1875 by the enigmatic Madame Helena Blavatsky, who drew on spiritual religions she had encountered on her travels. While spiritualism was fuelled by spectacle (with faked ghost and fairy photos, table turning, séances and so on), theosophy was led by the more reasonable medium of discussion. One popular theosophist of her day was **Kate Symmons**, who lived in Bristol in the 1920s, spoke for the Society regularly and was a well-published writer. Eva Longbottom became friends with Kate and wrote: "She lived in Bristol for some years, but later her family left for London. Soon after her arrival she

371 youhaventlived.com/qblog/2009/QBlog231109A.html
372 Arthur Conan Doyle, 1921, *The Coming of The Fairies*, p168-169.

became interested in the work of the Physiological Psychological Society, and it was for the members of the society that I wrote my impressions of colour as seen by me through the medium of music and the spoken word."[373]

Please also see: Clara Codd (vol one), Edith Gilliard (vol two), Elsie Howey (vol one).

LOUISA
died 1800, MAID OF THE HAYSTACK

Described as having "prepossessing appearance and graceful manners, but obviously of disordered intellect"[374], a strange young woman who "appeared to be under 20 years of age"[375] suddenly arrived at a house in Flax Bourton in 1776 politely asking for milk. In the days afterwards, she was to be found sheltering under a nearby haystack (which she decorated with trinkets) until local women took pity on her, and gave her food and drink. *The Lady's Monthly Journal* wrote with a hint of romanticism: "She was extremely young, and strikingly beautiful; her manners graceful and elegant, and her countenance interesting to the last degree. Her deportment and conversation bore visible marks of superior breeding; yet there was a remarkable wildness and incoherence in all that she said and did."[376]

However hard everyone tried, the maid could not be persuaded to come indoors and take shelter because she said she feared men

373 Eva Longbottom, 1933, *The Silver Bells of Memory*, p169-169.
374 Cited in Rosemary Clinch, 1987, *Curious Bristol*, p33.
375 'Death of Loisa: The Maid of the Haystack' in *The Lady's Monthly Museum*, January 1801, Volume 6, p214.
376 'Louisa: The Lady of the Haystack' in *The Lady's Monthly Museum*, June 1801, Volume 6, p421.

and asserted that "trouble and misery dwelt in houses".[377] After a week of this, she was declared insane and placed in St Peter's Hospital, Castle Park, where she remained for more than a year.

As soon as she was released from St Peter's, the maid immediately returned to the house at Flax Bourton, again sought shelter under a haystack and again refused offers of a bed under a roof. Nobody was able to determine her name or where she had come from, and although she spoke English she had a strange accent which nobody could place. The mysterious maid remained living under the haystack for four years.

The renowned Bristolian writer Hannah More was one of the many who, in 1781, came to meet the strange maid (whom she named Louisa, or Loisa in some spellings) and it was Hannah's opinion that Louisa would be best cared for at the Henderson Asylum in Hanham at Hannah's own cost. However, the benevolent writer was also keen to make further investigations to find out who Louisa really was and to locate her family.

Alongside a fascinated Queen Charlotte (wife of the reigning King George III), another esteemed visitor was the Methodist cleric John Wesley, who visited her at Hanham a number of times. He wrote in his journal in 1783 that Louisa was "pale and wan, worn with sorrow, beaten with wind and rain, having been so long exposed to all weathers, with her hair rough and frizzled, and only a blanket wrapping around her, native beauty gleamed through all." He added: "She appeared partly insane, partly silly and childish. She would answer no question about herself, only that her name was Louisa." However, when Wesley returned to visit "the poor machine" Louisa two years later in 1785, he declared her behaviour had deteriorated from "silly" to "furious".[378]

377 Cited in Anne Stott, 2003, *Hannah More: The First Victorian*, p55.
378 Cited in Quentin Bailey, 2011, *Wordsworth's Vagrants: Police, Prisons and Poetry in the 1790s*, p174.

As part of Hannah's campaign to identify Louisa, she circulated a pamphlet entitled *A Tale of Real Woe* throughout Europe. However, the only biographical information which Hannah could obtain from Louisa was that "her Father was a German, her mother an Italian, that she has one brother and one sister [and] her father had a very fine garden full of olive and orange trees".[379] It wasn't a lot to go on.

Following this, *The Lady's Monthly Journal* wrote about Loisa (as it called her): "In her general conduct she exhibited the various common evidences of the most confirmed insanity; which, in addition to the contraction of her limbs, from her exposure to cold in the open field, and from her future propensity to remain inactive, rendered her an object of the strongest pity ... However disordered and childish her affections and resentment, she could never be drawn into any explanation regarding her family, her connections or her country, however affable and unguarded she might sometimes appear."[380]

The Bristolian poet Ann Yearsley wrote about Louisa in her 1785 poem *Clifton Hill*: "Beneath this stack Louisa's haystack rose, Here the fair maniac bore three winter snows, Here long she shivered stiffening in the blast. The lightning round their livid horrors cast, the thunders roared, while rushing torrents pour, and add new woes to black affliction's hour." Louisa also features as the protagonist in William Wordsworth's 1798 poem 'The Mad Mother', which is a romanticised version of her story. A widely-shared drawing of Louisa exists which was created by William Palmer[381] in 1788 following the publication of 'A Tale of Real Woe'. Hannah endorsed the picture, hoping it would help to publicise

379 Cited in Anne Stott, 2003, *Hannah More: The First Victorian*, p55.

380 'Death of Loisa: The Maid of the Haystack' in *The Lady's Monthly Museum*, January 1801, Volume 6, p215-6.

381 The name of the artist varies. Others to whom this picture is attributed include G Scott and RS Kirby. I am unclear as to who the true artist is but Palmer's name appears most frequently.

Louisa's story and identify her. The picture shows a young girl, draped in a blanket with her hand at her breast, seated on straw beside a haystack and with a basket at her side.

It was not until 1785 and the anonymous publication of a bestselling French pamphlet titled *Unknown: A True Story* when anyone made a claim to identify the mysterious maid. And what a claim it was! The pamphlet asserted that the maid of the haystack was in fact the half-sister of the Queen of France (Marie Antoinette), and the daughter of the Emperor Francis I. It was alleged (with no proof) that in 1769, the maid had been in Bordeaux and socialising with dignitaries but once the Empress had discovered her husband's illegitimate daughter was mixing in high society, she had had the young woman arrested, removed to Belgium and left in Ostend with a meagre £50 and told to fend for herself. The pamphlet was a huge seller throughout Europe and Hannah reportedly believed every word (no doubt hoping to have solved the mystery of Louisa's origins), despite the fact Louisa was far too young to have fitted the description.

As Louisa's mental health continued to deteriorate, Hannah arranged for her to be moved to Guy's Hospital Lunatic House, London, which is where Louisa remained at Hannah's expense until her death in 1800. Thanks to Hannah's benevolence, Louisa was spared the horror of public 'madhouses' or asylums, and was instead afforded kindness and dignity from her doctors. Hannah and her sisters continued to visit Louisa for the remainder of her life and it was Hannah who paid for the cost of Louisa's funeral and burial in the hospital grounds.

Please also see: Catherine Andras (vol two), Mary Atlay (vol two), Hannah More (vol one), Sarah Wesley (vol two), Ann Yearsley (vol one).

ANNE LUTTON

1791-1881, PREACHER

The Portland Street Wesleyan Chapel in Cotham, built in 1792, was where the "eloquent preacher" Anne Lutton would speak to her congregation, something she was capable of doing in several languages. As a Methodist, she was noted for her piety, religious teaching, linguistic skills and musical ability. Anne would preach at locations all over England and Ireland (she had been born in Moira, County Down), although after the deaths of her parents in the late 1820s she travelled to Bristol to visit family friends the Westcotts, first at Elm Villa and then Llanberris Villa, both in Cotham; their daughter Jane Hicks Westcott would later edit Anne's letters and diaries into a published book.

In 1832, Anne spent ten months staying with the Westcotts, a family she loved very much but whose sociable way of life was very different from the quiet one she was used to. To help her cope with this newfound sociability, Anne made notes in her diary for how best to communicate with others. It was a six-stage process that went as follows: 1) pray for strength before meeting the guests, 2) find in advance passages of scripture which might be useful to the guest, 3) look for openings in the conversation to share those passages of scripture, 4) be mindful that the Lord was listening to every word she said and therefore not get carried away, 5) "make my parting words impressive", and 6) share a prayer with the guest as they departed.[382] We could all learn something here.

Her letters and diaries are full of Anne's concern for imparting her spirituality and lessons to those she met. However, despite being a somewhat serious presence, she did make friends in Bristol, including the writer Mary Anne Schimmelpenninck

382 archive.org/stream/memorialsaconse00luttgoog/memorialsaconse00luttgoog_djvu.txt

with whom she shared a passion for literature. And in a mid-1830s letter to a friend back in Ireland, Anne sounds like she's been having a positive blast here in Bristol: "I like the vicinity of my residence. I have been a few days in Bristol, visited Clifton, Kingswood, Westbury, Henbury and that now celebrated resort of all curious travellers, Blaize Castle [sic]. I have had a very dissipated time of it; sailing on the Avon when at Bristol, whirling about in carriages when our object could be better accomplished by land than water. And what was this very important object? Why, to gratify a certain taste for viewing all that is grand and beautiful in nature and art!"[383] Clearly taken by Bristol, Anne moved here permanently in 1837.

As was common for many early Methodists, Anne considered herself to be a member of the established church and, while in Bristol, she worshipped at St Mary Redcliffe (of which she wrote to a friend: "Redcliffe Church is the finest building in Bristol; it has all the grandeur and amplitude of a cathedral"[384]) as well as the Portland Square Wesleyan Chapel. However, for the final 20 years of her life she had become completely blind.

In 1883, two years after Anne's death, the Portland Street Wesleyan Chapel erected the Lutton Memorial Hall in her honour and it was situated next door to the chapel itself. However, in 1978, the Chapel was demolished and the modern Knightstone House was built in its place and combined with Lutton Memorial Hall to offer housing to those in need. Anne was buried in Arnos Vale Cemetery.

Please also see: Mary Anne Schimmelpenninck (vol one), Sarah Wesley (vol two).

383 Ibid.
384 Ibid.

BERYL McLEISH
1919-1995, WARTIME TELEPHONIST

As a Women's Auxiliary Air Force telephonist during World War Two, Corporal Beryl McLeish (who became Beryl Fawcus after marriage) of 9 Jutland Road, Avonmouth, received the very first telephone call to England from the Normandy frontline in June 1944, which was made via a special telephone cable that had been laid underneath the English Channel with the express intention of allowing communication between the frontlines.

Although hailing from the South West, during the war Beryl was stationed at Fighter Command Headquarters in Middlesex and handled hundreds of telephone calls conveying orders to Royal Air Force (RAF) airfields throughout the UK. One day, when one of the lights on her switchboard lit up, she was told to answer and expect a call coming through from an RAF base in Normandy. Beryl said: "It came through so clearly that it might have been an ordinary local call. I knew the person who was making the call and he told me where he was phoning from."[385] The news of this groundbreaking call from across the Channel was so exciting that it made the national newspapers.

MILLICENT MACKENZIE
1863-1942, EDUCATIONALIST

Forthright and determined, young Millicent Hughes (known as Hettie) grew up in an environment of stoicism following the death of her mother Hester when Millicent was just seven years old. Her paternal aunt took over the running of the Hughes household for

385 Ethel Thomas, 1989, *War Story*, p225-227.

Beryl McLeish illustration by Rhi Lee

the six years until Millicent's father Walter remarried in 1877, but those were formative years in a young child's life and Millicent's independent streak was firmly fixed.

She was born in the family home at 14 York Place, Clifton, as the middle child in the Hughes family. And following her initial schooling in Clifton, Millicent was sent to Montmirail, Switzerland, to attend a Moravian school... coincidentally (or not), this was in 1877, the same year that her father remarried. Either way, by 1878 Millicent was back in Bristol and a student of the University College, Bristol.

Around the same time, she started taking an active interest in local politics: Millicent was the head of a working men's school in east Bristol, she campaigned for trades unions for women, and was connected to both the Social Democratic Union and the Independent Labour Party. However, it was education which most interested her and in the autumn of 1888 she enrolled to study teaching at the Cambridge Teacher Training College. After qualification, Millicent held various teaching posts at women's schools and colleges in Wales, and became one of the recipients of the Gilchrist Travelling Scholarship for Women Teachers. She even travelled to the US to study how girls were taught overseas and wrote a report on her findings, which was published in 1894 as *The Training of Teachers in the United States.*

When, on 23 July 1898, she married John Stuart Mackenzie, who was a professor at the University College of South Wales and Monmouthshire, Millicent made a successful request to be permitted to retain her lectureship at a time when women were almost exclusively expected to give up paid work upon marriage. Speaking to the education section of the British Association in 1906, Millicent "read a paper full of valuable suggestions for the training of girls for the duties of home life. Mrs Mackenzie contended that in the education of young girls there is something radically wrong, and that they are taught subjects which are of no use whatever when they are called upon to face the circumstances of everyday life."[386] Millicent later wrote that it was the belief of both her and John that "the position I had secured for a woman should not be lost".[387] It was clearly worth her while because by 1910 she had become the first woman to achieve professorial status in Wales.

Alongside her commitment to educating women (particularly working-class women), Millicent was forming strong opinions about women's political status and it was her view the vote must be extended to women. As such she became a leading figure in the Welsh women's movement. In 1918, while living in Cardiff, she stood for Labour as the only female parliamentary candidate in Wales, although she was defeated by the Liberal candidate Herbert Lewis. She later said she stood "to emphasise the importance of the part that should be played by women in national affairs"[388].

Although much of her adult life had been spent in Wales, Millicent returned to Bristol for a few years in her retirement with John and they lived at 13 West Mall, Clifton. She was eventually cremated at Arnos Vale Cemetery on 15 December 1942. Meanwhile, Cardiff University's Mackenzie House on Newport Road is named in her honour.

386 'News' in *Western Daily Press*, 4 August 1906.
387 Beth Jenkins, 2018, 'Millicent Mackenzie' in *Oxford Dictionary of National Biography*.
388 Ibid.

ADA MARLEY
1887-1961, DRESSMAKER

In 2010, Windmill Hill resident Benedict Mackay was interested to find out more about who had lived in his house before him, and this was how he came to commission and erect a blue plaque to dressmaker Ada Marley on his 30 Stanbury Road home. He said: "I wanted to make a feminist statement and to find an 'ordinary' woman, thus provoking stale ideas about history. I was hoping, when I researched the records at the library, that I would find a woman who stood in her own right, not attached to a man, and I came across Ada."[389]

Born in 1887, Ada was baptised at the Portwall Lane Methodist Church in Bedminster and she lived initially with her family at 23 St Luke's Road, next to the then-new Victoria Park in Bedminster. She lived with her mother Elizabeth, deal-runner father William and siblings William, Annie, Ernest, Rosa and James; Ada was the second-eldest child. By 1911, the family had moved directly opposite the lush park to 26 Nutgrove Avenue and, now 23, Ada was listed in the census as a dressmaker.

Curiously, by the time of the 1939 register, Ada had moved around the corner to 39 Stanbury Road, where her occupation is listed as "dressmaker and house duties". Her mother Elizabeth was living with her but given her father did not die until 1948 we must wonder whether a) their marriage had broken down or b) Elizabeth was simply visiting Ada for the night of the register and was not actually a permanent resident at Stanbury Road. What we do know for sure is Ada herself never married or had children.

389 Email from Benedict Mackay to the author, 19 September 2018. With thanks to Benedict for uncovering Ada and for helping with information about her for this book.

LISELOTTE MARSHALL

1923-2017, WRITER

Born in Germany, Liselotte Marshall spent much of her childhood in a clinic in the Swiss Alps where she received treatment for bone tuberculosis. Because of this, she unofficially adopted a Swiss identity, speaking fluent French at the clinic and fluent German when she saw her family. However, as a Jew visiting her family in Germany in 1937 (a country now fully steeped in Nazi ideology), she was horrified by the anti-semitic abuse she experienced and promptly fled back to the relative safety of Switzerland. It wasn't long after this that her family also left Germany for the US after their business and home were seized by the Nazis.

Throughout World War Two, Liselotte stayed in Switzerland and worked as a nursing assistant at the clinic where she had been treated, before moving to the US to join her family and study at Hunter College, New York, and then Yale University, Connecticut. It was at the latter that she met her future husband, a British student called Peter Marshall, with whom she moved to the UK in 1953. It is in this way that Liselotte held German, American and British nationalities, although she maintained a lifelong abhorrence of nationalism due to the way the Nazis had made so many people feel stateless.

Peter's work took him to the University of Bristol in 1953, where he worked as a lecturer, and the couple's children Eleanor and Oliver were born in the city. It was while in Bristol that Liselotte discovered her passion for literature and a novel *Tongue-Tied* was published towards the end of her life in 2004. The novel concerned an interpreter who loses the ability to speak after her marriage breaks down, and draws on Liselotte's experiences of tuberculosis, family separation, anti-semitic abuse and a rejection of nationalism.

HANNAH MARSHMAN

1767-1847, MISSIONARY

Widely considered to have been the first female missionary in India, Hannah Shepherd began life as a farmer's daughter from Wiltshire. Upon marriage to the missionary Joshua Marshman, Hannah moved to Bristol where the couple became prominent members of the Broadmead Baptist Church, which has been based in central Bristol since 1640.

On 29 May 1799, Hannah, Joshua and two of their children[390] set sail from Portsmouth to India on the ship Criterion, eventually landing at Serampore on 13 October 1799. They made their home in the Danish colony and opened two boarding schools, which became popular with the well-to-do members of Indian society: Serampore College and a school for girls. A communal lifestyle was an integral part of the mission society, with an absence of hierarchical structures and no divisions made between servants and masters, and the Marshmans believed it was important they learn to speak Bengali in order to better understand the local community.

EMMA MARTIN

1812-1851, FREETHINKER, MIDWIFE

There was a proliferation of boarding schools run by single women during the 19th century, the most famous of which was established by social reformer Mary Carpenter at the Red Lodge on Park Row in 1860. But before then, in 1830, a young Clifton woman called Emma Martin (née Bullock) founded a ladies'

390 The couple had 12 children although only five survived into adulthood.

Baptist academy in Bristol. Emma was unusual in that as well as working, she was also a married woman with four daughters but her marriage to Isaac Luther Martin was desperately unhappy and was not to last. She later described him as "a husband ... whose company it was a humiliation to endure"[391] and after he tried to relocate the family from Bristol to London, Emma packed up her things and left both him and their daughters.

After founding her school (which, like her marriage, did not last), Emma went on to become the editor of *The Bristol Literary Magazine*, the author of a book called *The Exiles of Piedmont* (c1840) and, having denounced her Baptist faith, an Owenite socialist campaigner. Like others who shared her socialist values, Emma discredited the part played by clerical and religious orthodoxy in enforcing women's dependence on men, and favoured the Owenite thinking that men and women should be treated equally within a marriage.

It was while attending a lecture in Bristol in 1839 by the political reformer and feminist Alexander Campbell that Emma began to question her Baptist beliefs and eventually became a freethinker. In this capacity, she became a public speaker herself and wrote a number of pamphlets. One of these — *Punishment of Death?* — stated her opposition to capital punishment and she would go on to speak in front of a crowd of 5,000 on this topic in Nottingham Market Square (having been no-platformed from her original booking at the Nottingham Assembly Room). A further clash with the authorities took place in 1845, after she left placards in a Glasgow church announcing she was going to criticise the Sunday sermon; for this she was fined £3 for creating a public disturbance. Another topic which would cause controversy when Emma spoke about it in public was divorce, which was obviously

391 Barbara Taylor, 2016, *Eve and the New Jerusalem: Socialism and Feminism in the Nineteenth Century*.

an issue close to her heart following her own unhappy marriage and the loss of her daughters to her husband, although she resumed contact with them when they achieved adulthood.

By 1845, Emma was living at 100 Long Acre, Covent Garden, London, with an engineer called John Hopkins. They never married but John unofficially changed his surname to Martin. By this time, Emma was tiring of the freethinkers and their constant squabbles, as well as the accusations levelled at her that she was encouraging extremism. So she left the movement and began training as a midwife. Her daughter with John was born in 1847, which was the same year in which Emma completed her midwifery training. However, because she was an atheist, no hospital would employ her so she worked from home and gave lectures in midwifery, gynaecology and contraception, the latter being a highly controversial and taboo subject in the 19th century.

Emma died from consumption at the age of 39. In his obituary for her, fellow freethinker George Holyoake wrote: "She was one of the few among the early advocates of English socialism who saw that the combat against religion could not be confined to an attack on forms of faith – to a mere comparison of creeds – and she was attracted only as a secondary issue to the abuses of Christianity, when she saw that the whole was an abuse of history, reason and morality."[392] He added: "What do we not owe to a woman who, like Emma Martin, takes a heroic side and teaches us … the truth of a gentler faith?"[393]

Please also see: Mary Carpenter (vol one).

392 Terry Liddle, 2011, 'Priestesses of Beelzebub' in *Ethical Record*, Vol 116, No 3, p17.
393 Barbara Taylor, 2016, *Eve and the New Jerusalem: Socialism and Feminism in the Nineteenth Century*.

Emma Martin illustration by Rhi Lee

RUTH MARTIN

born c1920, SHEROIC DOCTOR

"A young woman doctor risked her life crawling along a tunnel through smouldering debris in a heroic but vain effort today to rescue one of ten persons who were killed when an underground petrol tank exploded in Bristol," reported the papers worldwide on 24 November 1951.[394] This sheroic young woman doctor was Ruth Martin who worked at the Bristol Royal Infirmary.

The explosion on Ashley Road was one of the worst accidents in Bristol since the end of World War Two. Nine people were killed outright, two more died later of their injuries and a further 13 were hospitalised with their wounds. The explosion happened when a petrol tanker was delivering fuel to the M&M Motor Mart and the ensuing inferno destroyed the garage, as well as the two flats above it. The force of the blast also damaged buildings nearby, with windows being shattered up to a quarter of a mile away. It took firefighters two hours to get the blaze under control.

John Masters was a sergeant in the army whose father was one of the owners of the M&M Motor Mart. He had been in the basement at the time of the explosion and was trapped by a fallen beam for five hours. Ruth risked her life to crawl through a narrow gap, surrounded by thick smoke and petrol fumes, in order to find him and administer morphine. Although John later died from his injuries, Ruth stayed with him throughout his ordeal and reported afterwards that he had been extremely brave and had even made jokes about how he was missing the football because of the explosion. While she was in the debris with John, Ruth also assisted other victims who were trapped nearby.[395]

394 'Ten Killed in Bristol Petrol Explosion', 24 November 1951, *Associated Press*
395 Marc Cooper, 'Fuel Tank Explosion Leaves 11 Dead' in *Bristol Post*, 19 November 2017.

And another thing... On the unfortunate theme of people being buried beneath fallen debris, let us remember **Mrs May** of Ellingham Lodge on Wellington Park, which is off Whiteladies Road, Clifton. During the great gale that tore across large parts of the UK on 14 October 1877, this "aged lady" was trapped underneath the rubble that was created in her house after the chimney stack fell through the roof and into the basement. Mrs May was imprisoned for quite some time until her rescuers finally "extricated" her and a kind neighbour, Miss Chappel, took her in. The gale across the UK took the lives of several people and caused a great deal of damage to properties nationwide.[396]

VIOLET MAUND

1899-1961, DIARIST

During World War Two, the keeping of records was strictly prohibited by Defence Regulations. This meant no records, no collating of information and definitely no diaries. It was feared that if these documents fell into the wrong hands they would provide valuable information to the enemy. Fortunately for future generations, several Bristolians broke this law. One such rule-breaker was Violet Maund, who describes herself as just an ordinary housewife in her book *The Diary of a Bristol Woman 1938-1945* (1950).

Violet lived with her husband at 52 Arley Hill, Cotham, and they had a daughter who attended Redland High School. Through her diaries, Violet comments on the impact of the war on Bristol as both a city and a society, and her writing is unique in being from a woman's perspective: all other surviving and publicly

396 'The Gale: Loss of Life and Great Destruction of Property' in *Western Daily Press*, 16 October 1877.

shared wartime diaries are by male writers. For example, the issue of how to extend clothing and food ration coupons is something which concerns her greatly, just as it would have done for other female householders whose stories were not recorded. As an example, in September 1941, Violet talks about how people would eat out more regularly during the war as a way of making their rations last longer. Bristol's first British Restaurant was opened in July 1941 on College Green (Bristol would have 13 of these community canteens by the end of the war), and Violet noted that one would get a good meal here for a shilling, plus three-pence for coffee. Historian Ethel Thomas noted of the British Restaurants: "This was the start of the self-service style of eating out, as in the present day motorway restaurants. Bristol's main British Restaurants were at the bottom of Park Street (College Green), Peter Street (Castle Green) and Belgrave Road (corner of Whiteladies Road), Clifton."[397]

Not everything in Violet's diaries is doom and gloom, and one aspect she highlights is the curiosity for Bristolians of having US forces in the city. For instance, on 4 February 1944, Violet recorded: "Walked on the Downs and watched American soldiers playing a team game, but could not make anything out of it. They were then drilled and had to march up and down several times, when one soldier cried out from the file: 'Have a heart, Sarge', and the Sarge said: 'All right then, stand easy.'" A few months later on 3 June 1944, she saw a baseball game for the first time although she didn't seem much impressed by it: "Went to the Rovers' Memorial Ground to see an American Baseball Match, Reversible Commandos versus All Black Star. The All Blacks won.

397 Ethel Thomas, 1989, *War Story*, p234. British Restaurants were communal kitchens that began springing up around the UK from 1940. They were a way for people who had been bombed out of their homes or who had run out of food coupons to still feed themselves and their families via the inexpensive but nourishing meals. The British Restaurants were officially disbanded by 1947 but some continued until as late as the mid-1950s.

I was amused to see how childish the Americans seem, decrying the opposition when it is their turn to hold the bat, and openly arguing with the umpire on his decisions ... As I was new to the game I could not judge if the decision was wrong, but the conduct of all was childish."

When peace was declared on 8 May 1945, Violet naturally recorded this in her diary: "Thank God! Thank God! How few bells can ring from their church towers in Bristol today? We are a sad City of ruins. The young lads will have noise to celebrate, so they have taken the lids of the pig-bins clashing them together as cymbals, as they pass this house on their way towards the City Centre. I stand on the veranda today and look towards Bath. I can see red glows in the sky and am grateful they are not the result of a blitz. Bonfires are lit and from the Centre comes the hum of a City rejoicing. My one regret is that somewhere in the far distant East, some fine young English or American boy may be killed or dying tonight. They are *not* the forgotten Army, for I, with many a mother, wife and sweetheart, pray: 'Please God, may that far distant war, too, soon cease.'"[398]

CAROLINE MAY
born c1860, TRADES UNIONIST

The Women's Co-operative Guild, founded in 1883, encouraged working-class women to voice their opinions and work together to build themselves a better future. The Guild worked on political campaigns and was particularly concerned about the rights of young wives and mothers. The issues of divorce law and votes for women were also of concern to members. Caroline May set

398 Although peace was declared in Europe in May 1945, the war continued in Japan until September 1945.

up the Bedminster branch of the Women's Co-operative Guild in 1892, having been an ardent member of the organisation for some time. Her energies clearly paid off and before long she had a membership of 73 at the Bedminster branch.[399]

KATE MEES

born c1875, RED MAID

The Red Maids' School was established in Bristol in 1634 and is the oldest surviving girls' school in England, although it is called Redmaids' High School following a merger with Redland High School for Girls in 2016. Originally located in the city centre on Denmark Street, the school was conceived as a home for orphaned or impoverished daughters of freeman or burgesses of Bristol, where the girls were taught to read and sew. The school is now on Westbury Road, Westbury-on-Trym.

A glimpse into the daily life of a Victorian pupil at the Red Maids' School can be seen in snippets of the diary of Kate Mees, who attended the school between 1891 and 1895. The range of subjects Kate and her sister pupils were taught included arithmetic, algebra, Euclid (aka geometry), history, geography, botany, Shakespeare, Scripture, English and French grammar, domestic economy, freehand and model drawing, perspective drawing and singing, plus shorthand and typing.

In 1891, there were 80 pupils at the school and the headteacher was a Miss Bowen. The pupils slept in just two dormitories and, because they did the school's housework and laundry, in addition to sewing their own uniforms and attending all of their lessons, they had very little free time. Life was by no means easy for

399 Madge Dresser, 2016, *Women and the City*, p123-125.

students of the school. Outlining a typical day at Red Maids' in 1891, Kate recalled: "Girls rose at 6.30am and attended prayers in the only school room, which was divided into four by curtains. Breakfast was at 8am, with household duties both before and afterwards. Lessons were from 9am until noon and from 2pm until 5pm. Homework from 6.30pm to 7.30pm and bedtime was at 8pm for the entire household. Breakfast and tea consisted of bread and butter and tea, with cake as a treat only on Founder's Day and the Head's birthday! The main meal of the day was either a hot meal and no pudding or cold meat followed by a pudding."

However, clearly Kate enjoyed her time at Red Maids' because she explained: "We had a school library but it did not contain many books and we had not much time for reading anyway. I hope I have not given the impression that we pupils felt crushed or repressed in any way; on the whole we were very happy on the principle of 'what you never had you never missed'. I am very proud of the fact that I was educated at the oldest girls' school in the country and the finest girls' school in Bristol."[400]

MARY MILGROVE

1765-1856, WOMEN'S REFUGE FOUNDER

When widowed Mary Milgrove (née Canvin) founded the Bristol Female Refuge Society in 1814 on Marlborough Hill (relocated to Lower Castle Street in 1860), she was not necessarily putting women's safety first despite the promising sounding name of the establishment. The refuge had space for 35 females aged 15-35 years, and in some cases offered free accommodation to those women who were most in need. The residents typically

400 rmsociety.org.uk/2018/10/life-at-school-in-1891/

stayed for two years before moving on. But this refuge was no early prototype of a contemporary domestic violence shelter, as we now often understand a women's refuge to be. Instead this 'refuge' was a form of punishment.

The Bristol Female Refuge Society was a charitable organisation which relied on donations. It was run as a Magdalen Home, which was a place for young women who had 'fallen' or otherwise brought shame upon their families as a result of either having had a sexual relationship with a man or, more commonly, having been sexually assaulted by a man and perhaps having become pregnant as a consequence. Although commonly associated with Ireland, Magdalen Homes were actually operational all over the UK and Ireland, and they were unpleasant and dangerous spaces because they blamed the woman entirely for the man's behaviour. At the same time, they canonised the people who worked at the institutions for 'saving' these women and heaped praise upon the businesses who gave charitable donations. They were effectively workhouses which demonised the women in their 'care' and punished them for their so-say bad behaviour, ignoring the fact that in the vast majority of cases the women were only there because they had been assaulted by (unpunished) men.

The Bristol Female Refuge Society managed to evade coverage in the local papers, save for a yearly report on its AGM and occasional reports of charitable donations. The AGM went from having a "highly respectable audience" in 1859[401] to "limited"[402] in 1869 and merely "good"[403] in 1891, which was the final year that its AGMs were reported on. By 1910, the Refuge was still in existence but in a dire state and the press was calling for help from its readership, citing the high cost of repairs to the old building and

401 'Bristol Female Refuge Society' in *Western Daily Press*, 3 March 1859.
402 'Bristol Female Refuge Society' in *Western Daily Press*, 5 March 1869.
403 'Bristol Female Refuge Society' in *Western Daily Press*, 20 March 1891.

the drop in subscriptions which were needed to keep the refuge self-supporting.

Observing Mary's death, the *Bristol Mercury* noted she was "a lady of superior intellectual endowments and deep piety. From the year 1814 until her decease, she lived in that house and acted as the unwearied and unpaid friend of that useful institution."[404]

Please also see: Bethlehem Dawes (vol two), Marion Linton (vol two).

VIOLET MINER

1905-1990, CLEANER

For ten years, Violet Miner from Sherwell Road, Brislington, was a cleaner at the Fry's chocolate factory and office blocks. In her retirement notice, the company observed: "Her cheerful approach made light of a dull job and made her very popular among those with whom she came into contact." Her husband Leslie, with whom she had a daughter called Sylvia, had also worked with Fry's as a "telecommunications linesman" and retired at the same time as his wife.[405]

MARY MITFORD

1787-1855, WRITER

Mary Russell Mitford was an author and dramatist who was well known in her day for a series of more than a hundred literary sketches which fell under the title of 'Our Village'.

404 'Deaths' in *Bristol Mercury*, 15 March 1856.
405 *Somerdale Magazine*, published by JS Fry. July 1968 edition.

Born in Hampshire, when she was ten years old Mary miraculously reversed her parents' ailing fortunes by winning £20,000 via a lottery ticket (equivalent to almost £890,000 in contemporary money). This should have been more than enough to keep the family going forever but by the 1820s, Mary's income as a writer was called upon to again prop up her parents (fun fact: her mother had been friends with a flourishing writer by the name of Jane Austen). As a teenager, Mary aspired to become the greatest poet in England and, while she never achieved quite that level of success, her work was certainly published in volumes alongside highly regarded poets such as Samuel Taylor Coleridge and Walter Scott. Further, her plays also saw success with, for instance, *Julian* being performed in Covent Garden, London, in 1823, with Bristol's beloved son William Charles Macready in the title role.

However, it was via her prose that Mary saw the greatest commercial success, particularly with the aforementioned 'Our Village: Sketches of Rural Character and Scenery' series, which initially appeared in *The Lady's Magazine* and was later published in five volumes of books, which were all bestsellers. The series ran from 1819 to 1832 and was based upon the life and characters of Three Mile Cross near Reading, where Mary lived. "These sketches of rural life were like Dutch paintings in their fidelity to detail, or like Bewick woodcuts in their charm and delicacy," noted Marguerite Fedden.[406]

The reason for including Mary in *The Women Who Built Bristol* is because after the deaths of her mother and father (in 1830 and 1842 respectively), unmarried Mary was free to do exactly as she wished, and what she wished was to travel the UK. Two places to which she travelled were Bristol and Bath, which she found

406 Marguerite Fedden, 1958, *Bristol Vignettes*, p7.

thoroughly charming cities... and declared Bristol to be her favourite of the two: "On Thursday I went to Clifton and prefer Bristol to Bath for its colour and its variety of street architecture, which I suppose is a great heresy! ... Bristol is warm, glowing, picturesque."[407] She spent a week staying at 11 Sion Row, Clifton, and wrote to a friend: "I have seen much that is worth the journey — the new steamship, the [SS] Great Britain, over which I was escorted by the chief engineer; [Thomas] Chatterton's fine old church [St Mary Redcliffe], Mr [Walter Savage] Landor's pictures and Mr Barker's. Of Bath, its buildings and scenery, I have heard much good; of Bristol, its dirt and its dinginess, its ugliness, much evil. Shall I confess — dare I confess — that I was charmed with the old city?"[408]

Charmed, indeed. Mary loved the pretty gabled buildings on Wine Street and the famous Dutch House (since destroyed during the Blitz), and compared walking around the winding cobbled lanes and steep little streets of 19th-century Bristol to climbing up a ladder. The area around the Avon Gorge was a particular favourite for her and, with the Clifton Suspension Bridge yet to be completed and travel at this time being via a wicker basket suspended from a metal bar, she wrote: "The airy line of the chain that swung from tower to tower of the intended Suspension Bridge with its basket hanging in mid-air like the car of a balloon making one dizzy to look at it, formed an enchanting picture ... I know nothing in the English landscape so lovely and so striking as that bit of the Avon beyond the Hotwells when the tide is in, the ferry boat crossing, and some fine American ship steaming up the river."[409]

407 Ibid, p9.
408 Ibid, p8.
409 Ibid, p9. See the entry for Frances Power Cobbe in volume one of *The Women Who Built Bristol* for a more detailed description of travelling across the Avon Gorge while suspended in a basket.

When a woman writes a love letter to Bristol as beautiful as this, it is impossible to exclude her from a book celebrating women who contributed to our city's heritage.

Please also see: Frances Power Cobbe (vol one).

LUCY MOORE

1877-1920, PERFORMER

There is nothing new about our fascination with people in the spotlight. Nor is there anything new about our interest in people who are famous just for being famous. One reality star of her day was Lucy Moore, an American-born performer who was living in Bristol when she met her untimely death at the age of 43 in 1920. Tens of thousands of people packed the streets around Lower Maudlin Street and Bristol Bridge as Lucy's coffin made its way to her final resting place at Arnos Vale Cemetery. But who was Lucy and why were people so interested in her?

Also going under the names of The Jersey Lily, The American Fat Girl, Alma Moore and Lovely Lucy, her real name was Eliza Elizabeth Moore and she was reported to be the largest woman in the world, weighing in at 48 stone — which is even more eye-opening when you learn she stood just five feet four inches tall.[410]

Lucy worked in the world of 'freak shows'. By the age of 12 she weighed more than 27 stone and by the age of 17 she was appearing at circuses and travelling 'freak shows' at home in the US. But it wasn't just Lucy's size which attracted attention; with a black American mother and a white English father, the fact she

410 For comparison, a US woman named Rosalie Bradford (1943-2006) is recorded by Guinness World Records as the world's heaviest woman ever, having weighed in at 85 stone in 1987: nearly twice Lucy's weight.

was mixed-race also caused Edwardian audiences to stare. She was touring Europe by the early 1900s and appeared before many members of a range of royal families. Wanting to retire from a life of touring, Lucy came to Bristol to join her sister Annie Moore at her home on Constitution Hill, Clifton.

However, it was a long battle with cancer which killed Lucy. And fans who wanted to gawp at the size of her coffin would have felt let down to learn that Lucy's cancer caused her to lose half of her body weight, although her coffin was still considerably larger than average and required eight men to carry it.[411]

MARY MOORE

1925-2006, CODE BREAKER

Fiercely intelligent, during World War Two, Mary Christina Davis was despatched to work for Bletchley Park as a member of the Enigma team led by Alan Turing, which is widely accepted to have shortened the duration of the war by several years, thanks to their work intercepting and decoding German messages. Between 1943 and 1945, Mary was stationed at Bletchley's bombe outstation[412] at RAF Eastcote, London, where she worked as bombe operator as part of her duty with the Women's Royal Navy Service. Bletchley Park is, rightly, still celebrated as the birthplace of modern information technology and the home of British codebreaking. Along with others who worked there during the war, Mary was later awarded a medal for her work at Bletchley.

Following the end of the war, Mary came to Bristol in October 1947, where she studied for a testamur in Social Studies, awarded

411 eugenebyrne.wordpress.com/2012/10/16/thousands-turn-out-for-funeral-of-american-mixed-race-celebrity-in-bristol-1920/

412 A bombe was an electro-mechanical machine which was used in the decryption of Enigma signals.

in 1949.[413] This was immediately followed by studying for the Diploma of the Institute of Almoners, which enabled her to work as almoner[414] at the Mid-Hertfordshire Hospital in St Albans until she married a Mr Moore (we do not know his first name), whom she had met while studying in Bristol.

Given Mary was a committed churchgoer throughout her life, it makes sense she chose to work as an almoner and, in that way, distribute charitable money to the poor. In addition to working in St Albans, she also worked as an almoner in Dumfries before retiring with her husband to Wincanton, where she became very involved with her local branch of the Women's Institute.[415]

Please also see: Rhoda Amine (vol two).

CHRISTINA MORE
born c1360, REBEL LEADER

Lollardy was a Christian movement which existed between the mid-14th and mid-16th centuries and was initially led by John Wycliffe (a University of Oxford theologian who was dismissed from post for his criticism of the Roman Catholic church). The Lollard community in Bristol was one of the largest in the UK and was centred around the parish of Redcliffe. The main tenet of Lollardy was an opposition to the Roman Catholic church and most members of the Lollard faith were dismissed as heretics.

Christina More was a prominent Bristolian Lollard. Her husband William More had been an alderman owning a

413 A testamur is a certificate confirming that someone has completed an examination, however it is not the same as a degree or other academic qualification.
414 An almoner is an old-fashioned term for a social worker employed in a hospital to look after the welfare of patients. In the past, an almoner would have also distributed charitable money (alms) to those in need.
415 bristol.ac.uk/news/2006/5214.html

significant amount of property, and after his death in 1412 she inherited not only his money but also his social status. Because of this, she had a strong position in the Lollard community and was one of the wealthiest people in Bristol at this time. Historian Charles Kightly notes: "It is probable that the More household was the principal centre of Lollardy in the Redcliffe area, if not in the whole of Bristol, during the years preceding Oldcastle's rising. Though obviously well known to the jurors in 1414, before this date the household seems to have enjoyed a degree of immunity from persecution, probably because of the social position of the Mores themselves."[416]

Christina maintained a Lollard chaplaincy and helped equip men for the notorious Oldcastle Uprising of January 1414; unlike in the Catholic church, Lollardy allowed women to have a much greater voice in public. That said, Christina was the only woman involved in the Oldcastle Uprising (so named because it was led by John Oldcastle); a coordinated attempt to overthrow both the Catholic church and King Henry V. The revolt was ultimately unsuccessful and resulted in a number of the men involved being sent to the Tower of London for execution. As a key organiser and bankroller, Christina was called before a Bristol jury for her part in the uprising. Among the many men also called before the jury were her servants Walter Blake (the leader of the Bristol rebels, whose costly armour was paid for by Christina) and James Marsh (whose weapons she paid for, along with the weapons for others in the Bristol group).

Christina was arrested and summoned for further questioning. As a patron of the faith and an employer of several accused men, the authorities felt Christina was guilty of heresy. But while others who were found guilty were hanged or burned

416 Charles Kightly, 1975, 'The Early Lollards: A Survey of Popular Lollard Activity in England, 1382-1428', PhD thesis, University of York, p248-249.

alive, Christina's sentence was a much lighter one: penance. Kightly states: "Any immunity from persecution that Christina may have had, however, ended in 1414, and it is obvious from the facts of her subsequent trial that both church and civil authorities regarded her with particular suspicion: indeed, it may have been only her connections with the Bristol ruling class that saved her from a worse fate than imprisonment and purgation."[417]

GLADYS NELSON

1910-2008, TEACHER, COMMUNITY CAMPAIGNER

Having been born in Tewkesbury, Gladys Nelson, who was known affectionately as "the grandmother of Yate", began her career in education as a teacher at Yate Church School (now St Mary's Church of England Primary School), where she worked for 16 years. She then spent 16 years teaching at the Ridge Junior School in Yate. In fact, such was her commitment to early years education that Gladys also helped to set up a local playgroup.

After meeting signalman Albert Nelson, Gladys was married at the town's St Mary's Church in 1937 and the couple had two daughters, Monica and Pamela. "She was a family lady," said Monica, after her mother had died. "But she was also very community orientated and missed every moment she was not doing something in the town."[418]

After many years working in education, Gladys moved her attention to politics, initially serving as an independent member on Yate Parish Council between 1964 and 1973, later becoming a Liberal Democrat councillor on Yate Town Council between 1987 and 1999 — not retiring from the post until the impressive

417 Ibid, p249.
418 Ali Dent, 'Tributes Paid to Grandmother of Yate' in *The Gazette*, 16 December 2008.

age of 89. During her time in office, Gladys helped to save the Victorian mansion known as Poole Court (which later became the home of Yate Town Council), reinstated Yate Carnival and was instrumental in the opening of the Yate Heritage Centre.

Monica said: "Yate was her life. She put every effort into the town and I think people have missed her greatly since she left the town council. She loved being involved in the community and doing what she felt was right." Mike Robbins, who was the Mayor of Yate at the time, added: "If children did not know her, their parents did and if the parents did not know her, the grandparents did. She did so much for Yate and was very well known locally."[419]

Commemorative trees were planted outside Poole Court in 2009 in memory of Gladys and in honour of her hard work in saving the important building.

AUDREY NOBLE

1915-2016, ACTOR

Early elocution lessons paid off for Bristol-born Audrey Noble after she was cast in her very first role at the age of 17, which was a walk-on role in *Hamlet* at the Prince's Theatre, Clifton. Buoyed by this taste of stardom, Audrey enrolled in drama classes with the Rapier Players and soon became Assistant Stage Manager for the company at the Little Theatre, which was attached to the Colston Hall. Her manager Ronald Russell told her: "You will never be a star, but you will always do good work in good companies,"[420] which turned out to be extremely accurate.

Audrey worked with the Little Theatre company from 1938 to 1941, until World War Two led her to join the Entertainments

419 Ibid.
420 Shirley Brown, 'Obituary: Audrey Noble' in *The Stage*, 7 December 2016.

Audrey Noble illustration by Tina Altwegg

National Service Association and work in army theatre productions to entertain the troops in France, Belgium and Germany. After the war ended, Audrey returned to Bristol and became a popular character actor for a range of theatre companies, and continued to work with the Little Theatre during the 1950s and 1960s, before joining Bristol Old Vic in the 1970s and 1980s. Alongside her stage career, Audrey was starting to find television roles, which included a regular spot as Mrs Scott in the soap opera *Crossroads* in 1973 and guest roles in long-running shows such as *Z Cars*, *Casualty* and *All Creatures Great and Small*, although her big TV break had been as Mistress Quickly in the 1959 series of *The Life and Death of Sir John Falstaff*. Such was her reliability, that she was known in the industry as "one take Audrey".[421]

Her final stage appearance was back with the Bristol Old Vic in a 1985 production of *Tartuffe*. Audrey died at her home in Bristol in 2016 at the grand age of 101.

Please also see: Peggy Ann Wood (vol one).

AMELIA NUTT

1845-1919, NURSE

Author's note: The subject of this entry is one which I found in an unusual way. I was out on a run to Chew Valley Lake one morning and the route took me through Withywood, where I noticed the Amelia Nutt Clinic on Queens Road. Curiosity piqued, I wanted to know who Amelia was but getting this information was not as straightforward as just asking the clinic, so some detective work was needed.

421 Ibid.

It seems Amelia was both nurse and "faithful friend" to the Jenkins family at Conway House, 58 St John's Road, Clifton, for whom she worked for 50 years as a nurse. From information in her death notice in the *Western Daily Press,* I was able to track Amelia down in the census reports and this led me to find out she had been born in Taunton and had never married or had children of her own.[422]

The Jenkins family was headed up by a chartered accountant called Frederick Augustus Jenkins and it seems reasonable to assume that Amelia initially joined them as nurse to their children and subsequently became a much-loved and valued member of the household. On the census reports for 1891 and 1911, she is listed as both 'nurse' and 'servant', so perhaps she earned her keep by assisting around the house as well as caring for those who needed her.

As to how the clinic in Withywood came to bear her name, this is another mystery. I can only assume the Jenkins family donated the money for the clinic in Amelia's name because of their high esteem for her but this is mere guesswork.

NELLIE O'CONNELL
born c1910, TOBACCO STRIPPER

Following the death of her mother when Nellie O'Connell was just five, Nellie and her three sisters were brought up by their father in Hotwells. The family stayed together through thick and thin, and even when the sisters married they stayed in the Hotwells family home with their new husbands. Nellie's story is also the story of the community of Hotwells.

422 'Deaths' in *Western Daily Press*, 5 July 1919.

Nellie worked at Franklyn Davey & Company (established in Bristol in the 18th century but bought out in 1901 by Imperial Tobacco) on Raleigh Road, Southville, where she stripped leaves that would be used for pipe tobacco; the 1912 Franklyn Davey building is now better known as the Tobacco Factory Theatre. Nellie worked the equivalent of a zero-hours contract: "They were always on short time so I never knew each week what I was going to get paid, but one time I earned 11 shillings! Two of my sisters worked at the Wills factory and they did 46 years of service in the end. Everyone worked hard in those days and longer hours. It wasn't at all easy at times to make ends meet."[423]

For her 21st birthday, Nellie's dad was determined to throw her a party she would never forget. And despite the family not having much money, he ordered a huge barrel of beer from Georges' Brewery on Bath Street, which was delivered by a horse and cart. "Goodness knows what the neighbours thought," remembered Nellie. "We had a house-full, all up the stairs and everywhere. What a time we had. We even laughed when someone left the tap in the barrel on and we were all nearly ankle deep in beer!"[424]

Recalling how Hotwells used to be its very own neighbourhood, Nellie says there were once three chemist shops, three churches (only the Holy Trinity survives), a dairy run by Mr Tool (who delivered his milk via horse and cart), and a rag and bone merchant called Mr 'Baggy' Bennett who was based near the Rose of Denmark pub. Community life centred around the river, which provided both work and entertainment: "We loved a trip to Barry [Wales]. It cost one shilling and sixpence for the ferry across the river to catch the train to Portishead, and two shillings and sixpence on the steamer to Barry."[425]

423 Rosemary Clinch, 1985, *Unknown Bristol*, p81.
424 Ibid, p82.
425 Ibid, p84.

Despite the horrors of World War Two, the Hotwells community could not be divided, even as bombs fell. "We could count the bombs by the splashes in the water," says Nellie. "I'll never forget the night my nephew went missing, he was only eight or nine at the time and he would keep wanting to sit on the doorstep collecting shrapnel. When we looked, he'd gone! Bombs were falling everywhere and we went frantic, it was so cold too being winter. He turned up in the end with two tins of fruit in his hands. While we had been turning grey, he'd been up in Clifton helping the firemen put the fire out at the Co-op which had been hit, and they gave him the fruit as a present — well, I suppose he had to do his bit!"[426]

Nellie married Terry O'Connell who worked on the tugs for Brown Brothers' Sand & Gravel Company and, after her wedding, she stopped working at the tobacco factory and instead became a cleaner who went into offices on Baldwin Street in the evenings. "After [an office] party, you might well come across someone still in a corner, and then we'd get the coffee on," she remembers. "I worked with a good team of women and we always had some laughs but it was hard work and I got home late at night, but it never bothered me. I wouldn't feel safe walking around at night now [1985], though, with all the muggings you hear about. When I was younger, a girl could go anywhere on her own."[427]

426 Ibid, p85.
427 Ibid, p87.

MARY ORCHARD

1650-1730, POTTERY OWNER

From 1696 to 1727, Mary Orchard from Redcliffe Street ran a successful pottery on Temple Street called (I'll have to tell you because you'll never guess) Temple Street Pottery. Born Mary Suter, she married sailor John Orchard at St Mary Redcliffe church in 1668 and is first recorded as having manufactured and sold tin-glazed earthenware pots on 15 May 1696. After this, she made and exported pots to Ireland as well as to places as far flung as Portugal, Jamaica, Barbados and the US until at least 1721. It seems that John died fairly young because by the end of the 1600s Mary is a widow. Her occupation during these years is variously listed as everything from 'mug maker' to 'gally pot making'.

Mary had up to nine apprentices in her own right between 1702 and 1720, which is an indication of the scale and success of her business, as well as the high regard in which she was held. Indeed, on 20 March 1701, Mary (and her business partners William Andrews and John Knight) signed a lease on a bigger premises on Temple Street from which to work. The lease stated: "Together with all the Garden Stable pothouse and warehouse thereto belonging thereon lately erected and built And alsoe all and singular Roomes Kitchens halls parlours Chambers Sollars Shopps Lofts Lights pavements wayes water Easements ... And Alsoe liberty for them the said William Andrews and — Orchard... to erect in some part of the said Garden one or more pothouse or pothouses." The lease was for a minimum of ten years with an annual rent of £35.[428]

Following her death in December 1730, Mary was buried at St Mary Redcliffe church, back where she had married John in 1668.

428 bristolpottersandpotteries.org.uk/potters-letter/o/

EMMIE OWEN

1871-1905, OPERA SINGER

Successful opera singer Emily Mary Owen may have only lived a short life but she certainly lived a full one. Growing up on St Michael's Hill with her parents Hester and Henry, plus a string of siblings, Emmie was thrust on to the stage at an early age and made her professional debut in the play *Proof* (produced by Bristol's theatrical Chute family) at the Prince's Theatre on Park Row at the age of 14: "A word of praise is due to little Emmie Owen for her intelligent acting as the child in the first act."[429]

By 1891, she had joined the world famous D'Oyly Carte Opera Company as a touring soprano singer and with them she regularly performed at the illustrious Savoy Theatre, London. As a member of D'Oyly Carte, Emmie rapidly progressed from the small role of Cheetah in *The Nautch Girl* to the starring role of Yum-Yum in *The Mikado*. The *Bristol Magpie* proudly noted in 1899: "The revival of *HMS Pinafore* at The Savoy will, I predict, be a big success ... Miss Emmie Owen plays Hebe. That appreciation of this clever Bristol artiste is not lacking in the proper quarters will be evident from the fact that Sir Arthur Sullivan has written and Mr Gilbert introduced a *pas suel* [solo dance] especially to improve her part. We know what Emmie can do on the light fantastic toe, and although the Savoyards do not yet, they soon will."[430]

Between December 1896 and June 1897, Emmie travelled with the company to South Africa, where she successfully took the lead in a range of touring operas. Further international touring followed in 1901 and 1902, with trips organised by her manager to Australia and New Zealand... but then disaster struck. Money she had been promised for a string of performances was

429 '"Proof" at the Prince's Theatre' in *Western Daily Press*, 6 April 1885.
430 'Stageland' in *Bristol Magpie*, 1 June 1899.

never paid and then Emmie fell seriously ill, ending up stranded and penniless in Auckland, New Zealand. Her "somewhat circumstantial and disquieting story"[431] made headlines back in the UK and her friends rallied around to rescue her and raise the £50 needed to help her travel back to England later in 1902: "The sad story of Miss Emmie Owen has already enlisted deep sympathy and substantial help. [Her father] received a letter from Mr W S Gilbert enclosing £10 10s, and saying how extremely sorry he was to hear of Miss Owen's distress. Mr Clement Scott has also promised to help, and Mrs D'Oyly Carte is believed to be interesting herself on Miss Owen's behalf."[432] Emmie's ship home was finally booked to set sail at the end of February 1902.

After a lengthy recuperation, Emmie did briefly return to performance and she was back on the London stage at Christmas 1902 at the Crouch End Theatre: "This little lady was at one time one of the most vivacious members of the Savoy company, excelling especially in dancing, in which, however, few opportunities were given to her."[433]

Emmie died in 1905 aged just 33 while in Kent, although what led to her unexpected death is not recorded.

Please also see: Elsie Griffin (vol one), Sarah Macready (vol one).

431 'Local News' in *Western Daily Press*, 28 January 1902.
432 'Local Notes' in *Western Daily Press*, 29 January 1902.
433 'Local Notes' in *Western Daily Press*, 23 December 1902.

BEATRICE PAGE
1889-1972, TRAM DRIVER

In the face of phenomenal opposition, the first ever female tram driver in the South West was Beatrice Page (née Granger) of Whitecross Road, Weston-super-Mare, who in August 1914 began to occupy the driver's seat after the directors of the Weston-super-Mare and District Electric Supply Company approved a proposal to permit women to drive the trams; although the women drivers were still known as 'motormen' in the industry.[434]

All of the healthy men in the country (including Beatrice's husband William) had been called up to fight in World War One, meaning there was a shortage of tram drivers and, with nothing else for it, the powers that be reluctantly allowed women to have a go behind the steering wheel for the duration of the war... on the understanding they would give the men their jobs back the very second they returned. The women were paid less than the men had been despite doing exactly the same job, so in August 1918 Beatrice and her sister 'motormen' went on strike demanding equal pay.[435]

Despite being obliged to give her job back to a man when the war ended in 1918, Beatrice was invited back to drive the final ever Weston tram on 17 April 1937. This was a somewhat eventful journey, as the tram was pelted with eggs and fireworks by disruptive onlookers, perhaps frustrated that they had not been able to secure one of the very limited tickets for this historic trip. Souvenir hunters promptly climbed aboard once the tram reached the depot and pulled it apart in order to have a piece of the tram to take home.[436]

434 'Weston's Trams 1902-1937', Autumn 1994, Weston Civic Society, *Weston View.*
435 somersetremembers.com/content/storys/the-home-front/beatrice-page-1882-1976-on-the-trams.ashx
436 'Eggs Thrown at Tramcar', 19 April 1937, *Western Daily Press*

Beatrice Page illustration by Carrie Love

WINIFRED PARRY

1871-1952, REBEL LIBRARIAN, SUFFRAGIST

Born at 6 St Michael's Park, Kingsdown, to Elizabeth and Owen Parry, Winifred Louise Selby Parry was the youngest of their three children and the only daughter. She went on to become Bristol's first female reference librarian and a quiet agitator in the best possible way.

As in pretty much every area of life, the history of libraries and librarians is dominated by men. However, as the Industrial Revolution rumbled on, the Victorian era was an exciting time of change and the Edwardian period brought about an era of women's revolution. As a woman working in Bristol Central Library, Winifred was well placed to make her mark on the world and her fierce story will make you think twice about daring to dismiss librarians as meek and mousy.

Until as recently as the 1950s, advertisements for library staff were written in such a way as to appeal only to men, even though in more recent decades our stereotypical image of a librarian is of a dowdy woman in sensible shoes. But until the 1950s "women were not considered seriously for higher administrative duties in libraries because they were seen to 'depress the status of an occupation'".[437] Winifred challenged these assumptions and became a campaigner not only for votes for women but also for increased pay for female librarians.

Winifred joined the staff of Bristol Public Libraries in 1888, qualified as a librarian in 1894 and was a Reference Librarian from 1906 to 1936. We know from her Library Association certificate that when she passed her exams on 18 June 1894, the qualification demanded more than just the ability to put books

437 Jane Simon, 1997, 'Women's Status Within Libraries 1950s to 1980s' in *The Australian Library Journal*, 46:3, p272.

in alphabetical order and to tell people to "shh". The certificate required candidates to prove their skills in commercial arithmetic, bookkeeping, English grammar and composition, history, geography and English literature. This was not an easy job. The very fact it took Winifred six years from starting work with the library to achieving qualification shows how demanding the training was.

Winifred's lengthy career with the library service is largely due to the fact she never married. As in other professions, female library staff were expected to stop work when they became engaged and this was a notion which lasted well into the 1960s. But as early in her career as 1899, Winifred was challenging this, writing: "It has been urged against women as librarians that the unstable tenure of their position, due to the demands of marriage, leads to such frequent changes in a library staff as to render then undesirable. But is this altogether an evil to be dreaded, or is it a blessing in disguise? Where there is an inefficient male staff there is scarcely any possibility of change ... but with women, who are occasionally leaving to be married, the difficulty is overcome; the staff is also kept comparatively young, and consequently energetic and up-to-date."[438]

But wait! Winifred hadn't finished. She continued to write in favour of women librarians over men: "Women workers were... constructed as lacking some qualities needed to be a satisfactory library worker. These qualities, of physical strength, social and vocational skills, were often assumed to be possessed by men. Women were also constructed as likely to work only for a limited time before resigning on marriage; this was often, but not always, understood as a negative factor. These accounts, which co-existed with accounts of women's suitability for library

438 Winifred Parry cited in Evelyn Kerslake, 1999, 'A History of Women Workers in English Libraries 1871-1974', doctoral thesis at Loughborough University, p93.

employment, outline various attempts to qualify that suitability. The dichotomous relationship of these accounts was significantly challenged, however."[439]

In addition to voicing her opinion that married women should be able to continue to work as a librarian should they so wish, Winifred also lobbied for votes for women *and* for a pay rise for the female librarians in Bristol. There is a suggestion the Bristol Central Library's collection of 1907-1913 *Votes For Women* newspapers (the official journal of the militant Women's Social and Political Union) is down to Winifred's influence, which seems entirely plausible. Not least because of a letter from Bristol Library bosses which is found in one of her scrapbooks and dated 13 June 1913.

Evidently, Winifred's employers had received a letter from someone at the National Union of Clerks asserting there was a nefarious character (ie Winifred) at work within the Bristol Library service. They had received a letter suggesting their investigation into accusations about Winifred's behaviour had not been properly carried out and they "denied the charges preferred in the letter with the utmost resentment at my command". The letter continued: "Certain female members of the staff influenced by the dominating personality of one of their members [Winifred] and mutually imbued with advanced suffragistic ideals have joined the National Union of Clerks and are exploiting their views through its agency; at the present moment a letter from the Secretary of this Union demanding increased wages, and other dictatorial provisions is awaiting the consideration of the Bristol Library Authorities. You will gather from this that insidious forces are at work which call for drastic treatment."[440]

439 Ibid, p93.
440 L Acland Taylor, 1913, June 13, Letter to Dr Ernest Baker, kept at Bristol Central Reference Library.

What were these 'suffragistic ideals'? Well, in addition to ensuring the Central Library subscribed to *Votes For Women*, Winifred was also writing to national suffrage newspapers about the 'anti-suffrage canvas' in Bristol. This followed an assertion that women such as Lady Fry, President of the Bristol Branch of the National League for Opposing Woman Suffrage (NLOWS)[441], claimed to have canvassed the women to see whether they would have bothered to take up the right to vote should they be granted it. A reply-paid postcard had allegedly been sent to all the Bristol women who would have become entitled to vote but, after asking around her friends and relations *and* knocking on a lot of doors, Winifred could find no woman who had been canvassed by the NLOWS. Nonetheless, the NLOWS published a report confirming Bristol women definitely did *not* want the vote. Winifred smelt a rat and set about uncovering it via an increasingly righteous series of letters to the national suffrage newspapers. Winifred concluded that all the NLOWS' report had done was strengthen the resolve of suffragists and suffragettes, and to prove women wanted and needed the vote more than ever.[442]

After 48 years of tireless work — and occasional rabble rousing — within the stacks at the Bristol Central Reference Library, Winifred retired on 24 March 1936, by which time she had acquired the title of Librarian-in-Charge. "During the whole of this period, Miss Parry performed her duties with rare devotion and ability. The [Libraries] Committee desires to record its high appreciation of the long and valuable services she has rendered to the Libraries of the city," wrote the chairman of the committee.[443]

As one might expect from a librarian, Winifred was a

441 The Honorary Secretary of the Bristol Branch of the NLOWS was Edith Long Fox, who is profiled elsewhere in this book. Edith wrote a lengthy response to Winifred's claims the 'anti-suffrage canvas' had been falsified, which was published in the *Common Cause*. Needless to say, Winifred wrote back, picking holes in every single one of Edith's points.

442 Winifred Parry, 1911, March 9, 'The Anti-Suffrage Canvass at Bristol' in *Common Cause*.

443 Cited in Annual Report, Public Libraries, 1935-1935, p23.

meticulous record keeper and, in the early 1980s, a historian discovered a box of her scrapbooks in the basement of a Birmingham secondhand bookshop. How they got there we do not know but he gave them to the Bristol Central Library, which is where they are now stored in the reference department. These scrapbooks are fascinating and include news cuttings, letters and other memorabilia which Winifred neatly pasted in, including dried flowers decorating some of the pages. Many of the cuttings were letters that Winifred herself had written to the local newspapers and, when they were printed, she would cut them out and stick them in her scrapbook: often accompanied by a cross little handwritten note along the lines of: "This is not what I said!"

Winifred enjoyed 16 years of retirement before her death on 16 March 1952 at her home at 35 Upper Belgrave Road, Clifton. Her funeral and burial took place at Arnos Vale Cemetery on 19 March 1952.[444]

Please also see: Edith Long Fox (vol two).

MAUDE PIGOU

1842-1927, PHILANTHROPIST

Described as an "energetic and devoted worker"[445], Hertfordshire-born Harriet Maude Pigou (née Gambier) was the second wife of Francis Pigou, the much revered Dean of Bristol Cathedral. "The pressure of her kindly hand will do more towards the reclamation of an erring girl than volumes of sermons,"[446] wrote a journalist in 1894, giving the impression of a very warm and matronly lady.

444 .With thanks to Dawn Dyer for the nomination of Winifred Parry to this book.
445 Sarah A Tooley, 1896, 'Ladies of Bristol and Clifton', in *The Woman at Home*, p442
446 Ibid, p442

Indeed, Maude came from a family that was opposed to slavery and which campaigned long and hard to see the end of that trade, so it was inevitable she would grow up to do good works herself.

Maude moved to Bristol from Halifax in 1890 because of her husband's job and they lived at the Deanery near the Cathedral. Despite being plagued by "delicate health", she remained committed to her charitable work, with which she tried to create a better quality of life for factory girls and to find employment for working-class people without any work. One of the key ways in which she enabled working-class men to help themselves was by sourcing wood for them to chop and sell for their own benefit, with the ultimate aim that they might set up their own business and become self-sufficient.

In order to source wood for the men to chop and sell, Maude turned to the local press to seek donations, as this letter to the *Western Daily Press* in 1895 shows (a similar letter was published in 1904 and doubtless every year in between): "I am anxious, during the present distress, to help some of the unemployed. I have made arrangements with the landlord of one of the lodging-houses which I visit to open a wood-yard, which he will himself superintend and take care to see that deserving persons are employed. I shall be glad to receive at the Deanery orders for firewood or chumps, which will be delivered as soon as possible, probably within four-and-twenty hours."[447] A journalist confirmed: "I have heard of her going daily, through the severe weather of last winter, down to a couple of men's lodging-houses, in a poor part of the town, which she has under her care, to superintend the distribution of work at the woodyards which she had opened to provide employment for these who needed it."[448]

Maude worked hard on "rescue and preventative work" with

447 'Mrs Pigou and the Present Distress' in *Western Daily Press*, 8 February 1895.

448 Sarah A Tooley, 1896, 'Ladies of Bristol and Clifton', in *The Woman at Home*, p443

girls from poor backgrounds, and after moving to Bristol she joined up with the Non-Conformist women who had already been doing a great deal of good work in this area via the Women's Conference of Workers which had been held in Bristol in 1891. True to her faith, Maude, who was also involved with the Mothers' Union and Girls' Friendly Society in Bristol, saw it as a "special gift from God" to accomplish her good deeds to the best of her ability. "Girls of that class are keenly sensitive, and know in a moment whether you are merely talking at them, or feeling for them," she observed. "We should try to realise that but for the grace of God we might be as these poor creatures are; so many have gone astray through a very little thing."[449]

HARRIETT & LILY PLASTER

born 1846 (Harriet) and born 1885 (Lily), GROCERS

In addition to Harriet Lewis, who we met earlier in this book, another shopkeeping Harriet of interest is local 'giantess' Harriett Plaster (née Bowles), who stood proud at 6ft 2" tall. Bristolian Harriett married Samuel Plaster and the couple relocated to 8 Wolverton Street, Bedminster, from where Samuel worked as a 'general haulier', according to the 1901 census. In reality he was a scavenger, and with his horse and cart he collected 'house scrapings' (aka rubbish) before municipal refuse collectors were a thing, deposited the rubbish in the meadows by Ashton Gate, and then filled his cart with vegetables which he would sell when he returned to Bedminster. How hygenic! The couple had six sons.

Samuel died in approximately 1907, around which time his youngest son Charles met his sweetheart, the future Lily Plaster.

449 Ibid, p444

Lily was employed at ES & A Robinson's paper bag factory on Bristol Bridge and Charles — who worked as a clippy on the horse tram between Knowle and Hotwells — used to wave at her every time his tram went by. The young couple were soon married and shortly afterwards Charles opened his first greengrocery shop at 14 West Street, where he employed four of his five elder brothers. By 1909, he had opened a second C Plaster grocery shop at 24 West Street, and it was here that he lived with his mum Harriett, wife Lily and their baby son Charles. While Charles, Lily and Harriett kept watch over the two shops, the four brothers did door-to-door grocery deliveries with a horse and cart. It was quite the family enterprise. Not shy of a hard day's work, Harriett was still capable of lugging around a hundredweight of potatoes well into her 70s.

By the 1930s, there were 17 members of the ever-growing Plaster clan working in the family business in Bedminster; Charles even branched out into pubs and, for a while in 1925, he was also the landlord of the Sportsman's Arms on West Street (now the Black Cat).[450]

Please also see... Harriet Lewis (vol two).

ISOBEL POWELL

1907-1995, SCIENTIST

It was love which brought German-born Isobel Artner to Bristol. Her mother was Scottish, her father was Austrian and Isobel spent her formative years in Vienna. Due to also spending time in Denmark and France, by her early 20s Isobel was multilingual

450 Anton Bantock, 1997, *Bedminster*, p66-67.

and she maintained a love of languages throughout her life.

While Isobel was in Paris, she worked as a secretary for the composer Sergei Prokofiev and through him she met Professor Cecil Powell, who was a Research Fellow at the University of Bristol and was visiting friends in Paris. Isobel and Cecil soon fell in love (Prokofiev's famous 1936 composition 'Peter and the Wolf' would become a favourite and much-played record for the couple) and in 1932 she moved to Bristol to marry him and become his secretary at the university. As her time at the university progressed, Isobel became a microscope scanner and this would lead to huge consequences.

Initially, Isobel was one of only a few microscope scanners (leading a team known within the university as 'Cecil's Beauty Chorus', which is a very uncomfortable way of referring to these talented scientists), who checked the plates which had been exposed to cosmic radiation at Mountain Observatories or to laboratory sources of particles. The scanners needed to search the whole plate under a magnification of 100 times to look for and record tracks which would assist the physicists. It was in this way that in 1946 Isobel became responsible for identifying one of the subatomic particles which led to her husband's 1950 Nobel Prize. After attending the prize ceremony in Stockholm, Isobel wrote in her diary: "It was a very curious sensation when you suddenly see yourself on the screen. It was the first time that television had been used in Sweden for the Nobel Prize-giving ceremony."[451]

Not content with helping Cecil achieve a Nobel Prize, Isobel was also instrumental in his work with Sir Joseph Rotblat concerning the politics of science, specifically campaigning against the use of nuclear weapons. Cecil had previously worked with scientists Bertrand Russell and Albert Einstein in this area and had been

451 Peter Fowler, 'Obituary: Isobel Powell' in *The Independent*, 28 November 1995.

one of the 11 signatories of the Russell-Einstein manifesto in 1955, which encouraged world leaders to think "in a new way" which did not involve nuclear weapons and to find peaceful ways to settle global disputes. This would become the Pugwash organisation in 1957 of which Cecil would become Chairman in 1967. The goal of Pugwash was to provoke the government to action during the Cold War and to make the people with power realise the drastic consequences of nuclear weapons. Cecil died in 1969, meaning he was unaware of the continued and ongoing effect of Pugwash in creating "a world free of nuclear weapons and other weapons of mass destruction"[452] in the ensuing four decades… which were so significant that in 1995 the organisation was awarded the Nobel Peace Prize.

Following Cecil's death, Isobel remained in Bristol and continued working at the university; in 1987 there was a celebration for Forty Years of Particle Physics and Isobel enjoyed being reunited with many of her former friends and colleagues. She further developed her already impressive language skills by taking a diploma in Spanish and was involved with the university's Wives' International Group. This was set up to help the families of overseas students and staff, almost all of whom she could speak to in their native language. There was certainly much more to the deeply intelligent Isobel than simply being dismissed as a part of 'Cecil's Beauty Chorus'.

And another thing… Brenda Perry (1924-2002) worked with Isobel in the wonderfully named Cosmic Ray Research Department at the University of Bristol, where she also assisted Professor Powell and was another member of 'Cecil's Beauty Chorus'. Thanks to her important contribution to his work, Brenda helped to develop a

452 pugwash.org/about-pugwash/

film which showed the high energy radiation that came in from outside the solar system. After leaving the University, Brenda moved to work at the British Aircraft Corporation (now British Aerospace) where she read instrument panels during test flights, which included the Canberra High Altitude record of 65,890 feet.

BARBARA PRICE

born 1927, WARTIME SCHOOLCHILD

When World War Two broke out in September 1939, Barbara Price was just 12 years old and a pupil at South Street Senior Girls School, Bedminster (now Compass Point School). Barbara wrote for the BBC's People's War website in 2005 about her experiences as a Bristol child during the war and this memoir provides an illuminating glimpse into what that extraordinary time was like for a child.

"We spent a lot of time out of doors, playing in the street, on roller skates, with skipping ropes, balls, marbles and generals [cigarette cards]," Barbara recalled of her childhood pastimes. The children also played at Ashton Park (now Greville Smyth Park), and went swimming at the Dean Lane Baths, sometimes twice a day: "[Sundays] was when Mr Harding the attendant, donned his Wellington boots ... drained all the water from the pool, a brick built open air one, then scrubbed the bath with a hard brush. This was done just once a week and always caused great interest."

By the summer of 1939, Barbara remembered how the parks and open spaces where the children used to play had largely been transformed into allotments and underground shelters as part of the Bristolian war measures. The family home had an Anderson shelter in the garden: "Dad made us a wooden frame unit of five bunks, Dad never used his because as soon as the siren sounded, he was out on fire duty. He used wire mesh to hold the mattresses, but this proved very uncomfortable, as you could not sit up straight on the bottom bunk without your hair catching on it. One night I singed my hair on the candle and didn't realise, until I started to smell the burning."

When the first Bristol air raid happened on a Sunday evening in November 1940, Barbara remembers it started at about 6pm and lasted a full 12 hours. She said: "Men and boys spent all that time fighting fires, and by the morning arrived home exhausted, filthy and were covered in soot, and much older and wiser. It had been a terrifying long night for everyone. The whole of the city centre was on fire." Of course, people feared for their nearby relatives and, as in other testimonies of the war, the Price family couldn't stay indoors not knowing if their loved ones were OK: "My mother and I walked up Chessel Street to see if my grandparents were safe and all the sky glowed red. The Clifton Suspension Bridge, silhouetted against it, was an unforgettable sight. The tiles on our roof were hanging off, and the outside toilet door had blown away, so a curtain had to suffice."

Everybody had to pitch in and help regardless of age, and children were called upon to fill buckets with sand and water to put outside all of the neighbouring houses, so they could be used to douse small fires. In winter, the top layer of water would turn to ice and need to be chipped through before it could be of any use. Children were also sent out to stand in shop queues for hours at a time, waiting to try and buy unrationed items and hoping that by the time they made their way to the front of the queue there would be something left.

When the American soldiers arrived in Bristol, they were typically stationed in the big houses in Clifton or at Ashton Court, which was turned into a massive army camp; camouflage nets hung from every tree, disguising a lorry or tank underneath.

The American soldiers brought treats galore for the Bristolian children who had almost forgotten what sugary sweets tasted like but, fresh from the US, the men had pockets laden with chocolates, sweets and gum which they shared with the youngsters. One night, everyone was invited to a party at the Ashton Court camp and lorries came to pick people up: "I think it was the first time anyone had been into the grounds of Ashton Court. We were very impressed with the park and the house, but mostly the music and vast amount of food. Suddenly this wonderful supply of good things disappeared as quickly as they came; as the Americans were part of the invasion force and went on their way to Normandy."

When she turned 14 in July 1941, Barbara left school and began work at the Wills Tobacco Factory. She remained living in Bristol for the rest of her life, where she married, had children and became a grandmother. When she told her story in 2005, Barbara concluded: "I still appreciate a new block of soap, hot water and a warm towel. Also I have always been an enthusiastic recycler, but in those days we called it salvage."[453]

Please also see: Emily Smyth (vol one).

PRINCESS MARINA, HRH THE DUCHESS OF KENT

1906-1968, BRISTOL AIRPORT AMBASSADOR

Princess Marina of Greece and Denmark married British Prince George, the Duke of Kent, in 1934, with whom she had three children and acquired the title of Her Royal Highness the Duchess of Kent. However, the marriage was short-lived after Prince George was killed during 1942 in an air crash while on

453 bbc.co.uk/history/ww2peopleswar/stories/98/a6078198.shtml

Princess Marina illustration by Tina Altwegg

active service with the Royal Air Force. The Duchess continued to be involved in royal duties following her husband's death and this is where her link to Bristol lies.

After two years on a small site in Filton, the fledgling Bristol Airport was relocated to an area of former farmland in Whitchurch, three miles south of the city centre and it was opened on 31 May 1930 by Prince George at an event attended by 30,000 people. It became only the third civil airport in the country (that is, an airport not intended for military use), seeing 900 passengers annually during 1930 and more than 4,000 annually by 1939, with most flights being short 'air taxi' services within the UK.

During World War Two, the Whitchurch site was requisitioned by the Royal Air Force and was used not only for training pilots to fly military planes, but also as one of the few still-functioning civil airports providing connecting services to the US, for instance. Famous names who used these international services via Whitchurch include pioneering aviator Amy Johnson, American First Lady Eleanor Roosevelt, wartime Prime Minister Winston Churchill and popular entertainer Bing Crosby. Some of the other passengers were almost certainly wartime spies. When the war came to an end, the Whitchurch airport returned to civil use but demand for flights was growing faster than the site could manage and with no space left to expand into, Bristol Airport needed to be relocated for a third time.

When the new and improved Bristol Airport was opened in Lulsgate Bottom, south Bristol, on 1 May 1957, it was the Duchess of Kent who was asked to cut the ribbon. While this may have seemed an odd choice given she was a relatively little known member of the royal family and not local to the area, the Duchess was pleased the Bristol Airport link to her late husband was being acknowledged and the invitation was maintaining a family connection for her.

The Duchess arrived at Temple Meads railway station that May morning, where she was met by a very welcoming crowd. She was then driven in an open-topped car through the streets of Bedminster towards the new airport site, where she received a fanfare from the City Trumpeters.

In her speech, the Duchess said the invitation to open the new airport was very touching because of her husband's link to the Whitchurch airport which, she pointed out, had "opened a new epoch of adventure and enterprise for the citizens of Bristol". She added: "It is abundantly clear that this airport will fill a very real and important need, not only for Bristol but for the West of England and the whole country."[454]

She confirmed her admiration for the bravery of Bristol during the Blitz saying: "The whole of England knows what Bristol endured and suffered in the last war. Many of your loveliest buildings were destroyed, your nights disrupted and the life of your citizens and the trade upon which they depended [were] in constant and continuous danger."[455]

ELIZABETH RAINFORTH

1814-1877, OPERA SINGER

As a child, London-born Elizabeth Rainforth's talent for singing was identified early and she benefited from excellent training before making her first public appearance at a concert on 29 February 1836, singing an aria from *Der Freischütz* to great acclaim. Elizabeth went on to become a star of the London opera scene, performing regularly at the English Opera House in London's Covent Garden, as well as other prestigious theatres around the

454 Eugene Byrne, 'How Time Flies: Bristol Airport Marks 60 Years' in *Bristol Post*, 14 May 2017.
455 Ibid.

capital and country. Following her retirement in 1871, Elizabeth came to live in Bristol at Chatterton Villa on Greenway Road, Redland, and remained there until she died on 22 September 1877.

MISS RAMSAY

born c1840, SUFFRAGIST, NOVELIST

The Bristolian writer Miss Ramsay wrote one of the earliest-known suffrage novels in the form of her 1874 book *Mildred's Career: A Tale of the Women's Suffrage Movement*. Miss Ramsay (her first name is regrettably unknown and even on her book cover she is simply 'Miss Ramsay') lived at 40 Royal York Crescent, Clifton, and was Secretary of the Clifton section of the Bristol and West of England branch of the National Society for Women's Suffrage during the 1870s. She honoured the President of the Society with a dedication in *Mildred's Career* which read: "To Lady Anna Gore Langton, to whose generous efforts the women's suffrage movement owes so much, this tale is respectfully dedicated." The Bristol office was based at 16 Park Street until 1880 (and then moved to 20 Park Street, which in 21st-century Bristol is — confusingly — 69 Park Street) but Miss Ramsay was not its only literary member, because sister suffragist Emily Spender also authored a suffrage novel around the same time (more on Emily in her own section in this volume).

Mildred's Career follows Mildred Randall as she attempts to find her voice in a world which demands women be quiet. The themes are clearly feminist: cruelty at the hands of men, women forced to marry a bad man for survival, cruel husbands denying a mother access to her children and strong women uniting to support one another. All of which are allowed by law but would not be so if women had the vote. *Mildred's Career* raises the important issue of how girls of social standing are taught no skills with which to support themselves financially and thereby achieve independence. When the business in which the Randall sisters are shareholders goes bust, orphaned Mildred and her sisters find themselves penniless. After she is rejected for a job as a lawyer's clerk and is told "There are men's occupations and women's occupations"[456], Mildred resolves to challenge this sexism and prove everyone wrong. It is perhaps inevitable that Mildred's attention is caught by a poster she sees advertising a forthcoming women's suffrage meeting to which she takes herself. Remember, this is 1874 and the suffrage movement is in its infancy: there are no militant suffragettes or Pankhursts to steal the limelight; instead we have the original suffragists campaigning peacefully and determinedly for their cause. With the impressive — if fictional — Althea Warburton as her suffrage sister, Mildred soon becomes embroiled in the campaign.

Miss Ramsay does not write in a subtle way. Her purpose is clear: she has points to make about the injustices women face and she makes them scattergun, one after the other. What is fascinating is that this is not historical fiction but a contemporary novel and it is rare to find a feminist book such as this set in the early 1870s. And this is where the value of *Mildred's Career* lies. As a writer, Miss Ramsay is neither gifted nor lacking but if you can find a copy, it is well worth reading *Mildred's Career* because the story is a thoroughly absorbing page-turner.

An 1897 review of *Mildred's Career* said: "This is rather a story of the general woman's movement, than of suffrage in particular, but it is well and spiritedly told. The heroine loses her property early in the tale, and her difficulties before she can find a profession by which she can support herself, and the obstacles

456 Miss Ramsay, 1874, *Mildred's Career*, p55.

thrown in her way by a trades union spirit, as well as by her own deficient education, are very real. When she obtains wealth, she founds a college for women, that other girls may not have the same disadvantages to struggle with that she had. The efforts made by a poor mother to obtain custody of her child are also touched upon."[457]

Miss Ramsay was not simply a novelist, because she also took her commitments to the National Society for Women's Suffrage very seriously and spoke on their behalf at a number of events around the South West. For instance, on 31 July 1874, she spoke in Torquay about why women should receive the vote, giving a "clear and spirited speech". A few weeks later she was in Teignmouth on 15 August 1874, where she responded at a public meeting to a clergyman who was troubled that there was no mention in the Bible about women having the right to vote (an argument which also appears in the early chapters of *Mildred's Career*). Miss Ramsay retorted that it was not the fault of contemporary women if the "early sacred writers had omitted to take into consideration the propriety of women having votes in the election of English Members of Parliament". The clergyman seemed horrified that a woman had spoken back and responded that women should simply not be allowed to speak! Yet he was reminded by Miss Ramsay that there were many instances in the Bible of women being permitted a voice, to which a man in the audience suggested that perhaps it was not necessary to look to the Bible for a clue as to whether women were entitled to a vote.[458]

Please also see: Anna Gore Langton (vol one), Emily Spender (vol two).

457 'Mildred's Career' in Janet Horowitz Murray, ed, 2016, *The Englishwoman's Review of Social and Industrial Questions, (Book 7: 1874)*, p160.

458 Janet Horowitz Murray, ed, 2016, *The Englishwoman's Review of Social and Industrial Questions, (Book 7: 1874)*, p160.

DOROTHEA RAMSEY
1904-1989, SOCIAL WORKER

Following a strong education in London and Cambridge (including studying flute under no lesser tutor than Gustav Holst), Dorothea Whiting Ramsey (sometimes known as Mary) moved to Bristol in 1939 upon the outbreak of World War Two, when she was assigned to the war emergency bureau by the Bristol Council of Social Service. It was here that she became aware of the social problems of elderly people, which would inform the remainder of her career. She was acutely aware that just as wartime left children in a precarious situation, it also threw vulnerable older people into increased distress.

Dorothea helped to set up the Bristol Old People's Welfare Committee in 1941 and became the organisation's first secretary. In this role, she became one of the very first people to stress the importance of residential care for older people, particularly those who felt isolated by their current living situation or who had health needs which were simply not being met in a traditional hospital, workhouse or home. As such, Dorothea established the West Town House residential care home in Bristol in 1942, which was only the second such boutique care home in the UK.

Although Dorothea returned to London in 1943, she continued her work supporting distressed older people and became a member of the advisory case subcommittee of social service, from which the National Old People's Welfare Committee grew (now known as Age UK). Dorothea was the first secretary of this charity in 1945 and remained in post for seven years, by which time the organisation had expanded to 831 local committees throughout the UK, all fighting hard to improve conditions for their clientele. Dorothea remained focussed on encouraging the building and maintenance of residential care homes for elderly people, and training others to better support older people with care and dignity.

LUCY READ

1834-1925, HEALTHCARE PIONEER

There is a small building on the corner of St George's and Anchor Road in Hotwells with a discrete foundation stone marking the site of the Read Dispensary for Women and Children. This was the first institution of its kind outside London. Dispensaries were created from the 1770s and were set up by wealthy people who paid subscriptions to enable poor people to access free healthcare; the dispensary system began to fold in 1948 with the establishment of the National Health Service.

Founded in 1874 by Lucy Anne Read of 33 West Mall, Clifton, the Bristol Dispensary for Women and Children initially opened in rented rooms on Berkeley Square, Clifton, and was the first place in Bristol where women could receive low-cost or free medical attention from a female doctor. The Dispensary was open from Monday to Saturday, and patients were admitted between 11.30am and 12.30pm. The Read Dispensary's Honorary Medical Assistant was Eliza Walker Dunbar, who was the first woman to practice as a doctor in Bristol and stayed with the Dispensary until 1895 when she founded the Walker Dunbar Hospital on Clifton Down Road with the assistance of Emily Eberle. It appears that Eliza and Lucy Read were friends and through this friendship Lucy became interested in the idea of a dispensary, at which Emily also assisted for many decades. The third female physician was Marion Linton and they were assisted by two male doctors, who were both honorary surgeons at the Read Dispensary.

Lucy was a champion for women's health who repeatedly

wrote and spoke about the need for the Dispensary. In 1876, she gave a series of lectures on improving one's health, and in 1878, she wrote to *The Times* about her motivations to "seek out" the only woman doctor in Bristol to set up specific provision for poor women and children: "It was the knowledge that many of the most respectable women of the poor allow ailments to become aggravated maladies before they will endure the publicity of the hospitals or run the risk of the young dispensary doctors that led me to introduce myself to Dr Eliza W Dunbar, who had settled here, and to ask her to give gratuitous advice to the poor. She consented... and has lately had no fewer than 53 patients in one morning. Women come from all parts of Bristol, from the neighbouring villages and even from other towns."[459]

At a talk in 1906 to the Bristol branch of the Royal Sanitary Institute (which she addressed alongside her colleague Marion Linton), Lucy "expressed the opinion that if lady doctors would support, encourage and help their poorer sisters, one of the great objects of [hygiene] would be accomplished"[460].

A letter to the *Woman's Gazette* in February 1876, from an E Scott, praised the Read Dispensary: "As you take a very great interest in the social and physical wellbeing of women, you will be pleased to learn that a dispensary for women and children has recently been established in Bristol and succeeds admirably. Women are required to pay on their first visit 1s, and children 6d, and on every succeeding visit the patients pay half these charges. This rate of payment it is to be hoped, will soon render the institution entirely self-supporting. This rate of payment and the slight self-denial it occasions on the part of those wishing to benefit by the medicines and gratuitous advice of Dr Eliza Dunbar

459 Cited in Michael Whitfield, 2016, *The Dispensaries: Healthcare for the Poor Before the NHS: Britain's Forgotten Health-Care System.*
460 'The Sanitary Institute' in *Western Daily Press*, 13 July 1906.

tend to foster the spirit of independence and self-reliance so much needed among working women. Many collateral advantages are offered. I was much delighted to find that a series of lectures had been given by Miss Read, the generous founder of the dispensary, on 'the Conditions of Health'. I had the pleasure of attending the last of the series on the subject of food constituents, and how best to preserve the nutritive qualities of ordinary food in cooking. Lectures of this description given with sufficient accuracy, and at the same time time enough to command the attention of the audience addressed, are much needed. The exertions of Miss Read and Dr Dunbar are highly appreciated by the women themselves."[461]

Following the demolition of the Berkeley Square building in 1905 because of "city improvements", the Dispensary was in urgent need of new premises while it made do with a temporary site. As Honorary Treasurer, Lucy set herself the task of raising the money: "The Committee finds themselves obliged to build, and have obtained a site … on condition that suitable premises be erected as soon as possible. £2,000 required; £1,000 still to be obtained. Contributions are urgently needed and will be received by the Hon Treasurer Miss Read."[462] The new building would, in addition to having medical treatment rooms, also have a space where lectures on health would be offered to the public. As part of the fundraising drive, there was a series of talks and concerts in aid of the new Read Dispensary, one of which at the Clifton Grand Spa was "not altogether on conventional lines, for two ladies played solos on wind instruments, and played them so well as to earn highly appreciative plaudits."[463] Well!

Clearly building work was happening at the same time as

461 Cited in Janet Horowitz Murray ed, 2016, *The Englishwoman's Review of Social and Industrial Questions, 1876.*

462 'Building Fund of the Read Dispensary' in *Western Daily Press*, 7 October 1905.

463 'Clifton Society Talk' in *Clifton Society*, 22 March 1906.

funds were being raised, because the foundation stone ceremony on the new building also took place in October 1905 and it was the Duchess of Beaufort who presided on the day. Describing the grand affair, *Clifton Society* wrote: "The site had been made gay with flags, and when the Duchess arrived from Badminton by motorcar she was received in an enclosure adorned with palms and flowering plants."[464] At the end of the speeches, a round of cheers was offered up for Lucy Read "who said that though she certainly began the work 30 years ago, the success of it was due to those doctors and others who had so well worked for and supported the Dispensary. She expressed the hope that the institution would be a blessing to the women of the neighbourhood for generations to come."[465]

In October 1906, the Read Dispensary moved to its purpose-built site in Jacob's Wells with the official opening ceremony being conducted by the Lady Mayoress of Bristol, and invited speakers including Eliza Walker Dunbar and the respected suffragist Edith Hoskyns-Abrahall, who regularly spoke around the UK on the topic of women's health and liberation. In 1907, the Read Dispensary saw 2,755 patients who, between them, made 10,728 visits.[466] This was a substantial increase on the 2,410 patients who had been seen at the previous Berkeley Square site during 1904.[467]

Contemporary newspaper reports describe her as a "well known Clifton lady" but very little is actually known about Lucy Read. What we do know is she was born in Chigwell, Essex, to a silk merchant, and she moved to Clifton in the mid-19th century with her widowed mother and they lived at 33 West Mall with three servants. When Lucy died in 1925 aged 92, she was recorded as a "spinster" who had effects worth £16,555. Alongside the

464 'Clifton Society Talk' in *Clifton Society*, 26 October 1905.
465 Ibid.
466 Anthony Beeson, 2017, *Central Bristol Through The Ages*.
467 Clifton Society Talk' in *Clifton Society*, 26 October 1905.

Read Dispensary, she was involved with many other good works including the Children's Country Visiting Society, the Salvation Army and the Christ Church Schools in Clifton. Her death notice in the *Western Daily Press* stated: "Many of the poorer class women and children owe much to the efforts and foresight of Miss Lucy Anne Read ... who first formulated a plan for establishing a medical institution in the city where women and children might consult specialist lady doctors."[468] Her funeral was held at Christ Church, Clifton, and she was buried at Arnos Vale Cemetery.

The Read Dispensary continued after Lucy's death and, during the great depression of the 1930s, the Dispensary found new ways to support struggling women. For example: "At the Read Dispensary in Anchor Road there was what was known as the Black Box. It contained baby clothes which could be borrowed and returned later."[469]

Rumours of the imminent closure of the Read Dispensary due to its financial problems began to circulate in 1929 but were quashed at a public meeting by GP Vicky Tryon, who also worked at the Dispensary. By 1934, these rumours were still bubbling away, as were suggestions that the Walker Dunbar Hospital in Clifton was in trouble, with both institutions still in debt for their building costs to the combined tune of £1,000.[470] By 1937, the two had merged and the Read Dispensary in Hotwells was now an out-patient department of the Walker Dunbar Hospital.

But despite its own troubles, the Dispensary continued to support Bristol in a wide range of ways. For example, from 1941,

468 'Death of Miss L A Read' in *Western Daily Press*, 6 October 1925.

469 Helen Reid in David Harrison, ed, 1989, *Bristol Between The Wars*, p74. It is a sad state of affairs that this service is still needed and is now provided by the Baby Bank Network, which was set up in Bristol in June 2015 and offers pre-loved baby essentials to those who cannot afford to buy them. babybanknetwork.com

470 'Bristol Effort to Remove Debt' in *Western Daily Press*, 15 June 1834.

after the Folk House nearby on Deanery Road[471] was destroyed in the Blitz, a limited curriculum of courses and classes were still run from the Read Dispensary building until the Folk House could be repaired. Similarly, when World War Two ended and many soldiers were returning to Bristol with permanent disabilities and disfigurements, the Read Dispensary led the way in running training courses to help those affected to train to find new jobs and get their lives back together, which was revolutionary. The Read Dispensary finally closed in the early 1960s after the National Health Service happily dispensed with the need for the Dispensary system.[472]

And another thing... Clifton-born **Alice Templar Short** (1875-1960) lived at 3 Dowry Road, Clifton. This was a property owned by Lucy Read, and which she bequeathed in her will to Alice and her second daughter, **Lucy Grace Short** (born 1902 and perhaps named in honour of Lucy Read, who is Lucy Short's godmother). Alice's four other children and her husband do not get a mention in the will! The Short family is still living at the Dowry Road property at the time of the 1939 Register, by which time daughter Lucy is working as an office clerk. But what was the relationship between Alice Short and Lucy Read which led to this generous situation? I wish we knew.

Please also see: Eliza Walker Dunbar (vol one), Emily Eberle (vol two), Marion Linton (vol two), Vicky Tryon (vol one).

471 The Folk House is the oldest adult education centre in Bristol and was formed in 1887. Originally located on Deanery Road, it moved to its current site on Park Street in 1964.
472 With enormous thanks to Lori Streich for her research and commitment to preserving Lucy Read's story. Lori researched and compiled the notes that formed the basis of this entry. Thanks also to the team at Arnos Vale Cemetery for locating Lucy's grave during the research for this entry.

ELSIE REEVES

born 1898, STEEL FACTORY WORKER

Proudly Bristol born and bred, Elsie Reeves spent the first 27 years of her life living and working in Hotwells. And even when she moved to the other side of the world for work, she would still always call Bristol home.

While growing up in Hotwells, Elsie attended the Dowry School and Holy Trinity Sunday School. Her family was fully embedded in Hotwells life, with her uncle George being a driver on the Clifton Rocks Railway. During World War One, she served in the Women's Land Army and was stationed at Leigh Court, where one of her roles was to drive cows across the Clifton Suspension Bridge.

After leaving school, Elsie was employed at an iron and steel company called John Lysaght & Co, based at St Vincent's Works in Netham. Lysaght's expanded quickly, exported around the world and employed more than 400 people at its Bristol site by 1878. In the same year, the business grew to add sites in Wolverhampton, Scunthorpe and Newport and even, in 1879, Newcastle in New South Wales, Australia. By 1901, the company had more than 3,000 employees globally, of whom Elsie was one.

There were opportunities for British employees to work at other sites and Elsie recalled the big change in her life that happened in 1925: "[Lysaght's] wanted Bristol workers out there [Australia] when they opened up their new factory in Newcastle. My sister and her husband went first, then they convinced us to join them. I'll never forget the day we left. It was 1926 and we lived in Purdown at the time. We got up at an unearthly hour and my husband, me and our little boy of three walked all the way to Temple Meads, complete with luggage, to catch the train. We sailed from Tilbury on the SS Berrima at 11 o'clock that morning;

I often wonder how we managed. When we arrived in Australia, Lysaght's had built rows and rows of red brick houses for their workers, wonderful it was, just like home."[473]

Elsie, her husband and their son stayed in Australia for the rest of their lives, but she always felt they had two homes and she visited her Bristol base as often as she could.

GRACE REEVES
born c1905, GEOGRAPHER

Author's note: The nomenclature of the Grace Reeves Study Centre at the University of Bristol has been a curiosity to me for some time. Who was Grace Reeves and why is a university building named after her? Finding the answer was a lot more difficult than I expected as initially nobody at the university seemed to know...

There are scant facts I have been able to obtain about Grace Reeves' early life but we do know she was one of the original 14 students to study Geography when it was first formally taught at the University of Bristol in 1920. She was also one of the original graduating students when she did so in June 1929. When staff at the university's Geography department wrote an essay in 1995 celebrating its first 75 years, Grace was one of the surviving students who contributed with anecdotes and photographs to illustrate the piece. At that time, she was living in retirement in Cheltenham, where she had worked at St Mary's College (now part of the University of Gloucester) between 1951 and 1973 as Head of the Geography department. By the time of Grace's retirement in 1973, the St Mary's annual report noted she had

473 Rosemary Clinch, 1985, *Unknown Bristol*, p77.

"organised one of the most successful departments in the college". Grace had died by the time the University of Bristol's essay was updated in 2009 although sadly we do not know her exact year of death. In October 2015, the University of Bristol renamed the Geography Library as the Grace Reeves Study Centre in honour of the role she had played in the inception of the department and her lifelong dedication to the science of geography.[474]

And another thing... Grace was one of the first students to stay at the then-new Clifton Hill House women's halls of residence which **May Staveley** fought so hard to get off the ground.

Please also see: May Staveley (vol two).

SARAH RIDLEY

died 1726, PHILANTHROPIST

The Ridley's Almshouses which once stood on the corner of Milk Street and Old King Street (now in the heart of Broadmead shopping centre, opposite where Debenhams stands) were built with money donated by Sarah Ridley in her will and named in memory of herself and her brother Thomas.

Sarah's will had stated: "Above all things in remembrance of my late brother, who died a bachelor, I thought fit, that something might remain to perpetuity, whereby to retain as well his memory as mine own, have resolved for that purpose on a lasting charity; and for that end and intent, I give to ... all of the city of Bristol ...

474 Peter Haggett et al, 1995, *Geography at Bristol: An Historical Account of the School of Geographical Sciences*, University of Bristol pamphlet. With many thanks to Maria Fannin and David Richards at the University of Bristol, who were extremely helpful with sourcing further information about Grace. I am also grateful to Louise Hughes at the University of Gloucester for taking the trouble to hunt through the archives on my behalf and to send me scans of letters handwritten by Grace.

the sum of £2,200, which I appoint to be placed forth at interest in their names, in trust, until sufficient money be raised by the interest of it, as well purchase some houses or lands, in or near some church or chapel within the city or suburbs of Bristol, and to erect and build thereon, or otherwise to convert, some buildings erected into a convenient almshouse for ten persons, over the door whereof should be engraved these words: 'In memory of Mr Thomas Ridley and Sarah Ridley, being brother and sister, never married.'" Her will went on in great detail to include many more stipulations and clauses for the building of the almshouses.[475]

The property included accommodation for ten people as well as a live-in 'master'; building work began in 1735 and concluded four years later in 1739. A parcel of land had been found which housed five very rundown messuages (a residential house with outbuildings) in what was then deemed a suburb just north of Bristol. An 1819 description of the almshouses said that they were "a neat building of freestone for five bachelors and five maids, each of whom receive 9s per fortnight"[476]. There was a small watch house outside on the corner of the pavement (later converted into a newsagent's kiosk), which was a rare early example of primitive policing. The watch house was demolished by the 1920s and the almshouses, which had been damaged by bombs during World War Two, were completely razed in 1954 to make way for the Broadmead shopping centre.

475 *The Bristol Charities' Report of the Commission*, 1831, p192.
476 Anthony Beeson, 2012, *Central Bristol Through Time*, p29.

MARY RIDSDEL
1849-1890, SALVATION ARMY OFFICER

"Fought a good fight as the first female officer in the Salvation Army." This is the inscription on the tombstone of Captain Mary Ann Ridsdel in Arnos Vale Cemetery. But who was this woman who laid one of the building blocks of Bristol?

Born Annie Davis, after marrying Commissioner William Ridsdel in 1878 her name became Mary Ann Ridsdel and she was fully entrenched in the recently formed Salvation Army, in which her new husband held the highest rank of officer and was one of the most respected people in the entire church. In turn, Mary would become the Salvation Army's first ever female officer: "Annie Davis became an officer and a very successful officer she proved. It was thought by some that female officers would not be equal to the work of the Army ... but Annie Davis did better than some of the men and God gave her a long run of victories."[477]

After becoming an officer, Mary was initially stationed in Essex but, following her marriage to William, the couple worked together for the Salvation Army variously in Cardiff, Bradford and Plymouth, where they recruited others to join and support their church. The family moved to Redland Road, Redland, in September 1879, when Commissioner Ridsdel was made Commandant of the Bristol Division of the Salvation Army, and as part of their work in the city the couple were fundraising for the building of a Salvation Army hall in Bristol (this would eventually open on Dean Lane, Bedminster, in 1909 and remains in use today).

The couple had a son, Stanley, who sadly died on 20 April 1890 at just eight months old. They also had four surviving

477 'General Booth in Bristol' in *Bristol Mercury*, 5 April 1890.

children, two of whom were twins aged only eight months when Mary died of tuberculosis in 1890. Her day-long funeral began with prayers from 8-9am, followed by a large procession through Bristol which was attended by Salvation Army officers from all over the UK, before a service at 1.30pm and the burial at Arnos Vale Cemetery at 4pm. A newspaper report said: "There were enormous crowds of people at various points of the route, notably at the Horsefair and at Bristol Bridge. At starting there were about 1,100 soldiers, but many hundreds of friends joined them on the way, and the procession, with four persons abreast, was about half a mile in length."[478]

It was a lengthy and solemn affair, and Mary's coffin was strewn with flowers. General William Booth, the founder of the Salvation Army, came from London to conduct the funeral ceremony and "as they marched through the streets of the city he wanted them to lift up their voices for the people of Bristol, and he prayed there would be a greater uplifting of souls than ever before. God would raise up warriors to take the places of Mrs Ridsdel and others, and also soldiers for the ranks: to fight as she fought and never give in."[479]

Please also see: Emily Smyth (vol one).

JANE JACKSON ROECKEL
1834-1907, MUSICIAN

As was sadly so often the way, pianist Jane Jackson Roeckel (Jackson being her surname before marriage) often worked professionally under an assumed male name or her initials in order for her work

478 Ibid.
479 Ibid.

to be taken more seriously by a society that largely only valued the work of men. As such, her surviving 200 compositions are credited to either 'Jules de Sevrai' or 'J L Roeckel'. For this entry, however, I shall reclaim her given name and call her Jane.

Having studied under such fine musicians as Charles Hallé and Clara Schumann, Jane lived and worked in Clifton, where she had been born. She made her professional debut in 1854 with a series of three concerts in London, performing a piano duet with Ernst Pauer. A reviewer wrote: "The pianoforte duet of Onslow, the best of the two by that composer, which is among the most exciting performances of the evening. It was admirably played by Miss Jane Jackson and Mr Pauer, and received with much favour."[480] After her London debut, Jane seemed to prefer staying closer to her home in Clifton and she largely performed in the Bristol and Bath areas, always to rapturous receptions.

In July 1864, she married the composer Leopold Roeckel at Clifton Church and, although she continued to perform as a pianist after her marriage, she seemed to reduce the number of concerts she gave, instead focussing on teaching. In addition, she was concerned with promoting the welfare of young musicians. One of those whom she helped was a 14-year-old working-class violinist from Newcastle called Marie Hall who, with Jane's patronage, was able to rise from being a street performer to a concert hall musician.

After recognising Marie's talent, Jane arranged for her to meet the composer Philip Napier Miles, a millionaire who enjoyed supporting aspiring musicians. With Miles' financial backing, Jane concocted a plan for Marie to spend three years studying with Professor Johann Kruse in London. Yet inexplicably, Marie's father was not keen on this patronage and Miles had to endow

480 sophie-drinker-institut.de/roeckel-jane

him the sum of £1 a week as compensation for the 'loss' of his daughter's domestic services around the home. Marie's career flourished thanks to this great start and she spent her entire life playing professionally to rapturous acclaim. None of this would have been possible without Jane's support.[481]

In what I am choosing to interpret as a feminist act, Jane also hosted themed concerts with the chosen subject often being 'women'. For instance, in 1885, she arranged a concert in Clifton featuring only compositions written by and performed by women. This was rather radical for the time. She also used money raised at these concerts to support children in the Bristol orphanages. Jane was buried at Shirehampton Church.

BLANCHE ROGERS

1867-1951, SUFFRAGIST

Author's note: For more than six months during my research for this book, Blanche Rogers was simply 'Mrs Rogers' and it infuriated me something rotten. In all the news reports about her, the minutes from meetings she had spoken at and scant records in existing history books, she was either 'Mrs Rogers' or 'Mrs FW Rogers' (her husband's initials and surname).

But by trawling the census reports and joining together some blurry puzzle pieces, I was eventually able to track her down under the typo of 'Blanche Rogerss' and the relief was immense. From simply knowing her first name, I was able to find out so much more information about this amazing early suffragist: from her birth and death dates, to the names of her children, who the Lyons family was and so much more. This really does show the importance of giving women their own names

481 Paula Gillett, 2000, *Musical Women in England, 1870-1914: Encroaching on All Man's Privileges*, p72.

and not, upon marriage, letting them lose all autonomy and becoming an identity-free 'Mrs Rogers'.

Bristol-born Blanche Mary Rogers (née Lyons) and her husband Frederick married on 17 October 1889 at St Mary Redcliffe and they set up home at 2 Kensington Villas, Royal Park, Clifton, where they had three daughters: Blanche, Eleanor and Mary. The family was supportive of the peaceful campaign for women's suffrage led by the National Union of Women's Suffrage Societies, although in later years they also joined the more militant campaign run by the Women's Social and Political Union (WSPU) and worked alongside the WSPU's Annie Kenney, who was based in Clifton for a few years from 1907. In addition, Frederick was Honorary Secretary of the Bristol Men's League for Women's Suffrage.

A drawing-room meeting was held in Clifton at 16 West Mall (the home of suffrage sisters Maud Duncan and Mabel Cross) in May 1907, which was part of a series organised by the Ladies' Club of Clifton as a warm-up to their full-on suffrage campaign. Chaired by the redoubtable Margaret Tanner, the speakers included some women who will be familiar to readers of *The Women Who Built Bristol*: the gymnastics teacher Theodora Johnson, local writer Amy Green-Armytage and our very own 'Mrs FW Rogers'. Blanche read out a humorous sketch by their host Mabel Cross entitled 'Latest Intelligence From the Planet Venus', which proposed that life on Venus was almost identical to life on Earth, except that all political, business and other significant decisions were made only by women, and when men on Venus started agitating for the vote, the women shut them down pointing out the mental inadequacies of the male sex.[482]

On 2 April 1911, when suffragists and suffragettes all over

482 'Drawing-Room Meeting' in *Western Daily Press*, 27 May 1907.

the UK were evading the national census completion, Blanche joined with other local women by spending the night at a house in Bath, so she was not at home and was therefore missing from the census report. The feeling was that if women did not count as citizens, then they should not be counted on the census. We find a mention of Blanche at the Bath census evasion house in her friend Mary Blathwayt's meticulously recorded diaries: "There were 29 of us. Mrs Mansel took the chair and spoke. Mrs Rogers came over from Bristol and recited but left again at midnight. Grace Tollemache played the violin and Aethel accompanied on a piano."[483] In sympathy, Frederick also seems to have evaded the census, because the report for 2 Kensington Villas shows the house as being completely empty on 2 April 1911.

Blanche regularly spoke at suffrage meetings around Bristol; for instance, in 1912, she was at another drawing-room meeting in Clifton hosted by Mabel Cross which also included Eliza Dunbar Walker, Amy Green-Armytage, Theodora Johnson and Marion Linton) debating whether or not imprisoned suffragettes were right to go on hunger strike and whether or not the government was right to force feed them. Naturally, the attendees of the meeting were on the side of the suffragettes: "Mrs FW Rogers urged that forcible feeding should never be used in any country for a political prisoner, which was what the suffragettes were. It should only be resorted to in medical science, and then as a last resort as it was too terrible for a civilised society. The women started the hunger strike as a protest and in order to be treated as political prisoners."[484]

Following World War One, Blanche became involved in the Women's International League for Peace and Freedom, as did

483 Jill Liddington, 2014, *Vanishing For The Vote: Suffrage, Citizenship and the Battle for the Census*, p163.
484 'Barbara's Budget' in *Clifton Society*, 28 November 1912.

many other suffragists of her generation. Frederick had died by the time of the 1939 Register of England, but we can see Blanche was still living at the same address, her profession was teacher of elocution and she had taken in a number of lodgers.

And another thing... Blanche was one of the suffragists who planted a bush at the Suffragettes' Wood created by the **Blathwayts** at their Batheaston home. On 27 February 1911, Blanche planted a Scotia Holly bush in the arboretum, and a photograph by Colonel Linley Blathwayt of the bush and its commemorative plaque can be viewed online at bathintime.co.uk

---

Please also see: Emily Blathwayt (vol one), Mary Blathwayt (vol one), Mabel Cross (vol two), Maud Duncan (vol two), AJ Green-Armytage (vol two), Theodora Johnson (vol one), Annie Kenney (vol one), Margaret Tanner (vol one), Aethel Tollemache (vol one), Grace Tollemache (vol one).

FLOSS ROGERS

born c1910, CHARGEHAND

When most women left work at the Fry's chocolate factory, it was to enjoy their retirement in peace and so they could spend their twilight years with their families. However, Chargehand Floss Rogers was forced out of work due to a fractured neck sustained in a workplace accident in May 1965. Having joined Fry's at the age of 14, she worked on conveyor packing at the Union Street factory and Floss went on to join the Somerdale plant, rising through the ranks until she was made a Chargehand in 1958. Despite also caring for her sick mother, Floss still carried on working during the mornings... until her awful accident forced her out of employment. Just imagine how different Floss' retirement would have been had she lived in 21st-century Bristol with the health and safety culture we now experience.[485]

ROSA ROUSE

born c1900, POLICE OFFICER

Initially working with the Bristol City Police Force, Rosa Rouse had a special skill which meant she was in high demand. Her skill was that she could ride a motorbike. As such, she was transferred to join the Gloucester Constabulary on 12 December 1927 and was stationed at Staple Hill… bringing the number of women on the Gloucestershire police force up to a grand total of seven (there was no dramatic change in this number until the 1960s).

By 1931, there were 64,693 police officers throughout the UK but only 167 of these were female.[486] Rosa was flying a flag for the future but she – and the six other female police officer – had to contend with a hell of a lot of sexism. They were snubbed by their male peers, who often refused to give them work. And although when working in Gloucester during the 1930s she was regularly taking witness statements for cases of incest, following a move to Cheltenham, Rosa found she was treated as little more than an errand girl by the men.[487] Despite Rosa and the other female police officers trying to explain to their male colleagues that they, as women, were more likely to gain the trust of vulnerable witnesses, they were regularly overlooked and bullied by their colleagues. As is revealed in this extract from a book about violence and policing in Britain, which concerns Rosa watching

485 Somerdale Magazine, published by JS Fry. August 1965 edition.
486 'News', *Gloucester Citizen*, 18 March 1931.
487 Shani D'Cruze, Ivor Crewe, 2000, *Everyday Violence in Britain, 1850-1950: Gender and Class*, p123.

a male colleague interviewing a young woman who was accused of concealing a birth: "While she was telling her story, she was contradicted and told she was telling a lot of lies ... I was so angry I called the officer aside and told him not to betray his ignorance and inexperience any further. The girl had burst into tears and was terribly upset, insisting that she was telling the truth. She had said that when the baby was born, there was no-one to cut the cord and she waited for the afterbirth to come away, still attached to the baby. This was said by the interviewer to be absolutely impossible. From previous experience, I knew that not only was it possible but probable."[488]

Causes close to Rosa's heart included child abuse, infanticide and the demanding of money with menaces, and she devoted time to raising awareness of these crimes. In 1928, Rosa was also one of the few women police officers called to give evidence during the Savidge Inquiry. This was a high-profile case attracting national interest and concerned Irene Savidge, who had been arrested for indecent behaviour following "a rather chaste kiss" with a well-known man in Hyde Park, London, in April 1928. During a police interrogation lasting five hours, the male police officers ordered the female police chaperone to leave the room and then instructed Ms Savidge to show them her underwear. She later complained about the appalling treatment she had received from the male police officers, which led to an enquiry — and ultimately reform — into the way the police treated female suspects in general.

Due to ill health, Rosa (by this time married and known as Rosa Ashby) was pensioned from the police force on 4 July 1941. Her photograph albums and other records have been stored with the Gloucester Archives and of particular interest is the unpublished manuscript of Rosa's memoirs.

488 Ibid, p123-124.

MARY RUDGE
1842-1919, INTERNATIONAL CHESS CHAMPION

Herefordshire-born Mary Rudge (one of seven siblings, which is relevant because we meet a few of them during her story) learned to play chess when she was still a young child and became the first Englishwoman to play competitively both to a high standard and for a long time. This is particularly notable because this was at a time when women were actively discouraged from playing this 'manly' game that required mental aptitude, which — of course — a woman would not have.

So Mary and her sister Emily adopted the pseudonyms 'Snowdon' and 'Vesuvius' when they played in a national correspondence chess tournament in *Cassell's Illustrated Family Paper*[489], not wanting to give away the fact they were mere girls. Between 1870 and 1873, the two sisters competed successfully in many more postal chess competitions yet they still did not consider themselves to be serious chess players.

When their father died in 1874, Mary and another sister, Caroline, both unmarried and with no assets of their own, moved to Bristol to live with their brother Henry, who was a curate at St John the Evangelist on Whiteladies Road. Fortunately, in 1871 the Bristol and Clifton Chess Association had become one of the very first chess clubs in the world to admit women as members, which enabled Mary to join up and really improve her game. It was noted in the Association's minutes from 1872: "During the year the vice-president proposed that ladies should be admitted to the Club as associates, at an annual subscription of 5s, which was agreed to. We believe that no members of the softer sex were

489 Correspondence chess is largely similar to chess played on a board except the players do not meet and their moves are sent via post. The game also, obviously, lasts a great deal longer, sometimes up to several months. An advantage for players is they have much longer in which to consider their moves, which means the games are often much more complex.

Mary Rudge illustration by Carrie Love

admitted as subscribers, by any chess club in this country, prior to this date."[490]

By only February 1875, the *Chess Player's Chronicle* had noted: "It is considered that Miss Rudge has not a superior among the ladies of this country."[491] She may not have had a superior but she did have a rival… in the shape of Eliza Thorold from Bath, whose brother Edmund was also playing a long series of matches against Mary. Regardless of the Thorold siblings' proficiency, Mary trampled them both in fairly swift time and was soon able to defeat most male opponents with almost guaranteed certainty. As a cautious player, Mary took few risks and won her games by sound technique, taking advantage of the gambles her opponents often took instead. The *British Chess Magazine* noted of her play: "Rudge in capital form … displayed those qualities of steadiness and tenacity for which she is renowned … Her play was marked throughout by care, exactitude and patience. Someone said of her, 'She doesn't seem to care so much to win a game as to make her opponent lose it.' She risked nothing, she never indulged in fireworks for the purpose of startling the gallery."[492]

By 1879, Mary, Caroline and Henry were running the Luccombe House Preparatory School for boys in Redland but, when the school no longer proved profitable, in 1885 Henry moved to Lancashire leaving his unmarried sisters in Bristol. It is thought they lived with their widowed sister Sarah Heslop. Despite her skill, chess was merely a hobby which brought in no money and, with no income from the school anymore, Mary was struggling to make ends meet. It is for this reason that an appeal was published in *British Chess Magazine* in June 1889 saying: "Our readers will be sorry to hear that Miss M Rudge, of Clifton, is

490 J Burt, 1883, *The Bristol Chess Club*.
491 *Chess Player's Chronicle*, February 1875, p197.
492 *British Chess Magazine*, 1897, pp285-296.

at present in very depressed pecuniary circumstances; so much so that she has felt obliged (though most reluctantly) to give her consent to an appeal being made on her behalf. We are sure English chess players will not allow one of their best lady players to remain in actual, though it is to be hoped only temporary, want, and contributions for its relief, however small, will be thankfully received." Consequently, Mary would receive a £20 donation from the Bristol club in recognition of her having just won the championship cup for them. Mary was also invited to Dublin as a paid companion of the chess problem composers and journalists Thomas and Frideswide Rowland, and she stayed there from July 1889 to May 1890.

During her time in Dublin, Mary became one of the strongest chess players in Ireland and made several further visits to Dublin to play chess in later years. For the 1889-90 Armstrong Cup (one of the earliest chess leagues in the world), Mary played second board below the Irish champion, James Porterfield Rynd. She remained unbeaten, winning eight games and drawing three. Mary also won the ladies' challenge cup in Cambridge in 1890 but then avoided women-only chess tournaments, because there were no other female competitors who came close to her in standard. However, she was a member of the Ladies' Chess Club, which was founded in 1895. She continued to compete against men… and beat them. She also continued to represent the Bristol and Clifton Chess Association at tournaments, usually successfully.

Mary's career high was winning the first ladies' international chess tournament in summer in 1897, which was held to celebrate Queen Victoria's diamond jubilee. Mary conceded only one draw against 19 opponents and won the first prize of £60, as well as the title of Lady Champion of the World. Her last known public appearance as a chess player was on 26 November 1898 at the Imperial Hotel on Whiteladies Road (now called Canynge Hall and part of the University of Bristol), when she played against the world champion Emanuel Lasker: the game was broken off when they ran out of time and, while he did not concede defeat, Lasker did say that Mary "would probably win if she played the best moves all the time"[493], which is surely all anyone needs to do to win anything.

After 1900, we rarely hear of Mary again. We know she certainly made no significant money from her chess triumphs and was largely paid in hospitality rather than cash, which is why in 1912 several chess magazines were asking for donations for a pension fund for Mary. By the time of her death in 1919, Mary was the last surviving sibling from the Rudge family and was living in Streatham, London, in very reduced circumstances and suffering terribly with rheumatism.

ANNA RUSSELL

1807-1876, BOTANIST

Born in Arnos Vale as one of seven children to a Unitarian sugar refiner, Anna Worsley was encouraged to develop her interests, including her passion for natural history. While her brother Samuel showed an aptitude for fossils, Anna was initially more keen on insects before settling on botany. Her contribution to HC Watson's 1835 book *New Botanist's Guide* brought her work to a wider audience and with Watson's patronage she was able to further develop her knowledge of plants. In the 1840s, Anna joined the Botanical Society of London and for years she actively contributed specimens to its annual exchanges of herbarium material. It was through the Society that she met her husband

493 *Bristol Mercury*, 3 December 1898.

Frederick Russell, whom she married in 1844. The couple initially lived in Brislington before moving, in 1856, to Kenilworth, Warwickshire, where Anna developed an interest in fungi: she would eventually complete more than 730 drawings of different species of fungi.[494]

SALOME

1976-2017, GORILLA

While Alfred the Gorilla is better known in Bristol's ape circles (you can visit his taxidermied carcass at the Bristol Museum and Art Gallery), his lesser-known successor Salome is equally important to remember. Apart from everything else, in 2004 Salome was the very first gorilla anywhere in the world to receive fertility treatment.

Salome was conceived at Bristol Zoo but born at London Zoo, where her mother Lomie lived. As an infant, she was hand reared before moving to Chessington Zoo, where she had her first infant in 1988 and then came to Bristol Zoo in 1997. At Bristol, Salome was one of eight Western Lowland gorillas and her keepers believed she was the most intelligent of the band. She amused visitors by building nests on the glass above their heads in the 360-degree viewing area inside the Gorilla House and, when the weather was good, she spent a lot of time outside on Gorilla Island.

In total, Salome had three infants, with her second and third being conceived following the pioneering use of human fertility drugs. Salome was given Clomid (which encourages the ovaries

494 With thanks to researchers at Arnos Vale Cemetery (including Marion Blackburn, Hildegard Dumper, Liz Johnson and Janine Marriott) for generously providing extra information for this entry.

to release eggs) and in 2006 gave birth to Komale. Her third baby Kukena was born in 2011. In the final months of her life, Salome's health began to fail and she was being treated for heart disease, which was what ultimately killed her when her keepers found her dead in the Gorilla House in November 2017 at the age of 41.

Bristol Zoo Chief Executive Dr Bryan Caroll said: "Everyone is extremely saddened by Salome's death. The zoo has lost one of its most popular animals and one of its great characters. So many of us feel we have lost a friend." He added: "So many people knew her and recognised her by a small ginger patch of hair on her head and they would return time and time again to see her. She was loved by our guests and by our keepers and staff alike."[495]

HILDA DIX SANDFORD

1875-1946, ILLUSTRATOR

As the fifth of eight children born into the Bristolian Dix family, Hilda Dix had to find her own way to make her voice heard... and she found her way via art. Hilda's religious father was an insurance salesman who exercised his own creative streak by writing hymns, while elder sister Gertrude Dix became a popular novelist thanks to socialist fiction such as 1895's *The Image Breakers* (based on the true story of striking Bristol factory women). There was clearly a strong creative streak in the Dix household.

As such, Hilda became a respected painter and illustrator thanks to the encouragement she received from her family as a child. Hilda won two prestigious *Studio* magazine competitions when she was young and, in the 1890s, she won further prizes for her illustrations. After marrying engineer John Sandford in 1898,

495 Heather Pickstock, 'Bristol Zoo's Favourite Gorilla Salome Has Died' in *Bristol Post*, 1 November 2017.

the couple moved from Bristol to New South Wales, Australia, for several years and, during their time in the southern hemisphere, Hilda created illustrations of Aboriginal children, which was to set her artistic style for the rest of her career.

The couple moved back to England in 1903, when Hilda took work producing illustrations of playing children for the greetings card companies Raphael Tuck & Sons and Hildesheimer & Co, which were both benefiting from the phenomenal popularity for posting cards at the turn of the last century. Taking her creativity in a different direction in her retirement, Hilda became an active member of local amaeteur dramatic societies near her final home in Winscombe, Somerset.[496]

Please also see: Gertrude Dix (vol one).

SARAH SEYMOUR

1838-1859, DROWNED BRIDE-TO-BE

One week before the vicar of St John's church in Bedminster had been expecting to marry Sarah Jane Seymour to her beau Harry Larcombe in June 1859, he found himself conducting a joint funeral for the doomed couple. Sarah (who lived on Harford Street, Redcliffe, and worked for ES & A Robinson's paper factory on Redcliffe Street) and Harry were drowned following a boating accident off the coast of Watchet, Somerset, in which at least six other people also died (the exact death toll varies considerably in newspaper reports).

Shortly before their wedding, the young couple (Sarah was 21 and Harry 22) were enjoying a seaside escape, as was common

496 With thanks to Dawn Dyer for the nomination of Hilda Dix Sandford to this book.

in the mid-Victorian era after the railways and steam power had made travel so much easier. Having taken a train to Weston-super-Mare, the couple joined the steam-powered, iron-built ship the Neath Abbey, which had been constructed in 1842 and was the pride and joy of the Welsh ironworks which had built it.

On 13 June 1859, there were several hundred pleasure seekers aboard the Neath Abbey for the trip along the coast. When the ship returned to Watchet at the end of the outing, boats were due to transfer passengers from the ship to the shore but when the time came there were just two small boats available, which could only safely carry eight people at a time. This was far from sufficient. Due to this lack of boats and the subsequent overcrowding, as well as problematic strong winds and high tides, the overloaded boats sank beneath the water line, became filled with water and many passengers fell overboard and drowned. Sarah and Harry were among them. It is important to remember that in the Victorian era, many people did not know how to swim and, in addition, women were particularly overwhelmed by their cumbersome and heavy layers of clothing. Harry's father George was one of those on the shore who watched, traumatised, as his son and future daughter-in-law whom he had come to greet drowned before his eyes. A Watchet coastguard who witnessed the tragedy later said he was horrified so many people had been squashed into the tiny boats in the first place.

The tragedy attracted a lot of press attention, and the angered and grieving people of Bristol wanted someone to blame. Was the Neath Abbey's captain responsible (he was eventually cleared of responsibility, not least because he immediately recognised the dangers posed and set off in a rowing boat to try and rescue those who had fallen in the water)? Were some passengers drunk (as certain reports claimed) and incapacitated? Even the misshapen pier at Watchet came in for condemnation and was subsequently rebuilt to a more satisfactory standard. Ultimately, it didn't matter: nothing would bring back the dead.

The burial of Sarah and Harry was the very first in St John's New Cemetery on the steep slope between St John's Lane and Cotswold Road in Bedminster. Due to the massive press attention the Watchet drownings had generated — and the particular focus given to the doomed couple — their funeral became a public event attended by around 5,000 people. Sarah's coffin was carried by six young women and Harry's was carried by six young men, and a huge procession followed the coffins from the church to the New Cemetery, which had only been consecrated two weeks before. In the 1940s, following devastating damage to the church and its grounds in the Blitz, St John's and the New Cemetery were demolished, and the space is now a small community park where only two gravestones remain. One of these is Sarah and Harry's joint tomb.[497]

'ELIZABETH SHAW'

born 1902, CHOCOLATIER

At the turn of the last century, the Smith family in Somerset welcomed their daughter Elizabeth Katherine Smith to the world shortly before making the move to Teddington, Surrey, in search of work. As soon as she was out of school and seeking employment, young Elizabeth began working with a Teddington confectioner called Patrick Joyce at Page & Shaw, whom she married in Streatham on 8 May 1926 and the couple set up home in the area. Marriage wasn't plain sailing for the Joyces, however, and they fell on tough times, having to give up their home and

497 'Daytrip Turned Into a Tragedy For Bristol and Ended a Young Couple's Dreams' in *South Bristol Voice*, August 2017, pp30-33.

move in with Mr and Mrs Bellchamber, who were Elizabeth's sister and brother-in-law.

One of Elizabeth's loves in life was cooking and making treats for her family. A favourite recipe was chocolate made from a honeycomb crisp which was flavoured with mint, a recipe that had been given to her by a friend from the US. In order to make a little extra money, Elizabeth started to manufacture mint crisps on her sister's stove to sell at her brother-in-law's shop, Bellchambers.

The chocolates were enormously popular and soon required proper branding and packaging in order to fully monetise them. In need of a name for her brand, Elizabeth and Patrick decided to combine her first name with the surname of their former employer, Shaw: the feeling being that 'Elizabeth Shaw' was a name which was both pleasing to the ear and reassuring in tone. This was the inception of the soon-to-be-enormous confectionery brand Elizabeth Shaw.

With Patrick's help, the chocolates were distributed to shops other than Bellchambers. But as the number of outlets increased, so too did the demand for a bigger kitchen: Elizabeth's sister's stove was no longer up to the task. The couple set up a kitchen at 25 High Street, Teddington but, before long, even this was too small and they moved again, first to The Mint House on Commerce Road, Brentford and, in 1953, to a bigger site in Camberley.

To make these moves possible, Elizabeth and Patrick invested every last penny in machinery and equipment for the Camberley factory and just when everything was going so well, disaster struck. A fire tore through the factory, destroying virtually everything within the building… taking all of the Joyces' investment with it. With no money left to start again, Elizabeth was forced to sell the Camberley factory site and, worse, the prosperous brand name of Elizabeth Shaw.

In 1968, Elizabeth Shaw (both brand and recipes) was bought by Cavenham Confectionery which relocated the business to Bristol. Cavenham invested heavily in boosting the brand and expanding the range so that, as well as mint crisps, the Elizabeth Shaw name was also producing quality boxed chocolates. Over the following decades, further mergers and changes to the ownership of Elizabeth Shaw took place but the one thing which remains steady is the production of high-quality and popular mint crisps in Stoke Gifford, which can still be bought at confectioners and supermarkets all over the country.[498]

MABEL SHAW

1883-1956, SCHOOL SECRETARY

Author's note: Something which has cropped up a few times while researching both volumes of The Women Who Built Bristol *is how little the roles of administrators have been recorded. Whether women such as Lucy Read (who coordinated the Read Dispensary for Women and Children in Hotwells) or Mabel Shaw (who was secretary for Redland High School), these administrative roles are often overlooked as being dull or unimportant. On the contrary, these roles are crucial for actually making things happen and the people who perform them well should not be underestimated.*

Mabel Grace Shaw, who lived at 3 Miles Road, Clifton, was the Secretary to the Headteacher of Redland High School for Girls (which merged with Redmaids' High School in 2016) from 1912 to 1940. Recording the retirement of Miss Shaw to Burnham, Redland High School lamented: "It does not need words of ours

498 With thanks to Lynda Brine at Elizabeth Shaw for her help with this entry.

to express the school's sense of loss in the resignation of Miss Shaw in July 1940. As Clerk to the Council and School Secretary, Miss Shaw held a unique position. Her knowledge of the school was unsurpassed and her very great love for Redland combined with this knowledge to produce an unflagging care for all that concerned the welfare of the school, the administration of its affairs, our beloved building and the welfare of each member of the school, past and present. None who were privileged to take part will ever forget the parties which Miss Shaw so often helped to organise, the sparkle given by her wit and her uncanny powers of invariably winning every competition."[499]

Miss Shaw also wrote the book *The History of Redland High School,* which she had begun in 1931 in advance of the school's jubilee in 1932. The book was praised for being brought to life by "that lively sense of humour which was one of Miss Shaw's most endearing qualities"[500]. Recording the school's growth from having just four pupils when it opened at Redland Grove in 1882 to 150 pupils by the time it moved to Redland Court in 1885, Miss Shaw wrote: "May 12 1885 must have been the most exciting day in the whole history of the school, for on that day the pupils, numbering 150 in all, assembled for the summer term in Redland Grove to migrate en bloc — led by Miss Cocks [the headmistress] to their wonderful new home on the hill... On arriving at Redland Court, Miss Cocks took the whole party on a tour of inspection. One can well imagine the excitement — yes, the awe — as they went from room to room and realised that this beautiful house was to be their school."[501]

In her obituary, which was written by teacher Dora Beatrice Weekes with whom Mabel shared a house, the school wrote: "No

499 Miss Berwick, 'Editorial' in *Redland High School Magazine,* June 1941, p4.
500 Dora Weekes, 'Obituary: Mabel Grace Shaw' in *Redland High School Magazine,* 1957, p33.
501 'Notes of the Day: Redland High School' in *Western Daily Press,* 30 May 1932.

one who knew Miss Shaw could fail to realise what Redland meant to her, or what Redland owed to her. She knew every girl in school and remembered all about her ... She served under four headmistresses, whom she supported with wisdom and loyalty through difficult times and during the two wars ... She died after a long illness which she bore with great patience and courage."[502]

Please also see: Elizabeth Cocks (vol one), Lucy Read (vol two).

WINIFRED SHORT

born 1910, SUPERVISOR

Winifred Clarion May Short dedicated her working life to the Fry's Chocolate Factory, spending 43 years with the firm. After attending Hanham Road School, Winifred joined Fry's at the age of 14 as a junior day worker at the Union Street factory in the Fancy Packing Department.

In 1930, Winifred's department moved to the large purpose-built factory at Somerdale, where she enjoyed multiple promotions until she reached a supervisory level in 1950. Like all Fry's workers, and all businesses run on Quaker principles, Winifred took part in extra-curricular activities with the firm. For her, this meant playing the piano at lunchtime concerts.[503]

502 Dora Weekes, 'Obituary: Mabel Grace Shaw' in *Redland High School Magazine*, 1957, p33.
503 *Somerdale Magazine*, published by JS Fry. July 1968 edition.

MAGGIE 'GRAN' SIMMONS
born c1880, COAL SELLER

There was once an island community at St Philip's Marsh, which was the housing area for the workers in the Old Market area. The area is now home only to faceless trading estates and car dealerships. But until the 1950s, it was a vibrant, close-knit and self-contained community of more than 6,000 women, men and children spread across 20 streets. St Philip's Marsh was a poor area and most homes only had outside toilets and no bathrooms, yet the sense of camaraderie and community spirit was second to none. The terraced houses were filled with life and colour, there were grocery shops on most corners, plenty of pubs to choose from and good schools for the children to attend.

There were also lots of local personalities, one of whom was Maggie Simmons, known simply as 'Gran' to most people. She was one of many street sellers in St Philip's Marsh and what Gran sold was coal. With her hand-drawn cart piled high with sacks of coal, she trundled it to and from the Bristol Gas Light and Coke Company (known locally as the Coke House) and around the streets of the Marsh to sell to her customers. Come rain or shine, Gran would be out there selling her coal. She was still working at the age of 75, which given the physically demanding nature of her work is very impressive indeed.[504]

Due to the poor-quality slum housing, infestations of rats and vermin from the nearby Feeder Canal and the general unsanitary living conditions, St Philip's Marsh was finally declared an industrial rather than residential area and, from the early 1950s onwards, families and householders were encouraged by Bristol City Council to move elsewhere. Eventually, those who refused

504 Bristol Broadsides, 1986, *St Philips Marsh: The Story of an Island and its People*, p5.

were issued with compulsory purchase orders and forced out by the late 1950s. The final residents left in the very early 1960s and today only a couple of residential houses remain, and almost everything was demolished from houses to shops, schools to pubs. However, the wrecking ball could not destroy the sense of community and even though residents were now spread out around Bristol, many former Marsh folk reunited in 1986 to perform the musical *Yesterday's Island* about their experiences as a community in the area. This has since been performed numerous times to sold out audiences, including at the Bristol Hippodrome.

And another thing... Another Marsh character who was also a street seller was **Emily Purnell**, who was a widow with a baby son to care for but no income. Emily took to wheeling a handcart piled high with firewood which she sold door to door around the streets of St Philip's Marsh as a way to earn money to care for her young family. Once she had saved enough money from selling firewood, Emily was able to buy a shop at 9 Albert Crescent and improve her quality of life.

Please also see: Barbara Faulks (vol two).

ELIZABETH SOMERSET

1742-1760, GHOST

Do you believe in ghosts? Whether you think the idea of the afterlife is hokum or whether you think there's something out there... the story of tragic teenager Lady Elizabeth Somerset is certainly a spooky one.

The Dower House in Stoke Park (the big yellow house on the hill that you see as you leave Bristol by driving up the M32) was originally built in 1553 for Sir Richard Berkeley, and rebuilt in 1760 for use by the widow of the estate. Perhaps a deciding factor for rebuilding the house was the death of the residents' daughter, Lady Elizabeth Somerset, who fell off her horse while riding in the grounds and fatally broke her neck.

Does Elizabeth still haunt the park? Despite the fact horses have not been ridden in the grounds for decades, there have been numerous reports of galloping hooves being heard in the area. As a child in the 1970s, Steve England played in the park and in 2018 told *The Mirror*: "I've heard the sound of thumping hooves behind me on numerous occasions. Once I was with a group of friends and we all grabbed each other and jumped out of the way thinking something was charging at us but there was nothing there. And a few years ago I was walking home after doing some work on the land and the image of a little girl wearing a petticoat and straw hat walked straight through me."[505]

Following Elizabeth's death, her family built an obelisk on the hill where she died and the monument remains. It is claimed that if you stand beside the obelisk and hear three knocks, then Elizabeth's spirit is close by. In January 1942, the obelisk was struck by lightning having survived unscathed for the preceding 182 years… how Elizabeth felt about this we cannot be sure but it is claimed that every year, on the anniversary of Elizabeth's death, her ghost can be seen walking on the estate, horses' hooves can be heard and, at night, you will hear the sound of a girl screaming. The area has been regularly visited by paranormal investigators, one of whom had his photograph taken next to the obelisk. When he looked back at the developed picture he saw a figure standing just behind his shoulder… despite there having been nobody there when the picture was taken. Make of this what you will.

505 Millie Reeves, 'What's it Like to Live in 17th Century Mansion Haunted by Dead Girl...' in *The Mirror*, 11 July 2018.

In the 20th century, the Dower House became the Burden Neurological Institute. It is now a Grade II listed property and has been converted into residential flats. The memorial to Elizabeth remains in the public grounds and can be visited by anyone walking in the area.

Postscript: there are some suggestions that Elizabeth did not in fact die following a horse-riding accident but instead she contracted consumption and died. However, because consumption was perceived to be a working-class disease, some people suggest her snobbish family fabricated the story about the riding accident to give her death (what they felt would be) more dignity.

Please also see: Rosa Burden (vol one).

JOANNA SOUTHCOTT

1750-1814, PROPHET

From *The Oxford English Dictionary*: "Prophet: A person regarded as an inspired teacher or proclaimer of the will of God." I include the dictionary definition of 'prophet' here because, modestly, Joanna Southcott claimed to be one. Moreover, she claimed to be the woman spoken of in 'The Book of Revelation' in the Bible. This extraordinary women does not hail from Bristol, nor did she spend a particularly long time here, although her story on its own is truly remarkable and is worth exploring if you are so inclined. But at least one notable thing happened to Joanna while she was in Bristol, so I am adding her here as a curiosity. But first, an incredibly potted biography.

Born in Ottery St Mary, Devon, as a child Joanna was fixated by reading the scriptures and interpreting the everyday events of

Joanna Southcott illustration by Tina Altwegg

her life as if they had a spiritual significance. When her mother died, Joanna promised she would live a pious life and spent her 20s and 30s working as a domestic servant for various households around Exeter. She was 51 before she was first published as a writer and even then it was simply texts about village life rather than anything more significant.

Yet in 1792, Joanna experienced her first millenarian vision: a voice spoke to her day and night, predicting a war in France, food shortages in the West Country and much more besides. Consequently, between 1801 and 1814, Joanna published more than 65 pamphlets sharing her visions with the world, almost 5,000 pages of prophecy. It is believed more than 108,000 copies of her work were published and circulated during those 13 years, making her one of the most popular writers of her era.[506]

Joanna repeatedly claimed that a female figure would bring about millennial change and referred to chapters in the Bible which apparently reinforced this.[507] Perhaps the wildest claim she made was at the age of 60 when she said she was pregnant with the next son of God. A surprising number of people believed her, although understandably many also did *not*. However, several doctors examined her and concluded she was pregnant. No child was ever born and the accuracy of those doctors was called into doubt. For example: "A most villainous report is in circulation, that Dr Reece, who vouches for Joanna Southcott's pregnancy, is himself an *old woman* and also *with child*!"[508]

In June 1804, to escape the Georgian equivalent of internet trolls who were hounding her and making life a misery (by writing scathing articles about her in journals and letters), Joanna came to hide in Bristol for a while. She stayed with sympathisers but while

506 Sylvia Bowerbank, 2004, 'Joanna Southcott' in *Oxford Dictionary of National Biography*.
507 For example: Genesis 3, in which God promises that the woman's seed shall bruise the serpent's head; and Revelation 12, in which the woman clothed in sun brings about a new order.
508 'Thursday Afternoon' in *Bristol Mirror*, 3 September 1814.

pacing up and down the house one evening, the entire building began to shake with her fury and despair, terrifying everyone in the building. Joanna fell into a frenzy, speaking uncontrollably and alarming absolutely everyone who saw her. Eventually, she composed herself and announced that her prophetic voice had asserted that, just as the Bristol house trembled, the whole earth would tremble and powerful men and doubting clergy would fall. To confirm Joanna's authority, the voice stated: "I will conquer in woman's form." However... it is now well over two centuries later and we are still waiting for women to conquer, so perhaps the naysayers were right to doubt her. Either way, Joanna certainly caused a storm during her lifetime.

LILY SPENCER

1883-1945, BOOTMAKER

Alongside her husband Albert, Midsomer Norton-born Lily Spencer was an outworker for a boot factory in Kingswood. Outworking was a popular way of earning a living for workers, especially women, who could collect jobs to take and complete at home. However, the onset of the Industrial Revolution and the rise in factory work largely put an end to outwork.

The Spencers, who married young at the age of 17 in 1900, lived at 41 Belgrave Terrace, Kingswood and, after Albert died in 1915 at the age of 32, his widow Lily was left to fend for herself and their children Florence, Wilfred and Doris. She took outwork at the Iles Brothers factory, also on Charlton Road, where she made children's boots. Wilfred later remembered how each pair of boots that Lily made would be fastened together at the back of the uppers with a piece of string. And each Friday, when he finished school, he would hold out his arms for up to 20 pairs of boots to be hung across them ready for him to take to the factory, so that Lily could be paid on the Saturday.[509]

By the time of the 1939 Register, widow Lily was still living on Belgrave Terrace with her children. By this time, she was working at the 'Guide Deaf and Dumb School', while Florence was a corset stitcher and Wilfred a dairy transporter. Doris had "unpaid domestic duties" listed as her occupation.

Please also see: Rose Thorn (vol two).

EMILY SPENDER

1841-1922, SUFFRAGIST, NOVELIST

Although technically a resident of Bath, I am including Emily Spender here because her contribution to the early suffrage movement in the South West was significant, not least to the Bristol suffrage societies of which she was an active member. Emily was a suffragist and novelist with strong literary connections on the male side of her family; her brother-in-law was the radical publisher William Saunders, and her pro-suffrage brother Edward Saunders was Editor of the *Western Morning News* and a subscriber to the Central Committee of the National Society for Women's Suffrage.

Emily's debut book was *Son and Heir* (1864), a conventional novel which was the first of six that she would write over a 20-year period; in the 1861 census her occupation is already listed as 'authoress' showing the ambition she held. However, her second novel *Restored* (1871) is thought to have been one of the very first suffrage novels that was printed, although it was initially

509 flickr.com/photos/brizzlebornandbred/3217824187/in/album-72157615256360197/

published anonymously — perhaps due to the stigma attached with a respected lady being linked to the suffrage movement. *Restored* was stridently feminist and dedicated to the woman who had been Secretary of the Clifton section of the Bristol and West of England branch of the National Society for Women's Suffrage during the 1870s and was a committed campaigner for women's suffrage in the South West. The dedication reads: "To LSA. My honoured chief and dear friend, who is all that I aspire to be and who has unconsciously inspired much that I have written."[510] In *Restored,* Emily covers the topic of a bullish husband who represses his wife's dreams to express herself. As with other suffrage novels of the pre-1900s, *Restored* didn't explicitly address the topic of suffrage but covered the issues in a more general manner.

From 1870 for several years, Emily was touring the South West giving speeches about the importance of votes for women and her name appears in the minutes of a range of early suffrage organisations, most notably the National Society for Women's Suffrage. Her obituary noted: "Miss Spender was ... one of the pioneers of the early suffrage movement, and in the early seventies of the last century toured the West of England making speeches for Votes for Women, at considerable personal risk to herself on some occasions, when she had to be protected by the police, so violent was the prejudice on the subject."[511]

In addition to working with the Bristol branch, Emily was Secretary of the Bath Women's Suffrage Society and often represented the society by speaking at meetings. Her name appears frequently in the press, both locally and nationally, showing the range of suffrage events she spoke at in the 1870s. She seems to have been forever organising petitions to be sent to Parliament showing the weight of support behind the notion of votes for

510 LSA is Lilias Sophia Ashworth.

511 'Bath & County Notes' in *Bath Chronicle and Weekly Gazette*, 8 April 1922.

women, as well as writing letters to the local papers informing other women of how they could join her and the societies she represented to help them campaign for women's suffrage.

Emily was clearly an admired public speaker, as this one report — of an event in Grantham, Lincolnshire, which she spoke at alongside a sister campaigner — shows: "Both ladies spoke at some length, and however undesirable the proposed change may seem to many people no one could take exception to the clear and logical character of their arguments, nor fail to admire the modest and persuasive manner in which they were delivered."[512] However, by the end of the 1870s, Emily's literary career began to take on a life of its own and her suffrage activities seem to have taken more of a back-seat role from this point. Despite this, in 1884, Emily was one of the signatories to the Letter from Ladies to Members of Parliament from heads of households in support of their inclusion in the government's franchise bill.[513]

During the middle years of her life, following the deaths of both parents, Emily lived in London (the 1881 census shows her at 62 Langham Court Road, Streatham) and then Italy (which inspired her final novel, *A Soldier For a Day*, in 1901) with her sister Alfrida Spender, before returning to Bath and moving to 40 St James' Square in 1905 after Alfrida died. Emily remained single and child-free, meaning her time was hers to spend as she wished. Her final address was 13 Springfield Place, Bath, where she died in 1922 after contracting pneumonia at the age of 80.

And another thing... Emily Spender was the inspiration for the character of Miss Lavish in EM Forster's 1908 novel *A Room With A View*. Forster had met Emily while she was staying at a pensione

512 'News' in *Stamford Mercury*, 28 February 1873.
513 Elizabeth Crawford, 1999, *The Women's Suffrage Movement: A Reference Guide 1866-1928*, p649.

in Italy with Alfrida, and he was struck by the military cape Emily wore, the thin cigarettes she smoked and the air of drama she created when she flounced into a room. The character's name is itself a flamboyant pun: Lavish Spender.

Please also see: Lilias Ashworth Hallett (vol one), Miss Ramsay (vol two).

DOROTHY STANLEICK

1924-2004, AIRCRAFT DESIGNER

Two years after leaving school, in 1943 Devonshire teenager Dorothy Mary Stanleick was advised to train as a draughtswoman at the Government Training Centre on Radnor Road, Horfield, by the Women's Technical Service Register. A year and a half later, now fully trained, Dorothy was dispatched to the Bristol Aeroplane Company's training school on The Promenade, Clifton, and despite being promised a nice office job, she was actually sent to the flight test drawing office to work as one of the first female instrument panel designers and testers. By the end of the war, only eight woman would have worked in this male-dominated job and the men whom Dorothy worked with were instructed that wolf-whistling and swearing were strictly not permitted in front of their female colleagues.

As part of her work, Dorothy helped design static flight observers for aircraft including Bristol Freighters, Wayfarers, Britannia and Brabazon, and she was also involved in the very early development of the Concorde aircraft. Dorothy also used to photograph the aeroplanes as they landed and, during her first week, she witnessed three plane crashes as a result of the undercarriage not operating correctly, which was terrifying.

Dorothy's work was well paid and she earned extra money by joining test flight observations on board the new aircraft. She later said: "We knew it was dangerous, but we were absorbed by the task and it did not stop us as we thought it was a good thing we were doing and we were getting paid for it."

Remembering a wartime bombing raid which fell on the Filton airfield, Dorothy recalled that the song 'Marching Through Georgia' would be played across the Tannoy to instruct everyone they needed to get to their designated bomb shelter as soon as possible. Stopping to help a blind colleague find her way to her own shelter, Dorothy became anxious because it was taking them longer than it should have done to find their appointed shelters, so she directed them both into the nearest one. In doing so, she saved their lives… because their appointed bunkers were both completely destroyed by bombs and 92 colleagues at Filton lost their lives that day. Dorothy and the blind woman she stopped to help would have been among the casualties.

In 1950, Dorothy married Malcolm West, who was a Chief Flight Test Observer at the Bristol Aeroplane Company, and the couple had one daughter, Lesley. Unusually, Dorothy kept her job after marriage because she enjoyed it so much and found it so stimulating. In this way, she proved she was always one to buck conventions for what a woman was supposed to be doing.[514]

Please also see: Rosina Jones (vol two).

514 bbc.co.uk/history/ww2peopleswar/stories/75/a5091275.shtml

MAY STAVELEY
1863-1934, EDUCATIONALIST

When Sir George Wills bought Goldney House in Clifton in the early 1920s and announced his plans to build a men's halls of residence on the site, May Christophera Staveley nearly exploded with fury. She was the Tutor to Women Students at the University College, Bristol,[515] and the warden of the institution's women's halls of residence at Clifton Hill, just 16 feet away from Goldney Hall. The risks to her girls' reputations by having young university men sleeping so close by was more than May would stand for, so she threatened to resign in anger. So intimidating was her wrath that Sir George soon backed down and eventually found a site two miles away to build the men's halls of residence, putting the entire length of the Durdham Downs between the two sexes. It would be the mid-1970s before a mixed-sex halls of residence first appeared in Bristol... at the Goldney House site.[516]

It was no surprise May was so adamant that the women's halls of residence must be defended because it was purely down to her that there even *was* a women's halls of residence at the future University of Bristol. The site at Clifton Hill became available in 1909 and, with May's help, a local committee was formed to raise the funds to buy it with the express intention of building a women's halls of residence, copying a similar scheme which had been successfully opened at Birmingham University (where May had been the warden between 1899 and 1905): "This act of 'almost reckless initiative' was made possible by two anonymous donors 'keenly interested in women's education'."[517] Thanks to wardens such as May (similar fledgling initiatives were happening at other

515 University College Bristol had admitted women since its opening in 1876.
516 Helen Reid in David Harrison, ed, 1984, *Bristol Between the Wars*, p116.
517 Carol Dyhouse, 1995, *No Distinction of Sex?: Women in British Universities 1870-1939*, p99.

universities across the UK around this time), it became much easier for future generations of young women to safely attend a university away from their home city without any potential risk to their reputation.

In addition to her work at the university, May had been involved with the pioneering Barton Hill University Settlement in East Bristol since its inception back in 1911, and she was employed there as both a lecturer and social worker. Having studied history at Somerville College, Oxford, May later became a history lecturer at the University of Bristol and as such was appointed President of the Bristol Association of University Women.[518]

As a Quaker, May would spend time in France during World War One, working in the Somme with the Friends Relief Commission. Back home, she was also Honorary Secretary of the University of Bristol's Women's War Work Fund which, among other things, ran the university's hostel for Belgian refugees.[519]

And another thing... Two fun facts about May Staveley follow. One thing she detested with a passion: smoking. One thing she loved without question: Pekingese dogs. Remember these facts in case they ever come up in a very niche pub quiz.

Please also see: Grace Reeves (vol two).

518 Madge Dresser, 2016, *Women and the City*, p129.
519 historiansatbristol.blogs.bristol.ac.uk/archives/239

FLORA STEEL

1847-1929, AUTHOR

Although born in Middlesex, Flora Annie Steel spent 22 years living in British India, where her husband worked in the Indian Civil Service (which Flora criticised for inefficiency and corruption) and she forged a successful career as a writer. The majority of her books are connected to the Punjab and reveal her strong interest in Indian life. It was after the birth of her daughter that Flora's interest in Punjabi life really escalated, because becoming a mother gave her more opportunity to interact with local women and learn the language. By listening to the women there, Flora collected their folk stories and published them as *Tales of the Punjab* (1894). While in India, Flora also campaigned for better educational standards to improve the prospects for citizens and she became a school inspector (or 'inspectress', as the term rather quaintly was for a lady). Throughout her life, Flora wrote and published extensively and her bibliography includes both fiction and non-fiction, most notably *The Complete Indian Housekeeper and Cook* (1898), which instructed European housewives on how Indian women ran their homes. Flora was subsequently buried in Arnos Vale Cemetery.

ENID ST JOHN

1889-1976, TEACHER

Born in Argentina, Enid St John came to Bristol in October 1900 to commence her studies at the Redland High School, and the St John family lived at 9 Oakfield Road, Clifton. Mother Eliza was the head of the household but the census shows no father… perhaps he had died and this prompted the move to England?

"One of my early recollections is of the death of Queen Victoria," wrote Enid in 1953. "A wreath went from Redland [High School] to the statue in College Green with the slightly adapted quotation from Tennyson's *Ode on the Death of the Duke of Wellington* — 'she wears a truer crown than any wreath that man can weave her.'"[520]

Enid soon became a prefect at Redland High School and had a great respect for her headteacher, Elizabeth Cocks: "As prefects we were trained to take real responsibilities. In carrying out these duties we realised how human a person our headmistress was, with a keen sense of humour."[521] By 1916, Enid had become a teacher at Redland High School, where the headteacher during World War One was Emily Shekleton: "I was privileged to become a member of Miss Shekleton's staff in 1916, and to witness the wonderful spiritual leadership which she gave to the school. There were no air raids, and the school maintained a high standard of academic work, and was also extremely active in many forms of war work. Miss Shekleton even offered the services of the school to the City Engineer, and Redland girls had a glorious time clearing snow from adjacent roads."[522]

In time, after having been the first former student from Redland High School to finish her degree at Cambridge University, Enid became headteacher of the school where she had been a pupil. Supplementing her interests in the welfare of women and girls, Enid was also on the committee for the Read Dispensary in Hotwells and was a supporter of votes for women: for instance, in 1908 she helped to decorate the Women's Social and Political Union shop on Queen's Road, Clifton.

For a time, Enid shared a house with Eliza Walker Dunbar, who had been a visiting lecturer at Redland High School. Given

520 Enid St John, Summer 1953, 'Redland Memories' in *Redland High School Magazine*, pp16-17.
521 Ibid, pp16-17.
522 Ibid, pp16-17.

Enid was on the board for the Read Dispensary which Eliza had helped to establish, it is likely the two had crossed paths for a number of years and had a great deal of shared interests.

By 1939 her address was 19 Downs Cote View near the Durdham Downs, where she lived with fellow teacher Muriel Andrews. Enid died in 1976, while living in Westbury-on-Trym.

Please also see: Elizabeth Cocks (vol one), Eliza Dunbar Walker (vol one), Lucy Read (vol two), Mabel Shaw (vol two), Alice Walters (vol one).

SARAH STONE

died c1740, MIDWIFE

Following in her mother's footsteps, Sarah Holmes of Bridgwater trained to be a midwife and for the first six years of her career worked as her mother's deputy. By 1701, Sarah had set up in practice on her own, and by 1703 she had moved to Taunton, married an apothecary and become Sarah Stone. The couple had at least one daughter, and it is known she also trained and worked as a midwife from the 1720s.

Sarah was concerned that weaving, the main trade in Taunton at this time, was extremely bad for pregnant women, and felt the male midwife or obstetric surgeon had no understanding of what pregnancy and childbirth was really like for a woman, often because the barber and the doctor were one and the same person. She was greatly concerned by the rise in male midwives, and felt that rural midwives were generally unskilled, which was why she was often called upon to assist when complications had arisen in a birth. Typically, she delivered around 300 babies a year. Sarah was considered capable of both empathy and detachment, and was sensitive to the mother's pain and fear, as well as her need for autonomy during the birth.

Around 1720, the Stone family moved from Taunton to Bristol because Sarah felt the overwork was damaging her health. It may also have been that the lure of fashionable Bristol was just too tempting. But she was confronted with a new problem in Bristol, which was the consequences of babies being injured by the forceps which had been used by poorly trained barber/doctors. Through education, Sarah tried to address this problem and encourage women to go to trained female midwives rather than unskilled male barbers, and she worked to train midwives to better understand the female body and how a healthy pregnancy and birth should progress.

Furthering her commitment to re-educating midwives, Sarah began work on a fully comprehensive book that she hoped would put an end to all the ignorance and misconceptions in the health profession that surround birth. In 1737, her book was finally published with the all-encompassing title of: *Sarah Stone's Complete Practice of Midwifery Consisting of Upwards of Forty Cases or Observations in that Valuable Art, Selected from Many Others, in the Course of a Very Extensive Practice, and Interspersed with Many Necessary Cautions and Useful Instructions, Proper to be Observed in the Most Dangerous and Critical Exigencies, as well when the Delivery is Difficult in its Own Nature, as When it Becomes So By the Rashness or Ignorance of Unexperienc'd Pretenders, Recommended to all Female Practitioners in an Art so Important to the Lives and Well-Being of the Sex.* I have included this lengthy title in its entirety because it helps to summarise exactly what the book was for and about; several of the cases used as examples in the book are from her time working in Bristol. Sarah writes the case studies up with a strong narrative arc and they could almost be read as literature on their own terms. Sarah moved to London after her book was published and she becomes hard to find in historical records after this point.

MATILDA STURGE

1829-1903, QUAKER

Born on Wilson Street, St Paul's, Matilda Sturge was part of the large Quaker family of Sturges based in Bristol and five of her nieces were profiled in the first volume of *The Women Who Built Bristol*. Matilda's family were very quiet Quakers who upheld strict restrictions on dress, speech and entertainment, even while other Quakers were starting to relax their rules. Although Matilda was educated at home, by 1868 she was attending the Lectures for Ladies series organised by the University College, Bristol.

Matilda was very involved with the Society of Friends at Bristol. She was initially a teacher at the First Day School (an early form of adult education) in Bristol, before becoming superintendent of the Sunday School for Girls. She also organised a mothers' meeting for more than 90 working-class Bristol women, which ran for many years. By 1880, Matilda was recognised as a minister, clerk of the monthly Bristol women's meetings and assistant clerk of the annual national women's meetings. She prioritised work that supported people in poor communities and strived to improve their circumstances and education.

As a writer, Matilda wrote many essays on topics as varied as religion, biography (including women such as Bristolian reformer Mary Carpenter, Indian reformer Pandita Ramabai and Anglican nun Sister Dora Pattison), history and also social issues, of which she had a particular concern for temperance and women's rights.

Please also see: Mary Carpenter (vol one), Caroline Sturge (vol one), Elizabeth Sturge (vol one), Emily Sturge (vol one), Helen Sturge (vol one), Mary Sturge (vol one).

CATHERINE SUGO

Born 1776, ACCIDENTAL SHOOTING VICTIM

Hailing from Cork, Ireland, Catherine Sugo was living in Bristol by 1809, where she had come with her husband… although he had set sail on a voyage in 1808 and not been seen for the 14 months since, leaving Catherine to bring up their infant child alone and to earn a tiny income from selling fruit. Catherine was struggling so much that her landlady, Mrs Chilcott, kindly turned a blind eye to the fact she had received no rent for months "in consideration of her good conduct and knowing her distress". Indeed, everyone seemed to agree Catherine was a very kind, quiet and unassuming woman who did not cause any bother to anybody. This makes it all the more unfortunate that it was Catherine who was the poor woman who was accidentally shot in the chest by a horse pistol during King George III's Jubilee celebrations in Bristol on 25 October 1809. Subsequently confined to her bed and experiencing awful pain, it was doubted whether Catherine would recover and an appeal was made to the public for donations to help her and her child in their time of crisis. Although we don't know what fate ultimately befell Catherine, we can only hope it was brighter than the one feared for her.

ANN TABBERNER
1774-1855, TEACHER

The Priory Church of St James is thought to be the oldest building in Bristol, dating from 1129. And the church — or a version of it which has been regenerated over the centuries — still exists, squashed into the space between the massive Primark in Broadmead and Bristol Bus and Coach Station. Throughout the years, the parish records for St James Priory (as it was originally known) detail all manner of fairs, charities, celebrations and other events that took place in the area, including a number of schools. One of these was a ladies' school run by Ann Tabberner from her home at 13 St James' Churchyard. However, by the time of her death in 1855, Ann was buried in Clifton rather than in the parish where she had lived or worked for most of her life.

ELLEN TANNER
1874-1937, ARCHAEOLOGIST

In summer 2018, the Holburne Museum in Bath made national headlines with its inclusion of an antique Persian bikini top as part of its display of the artefacts belonging to Victorian amateur archaeologist Ellen Tanner. When Ellen toured the Middle East during the 1890s with just two guides for company, she was one of the very first women to do so, and the wool and silk bikini top was one of the many unusual items she picked up on her travels. Other pieces she brought back included enamelled tea cups, metal vases and lacquered playing cards. Much of Ellen's substantial collection is now kept at the Bristol Museum and Art Gallery.

Ellen was born just outside Bristol and it was thanks to a substantial inheritance of £18,000 that she was able to fund her adventures in 1894. Describing her first impressions of Baghdad, she wrote in her diary: "As we came in sight of Baghdad, it looked like a fairy city with the palm-fringed river, orange gardens, the houses on the waterside like Venice, and all her mosques and minarets gleaming in the yellow evening sunlight."[523] Her travels also took her overland through Iran, on horseback in Iraq and into Baghdad via a steamer. She stayed in caravans and explored everywhere she came to, with markets proving a particular fascination, hence her substantial collection of artefacts.

Following three adventurous trips abroad, Ellen returned to the South West and settled near Bath, where she began to donate pieces to the Holburne Museum. When talking about the exhibition, the museum's curator Caitlin Jones said: "Tanner's story can tell us so much about our own troubled times: it's a chance to celebrate a pioneering woman and the extraordinary artistic and cultural output of the Middle East, but also a salient reminder of Britain's history of empire."[524]

After her death in 1937, Ellen was buried at Lansdown Cemetery, Bath. The pieces in her collection tell an extraordinary story about one woman's life and offer a uniquely Victorian woman's view of the world in the age of Empire.[525]

523 museumcrush.org/the-forgotten-victorian-woman-traveller-and-her-collection-of-middle-eastern-art/

524 Ibid.

525 With thanks to Lori Streich for the nomination of Ellen Tanner to this book.

MARY TAYLOR
1844-1926, STREET SELLER

'Paper Sally', as Mary Ann Taylor was known, has become a part of our city's folklore. She was one of those classic Bristolian characters who has gone down in history surrounded by almost as many mysteries as the treasures she hoarded.

Paper Sally was said to be a well-spoken woman who had been abandoned on a doorstep as a baby by her mother. Another story claimed she had been cheated out of her inheritance by crooked relatives or a dodgy lawyer. Either way, as an adult she lived in poverty. Sally always wore a black dress and pushed a pram around, piled high with whatever she had been collecting: wood for fires, coal for fuel or her namesake newspapers. Sally never swore and rarely drank, but she would take care of the stray cats in the area by leaving food out for them so they didn't starve.

Her home was initially in Redcross Street, St Philip's, and she lived surrounded by piles and piles of newspapers. She would collect old but clean newspapers to take to a fish and chip shop around the corner on Lawford Street for them to wrap their sales in, and they would repay her with a twist of scrumps: aka the crunchy bits at the bottom after the fish and chips have been fried.

By the time of her death, Sally was living at Deep Street, which is opposite the White Hart pub on Lower Maudlin Street. She died in a house fire on Christmas morning in 1926, suffocated by smoke and unable to escape because of the mountains of stuff hoarded in her home; she was buried at Greenbank Cemetery, Fishponds. Police officer Stanley Knight was the person who found her body. Long after his retirement, Knight told the *Bristol Evening Post* in 1983: "She was a very short lady who was given six free local papers every day. These she sold to pay for breakfast."

There were also claims a café on the Welsh Back gave her

Mary Taylor illustration by Carrie Love

tea and cakes every morning, and that the police kept a friendly eye on her. Add in the fact that Sally would give pennies to local children and the impression is one of an eccentric lady who was cared for by her community. Both the police and fire brigade sent flowers for her grave.[526]

SARAH THOMAS

1831-1849, SERVANT, MURDERER

In ye olden days, going to watch a public execution was considered a grand day out, accompanied by merchandise of papers and pamphlets relating to the soon-to-be-deceased; times were very different then. The last-ever public hanging at Bristol Prison on Cumberland Road was that of Sarah Harriet Thomas and it took place on 20 April 1849.

Sarah, who was just 18, had been employed as a servant by Elizabeth Jeffries at her 6 Trenchard Street home in the city centre. However, Sarah grew resentful and frustrated by her employer, whom she considered a hard taskmaster. It seems Sarah wasn't the only one to find Mrs Jeffries trying, because the woman had worked her way through a long list of other servants prior to Sarah's appointment, and some of these young women testified at Sarah's trial to confirm what a difficult person their former employer had been.

Finally, on 4 March 1849, Sarah snapped and she beat Elizabeth to death with a stone and even killed her dog, who she later threw down the outside toilet. Sarah then left the Trenchard Street house and returned to stay with her parents in Horfield. It was three days before Elizabeth's body was discovered.

526 flickr.com/photos/brizzlebornandbred/2093606935/

When police questioned Sarah about the murders, she proclaimed her innocence and initially tried to blame a previous servant but the police didn't believe her. Neither did the court, and Sarah was convicted and sentenced to death for her crimes. Shortly before going to the gallows, she gave a detailed confession, perhaps to clear her conscience or perhaps under duress. A local crime reporter named E Austin alleged the confession had been written *for* rather than *by* Sarah.[527] This young woman was not going to go quietly and it took six prison officers to drag Sarah, kicking and screaming, from her cell to the gallows… where she continued to scream until the very last moment. According to reports, the scene was so awful that even the prison governor became so overwhelmed with emotion that he fainted, and many members of the crowd also claimed to feel repulsed by what they had just witnessed.

ROSE THORNE

1870-1953, BOOTMAKER

Born in Shepton Mallet, Rose Colston married Francis Thorne in 1888 when she was just 17 years old and he was 21. Rose's mother Louisa Colston was widowed shortly after Rose's birth and, with Rose being the youngest of six children, there was pressure on the children to become independent as early as possible. Rose and Francis had their wedding at St Luke's Church, and settled at 48 Philip Street, Bedminster where they founded the boot manufacturing business F Thorne & Sons. Rose was also a member of the Salvation Army and wore her uniform with pride to meetings at the Dean Lane chapel after it opened in 1909.

527 britishexecutions.co.uk/execution-content.php?key=4768&termRef=Sarah%20Thomas

Rose and Francis soon started a family, with their first son born in 1890. By 1911 they had eight children to look after, all of whom followed their parents into the family boot business once they were old enough. Francis died in 1933 so, by the time of the 1939 Register, Rose was a widow living at 27 Duckmoor Road, Bedminster, with two lodgers to help with the living costs.

Please also see: Mary Ridsdel (vol two), Emily Smyth (vol one), Lily Spencer (vol two).

EUNICE and IRIS THWAITES
born c1930, PUB LANDLADIES

Back in the day, there were five bustling pubs along the short stretch of Philip Street in Bedminster. Now, owing to a combination of a change in how we live and bomb damage, just two remain: the Apple Tree opposite Windmill Hill City Farm and the Barley Mow on the corner with East Street.

Opened in the 1850s, the original Barley Mow pub was built around a small courtyard and was used for coroner's inquests during the 1860s, when its landlady was a Mrs Slocombe. This enterprising woman also owned a number of houses and shops nearby which she rented out. In the late 1870s, the Barley Mow was rebuilt and this was when it achieved the ornate Victorian brickwork and shiny green tiling for which it is now most recognisable: the external features still survive today and are a protected characteristic of the building.[528]

A number of landlords followed Mrs Slocombe but it was the arrival of the Thwaites family that really brought the Barley Mow

528 Fiona Fisher, Rebecca Preston, 2015, 'The 19th and 20th Century Public House in Bristol', English Heritage report, pp59-60.

to life. Gladys Florence Thwaites (1896-1985) and her husband George were landlords from the late 1930s; they lived above the pub with daughters Eunice and Iris, and son Edward (a carpenter). Under the Thwaites' reign, the Barley Mow was a central point of Bedminster life. With its location directly opposite the thriving HO Wills tobacco factory on East Street (where Asda now stands), there was no shortage of workers from Wills and the many other nearby businesses who were keen to come in and drink their cares away. The hub of the local community, under the Thwaites family the Barley Mow not only had its own football team but also organised regular fundraising drives in aid of the Bristol General Hospital on Guinea Street. By the time of the Great Flood of Bristol on 10 July 1968, George had died and the Barley Mow was being run by the indomitable forces of sisters Eunice and Iris, with mother Gladys (now in her 70s) unable to resist pitching in with her beloved pub from time to time. The Great Flood occured when two months of rain fell in just two days, causing the River Avon to burst its banks and the lower parts of Bedminster and Ashton Gate were more than six feet under water in some places.

Iris and Eunice were just closing up for the night on 10 July when the first of the flood water hit East Street. Panicked attempts by the sisters to barricade themselves into the pub were as unsuccessful as the drinkers' attempts to catch a bus home. As the hapless punters stood at the bus stop opposite, a strong wave of water gushed down East Street, pinning them against the wall of the Wills building... the water was so deep that it came up to their armpits. They splashed their way back to the pub where Iris and Eunice took them in as refugees for the night. Grabbing a few bottles of whisky from behind the bar, the landladies invited everyone upstairs where it was still dry and they all passed a rather uncomfortable night sleeping in chairs and on the floor .[529]

The Thwaites family continued running the Barley Mow for a few more decades and, in 1985, Gladys eventually died upstairs in the pub she had loved so much. It is unfortunately not known when Eunice and Iris left the pub or what became of them, but the Barley Mow remains in business today and is a very recognisable cider house on East Street with a loyal stream of regulars.

And another thing... Anecdotally, someone who was a regular in the Barley Mow during the 1980s remembers an amazing older woman called **Gertie** who lived in a flat in Redcliffe and regularly used to get up on the pub tables, lift her skirts high and dance along to the live piano accompaniment. By all accounts, even in the 1980s, drinking in the Barley Mow was like stepping back into the 1930s.

And another other thing... The Great Flood of Bristol in 1968 was not the first time the city had been overcome by a sudden deluge. In March 1889, during an earlier bout of exceptionally heavy rainfall, **Mary Sherman**, 71, was swept into a flooded cellar outside her home at Viacoff Parade, Broad Weir, and fractured her thigh. Gushing water had washed away the grating which usually covered the cellar opening and the *Bristol Mercury* noted: "There was between seven and eight feet of water in the cellar, and had it not been for the promptitude of two men, she must have been drowned."[530] Mary was taken to hospital and received good treatment.

529 Anton Bantock, 1997, *Bedminster*, p126.
530 'A Woman Nearly Drowned' in *Bristol Mercury*, 11 March 1889.

MARY TISDALL

1932-2017, JOURNALIST

Redcliffe provided an early stomping ground for Mary Pritchard. Because her family were of modest means, a scholarship meant Mary was able to attend Merrywood Grammar School for Girls in Knowle (now closed) and was an excellent pupil — although her dreams of attending university were cut short when her father insisted she leave school and start earning some money.

Mary's first job was as a typist at the *Bristol Evening World* newspaper, and the journal evidently recognised her promise because she was soon promoted to the role of Junior Reporter. It was while working here that she met John Tisdall, whom she married at St Mary Redcliffe in 1951. Mary's career was put on hold while she had their three children; her youngest child Nicholas had severe disabilities, which made combining motherhood and a career even more challenging.

By the 1960s, the Tisdall family had moved to Newcastle and once the children were at school Mary resumed her work, this time as a freelance journalist for the BBC, Tyne Tees Television and the *Northern Echo* newspaper. At the *Echo* she wrote a weekly column, which was innovative for a woman at this time: her pen name, linking to her Bristol roots, was Mary Redcliffe. In this column she addressed taboo topics ranging from how contraception should be made widely available to young women, how sex education *must* be taught in schools, how to access divorce, the way society discriminates against women, and the poor treatment of pregnant women by the medical service.

Her editor was the renowned newspaperman Sir Harold 'Harry' Evans, who would go on to be the editor of *The Sunday Times* among others and, at the time of writing, is Editor-at-Large of *Reuters*. His mini CV is intended to show that Evans knew what he was doing when he gave Mary a chance and when he let her have free rein (it is also interesting to remember that, once upon a time, working on a local newspaper really was a stepping stone to great things in a journalist's career). Mary is recorded in Evans' biography with a note saying: "Evans hired a young woman named Mary Redcliffe as a weekly columnist, and she promptly disrupted the equanimity of local Anglican bishops and other moral arbiters by writing about abortion and contraception, as well as the interesting divorce of the Duchess of Argyll, who had had oral sex with one of her partners — as a famous photograph at her trial purported to show. 'I'd better ask Enid [Parker, his first wife] about that — hang on,' Harry ordered Redcliffe when she phoned in her copy. A few minutes later he came back on the phone. 'Enid says you're right to write about it.'"[531]

As a broadcast journalist, in 1964 Mary created an important piece for the BBC's *Woman's Hour* radio programme about a woman who had undergone an illegal abortion, and the report was so shocking and disturbing it prompted a national debate about abortion which ultimately led to a change in the law in 1967. "*Woman's Hour* recently re-broadcast a powerful archive interview Mary recorded in 1964 with a woman in Newcastle who had undergone a backstreet abortion," wrote Mary's colleague Jill Burridge in 2017, about the famous piece which was re-broadcast to mark the 50th anniversary of the 1967 Abortion Act.[532] "It was a horrific reminder of the kind of traumatic experiences that many women endured before the Abortion Act of 1967. Those items generated a huge reaction from the audience, some sharply critical but many who were deeply moved."[533]

531 Judy Bachrach, 2001, *Tina and Harry Come to America: Tina Brown, Harry Evans and the Uses of Power*, p58-59.
532 The Abortion Act of 1967 meant abortions could be obtained free of charge in England, Wales and Scotland via the National Health Service providing certain conditions had been met.
533 Jill Burridge, August 2017, 'Mary Tisdall: Obituary', *Prospero*, p9.

Mary had been a reporter and producer on *Woman's Hour* since the 1960s and presented the innovative series *Diary of a Pregnancy* (following a listener through her pregnancy until the birth of her baby) and *Diary of an Engagement* (as another listener planned their wedding day; reportedly everyone at the BBC was in tears the day the marriage was broadcast).

In the obituary for her friend, Jill Burridge said: "[Mary], and her office, became my refuge in times of need ... Mary had come to *Woman's Hour* some years before, also from local radio (starting as a contributing freelance in 1969 and joining the staff a couple of years later), and brought with her a strong resolve to take the programme to women around the country, putting 'ordinary' voices on national radio." Jill added: "Mary had an ability to get on with everyone and a gentle but firm style of interviewing which ensured the challenging questions were not missed ... Mary brought to *Woman's Hour* a pioneering spirit of broadcasting that took radio outside the studios, away from London and was inclusive of all walks of life. It was Mary's humanity, sensitivity and humour, coupled with her own experience of parenting and family life that shone through – not only in Mary's broadcasting, but through to me, as a colleague and a friend."[534]

Throughout her entire career, Mary's work was dominated by showcasing the lives of ordinary women and by trying to improve the situation in life for women who, like her, had not had the best starts to life or the benefits of a university education.

Please also see: Barbara Buchanan (vol one).

534 Ibid, p9.

ANN TOBIN

born c1750, FREE DAUGHTER OF ENSLAVED AFRICAN

Volume one of *The Women Who Built Bristol* shared the story of Fanny Coker, who was a slave 'owned' by John Pinney, who brought her from the West Indies to his home in Bristol where she was freed and worked for his wife as a paid maid.[535] Pinney's business partner in the slave trade was a man named James Tobin, who had a half-sister named Ann Tobin who was of mixed heritage because her mother was, or had been, an enslaved African. Ann came to live in Bristol and socialised with the white merchant class, which was very unusual at this time given her skin colour and background.

Ann had been born in Nevis but brought to Bristol by her half-brother in 1774 and she remained here for the rest of her life. A few years later, James Tobin also brought slaves including Priscilla Gould from his sugar plantation at Stoney Grove in the West Indies to live in England and work in his home on Berkeley Square, Clifton. As a vocal anti-abolitionist, Tobin produced a number of pamphlets outlining how catastrophic he felt ending slavery would be for the defence and wealth of the British Empire. In 1790, he even gave evidence on this matter to the House of Commons.[536]

Please also see: Fanny Coker (vol one).

535 An area named Pinney's Beach remains on the island of Nevis, West Indies. The Pinney family owned land and plantations on Nevis for several generations, which were all run by slave labour and fuelled by the slave trade.

536 With thanks to Ruth Hecht and Mark Steeds for the nomination of Ann Tobin to this book. selectsurnames2.com/tobin2.html

Dolly Tree illustration by Rhi Lee

DOLLY TREE
1899-1962, COSTUMIER

During the golden age of Hollywood, stars such as Myrna Loy, Judy Garland, Jean Harlow and Rosalind Russell were well known for their acting but also for their glamorous outfits... some of which were designed by Bristol-born costumier Dolly Tree. She wasn't just a fashion designer, however, because Dolly also designed the costumes for almost 50 movies during the 1930s and 1940s, including *David Copperfield* (1935, George Cukor) and *A Tale of Two Cities* (1935, Jack Conway).

Born in Westbury-on-Trym, as a child, Dorothy Marian Isbell discovered she had a talent for drawing and a love for attention. This led her to try her luck on the stage (where she changed her name to Dolly Tree) and initially Dolly pursued a career as an actor. Her family moved to London in 1912 when Dolly was 13 and seeing some of the glitzy West End shows cemented the idea in her mind that performance was where her heart lay. After seeing a production of *Vanity Fair* at the Palace Theatre in 1916, an excited Dolly went home and designed a flattering poster of the lead actor Regine Flory, which ended up under the nose of theatre impresario Sir Alfred Butt. She recalled: "I was fascinated by the wonderful dancing and art of Regine Flory and admired her so much that I started to design a special poster of her, really to amuse myself, based on my recollections of this vivid artist seen across the footlights."[537]

Butt loved Dolly's artwork, bought it *and* gave her a two-year contract designing programmes and posters for all of his upcoming shows. Through this connection, Dolly's work also began to appear in newspapers and magazines such as *Tatler, The*

537 jazzageclub.com/jazz-age-club/dolly-tree-illustrations/

London Mall and The Royal Magazine. She said: "I drew tons of things in black and white and carted them solemnly around Fleet Street, knowing not a single soul. [Eventually I sold sketches] at five shillings each, I got rid of quite a lot of things. I did quite well with such subjects as fluffy flappers and lightsome lingerie."[538] For *Tatler,* Dolly took over the illustration slot on its popular 'Letters of Eve' series which had previously been drawn by sister-Bristolian Anne Fish.

Between 1915 and 1918, Dolly had small roles in five British silent films but it was her skills as a costume designer that really set her apart in the movie industry. The very first film that she designed the costumes for was *Woman to Woman* in 1923, for which the assistant director was a relative newcomer by the name of Alfred Hitchcock. By 1926, Dolly was living in the US, working as a costumier for both Broadway and Hollywood productions.

A succession of ill-fated marriages led to a battle with alcohol, which ultimately caused her to become unreliable with her work and she found herself cast out of the profession that had once adored her. Dolly died in 1962 as a patient of a psychiatric hospital in New York City. A very sad end for the once-glittering girl from Bristol.

Please also see: Anne Fish (vol two).

538 Ibid.

ANN TROTMAN

1952-1997, PARALYMPIAN

A wheelchair user for almost her entire life, Elizabeth Trotman (known by her middle name of Ann) was an exceptionally high achiever. Via remote learning with the Open University, Ann achieved a PhD in Disability Studies. She was also a paralympian, representing Great Britain at the International Games for the Disabled (as the paralympics was then known) in 1984, which was held in New York, US. This was the seventh paralympics to be held and included more than 1,800 athletes. Ann won three silver medals (for women's club throw, javelin and slalom), as well as a bronze medal for discus. That year, Great Britain came second overall and was beaten only by the US.

Following her sporting career, Ann worked for Bristol City Council as its Disability Sports Officer. One of her appointments was attending a lunch for disabled athletes at London's Grosvenor House Hotel organised by the British Sports Association for the Disabled, where she met and was photographed with Diana, Princess of Wales. This fundraising event generated more than £20,000, which was used to send the British team to the 1988 Seoul paralympics. Consequently, in June 1989, Ann was awarded the MBE for services to disabled sports.

ALICIA TYNDALL

1733-1764, LANDED GENTRY

Have you ever visited the beautiful Royal Fort Garden at the top of St Michael's Hill, which are now a part of the University of Bristol? Originally known as Windmill Fort, it was designed to be the strongest defence in Bristol and was the headquarters of the Royalist Army… until they surrendered in 1645 to Oliver Cromwell, who demolished the fort after which the gardens are named. The land was later bought by the Tyndall family, who had made their fortune by establishing Bristol's very first bank and they bought the land in order to build themselves an impressive home. As such, the three-storey house which currently occupies the site was built between 1758 and 1762 by merchant Thomas Tyndall for himself and his wife Alicia. She died in 1764 while giving birth to their son Thomas, who would grow up to have many children including a daughter called Alicia, who sadly died aged five and was buried alongside the grandmother she never met. Thomas Sr and Alicia Sr are buried with Alicia Jr at Christ Church With St Ewen on Broad Street in Bristol, and are commemorated inside the church with a flamboyant plaque.

ELIZABETH TYNDALL

1930-2017, PRIEST

When Bristol-born Reverend Elizabeth Tyndall was ordained as a Church of England priest in 1994, she was one of the very first women to take on this role. Despite hostility to the idea of female priests from some within the church, Elizabeth's compassion and determination helped her to keep going and achieve gender equality. *The Church Times* noted: "It was not just the idea of being equal with men that made Elizabeth rejoice in the ordination of women, but the conviction that women also had a vital part to play in God's ministry."[539]

Elizabeth was the youngest of six children in the Bristolian Ballard family, and the fact her father Frank was a Congregational

539 Anon, 'Obituary: The Revd Elizabeth Mary Tyndall' in *Church Times*, 9 June 2017.

minister must have influenced her own path in life. She initially trained as a teacher, where she was drawn to work in prisons as well as schools. After marrying Nicholas Tyndall, she had four children who understandably became her priority while they were young.

It was during the 1950s that Elizabeth began to consider a career in the church, although it would be 1983 before she was admitted to the office of Deaconess in the Church of England (becoming one of the first women to be ordained as a Deaconess in 1987). In this way, she was a part of the Movement for the Ordination of Women. The very first female priests were ordained in March 1994 and Elizabeth joined their number in April of the same year. Three months after her own ordination, Elizabeth became the first female priest to assist in the ordination of her own son, Nicholas. After her ordination, Elizabeth worked as a priest in Oxford until her retirement in 2002.

HANNAH TWYNNOY

1669-1703, BARMAID, TIGER'S VICTIM

Boasting the dubious title of being the first-known person in the UK to be killed by a tiger, barmaid Hannah Twynnoy is now firmly embedded in our folklore.

Based in Malmesbury, Hannah worked at the White Lion Inn and it was in this pub's back garden that she met her terrible fate. A travelling circus and its menagerie had set up camp in the White Lion's grounds and, after a caged tiger who Hannah had been teasing escaped its enclosure, the animal seized the hapless barmaid and mauled her to death on 23 October 1703.

Hannah's gravestone in the grounds of Malmesbury Abbey reads: "In bloom of Life, She's snatchd from hence, She had not room, To make defence; For Tyger fierce, Took Life away, And here she lies, In a bed of Clay, Until the Resurrection Day." Given that a burial and gravestone outside an abbey was highly unusual for a working-class woman in the 18th century, it would seem likely that a wealthy benefactor took an interest in Hannah's story and paid for these tributes on her behalf. However, who this person was has not been recorded in history. The White Lion Inn remains in business today.

And another thing... Marking the 300th anniversary of Hannah's death, on 23 October 2003 an unusual ceremony was held at Hannah's graveside where every local schoolgirl named Hannah, who was under the age of 11 years, was invited to place a posy upon her grave.[540]

KATE UNDERWOOD
1874-1944, HOSPITAL MATRON

As matron of the Beaufort War Hospital between 1916 and 1918 (which the Bristol Psychiatric Hospital was requisitioned to become during World War One), Kate Underwood had a serious role to play. She was duly awarded the Royal Red Cross military decoration for services to nursing in 1919. A letter, written on 13 November 1916, from Kate to the family of Royal Edward Penna (a soldier who died in her care) gives an indication of her compassion for her patients and their loved ones: "Private Penna was a man of whom we were all fond, such a nice man, and the sister over him could not have done more for him had she been his mother. He died of septicaemia following bad gunshot wounds of the

540 Anon, 'Memorial for Tiger Death Woman' on *BBC News*, 23 October 2003.

thigh. I can truthfully assure his friends that everything possible was done for him, he was so much liked by all who came in contact with him, and we felt so sad to think his own people was not with him."[541]

Please also see: Prudence Early (vol two).

VEILED WOMAN
MYSTERIOUS STATUE

There are precious few statues of women in Bristol. We have only Queen Victoria near College Green, Wendy the wooden elephant at Bristol Zoo and the goddess Sabrina by Broad Quay. NB: only one of these is of a human woman, albeit a human woman with no connection to Bristol whatsoever. This means we need to celebrate those who we can. Therefore, in desperation, I also list in this category: Banksy's painted angel at the Bristol Museum and Art Gallery, the filthy-with-exhaust-fumes rendering of Lady Justice above the former entrance to Bridewell Police Court (although, ironically, someone pinched/broke her scales decades ago)[542], and — for a few weeks in spring 2018 — Ruth, an elderly lady equipped with hammer and handbag, who was positioned outside the offices of the charity Age UK on Victoria Street near the city centre.

In this clutching-at-straws-for-carved-depictions-of-women-in-Bristol category, we also find an unusual mask of a woman above a former pub at 18 St Nicholas Street. This enigmatic (dare

541 glensidemuseum.org.uk/beaufort-war-hospital-home-page/matrons-and-nurses-march-18/kate-underwood/

542 Fun fact: this statue of Lady Justice was created by the Bristolian sculptor Edward Hodges Baily (born 1788), among whose other notable pieces are the statue of Lord Nelson which sits atop Nelson's Column in Trafalgar Square, London.

I say spooky?) veiled woman was carved in 1868 by an unknown sculptor. Being a woman she, of course, is not alone, lest she get ideas above her station. No, she is flanked by three male heads. There is a lot of debate about what the four heads represent, with one theory suggesting they are the four seasons and the veiled woman represents autumn. Another theory posits that she is a rare depiction of death as a woman; death being more commonly pictured as a cloaked male figure with a scythe. However, like all art, the veiled woman remains open to interpretation.

Please also see: Sabrina (vol one), Wendy (vol two).

ANNA VINER

1731-1805, PIPE MAKER

Following the death of her husband George, Anna Viner took over his pipe making business and moved it from St Stephen's Parish to Horse Street (now Host Street) in St Augustine's Back. She advertised herself as supplying "captains and merchants with tobacco pipes for the African and American trades". Showing she was capable of big things, Anna expanded her late husband's business and in this way worked as a manufacturer, retailer and small merchant who made and exported pipes to Africa, the US, Canada and Barbados, using slave ships to transport her wares from Bristol. This is an example of how the slave trade was exploited by women working in trades and crafts.[543]

543 Madge Dresser, 2016, *Women and the City*, p62.

PENNY WADE
1930-2008, CHARITY WORKER

Born at Frenchay Hospital into a military family, Penny Ladds travelled with her parents to Mhow, India, when she was still a toddler and the family lived a life of luxury with a cook, butler, gardener, groom, night-watchman and other domestic help. However, the Ladds believed everyone should be treated equally and they looked after their staff well. Penny was educated in Rangoon, Burma (now Yangon, Myanmar), until the threat of a Japanese invasion in 1941 became too great; Penny later recalled seeing "bombers like huge birds of prey" and "the bodies of people killed in the raids". Women and children were promptly evacuated to Calcutta (now Kolkata), although bandits intercepted the train: "We lay on the floor of the carriage like sardines, as bullets came through the window," remembered Penny.[544]

By the 1950s, Penny was living in London and working as a nurse at St George's Hospital, where she drew on her childhood experiences in India to learn how to stay calm and detached while dealing with gravely ill or dying patients. In 1953, she married an Australian man called Robin Wade and the couple started a family of their own. Her experiences as a mother of three children prompted Penny to want to do more and, after answering an advert from another woman looking for someone to work with promoting natural childbirth, the two set about initiating what would become the National Childbirth Trust. In her obituary, *The Guardian* wrote: "It is difficult to overstate the difference that this movement has made to women's experience of childbearing and the early stages of motherhood. Before, a medical model had dominated the maternity hospitals, a mother's role was largely

544 Ann Thwaite, 'Penny Wade: Worker for the Homeless' in *The Independent*, 12 August 2008.

passive, and husbands were kept far from the action."[545]

As well as being a member of the National Childbirth Trust, Penny also became involved with the homelessness charity Shelter and she started her own organisation to support those who were marginalised in the Richmond area of London, which she called the Vineyard Project.

MRS WALTER

born c1840, DISCIPLINARIAN

Here's something you don't read about every day. In Victorian Bristol, parents of unruly middle-class daughters could employ the services of a third party to administer corporal punishment to their female offspring. Yes, you read that right. Parents would send their spirited daughters off to a boarding 'school', knowing those young girls would be caned into submission.

Operating from 53 Oakfield Road, Clifton, Mrs Walter advertised in the national newspapers stating: "Bad temper, hysteria, idleness etc, cured by strict discipline and careful training." And: "Intractable girls trained and educated. Excellent references." Mrs Walter also offered advice by mail at a cost of five shillings. Indeed, all aspects of her time were monetised and any reporters wishing to interview her were likewise requested to pay Mrs Walter half a guinea for her troubles.

As a bit of background information, 'Mrs Walter' was really Mrs Walter Smith: Walter Smith being her late husband, who had been the clergyman headmaster of All Saints School, Clifton. After her husband's death, she established a girls' school and, by calling upon the good name and reputation of her late husband, she was

545 Penny Lee, 'Obituary: Penny Wade' in *The Guardian*, 17 September 2008.

able to summon excellent references from people including an admiral, a general and a range of lords and ladies. It was these references for her husband's teaching which she dishonestly claimed as references for her own disciplinarian services. When these referees found out how their names were really being used they were understandably appalled.

As horrifying as this idea of corporal punishment is to contemporary sensibilities, it is comforting to know that some Victorians — not traditionally known for their mollycoddling of youngsters — also found the concept startling. The sensationalist magazine *Truth*[546] sent an undercover reporter to investigate, with the journalist claiming she had a troublesome daughter whom she wanted "broken in". Mrs Walter promptly accepted the challenge and named her price as £100 a year, assuring the fictional mother her golden rule was simply: "Never birch when angry."

Truth described Mrs Walter as a tall, strong woman, dressed like a nurse, who was quite happy to describe her methods to potential customers who were considering sending their children to her. She used a strong narrow table which had straps for the waist, wrists and ankles, and she struck the children with a long and pliable birch rod. The girls were ordered to remove all of their clothing and put on a backless gown (rather like a contemporary hospital gown) before they were buckled to the table.

Mrs Walter told *Truth* (not knowing she was speaking to a reporter): "Taking the birch, I measure my distance and, standing at the side, I proceed to strike slowly but firmly. By moving gently forward, each stroke is differently placed and six strokes may well be enough if given with full force. If the fault has been such as to need severe correction, then I begin on the other side and work

546 *Truth* was published between 1877 and 1957. It was known for its exposure of a range of fraudulent activities and as such found itself at the centre of several (generally unsuccessful) lawsuits. By the late Victorian period, it had a readership of about one million people per issue, so it had quite some influence.

back again. For screams, increased strokes must be given. If a girl tries very hard to bear it bravely, then perhaps I give ten instead of 12."

Following the exposé in *Truth,* Mrs Walter lost the respectable names who had supported her and the ongoing revelations kept the letters pages of the Bristol newspapers busy for quite some time. Even the woman who had sold Mrs Walter her birch rod (a Mrs Clapp, based on St John's Road: "A family who have made them for generations") felt the heat and denied ever having sold Mrs Walter the tool of her trade in the first place.

And another thing... On a corporal punishment note, let us remember **Mrs Willingale**. By 1937, Mrs Willingale was a patient at the Manor House for the Aged and Infirm on St Michael's Hill, but she vividly recalled the time her grandfather – who had been a royal coachman – escorted Queen Victoria to Cliftonville (which seems to be a quaint way of referring to Clifton Village). Young Mrs Willingale (who presumably wasn't yet known as Mrs Willingale and had a name all of her own before she became a man's chattel) had behaved very badly in front of the Queen. And upon seeing that the child's grandfather wasn't going to dish out any form of punishment himself, the monarch took matters into her own hands and gave the truculent child a smacking.[547]

547 'Hidden City Mansion with Notable Work', 17 June 1937, *Western Daily Press*

JESSICA WALTERS
1877-1954, SUFFRAGE ARTIST

Bristol-born Jessica Walters was the youngest daughter of a building society secretary from Clifton. She was christened 'Jessie' but seems to have preferred 'Jessica' as this was the name she used on many formal documents. The Walters family (who lived during this period at 12 The Polygon and then 4 Clifton Park Road, both in Clifton) had seven children. Jessica attended the Queen's Road Art School, from which she earned three prizes for her work: the 1899 National Competition for Schools of Arts and Sciences, a bronze medal for a chalk drawing in 1900 and, in 1901, she was awarded first-class certificates for both her life drawing and design. These achievements led her to travel to Paris, France, where she continued studying art.

When Jessica returned to Bristol in 1908, the family was living at 129 Redland Road, Redland, and she soon became involved with the women's suffrage movement and used her artistic skills working for the Suffrage Atelier to design postcards and posters. The Suffrage Atelier was founded in 1909 and was an artists' collective which campaigned for votes for women in the UK. Much of its artwork was reproduced and sold in Women's Social and Political Union (WSPU) shops around the country to raise money to help fund the women's suffrage campaign. The black-and-white postcard that Jessica created shows women carrying 'Votes for Women' banners and marching to the House of Commons.

She also produced at least three posters for the Suffrage Atelier, all of which mocked Prime Minister Herbert Henry Asquith. Jessica's reasons for despising Asquith went beyond merely resenting his refusal to grant women the vote, because she was also extremely angered at the treatment her suffragette sister Alice had received in prison following numerous arrests for militancy.[548]

The Walters family were some of the original supporters of the Women's Reform Union, a Bristolian society which centralised women's suffrage within the wider social reforms that were needed to achieve overall societal equality; the Union amalgamated with the Bristol branch of the National Union of Women's Suffrage Societies (NUWSS) in December 1909. However, rather than join the peaceful NUWSS, Jessica and Alice were members of the militant WSPU led by the Pankhurst family. As established above, although Alice was a militant suffragette, Jessica does not seem to have engaged in illegal activities for the cause and she was certainly never arrested. However, Jessica supported the WSPU via other means; for example, alongside her art she appeared as a maid in a production of the suffragette play *How The Vote Was Won* in November 1910. In addition, Jessica and her mother joined the suffrage boycott of the 1911 census: "On the family's census form was written 'information refused' to which the enumerator added, 'Stated to be a Suffragette'."[549]

Jessica continued to submit artwork to the Suffrage Atelier well into 1914 and her work was widely published in suffrage journals such as the *Common Cause* as well as *Votes For Women,* and was also reproduced and sold in WSPU shops. One example of a poster she designed is 'Eliza Comes To Stay', which is a spoof of a 1913 play written by HV Esmond, whose wife was the suffragette actor Eva Moore: this poster was exhibited in the Women's Kingdom Exhibition in April 1914 and was described

548 Jessica's sister Alice Walters is profiled in volume one of *The Women Who Built Bristol*: it was she who helped run the WSPU shop on Park Street and was working there the day it was attacked by university students.

549 In protest at the government wanting to count women as citizens while also denying them the right to vote, suffragists all over the UK organised a mass boycott of the 1911 census. Elizabeth Crawford, 2018, *Art and Suffrage: A Biographical Dictionary of Suffrage Artists*, p216.

as "an adorable piece of work".[550] It is now part of the Museum of London's extensive suffrage collection.

Following the death of her mother in 1917, Jessica left Bristol and moved to London with her sister Ida. She continued to draw and exhibit her artworks but, with the suffrage movement ebbing away due to the Pankhursts calling for the suffragettes to stand down in favour of the war effort, Jessica's work moved in a less political direction. In the 1950s, she returned to Bristol to live with some of her siblings and died in Stapleton Hospital in 1954.[551]

Please also see: Alice Walters (vol one).

ANNA WARING

1823-1910, HYMN WRITER

Born in Neath, Wales, to a strict Quaker family, at the age of 19 (and now living in Clifton), Anna Laetitia Waring decided it was time to leave the Quakers and become baptised into the Church of England. Despite their own firm beliefs in the teachings of the Quakers, her family was supportive of this bold decision, which was clearly the right move for Anna who went on to express her devotion by becoming a respected hymn writer.

Initially, Anna and her family lived at 12 Royal York Crescent, Clifton, and it was here at the age of just 23 in 1846 that she wrote some of her most well known hymns, including "In Heavenly Love Abiding" and "Go Not Far From Me, O My Strength".

In 1850, Anna's collection called *Hymns and Meditations* was published, which was reprinted and expanded many times. She

550 'A Mine of Interesting Information', *The Common Cause*, 24 April 1914.
551 Information for this entry was drawn from: Elizabeth Crawford, 2018, *Art and Suffrage: A Biographical Dictionary of Suffrage Artists*, pp215-218.

followed this in 1858 with a collection called *Additional Hymns*. A book of Anna's writings which was published after her death was extended to include not only hymns and poems but also essays, including a light-hearted piece about her beloved pet cat.

In her later years, now living at 3 Pembroke Road, Clifton, Anna became a regular visitor to inmates at the Bridewell and Horfield prisons "where her winning personality was instrumental in bringing home the divine message to many prodigals".[552] She had a typically Victorian outlook in that, as an unmarried woman of strong faith, she lived a pious life and devoted herself to good works. As an extension of her prison visiting she also became a supporter of the Discharged Prisoners' Aid Society. Talking about her work with the prisoners, Anna said: "It is like walking by a filthy gutter to pick out a jewel here and there, as the foul stream flows by."

Anna died peacefully in her sleep at her home in Clifton and was buried at Arnos Vale Cemetery. Her most well known hymn, "Father, I Know That All My Life is Portioned Out for Me", was performed at her funeral service.

And another thing... Another Bristolian hymn writer in the Victorian era was **Mary Peters** (1813-1856), a vicar's wife who was widowed at a young age. Mary found comfort from her grief in writing, and a not-inconsiderable project she worked on was a seven-volume history of the world published in 1840, called *The World's History from the Creation to the Accession of Queen Victoria*. However, she is best known for her hymns, having written more than 60, including "Around Thy Table, Holy Lord" and "Through the Love of God our Saviour", which were both popular in their day. Mary died of consumption at her home at 7 The Mall, Clifton.

552 AJ Green-Armytage, 1922, *Concerning Clifton*, p63.

KATHLEEN WARNER
1903-1996, BROADCASTER

Born in Trinidad, Kathleen Warner (née Davis) is best remembered for presenting the phenomenally popular *The Aunty Kay Show* on Radio Trinidad every Sunday afternoon from 1942 to 1985, which was aimed at children. However, I concede it is unlikely many Bristolians tuned in. Kathleen's Bristol connection is that she, and her sisters Meta and Beryl, were boarders at Redland High School, where they all came to finish their education. As 'Aunty Kay', Kathleen was known for her excellent elocution and perhaps this is something she picked up while at school in Bristol.

CATHERINE WAUGH
1870-1954, MATRIARCH

In his 1964 autobiography *A Little Learning*, the writer Evelyn Waugh records that his mother Catherine grew up at Priory House, 61 Pembroke Road, Shirehampton. Waugh wrote: "Her rustic tastes were formed by her childhood at Shirehampton, where she and her sisters were sent from India at an age which left them no memories of their place of birth, to the care of two maiden great-aunts and a bachelor great-uncle, a retired sailor … Shirehampton is now a suburb of Bristol. The Priory has become a vicarage and its meadows have been overbuilt. In my mother's childhood the place was rural and my mother was entirely happy there. All her life she looked back on that elderly ménage as the ideal of home."[553]

As Waugh noted, his mother Catherine Charlotte Raban

553 Evelyn Waugh, 1964, *A Little Learning*, p46-47.

was born in Bengal, India, where her father Henry worked in the Bengal Civil Service. As children, Catherine and her sisters Lilian and Henrietta were sent to relatives in Shirehampton to benefit from an English education. It was also felt by the Rabans that the sweltering Indian climate was unsuitable for delicate young girls and women generally, and so female family members were dispatched to the UK to cool down: "[The Rabans] built a commodious bow-fronted house, now a nursing home, in Hatch Beauchamp, Somerset; there, and to an old house named The Priory in Shirehampton, they sent their women-folk and children as refugees from the climate and there, those of them who survived, retired."[554]

In 1893, Catherine married the writer Arthur Waugh at Christ Church, Weston-super-Mare, with whom she had two children: Alexander and Arthur (who published under his middle name of Evelyn). Reporting on the wedding, the *Bristol Mercury* wrote: "The bride, who wore a handsome dress of ivory corded silk, with a long train and trimmed with real orange blossoms, was given away by Mr Spender Thomson of Edinburgh [her father had died in 1871]; she also wore a diamond and pearl brooch, the gift of the bridegroom."[555]

Catherine's husband Arthur had already made a name for himself as a talented writer by the time of their marriage. He had published a biography of Alfred, Lord Tennyson and was a regular writer for various New York journals. Arthur continued to write successfully and sometimes his plays were performed locally. Indeed, both he and Catherine made appearances performing in some of his plays when they were produced by local amateur dramatics groups.

554 Ibid, p36.
555 'Wedding at Weston-super-Mare' in *Bristol Mercury*, 6 October 1893.

JANE WELSH

1905-2001, ACTOR

This prolific stage and screen actor was born in Bristol in January 1905, and became interested in acting even as a young child. Having excelled in school plays, she was encouraged by her English teacher to join a repertory theatre group and it was in this way that she made her stage debut in *Charley's Aunt* in Bournemouth in 1923. Just one year later, she made her London debut with a production of *Alf's Buttons* at the Prince of Wales' Theatre. By 1926, Jane was working almost exclusively in London's West End, such was her popularity.

In the 1930s, she began to appear in movies, making her debut in 1931's *Two Crowded Hours* (Michael Powell). Off the back of this, she was making up to four films a year for British Gaumont, to whom she was contracted in the Hollywood studio system. She met her first husband Henry Mollison in 1932; an actor to whom she had been introduced by their mutual friend Noël Coward. However, the marriage was not a good match and the couple later divorced. Her second marriage was in the 1960s to Leonard Ritte, with whom she settled in London.

In 1948, Jane was cast as Mrs Brown in the popular *Just William* series of films, which have since enjoyed a renaissance with contemporary audiences and Jane's performance is a highlight. And by the 1950s, she had moved into the popular new medium of television, often appearing in the BBC's Sunday evening dramas. Her movie appearances were more sporadic by this time as her Gaumont contract had ended, but she can still be seen alongside Lana Turner and Sean Connery in the movie *Another Time, Another Place* (1958, Lewis Allen), among other films.

Jane retired from acting in the 1960s although her fans never forgot her, and she continued to receive fan mail from as far away

Jane Welsh illustration by Rhi Lee

as South Africa, Canada and the US for the rest of her life: "I'm absolutely amazed that I am remembered by so many who were born at least 20 years after I retired."[556]

WENDY
1960-2002, ELEPHANT

Housed at Bristol Zoo Gardens in Clifton, Wendy was the second-oldest Asian elephant in the UK at the time of her death, aged 42, in September 2002. Wendy was also the last elephant to live at Bristol Zoo after urban zoos began phasing out keeping these huge animals in the enclosures. It was only because of Wendy's great age that the decision was made to keep her at Bristol until she died rather than move her to the more spacious Whipsnade Zoo in Dunstable.

Born on a logging camp in Thailand, Wendy arrived in Bristol when she was one year old and, for the first 20 years of her life at Bristol Zoo, she enjoyed the companionship of an African elephant called Christina. Wendy and Christina were both very young when they came to Bristol and needed to be bottle fed. They were also taken for walks not only around the zoo grounds but also the streets of Clifton, including on Whiteladies Road. After Christina died in 1986, attempts to find a new companion for Wendy were unsuccessful, because she did not get on well with the other elephants she was introduced to, although she seemed happy in the company of humans and was gentle towards her keepers.

It was with sadness that Bristol Zoo took the decision to put Wendy to sleep in September 2002. The zoo's vet Sharon Redrobe

556 Howard Mutti-Mewse, 'Jane Welsh' in *The Independent*, 15 December 2001.

said: "Wendy had a severe degenerative joint disease; despite intensive veterinary care her welfare became a matter of great concern to the zoo. We realised that the condition was incurable and the prognosis gloomy. Wendy was suffering from significant joint pain despite strong medication and more recently was unable to have the comfort of restful sleep."[557] Wendy is the focus of a wooden statue that was created by Diane Gorvin and Philip Bews, which was unveiled at Bristol Zoo in 2013.

SARAH WESLEY

1759-1828, METHODIST WRITER

Born on Charles Street, Kingsdown, Sarah was the fourth child and only surviving daughter of Methodists Sarah and Charles Wesley. Her beloved uncle John Wesley had founded the Methodist church: a visit to his restored chapel in Broadmead is highly recommended to readers of this book.

A quiet child, Sarah was partly educated at home and partly at school in Bristol but she was most happy when left alone with her books. Although she enjoyed writing poetry, she was fearful of her father's criticism and felt too shy to show her work to anybody so never tried to become published. However, her aunt Martha Hall nurtured Sarah's talent for writing and introduced her to the writer Samuel Johnson, who heaped praise upon her. Once her writing developed, Sarah started to move in more literary circles and counted the acclaimed writer Hannah More among her friends. She was a member of City Road Chapel and a part of the ladies' working circle there, which sewed clothes for the poor while discussing religious and moral issues.

557 Anon, 'Zoo Favourite Wendy Dies, Aged 42' on *BBC News*, 12 September 2002.

Because Sarah never pursued publication for her creative writings, these have sadly been lost to time. However, what survives and is of most interest to historians is her biographical writing about her family.[558] Given the significance of the Wesley family both to Bristol and to wider Methodist circles, these family stories are invaluable.

Sarah lived in London for a while as an adult but was in Bristol at the time of her death and was buried in the churchyard of St James, which is also the church where she had been baptised.

Please also see: Hannah More (vol one).

MARGERY WESTBROOK

1910-1999, HOSPITAL MATRON

When the National Health Service was formed in 1948, Margery Westbrook became the first practising nurse to be elected as Chair*man* of the Staff Side of the Nurses and Midwives Whitley Council (effectively a trade union for medical workers), which decided the salaries of nurses, midwives and health visitors. And this remained the case until those workers and doctors finally got a review body in 1984, although Margery was no longer on the Council by this point, having stepped down in 1969. It is thanks to Margery and her colleagues on the Council that medical workers received anything close to a fair wage.

Margery was more than a practising nurse and politician. She soon became Matron of Southmead Hospital in Bristol and remained in this post until her retirement — at which point the title of 'matron' was abolished altogether. This change was in no

558 Sarah's letters and some of her writing are kept in the archives at the University of Manchester.

small part due to her own work on the Salmon Committee, which was concerned with the administration of the NHS.

Margery was born in Rotherham, Yorkshire, and was blessed with a toughened can-do attitude to life which she carried through everything that she did. Having worked in her father's pharmacy as a teenager, she went on to train as a State Registered nurse at Sheffield Royal Infirmary, from where she qualified in 1935. After this, she went to work at the Queen Elizabeth Hospital in Birmingham, where many of her patients would be soldiers gruesomely wounded during World War Two. After becoming Night Superintendent, then qualifying as a Sister, Margery took further qualifications in Administration and became Assistant Matron at the General Hospital in Bristol. Via a post in Weston-super-Mare, she settled into her final post as Matron at Southmead Hospital. Her widowed mother lived with Margery in her matron's flat and, when she was not at work caring for patients, Margery would be at home caring for her elderly mother.

Margery had progressive ideas about nursing and how nurses should be treated. She joined the council at the Royal College of Nursing as well as the Matrons' Association, was a member of the South West Regional Hospital Board and spoke at a committee of the International Council of Nurses in Geneva, Switzerland. She was appointed CBE in 1970 for her services to nursing.

After her retirement, Margery and her mother moved to Stoke Gifford, where Margery — of course — threw herself into work on the parish council and helped transform the area into a satellite town for Bristol. By the time of her death, Margery was living in Almondsbury.

RACHEL WHITTARD
1885-1968, VAD NURSE

Voluntary Aid Detachment (VAD) nurses were indispensible during World War One, although their stories are little shared. VAD nurses were often young women from upper-class families who typically had little nursing knowledge or experience and were instead trained in first aid. During the early years of World War One, VAD nurses were employed more as companions to the recovering soldiers than as actual nurses but, as the war progressed, the VADs were increasingly called on to assist trained nurses in their work.

During World War One, Rachel Whittard joined the Red Cross' team of VAD nurses stationed at a military hospital. Her work as a nurse during the war inspired her to take further training once war ceased and in 1920 she qualified as a midwife (during her career, Rachel delivered more than 900 babies), although she also worked as a district nurse. In 1926, she moved to Marshfield and such was her commitment to her patients that, during the harsh winter of 1940, she crawled on her hands and knees across icy and snowy terrain to reach the patients who depended on her visits. When Adolf Hitler declared war, Rachel found herself again thrown into nursing soldiers during World War Two, after which point ill-health forced her to retire.

During her retirement, she volunteered as Superintendent of the Congregational Chapel Sunday School and was a keen member of the Marshfield Women's Institute. Committed to her community, Rachel also enjoyed appearing in the Marshfield community pantomime every winter.

And another thing... Another Bristolian VAD with a special story was **Edith Hemingway**, of 18 Downleaze, Stoke Bishop. She was employed at the Beaufort War Hospital, Glenside, and her story is both typical of the unsung VAD experience and curious to contemporary readers because of the nature of the therapy she specialised in. Edith was primarily employed at the Beaufort War Hospital as a masseuse. She joined the hospital in November 1917, was paid £1 7s 6d a week and remained there until the hospital closed in February 1919. By this time she had become Senior Masseuse and worked three-and-a-half hours per day, with her duties involving massage and 'electrical therapies'. Her training records show she had spent nine months studying massage training in 1916 and a further two weeks learning 'electrical treatments'.[559] Edith, who remained unmarried, died in 1942.

Please also see: Kate Underwood (vol two).

BETTY WILKINS
died 1788, SERVANT

Servant girl Betty Wilkins worked for the miller of Willsbridge and lived at the Clack Mill (a corn mill) on the road heading out to Keynsham. By all accounts, her life was rather tedious and repetitive. Which makes the story of her death even more confusing. Betty died on 23 September 1788 and the postmortem concluded she had died from arsenic poisoning. Yet her body was found floating in the mill pond, washed up by the willow trees.

She was pregnant at the time of her death, so the court conducting her inquest presumed Betty had taken her own life out of shame. Because although she was married, Betty had not seen her husband for quite some time, meaning her unborn

559 glensidemuseum.org.uk/beaufort-war-hospital-home-page/matrons-and-nurses-march-18/vads/

child must be illegitimate. In the 18th century, suicide was considered to be a heinous crime and someone who took their own life was not permitted to be buried in a churchyard. Instead, as was customary for a suicide, Betty's body was buried "in the crossroads" and staked through the heart. The thinking being that this would prevent the dead from waking and haunting the living. But somehow Betty's spirit survived the stake. There is a site known as Betty's Grave which dates from the time of her death and stories about sightings of a restless soul around that area linger to this day.

ELIZABETH WILKINS

1922-2015, HOLOCAUST SURVIVOR, MIDWIFE

German-born Doris Wolf, known by her middle name of Elizabeth, fled Nazi Germany as a teenager in August 1939, just before the start of World War Two. The Jewish Wolf family was torn apart by the war with Elizabeth being taken in by a family in Hampshire. She was the lucky one: her father died in Colombia, South America (where he had fled for safety), and her mother and brother were murdered in Nazi concentration camps. The Wolf family are commemorated in a Stolpersteine memorial in Langen, Germany, which remember the names of local families who were killed or forced to flee during the Holocaust.

Elizabeth could barely speak English when she arrived in Hampshire but she quickly picked up the language and went on to study music, becoming an accomplished pianist. However, her vocational training was in nursing and she became a midwife, completing her training at Bristol's Southmead Hospital. She worked at Southmead for most of her professional career.

In 1948, Elizabeth married the recently widowed Lionel

Wilkins and moved to live with him and his daughters in Filton, where she stood out as a European Jew in this quiet English suburb. Although Elizabeth converted to Anglicanism, she remained proud of her Jewish ancestry and heritage. The couple moved to Cornwall for a period following Lionel's retirement but, after his death in 1980, Elizabeth returned to Bristol and resumed work as a maternity nurse in order to support herself.[560]

DEBORAH WILLET

1650-1678, MAID

Deborah Willet was born in Marsh Street in the city centre to a respectable merchant family... so respectable that she enchanted a certain navalman, politician and diarist named Samuel Pepys (who met her in September 1667 when she was working as a maid for one of his friends) and he poached 17-year-old Deborah to become his wife Elisabeth's companion at their home in London.

Introducing Deborah's family in his diaries, Pepys wrote that her uncle Mr Butts (who, along with his wife, brought Deborah up following the deaths of her parents Elizabeth and Robert) was "a sober merchant, very good company, and so like one of our sober, wealthy London merchants as pleased me mightily ... His wife was a good woman and so sober and substantial as I was never more pleased anywhere".[561] Of Deborah herself, Pepys wrote that she was "very pretty and so grave as I never saw a little thing in my life. I wish my wife may use her well"[562]. The fact he was so smitten with her prettiness is something we will return to.

Deborah was such an asset to Pepys that on subsequent visits

560 Alex Powell, 'Doris Elizabeth Wilkins Obituary' in *The Guardian*, 10 March 2015.
561 Marguerite Fedden, 1958, *Bristol Vignettes*, p38.
562 Samuel Pepys in JF Nicholls et al, 1882, *Bristol Past and Present*, p79.

to Bristol, the diarist made sure to visit Mr and Mrs Butts and, on occasion, bring Deborah with him so she could call upon her relatives. Pepys describes one such visit to Marsh Street, writing that it was "a substantial good house, and well furnished, and [Mr Butts] did give us good entertainment of strawberries, a whole venison pasty, cold, and plenty of brave wine, and above all, Bristol Milk[563]; where comes in another poor woman, who, hearing that Deborah was here, did come running hither, and with her eyes so full of tears, and heart so full of joy, that she could not speak when she came in, that it made me weep too."[564]

Travelling with Mr and Mrs Pepys, Deborah seemed to fit in extremely well, as he writes of one journey to Bristol: "My wife and girl talking and telling tales and singing." However, after a while, Elisabeth began to tire of Deborah's lack of formality and, during a trip to the theatre with her husband, Elisabeth complained to him that Deborah was too familiar with her and six months later, Pepys wrote that he found Deborah "crying that her mistress has been angry with her … I would take no notice of it."[565] However, Deborah remained a regular character in Pepys' diary for some time to follow… although no longer as Elisabeth's maid.

From October 1668, Pepys chronicles that Deborah is one of the many young women with whom he had an affair but he seems to have been more besotted with Deborah than his other flings. After discovering the affair (which is described in lurid detail in Pepys' diaries), Elisabeth sacked Deborah but Pepys continued to seek the teenage girl out and support her financially; this was made easier following Elisabeth's death from typhoid in November 1669. Such was his affection for her that, even after Deborah married a theology graduate named Jeremiah Wells

563 Bristol Milk was a type of sweet sherry.
564 Samuel Pepys in JF Nicholls et al, 1882, *Bristol Past and Present*, p81.
565 Ibid, p81.

in 1670, he helped her husband find work as a ship's chaplain. However, Pepys' diaries show he had helped the husbands of some of his other lovers find work on the ships... often as a means to get the men out of the way so he could continue wooing their wives. Academic Kate Loveman notes: "Given Pepys' past obsession with Deb, his continued contact with her family raises suspicions about the nature of their relationship. He may have assisted Deb and her husband out of simple benevolence. However Pepys's wife was now dead, Deb was living close by, and Pepys knew she was without her husband, indeed he had helped send her husband elsewhere. The situation is particularly suspicious because Pepys' diary reveals his affairs with women had more than once led to him helping their husbands to a position on board ship."[566]

Deborah and Jeremiah had two daughters, born in 1670 and 1672. However, as Mrs Wells, Deborah died young in 1678, with her husband following her to the grave just 18 months later.

MARY WILLIAMS
born c1780, MILL WORKER

While contemporary readers may bemoan the fact that these days we live in a culture of health and safety overload, mill worker Mary Williams stands as a stark reminder that we don't know how lucky we are. Mary was employed as a grinder at the mill on Little Ann Street, St Philip's, owned by a Mr Simmons. But in June 1809, her usual day at work took a horrible turn for the unusual. Mary's hands and arms became caught in the grinding machinery she was using, leaving them mangled "in a manner too horrible for description". Upon being rushed to the Royal Infirmary,

566 Anon, 'Mystery of Pepys' Affair Solved' on *BBC News*, 14 October 2006.

a surgeon called Mr Noble amputated both of her arms. Mary showed great resilience and strength of character throughout and made a good recovery from her ordeal, returning home to her husband and children.

LOUISA WILLS

1862-1936, HOMEOPATHIC MEDICINE ADOPTER

Louisa Gertrude Wilson was born in Hankow (now Hankou), China, but became a British citizen after her family returned to England. She married Walter Melville Wills in 1887 in Hampstead, London, and they had five children. Walter was the fifth son of tobacco tycoon Henry Overton Wills, after whom the Wills Memorial Building at the University of Bristol on Park Street is named.

Louisa and Walter lived with their children at Bracken Hill House in Leigh Woods, which Walter had commissioned for his family. The five-bedroom house still stands, complete with five acres of beautiful landscaped gardens which Walter had commissioned.[567] Owing to the family's interest in homeopathic medicines, it is not surprising to learn that some of the plants grown — and still growing — in the gardens include medicinal Chinese plants such as the Bristol onion and Babbington's leek.[568]

Walter was managing director of the profitable Wills tobacco industry, meaning Louisa and their children lived a luxurious

567 Louisa and Walter's son Douglas donated the house and gardens to the University of Bristol in 1959 and it then became home to the university's Botanical Gardens until 2004, when the university sold the gardens to generate income and the house returned to residential use. For more information: Ben Flanagan, 'Bracken Hill House: Plant Yourself in Paradise' in *The Guardian*, 8 August 2004.

568 Aside from in the Bracken Hill House garden, the only other place in the UK where the Bristol onion can be found is on the Avon Gorge. Babbington's leek is a variant of the leek which is usually only found on the British seashore.

Louisa Wills illustration by Tina Altwegg

lifestyle. Outside of work, the couple were very interested in homeopathic medicine and it was Walter who financed the building of the Bristol Homeopathic Hospital on Cotham Hill, for which the foundation stone was laid in a grand ceremony on 10 June 1921, before the hospital finally opened in 1925. Because Walter and Louisa's son Bruce had been killed during World War One, the hospital was officially referred to as the Bruce Melville Wills Memorial Hospital.

A brief history of homeopathy in Bristol: Dr Francis Black opened a homeopathic dispensary on Upper Berkeley Place in 1832, which expanded to a property on the Triangle in 1852, the first homeopathic institution in Bristol. Such was the influence of Dr Black's dispensary that in 1883, a number of patrons (including a Miss Charles and Miss Rich, both of Clifton) contributed sizeably to a fund for a homeopathic hospital in Bristol. Properties at 7 Brunswick Square, as well as the neighbouring Pembroke Cottage in St Paul's, were bought for the purpose of building this new hospital. It finally opened in 1903 after further investments from Miss Charles. By 1907, the homeopathic hospital in Brunswick Square had been enlarged to include an operating theatre, lift and verandah, and could accommodate 12 in-patients. It was a grand and imposing building with a turreted frontage, balustrades on the roof and columns flanking the front porch.

As further extensions to the popular hospital were needed in 1911, support was lent to the project by the Lord Mayor Frank Wills, while Louisa raised funds to provide a free bed for any in-patient who needed it but could not afford to pay. By 1914, the Brunswick Square hospital was being used by soldiers returning wounded from World War One and, by 1917, the demand for the hospital and its facilities had grown so much that Louisa and Walter purchased Cotham House and its grounds for £10,000, so that the new Bristol Homeopathic Hospital could be built. After the hospital's removal from Brunswick Square to Cotham House, the former homeopathic hospital in St Paul's was sold to the Bristol Maternity Hospital; the original building has since been demolished and modern flats erected in its place.[569]

The new Bristol Homeopathic Hospital had all mod-cons, including x-ray equipment, laboratories, a laundry, steam disinfector and a kitchen which could cater for up to 80 people. All of this was in addition to the wards, beds, medicines etc provided for the patients, and accommodation for nurses and other staff. However, none of this came cheaply, especially given that Louisa and Walter wanted to provide free treatment for those who could not afford to pay, so Louisa headed an impressive fundraising arm of the operation.

The hospital benefitted from lavish gardens in which some of the plants used in the medicines were cultivated and the gardens survive to some degree but they are not publicly accessible. The hospital was given to the National Health Service (NHS) once it came into operation, although the NHS sold the hospital to the University of Bristol in 1994.

Homeopathy services were still offered from a smaller part of the building until 2004, when the department was relocated several times until settling at its current base of the Portland Centre for Integrative Medicine on Clifton Down. The Grade II-listed building is now known as Hampton House and remains owned by the University of Bristol.

569 'The Bristol Homeopathic Hospital and Dispensary: A Short History' in *Bristol Homeopathic Hospital: Laying of Foundation Stone* commemorative booklet, 10 June 1921, pp7-8.

MONICA WILLS

1861-1931, CARE HOME PIONEER

Another woman who married into Bristol's influential Wills tobacco dynasty, Monica Wills used the family fortunes to benefit others. It was in 1911 that London-born Mary Monica Cunliffe Wills first talked about her dream of buying a small rest home for a handful of missionary friends, and from this small acorn a big oak grew. The modest rest home rapidly escalated into a "purpose-built haven for chronic and incurable sufferers"[570] and, in this way, the seed for the St Monica Trust retirement village was sown.

In 1887, Monica had married Henry Herbert Wills, who was a partner in the Wills Family Tobacco Company. It was he who, with his brother George, oversaw the building of the Wills Memorial Building. The couple lived in Clifton and, while walking across the Durdham Downs one morning, he spotted the Cote House estate in Westbury and felt this would be the perfect place for Monica's rest home. They bought the 27-acre site in 1919 and established the St Monica Home of Rest with architect George Oatley, who had worked on the Wills Memorial Building. Monica was a woman of strong religious faith and she prioritised the building of a new chapel on the estate, with the foundation stone being laid on 4 May 1920, ie St Monica's Day. It was a further five years before the St Monica Home of Rest was completed and ready to open in 1925 (three years after Henry's death in 1922).

Initially, up to 80 residents were housed in the main building on the Cote House estate with Oatley Court accommodating nursing staff, and Monica herself was very hands-on. Monica's belief was that the residents should be ladies of "gentle birth" who

570 stmonicatrust.org.uk/our-expertise/history

shared her High Church Anglican faith. In acknowledgement of her work, Monica was made a Dame in 1925 and was the first Chair*man* of the council at St Monica's Home of Rest.

Now known as St Monica's Trust, the spirit of the care home lives on and has extended to five residential sites in Bristol, of which the original Cote Lane site is still one.

And another thing... If you visit All Saints church in Wrington and make your way up to the bell tower, you will find that the name 'Mrs Mary Monica Cunliffe Wills' appears on one of the bells. This was to acknowledge the fact that in 1923, she laid the foundation stone for Wrington Village Hall, and opened the new building in 1924. Her husband Henry had provided the money to pay for the hall because, by the time of the 1911 census, the couple had moved to live in Wrington.

EDITH WINFIELD

born 1891, WHISTLER

"You know how to whistle, don't you? You just put your lips together and blow."[571]

When Edith AE Winfield won the whistling prize at the Bristol Baptist Union Eisteddfod[572] in April 1932, her talent called a judge to question "why this natural means of music-making was not used more".[573] We have a string of news reports throughout the entire 1930s of Edith winning trophy after shield after cup

571 *To Have and Have Not* (1944, Howard Hawks).

572 'Eisteddfod' is a Welsh term for a festival of literature, music and performance. Following a rise in Welsh emigration during the Industrial Revolution, the concept spread outside of Wales but eisteddfods held in England generally have no link to their Welsh origins beyond the name. The Bristol Festival of Music, Speech and Drama was founded in 1903 as the Bristol Eisteddfod and the name continues in the Bristol Dance Eisteddfod.

573 'Whistling As Means of Music', in *Western Daily Press*, 7 April 1932.

for her whistling prowess and it seems somewhat regrettable that whistling is no longer considered such a treasured musical artform in the 21st century. Not content with merely whistling, as a member of the Bristol Baptist Union, Edith also performed in various plays and tableaux which the organisation put on, for example appearing as the Virgin Queen in a 1932 production of *Good Queen Bess*, where she apparently "provided quite a diversion from the rest of the programme".[574]

By the end of the decade, Edith was firmly established as a whistling teacher in Bristol alongside running the Hawthorns Hotel (now the accommodation office for the University of Bristol) on Woodland Road, Clifton. With World War Two having started to make its unwelcome presence felt, and when there was a public call for furnishings to equip a local hostel for visiting servicemen, Edith immediately offered up chairs, rugs, china and even a sideboard from the hotel for use in the hostel.[575] She clearly kept up this generous spirit throughout the war and later reports show her donating a wireless radio and handwoven rugs to support those servicemen in need of some comforts.

And another thing... A bonus whistling woman: in December 1891, the American superstar **Alice Shaw** performed at a packed Victoria Rooms, Clifton, to rapturous reception. "The range of her whistling gamut, the delicacy and variety of her tones, the rapidity of her execution, the tunefulness of her whole rendering, and the artistic feeling which she threw into her performance were such as to evoke loud applause," gushed the *Clifton Society* on 3 December 1891.

574 'Reformation Story in Tableaux', in *Western Daily Press*, 8 October 1932.
575 'Thanks, Miss Winfield', in *Western Daily Press*, 19 December 1939.

LUCY WISDOM

1956-2009, PERFORMER, CONSERVATIONIST

Multi-talented performer Lucy Wisdom channelled her energies into music, theatre and the performing arts from a young age. As a member of the performance group Mutoids Waste Company, she helped recycle old cars, cranes and even fighter planes into sculptures which they used in performances all over Europe.

However, her academic background was in geology and archaeology, which she read at the University of Bristol. Following her degree, Lucy trained in circus skills in Bristol before helping to crew a yacht to Barbados in 1982, where she founded the Barbados Archaeological Society.

After being diagnosed with breast cancer in 1994, Lucy re-evaluated her priorities. She visited Sumatra, Indonesia, to volunteer at the Bohorok Rehabilitation Centre, which cared for orangutans whose mothers had been shot or sold. Using the acrobatic circus skills she had learned in Bristol, Lucy was able to teach the young apes how to survive once they were released back into the wild. Realising that helping individual baby orangutans was not enough, Lucy founded the Sumatran Orangutan Society in 1997 to challenge the illegal logging and palm oil plantations which were threatening the apes' natural habitats, and leading to their demise. In acknowledgement of her achievements, Lucy received numerous awards including Ethical Businesswoman of the Year in 2009.

Lucy was buried in a pink papier-mâché coffin that was carried to her funeral in Epping Forest on a vibrant hearse created by her friends from The Mutoids.

BEATRICE WISE

1876-1944, FOUNDER OF FIRST GIRL SCOUTS GROUP

In 1907 when Robert Baden-Powell came up with the idea for a scouting movement to teach youngsters survival skills and to help build useful members of society, it was known as the Boy Scouts. But as early as March 1908, there was support for girls to join the movement. And one woman who pushed for this was Bristol's Beatrice Ethel Wise.

When she was born, Beatrice lived with her family at 6 Park Place, Clifton. Her parents Sarah and James had eight children, of whom Beatrice was the youngest. By 1891, the family had moved to 15 Whiteladies Road, Clifton, where James worked as a butcher. By 1901, following Sarah's death and James' retirement, the family had relocated to the suburbs and were now living at 43 Hemplow House, Bath Road, Brislington (since demolished). Although she was 23 by 1901, Beatrice has no occupation listed on that census but it seems she was not entirely without activities to occupy her.

One such activity was a keen interest in the scouting movement. Her young niece May Jones wrote directly to Baden-Powell in early 1908 to say that, thanks to her aunt, she was taking up scouting herself. Baden-Powell replied positively: "I am glad to hear you are taking up scouting. I think there can be girl scouts just as well as boy scouts, and hope you will form a patrol, and let us know as yours will be the first girl scout patrol. You can work on just the same lines as the boys, and so need not do much more dusting and sewing than they, although a little of both are often necessary for a scout."[576]

May included a photograph with her letter and that photograph showed the six female members of The Owl Patrol

576 scoutcollecting.co.uk/post-girls_in_scouting___when_did_it_all_begin.html

of Brislington, with Beatrice Wise ("a very nominal Head") seated in their middle.

While The Owl Patrol was an unofficial branch of the Boy Scouts, it can also be recognised as the very first girls' branch of the scouts. The Girl Guides (now Girlguiding) was officially set up by Baden-Powell in 1910. Beatrice remained unmarried and was buried at Arnos Vale Cemetery.[577]

Please also see... Rotha Linton-Orman (vol two).

HELEN WODEHOUSE

1880-1964, EDUCATIONALIST

By the time Helen Wodehouse moved to Bristol, she had already gathered a long string of qualifications. As well as a first-class degree in Mathematics from Girton College at the University of Cambridge (1902), she spent a subsequent year at Girton studying Moral Sciences (1903) and had a higher diploma in Teaching from Birmingham University, where she read for an MA (1904) and DPhil (1906), and subsequently lectured there in Philosophy until 1911.

In 1919, Helen came to Bristol, where she was the first woman to hold the post of Professor of Education and Head of Department at the University of Bristol. She was also the first-ever woman to hold *any* professorial chair at this institution. Under her care, the University of Bristol's education department became one of the leading education departments in the entire UK.

577 The 2018 novel *Old Baggage* by Lissa Evans is an interesting take on the idea of women proactively inventing a scout-esque movement for girls. However, Lissa's book is set in 1928 and follows a former suffragette, Mattie Simpkin, who becomes disillusioned with the apathy she sees in contemporary young girls and resolves to teach them some skills with which to claim their independence.

Owing to her experience in educating teachers, Helen spearheaded the merging of the (at that time separate) women's and men's Departments for Education at the University of Bristol, despite heavy opposition. She followed this by instigating a new assessment system for the Diploma for Education, which has continued to this day.

Described as variously "austere", "shy" and "inspirational", a former pupil wrote of Helen in a memorial pamphlet: "Teaching, she told us, is not so much handing on the torch of knowledge as fumbling with a box of matches, trying to strike one so that your pupils can find the electric light switch for themselves." Another memory from the same former student was: "She advised us to be wary about introducing innovations too soon: 'Write down your ideas on a piece of paper and put it away in a sealed envelope for two years and then bring it out and, if you still think it advisable, act on it'."[578]

Such was her influence that, in 1964, the new Graduate School of Education at 35 Berkeley Square, Clifton, was named the Helen Wodehouse Building in her honour. It is worth noting that, by the time of her death in 1964, Helen was *still* the only woman to have held a professorial chair at the University of Bristol.

And another thing... Helen's nephew was the popular author PG Wodehouse, who wrote prolifically throughout his life and is best known for his enduring Jeeves and Wooster series.

Please also see: Geraldine Hodgson (vol two).

578 100stories.edn.bris.ac.uk/education/centenary/stories/story/in-1964-when-she-died-helen-/50/

ANN WOOD-KELLY

1918-2006, AVIATOR

If you were to have seen any vehicle travelling underneath the Clifton Suspension Bridge in the early part of the 20th century, it would most likely have been a boat of some kind. But not always. American Ann Wood-Kelly was a woman with a passion for flying and, seeking adventure, in 1942 she sailed from Montreal to Liverpool to join the British Air Transport Auxiliary during World War Two.

It was this which brought her to Bristol, where she became the first woman to fly a plane beneath the Clifton Suspension Bridge… not once but twice. On the first occasion, Ann was flying a Spitfire and was leading two other Spitfires which were both piloted by men. On the second occasion, Ann flew solo: although her second trip was a little more hair-raising, owing to the the high tide at the time, giving her less room for manoeuvre.

Please also see: Elsie Davison (vol two), Princess Marina (vol two).

ELIZABETH WOODWARD

1924-2002, BOTANIST, EQUESTRIAN

Despite a horse-riding accident in October 1968 that left her using a wheelchair for the rest of her life, Elizabeth 'Liza' Woodward refused to let her disability stop her from continuing to play a key part in the world of dressage which had always been her life.

Born into the Davies family in Bristol, Liza developed inner strength from an early age because her father died when she was just two years old, following injuries that he had received in World War One.

Ann Wood-Kelly illustration by Carrie Love

She had a solid education, starting at Badminton School in Bristol and graduating to complete an MA in Botanical Genetics at Newnham College, Cambridge, and a PhD in ferns at the University of Leicester. While completing her PhD, she identified a type of sedge (a grass-like plant) new to the British Isles, which was named after her: the Carex scandinavica E W Davies.

At the same time, Liza maintained her interest in horses, which saw her dealing in the animals, riding at point-to-point events and taking up the then-new sport of eventing. In 1952, she reported on the equestrian activities at the Helsinki Olympics for *The Daily Telegraph*.

By the mid-1950s, Liza had settled back in Bristol and taught pharmacy to dental students at the University of Bristol, even though she knew nothing about this topic and had to spend her evenings swotting up for the next day's lectures. After marrying Peter Woodward in 1958 (he was a chemist at the University of Bristol), the couple moved to Chewton Mendip in the south of Bristol to start their family and Liza left academia to return to her main passion of horses.

However, in October 1968, she had a life-changing accident. While competing in a cross-country event at the Tweseldown Horse Trials in Hampshire, Liza's horse tripped on a parallel bar causing both the horse and Liza to fall... with the horse landing on top of her causing catastrophic spinal injuries.[579] After this accident, she used a wheelchair for the rest of her life. However, Liza "never complained and with characteristic determination set to work to overcome her disability".[580]

In the coming years, Liza became Chair of the Community Health Council in Bristol, worked with Somerset County Council,

579 I want to know what happened to the horse and if it was also injured but have not been able to find out.
580 'Elizabeth Woodward Obituary' in *The Telegraph*, 15 March 2002.

and became the chief instructor at the Mendip Pony Club, where she also oversaw proficiency tests for the West Country. Not only that: in 1996 Liza also qualified as the highest level of dressage judge and became regional chair for dressage training in the West of England.

Alongside this, Liza maintained her interest in botany, returning to lecture at universities and to write for academic journals. She also taught biology at Millfield School, Street, and Sunny Hill School, Bruton, both in Somerset.

JULIA WOODWARD

1850-1910, BIBLIOPHILE

Born in Cheltenham to a very privileged family, Julia Lucy Woodward enjoyed a life of absolute luxury: her father Richard Woodward was a prominent landowner and fundholder. Originally from Kent, the surviving family moved to Clevedon following Richard's death in 1875 and they settled at a grand house called The Knoll, which Julia inherited in 1892 after her mother died.[581]

While at The Knoll, Julia took care of her Clifton-born uncle Vincent Stuckey Lean. He was descended from the Stuckey family who had made their fortune in banking, which meant Vincent was an extremely wealthy man with all the time and money he desired to indulge his passion for books. While caring for Vincent, Julia assisted him with collating four volumes which he called *Lean's Collectanea*, which were miscellanies of prose and poetry from existing works, and she shares an editorship credit for the books alongside her uncle.

581 In subsequent years, The Knoll became a maternity hospital and residential home, but more recently there have been plans to convert it back to a residential dwelling.

After Vincent died in 1899, Julia became fantastically well off because his estate was valued at almost £42,000 (more than £5 million in contemporary money) and, despite a sizeable chunk of this being donated to various organisations (including his beloved Bristol Library), there was more than enough left over for Julia to live a very charmed life. But she used this money for good. For example, she bought some land at Highdale Farm in 1897 and commissioned the Excelsior Club to be built for young men from St Andrew's Church: she also bought land at 17 Old Church Road and commissioned a coffee shop to be built which would benefit the Young Men's Christian Association.

When Julia died in 1910 with no family of her own, she left an additional sum of £500 and a bequest of her own collection of books to Bristol Library. Consequently, there still exists a large number of books in Bristol Reference Library than retain Julia Woodward's personal bookplate. Most donations of books to public libraries in the Victorian and Edwardian era came from men, so it was very unusual for such a large collection of books from a woman's personal library to have been donated. The readers of Bristol have much to thank Julia — and her uncle Vincent — for.[582]

MARY WYNTER

1650-1691, CHATELAINE

Captain John Wynter was a naval man who counted Francis Drake (sea captain, slave trader, explorer) as a friend. However, an accusation of piracy almost ruined the Wynter family and placed their ownership of Dyrham Park, which they had bought in 1571,

582 With thanks to Dawn Dyer for the nomination of Julia Woodward to this book.

at risk. Throughout the Civil War of 1642-1651, the Wynters clung on to Dyrham Park, although the Tudor estate was fast falling into a state of disrepair.

John's daughter Mary Wynter was the only one of his five children to survive into adulthood. In 1686, she met William Blathwayt following an introduction by Sir Robert Southwell, who owned the nearby Kings Weston Estate, and the couple were soon married and had four children, although one died in infancy.

Mary died just five years after her wedding due to complications in childbirth, but her surviving children (William, John and Anne) lived to see Dyrham Park transformed into the grand estate it now is, which is so closely associated with the suffrage sympathising Blathwayt family.[583]

Please also see: Emily and Mary Blathwayt (vol one).

ISABEL YEAMANS
1637-1704, QUAKER PREACHER

Lancashire-born Isabel Fell converted to Quakerism in her late teens and by 1660 had become a travelling Quaker, beginning her adult life of preaching at meetings all over England. After marrying Bristolian merchant William Yeamans in 1664, Isabel moved to live with him in the city and they had at least four children together. Following her father's death, Isabel's mother also moved to Bristol for her second marriage and Isabel was a signatory on the marriage certificate.

While in Bristol, Isabel helped to establish the women's monthly meetings in 1671, in response to a call encouraging

583 nationaltrust.org.uk/dyrham-park/features/history-of-dyrham-park

Quaker women to meet separately from men and work together to promote women's rights. Alongside the women in her monthly meetings, Isabel and the other Bristol women challenged the all-male Bristol leadership, and the men promptly admonished the women for overstepping the mark in what they were permitted to do. Rather than object, the women simply stepped back down.

After William's death in 1674, Isabel returned to Lancashire with her surviving children and immersed herself in the Quaker women's meetings there.

JOAN YOUNG
1533-1603, LAND OWNER

If you head into the (appropriately for us) Elder Lady Chapel at Bristol Cathedral, you will see a number of interesting things, one of which is a buxom lady atop a tomb in the west end of the nave.[584] As surprising as such a saucy sculpture seems in a religious environment, it was not actually that unusual for its day and is a fitting and remarkable tribute to the Tudor woman who lies beneath it: Lady Joan Young.

Born Joan Wadham, she married twice, first to Sir Giles Strangways and, following his death, to Sir John Young. Astonishingly, she bore nine children: six with Giles and a further three with John.

Together with John, she built the Great House on Park Row in the 1570s, on the site of the former Carmelite Friary, of which the Red Lodge is the only segment still remaining: the Colston Hall now stands on part of their former land. This grand construction

584 Here's a fun fact about the Elder Lady Chapel at Bristol Cathedral: it had been boarded up behind plaster and whitewash for a very long time and forgotten about until Dr Pigou, the Dean of Bristol Cathedral (and husband of Maude Pigou who is profiled in this book), discovered and restored it during the late Victorian era.

was only made possible for John thanks to Joan's money, which she had inherited following the death of Sir Giles, who had owned a great deal of land in Devon and Somerset. With its knot garden and impressive Great Oak Room, the Red Lodge Museum (which now occupies the building, although it had previously been home to the Red Lodge Reformatory for Girls run by Mary Carpenter) is well worth a visit. Even more so when you learn the Youngs entertained Queen Elizabeth 1 at this address in 1574, when the monarch visited Bristol.[585]

John had died in 1589, which made Joan an even more wealthy woman. But upon her death on 14 June 1603, everything passed to her eldest son John Strangways, which included the monastery, rectory and advowson (the right to appoint a member of the clergy) for the village of Abbotsbury, Dorset. Portraits of Joan can be viewed at the Red Lodge Museum.

Please also see: Mary Carpenter (vol one), Lucy de Newchurch (vol two), Maude Pigou (vol two).

585 Here's a fun fact about Queen Elizabeth 1: her visit to Bristol to stay with the Youngs at the Red Lodge was at the same time as her visit to Bristol when she reportedly gave the washerwomen of Jacobs Wells the freedom to dry their clothes on Brandon Hill (see the entry for Lucy de Newchurch in this book).

FURTHER READING

Author's note: This is not a list of all the books and sources used as references in this volume (please see the relevant footnotes for those). This is a limited list of books about women's history generally, women's history in Bristol and a few pertinent novels. It is, of course, far from an exhaustive list.

Lucienne Boyce (2013). *The Bristol Suffragettes*. Bristol: SilverWood Books. This book is a detailed celebration of militant suffragette activity in Bristol.

Lorna Brierley, Helen Reid (2000). *Go Home and Do The Washing: Three Centuries of Pioneering Bristol Women*. Bristol: Broadcast Books. An independent book providing a good examination of different areas where Bristolian women have had an influence.

Shirley Brown, Dawn Dyer (2002). *100+ Women of Bristol*. Bristol: Bristol City Council.

Elizabeth Crawford (1999). *The Women's Suffrage Movement: A Reference Guide 1866-1928*. London: Routledge. Quite possibly the most detailed and exhaustive book about the British suffrage movement that you will ever find, apart from...

Elizabeth Crawford (2006). *The Women's Suffrage Movement in Britain and Ireland: A Regional Survey*. London: Routledge ... this book.

Madge Dresser (2016). *Women and the City: Bristol 1373-2000*. Bristol: Redcliffe Press. A comprehensive and academic look at six centuries of Bristol's history.

Helen Dunmore (2017). *Birdcage Walk*. London: Hutchinson. This absorbing novel is set in 18th century Bristol during a period of political upheaval and boasts a strong feminist focus.

Anna Freeman (2015). *A Fair Fight*. London: Weidenfeld & Nicolson. A pageturner of a novel focussing on the little-known true story of female bare knuckle fighting in Georgian Bristol.

Sheila Hayward (2008). *Harriet's Family*. Canada: Trafford Publishing. Sheila recreates the true story of her grandmother's fascinating life as a working-class woman in Bristol.

Marie Mulvey-Roberts (2015). *Literary Bristol: Writers and the City*. Bristol: Redcliffe Press. A detailed and academic look at all of the writers who hailed from our city.

Caroline Criado Perez (2019). *Invisible Women: Exposing Data Bias in a World Designed for Men*. London: Chatto & Windus. A fascinating and revealing look at how both history and society have forgotten to include women on an everyday basis. Until now.

Sheila Rowbotham (1973). *Hidden From History: 300 Years of Women's Oppression and the Fight Against It*. London: Pluto Press. Groundbreaking and influential feminist text by a deeply inspirational writer.

Sheila Rowbotham (2010). *Dreamers of a New Day: Women Who Invented the Twentieth Century*. London: Verso. Exciting and important text exploring how modern woman came to be… and lots of the sheroes who made that possible.

Helen Thomas, Rosie Tomlinson, Mavis Zutshi (2015). *Bedminster Tobacco Women: A Local History Project*. Bristol: Fiducia Press. This is a brilliant project examining the working and home lives of many of the women who worked in Bristol's famous tobacco industry.

ACKNOWLEDGEMENTS

People who simply must be thanked for giving up their valuable time to share wisdom, advice and articles, offer unbridled support and — in some cases — to trawl through stodgy drafts of this book, include: Jane and Alan Bambury, Eugene Byrne, Claire Cavanagh, Naomi Clifford, Elizabeth Crawford, Thangam Debbonaire MP, my husband Dr Paul Duffus, Prof Peter Fleming, Penny Gane, Arthur Girling, Peaches Golding OBE, Viv Groskop, Andrew Kelly, Doreen Lindegaard, Janine Marriott and the team at Arnos Vale Cemetery, Dr Naomi Paxton, Prof Steve Poole, Tim Popple, Wendy Tippett, Philippa Walker and — a very welcome addition to the Duffus family — young Marcie. While Richard Jones at Tangent Books has yet again proved himself to be an extremely patient chap, tolerating my endless texts and emails with good grace and unflappable calmness. And we remember Beryl Jones (1923-2019).

Plus, for nominating women who had previously escaped my attention, my immense gratitude to: Edson Burton, John Cooper, Elizabeth Gould, Ruth Hecht, Mark Small and Mark Steeds. And extra special thanks to Dawn Dyer (and the all-knowing staff at a range of Bristol libraries), Mike Manson and Lori Streich for being so continually supportive and encouraging, and for repeatedly coming up gold with truly amazing suggestions of brilliant women.

Extra special thanks go to Kim Renfrew who, once again, has helped me beyond measure by whipping the copy into line, pointing out holes in the text and generally being wonderful. She also kept chugging away through the very messy first draft while I was lost in grief, helpfully providing me with something solid to take my mind off things for a few moments here and there. Everyone should know a Kim.

On the design side, a double thumbs up to Joe Burt (**wildsparkdesign.com**) for making everything ship shape and Bristol fashion, and to Tiitu Takalo **(tiitutakalo.net)** for once again providing a striking picture for the cover. They say you shouldn't judge a book by its cover but, since everybody does, having an illustration as bold as Tiitu's really does help. In addition, I was delighted that Tina Altwegg (**wingedfoxdesigns.co.uk**), Rhi Lee (**rhileedesign.com**) and Carrie Love (**c-love.co.uk**) were willing to pull out all the stops to bring some of these warrior women back to life via their beautiful illustrations.

Any mistakes in this book are my responsibility alone and I would be happy to correct them in any future prints of this book.